S0-AGP-748

A Woman's Nation Changes Everything

A Study by Maria Shriver and the Center for American Progress

Edited by
Heather Boushey *and* Ann O'Leary

with
Karen Skelton *and* Ed Paisley

Leslie Miller *and* Laura Nichols

Preface

By John D. Podesta

Earlier this year, the Center for American Progress decided to closely examine the consequences of what we thought was a major tipping point in our nation's social and economic history: the emergence of working women as primary breadwinners for millions of families at the same time that their presence on America's payrolls grew to comprise fully half the nation's workforce. In addition, we were watching the Great Recession amplify and accelerate these trends. We are in the midst of a fundamental transformation of the way America works and lives.

But my own interest wasn't just academic. It sprang from a very personal source: my mother. My family wasn't much like what we were watching on TV in the 1950s. My parents had a tag-team work life—my father working in a factory during the day; my mother in a pink-collar job from 5 p.m. until midnight. Like millions of families today, they juggled, struggled, nurtured, laughed a lot, and fought a little so that their kids could lead good lives and get ahead. I don't think my mother ever really thought of herself as a trendsetter, but she was at the leading edge of a wave that shaped America in the last half of the 20th century—a wave we call "a woman's nation." Though she recently passed away, she still serves as a role model for my daughters.

So I was delighted when Maria Shriver, who cleverly conceived of the phrase "a woman's nation," came to me with the idea of combining a project she envisioned with CAP's work and together producing a landmark examination of this fundamental change in American society. We realized that Maria could add invaluable depth to the efforts underway because she recognized not only the enormous impact of these changes on the workplace, but their import for every aspect of the American life and culture, as well. A partnership was born, and it produced a document that goes far beyond the typical findings of your standard economic policy report.

This report brings together the relentless intellect of a Peabody and Emmy Award-winning journalist who pushes beyond statistics to fully reveal the complexity of women's lives and the academic muscle of a progressive think tank that understands how to comb through data and illuminate the trends re-shaping the American landscape.

In the summer of 2009, Maria packed her bags and crisscrossed the country and, with her team, engaged in conversations with everyday women and men in Atlanta, Detroit, Los Angeles, Seattle, and Silicon Valley, hearing and understanding from both sexes how this cultural upheaval has changed their lives. Maria used the diverse voices she heard to stitch together the work CAP was doing.

CAP's contribution—led by senior economist Heather Boushey, the leading authority on the study of working families and the U.S. labor market, and Ann O'Leary, a CAP senior fellow and executive director of the Berkeley Center for Health, Economic & Family Security—shines a light on America's defining institutions. We examined government and businesses; faith, culture, and media; and our health care and educational institutions, and then we considered meaningful ways they can adapt to this sea change in Americans' lives.

And the Rockefeller Foundation, which generously funded a nationwide poll in collaboration with *Time* magazine, conducted a comprehensive examination of American attitudes about the role of women in today's world.

The result is an exhaustive, multifaceted report. CAP's economic team commissioned work from a variety of scholars and experts. Maria inspired and assembled a collection of diverse, incisive, and illuminating essays and brought to us her conversations with dozens of Americans around the country. And then there is the landmark national poll that closes the report. Together, we've created a provocative study that we expect will spur a national conversation about what women's emerging economic power means for our way of life.

When we look back over the 20th century and try to understand what's happened to workers and their families and the challenges they now face, the movement of women out of the home and into paid employment stands out as a unique and powerful transformation. Unlike the America our parents still remember and even helped to build, today:

- Moms aren't home all day caring for younger children, waiting for the cable guy or to pick up the kids from school, yet quality child care and flexible hours at work are in short supply.

When we look back over the 20th century and try to understand what's happened to workers and their families and the challenges they now face, the movement of women out of the home and into paid employment stands out as a unique and powerful transformation.

- Workplaces are no longer the domain of men. The last remnants of those days can scarcely be found at all, save on episodes of "Mad Men" or on "Leave it to Beaver" reruns. Women now comprise half the workers on employers' payrolls. And while men and women still tend to work in different kinds of jobs, most workers under 40 have never known a workplace without women bosses and women colleagues.

- Schools still let kids out in the afternoon, long before the workday ends, and they shut their doors for three months during the summer, even though the majority of families with children are supported by a single working parent or a dual-earning couple.

- Most workers—men and women—now have family responsibilities they negotiate daily with their spouses, family members, bosses, colleagues, and employees. But it is still a rare doctor's office that is open evenings or weekends, even though so many people work at all hours in our 24/7 economy.

Women becoming primary breadwinners or co-breadwinners changed everything. But, even though we were all witness to this phenomenon's slow emergence over many years, these changes seem somehow to have snuck up on us. As a result, our policy landscape remains stuck in an idealized past, where the typical family was composed of a married-for-life couple with a full-time breadwinner and full-time homemaker who raised the children herself.

Government policies and laws continue to rely on an outdated model of the American family. And, despite the existence of innovative practices in corporate America, most employers fail to acknowledge or accommodate the daily juggling act their workers perform, they are oblivious to the fact that their employees are now more likely to be women, and they ignore the fact that men now share in domestic duties.

Our policy landscape remains stuck in an idealized past, where the typical family was composed of a married-for-life couple with a full-time breadwinner and full-time homemaker who raised the children herself.

Slow, too, have been our institutions of faith in recognizing this transformation of male-female dynamics at a time when increasingly urgent lives make spiritual support more needed—and, perhaps, less available—than ever before.

And the media present flawed images of the real challenges women face, embracing glamour, power, and sex while ignoring the daily struggle to raise children and pay bills.

At one level, everything has changed. And yet so much more change is needed. This report contemplates what a new America should look like after we finally embrace this important new dynamic in our lives and the changes it has caused in our homes and businesses.

At CAP, our work builds upon the progressive ideals of leaders who brought needed change to our national life, people such as Theodore and Franklin Roosevelt, Jane Addams, and Martin Luther King. We draw from the great social movements of the 20th century, from labor rights and worker safety to civil rights and women's suffrage.

"A Woman's Nation Changes Everything" is work in the best tradition of those ideals. It flips a switch in our culture, sparking a collective acknowledgement of the interdependence of men and women today. With that switch we hope will come changes in the collective mindset of our government, business, faith institutions, our culture, media, and most importantly, men and women. Embracing these new dynamics and sparking new conversations is what "A Woman's Nation Changes Everything" is all about.

But this report is only the beginning of that conversation. In the months and years to come, we at the Center for American Progress hope you will join us in our efforts to transform our ideas into actual policies that make the world around us work better for families—as they really are. We hope you enjoy this report and that you'll join us on the road ahead.

John D. Podesta, President and CEO,
Center for American Progress

Contents

LET THE CONVERSATION BEGIN

A Woman's Nation

By Maria Shriver

I sit down to begin writing this not too long after my mother died. I held her hand as she took her last breath and left this world. She was my hero, my best friend. I spoke to her every day of my life—and the truth is, I can't imagine my life without her. And so I sit here now, trying to write this opening to a report on the American woman that bears her last name and my own. I find it hard to concentrate, hard to gather my thoughts. For a moment, I consider not writing it. But I close my eyes and hear her telling me, as she always did, "You can do it, Maria! Get going! Get moving!"

My role model, like most daughters, was my mother. She was my first image and idea of what it meant to be a woman. It didn't matter to me that she wasn't like the other mothers. She wore men's pants, smoked cigars, and worked outside the home. She was my mother, and she was fearless. She raised me exactly the way she raised my four brothers: to believe I could do anything. She sent me right in there to play tackle football with the boys. She said, "Maria, this may be a man's world, but you can and will succeed in it." I admit I wasn't exactly sure what that meant the first time I heard it. After all, I was only in the second grade. But I didn't question her. You didn't say no to Eunice Kennedy Shriver.

My mother was indeed a trailblazer for American women. She was scary smart and not afraid to show it. With all her energy and ingenuity, she didn't buy into the propaganda of her day that women had to be soft and submissive and take a back seat. That took courage back then, because she grew up in a family that expected a lot from the boys and very little from the girls. Women stayed behind the scenes in supporting roles. Not my mother.

She was tough, but also compassionate. She was intimidating, but also approachable. Driven and also fun. Restless and patient—and curious and prayerful. My mother understood power and wanted it, then wielded it to help those who had none.

And while she liked to hang with the boys, all her heroes were women—first and foremost, her own mother, and the millions of other mothers of kids with intellectual disabilities. She introduced me to other role models who changed the world: Dorothy Day, Mother Teresa, Claire Booth Luce. She told me their stories, because she wanted me to appreciate the gift and the power of women to change the language, the tempo, and the character of the world.

And she was right. Cut to 2008. No one was cheering louder than my mother during an election campaign that was all about change. At last, during the same presidential campaign season, we saw one woman run for president and another for vice president. As for me, I watched the change unfold from a unique vantage point, as first lady of the biggest state in the union—home to more than 18 million women—and head of The Women's Conference, an annual conference for and about women held in California.

My goal has been to make The Women's Conference a nonpartisan meeting place where women could come together and share experience, information, and motivation with one another. Participants come from all walks of life—from foster-care graduates to heads of Fortune 500 companies, from stay-at-home moms and retired grandmothers to college students and small-business owners. Every age, every ethnic group, every economic circumstance. They come to be inspired by speakers from all over the world, who share their wisdom and strategies on finances, spirituality, health, political power, relationships, how to overcome obstacles, how to navigate every area of human life.

In the past few years, The Women's Conference has exploded in size and impact. It has developed programs beyond its walls, granting scholarships to needy girls, investing in micro-lending to women, connecting poor women to services that can improve their lives, and working to end emotional, physical, and sexual violence against women. We're now hosting about 25,000 attendees, and thousands more can participate online.

When the 2008 Conference sold out in just a couple of hours, it hit me that something profound was going on with women. We'd program a workshop on caring for aging parents, and it was standing-room-only. We'd bring in speakers to talk about how to start up a business, and the rooms were packed. We couldn't book enough sessions on empowerment, activism, and spirituality. All of them were filled, and people were asking for more.

Women say they feel increasingly isolated, invisible, stressed, and misunderstood.

I wondered what was going on. I talked to the women, and they filled out our questionnaires. I learned women are hungry for something that's missing in their lives—a place to connect. They say they feel increasingly isolated, invisible, stressed, and misunderstood. They say the news media, where I'd worked for 30 years, don't accurately reflect their lives anymore. They say women on TV shows and in the movies certainly don't either. They can't believe how out-of-touch government is with who women are today and what they need to survive. They can't understand how slow business has been in figuring out how to retain, support, and promote women. They lament that many faith institutions want women to be volunteers, but won't give them a seat at the table, let alone a place at the altar. They're terrified how quickly their family finances could be wiped out by a child's catastrophic illness or a parent's Alzheimer's. And they're exasperated that pundits and pollsters continue to jam women into convenient boxes with labels like "soccer moms" or "security moms."

Of course, women are as diverse as men. They are successful businesswomen, single mothers living below the poverty line, college graduates making their own way, blue-collar wives in two-career families, gay mothers, foster mothers, childless women who've been laid off, women setting up Internet businesses from home, soldiers in combat units overseas. They don't dress the same way or vote the same way or have the same color skin. They don't speak with one voice. And they don't have one issue.

We decided we needed to learn some new, hard facts about today's American woman. Who is she? How does she live? What does she think? What does she earn? What are her politics? How does she define power? How does she define success? What does she think of marriage? What does she really think of men? How does she want to live her life moving forward?

We went to the Center for American Progress, where the president and chief executive, former Clinton presidential chief of staff and author John Podesta, told us CAP was right in the midst of studying the impact of the changing economy on women. In fact, CAP's chief economist, Heather Boushey, who is an expert on women and workforce issues, told us that women were right on the cusp of a huge change. Women were about to break through and account for fully half of all American payrolls for the first time. Bingo!

We decided we needed to learn some new, hard facts about today's American woman. Who is she? How does she live? What does she think?

We told CAP that we wanted to study how women's changing roles were impacting not only the economy but also all the other areas of American culture that our conference participants had pointed out to us. And we especially wanted to know what men thought about it all. CAP said, "We're in!"

This report builds on the extraordinary work of so many women's groups who have gone before us, and the more than 200 state, county, and local women's commissions that day in and day out investigate and monitor the status of women and work diligently to promote equality. Their work and the groundbreaking reports of the Institute of Women's Policy Research have played critical roles in examining the status of the American woman.

Our report breaks new ground by taking a hard look at how women's changing roles are also affecting our major societal institutions: our government, businesses, religious and faith institutions, educational system, the media, and even men and marriage. And we examine how all these parts of the culture have responded to one of the greatest social transformations of our time. We look at where we are and where we should go from here.

It was back in 1961, when my uncle, President John F. Kennedy, asked former First Lady Eleanor Roosevelt to chair the very first Commission on the Status of Women. According to anthropologist Margaret Mead, who co-edited the final report, the goal was "a review of the progress that has been made in giving American women practical equality with men educationally, economically, and politically."[1]

The Commission's 1963 report, *American Women,* said that the role for women "most generally approved by counselors, parents, and friends [is] the making of a home, the rearing of children, and the transmission to them in their earliest years of the values of the American heritage."[2] Back then, only 10 percent of families were headed by unmarried women—and in families where both parents worked, less than a fifth of the wives earned as much or more than their husbands.[3] In fact, most women's jobs were in what the report called "low-paid categories" such as clerical work. And the Commission also found a "widening gap [between] the educational and career expectations for boys and for girls."[4] The gap in political participation was wide, too. There were only two women senators and 11 congresswomen, and just two women had ever held cabinet posts.

Among the Commission's policy recommendations: equal pay for equal work, access to child care and paid maternity leave, and enhanced educational opportunities for women. Mead signaled in the final report, "The climate of opinion is turning against the idea that homemaking is the only form of feminine achievement."[5]

Indeed it was. The report was published within months of Betty Friedan's *The Feminine Mystique*, the opening salvo of the Women's Lib movement, which promoted the idea that women's true fulfillment could come only outside the home with "liberation" from wifely and motherly duties. With that, the pendulum of opinion seemed to swing all the way in the other direction.[6] You could understand why women got whiplash.

All of a sudden, so many women became activists, taking to the streets and the halls of power. Many of these women risked their reputations, their security, their jobs—sometimes even their lives and marriages—to knock down walls of inequality. They got many outdated work laws changed and new anti-discrimination laws put in place. Their work and their courage created opportunity for many women, enabling more women to go to college and professional schools, more women to play sports, more women to get on career tracks. Today we stand on their shoulders. Their work freed so many of us to dream new dreams and fulfill them. And with the simultaneous sexual revolution, the advent of the pill, and the *Roe v. Wade* decision, many women postponed or even said no to marriage or children. Women were moving up the ladder in just about every area of endeavor.

Fast forward to 2009. For the first time in our nation's history, fully half of U.S. workers are female—and mothers have become the primary breadwinners in 4 in 10 American families.[7] That's a sea change from 40 years ago. What had been a slow and steady shift has been accelerating during the current recession, when more than three-quarters of the jobs lost have been men's jobs, especially in areas such as construction and manufacturing.[8]

With more and more men forced to stay home, more and more women are bringing home the bacon. Women are more likely than ever to head their own families. They're doing it all—and many of them have to do it all. When they work, it's no longer just for "the little extras." Their income puts food on the table and a roof over their heads, just like men's income always did. In fact, half of all families rely on the earnings of two parents and in more than 20 percent of all families a single mother is the primary breadwinner.[9] Seventy percent of families with kids include a working mother.[10] And more and more of them, like me, are moving into what I call "the squeezed generation," caring for both kids and our own aging parents.

Welcome to A Woman's Nation

As you'll read in this report, women have now taken their place as powerhouses driving the economy. Consider this: Today, women now earn 60 percent of the college degrees awarded each year and fully half of the Ph.D.s and the professional degrees.[11] Almost 40 percent of working women hold managerial and other professional positions.[12] Women make 80 percent of the buying decisions in American homes.[13] Companies led by women generally are proving to have healthier bottom lines.[14]

It's a transformational moment in our history—much as the opening of the West, industrialization, the great 1960s civil rights campaigns, and the flowering of the Internet age have all irrevocably altered the fabric of American life. With working women now the New Normal, striving and succeeding in areas where they never have before, so many assumptions and underpinnings of our society are cracking open. The rumbling is shaking the ground in every corner of the culture, and many women and men are struggling to get their footing. The effect on every sector of our society will be deep, wide, and profound. We hope this report will help us all come up to speed and begin a national conversation about how our institutions need to adapt to the unfolding of A Woman's Nation.

To take the pulse of Americans—their realities and their expectations, their hopes and dreams—I put back on my journalist's hat and together with our team crisscrossed the country holding conversations with an array of women and men on the frontlines of this new American revolution. In addition, the Rockefeller Foundation, in collaboration with *Time* magazine, commissioned a nationwide poll of 3,413 men and women to substantiate what we were hearing on the ground and flesh out the academic research.

An overwhelming majority of both men and women said they're sitting down at their kitchen tables to coordinate their family's schedules, duties, and responsibilities, including child care and elder care, at least two to three times a week.

Together, the results of these efforts provide a fascinating window into the changing American landscape. What we heard loud and clear is that the Battle Between the Sexes is over. It was a draw. Now we're engaged in Negotiation Between the Sexes.

Virtually all married couples told the pollsters they're negotiating the rules of their relationships, work, and family. An overwhelming majority of both men and women said they're sitting down at their kitchen tables to coordinate their family's schedules, duties, and responsibilities, including child care and elder care, at least two to three times a week. Men said it was more like every day!

Indeed, during my conversation with powerful businesswomen on the West Coast, one told me she and her husband "are constantly renegotiating our agreement about what gets done, who does it—or do we hire somebody as opposed to doing it ourselves." And a man in Seattle told me he and his wife have to work out "who's gonna take care of the light bill? Who's gonna pay for the mortgage? It doesn't matter who's bringing the money in. The money is coming in, but decisions have to be made about how the money is going out."

In the Rockefeller/*Time* poll, more than three-quarters of both men and women agreed that the increased participation of women in the workforce is a positive change for society. Both sexes also agreed that men are becoming more financially dependent on women. And both women and men said they're still adjusting their lives, their expectations, and their assumptions to the change.

Women and men said they're still adjusting their lives, their expectations, and their assumptions to women's participation in the workforce.

The findings matched what I heard in the street. Everywhere I went, people talked to me about how overstressed and in crisis they feel, especially when it comes to financial security. Women said that never before has so much been asked of them, and never have they delivered so much. Divorced mothers talked to me about trying to make do without child support. One single mother who had just lost her job told me she was utterly dependent on her family and friends just to stay afloat.

Men are feeling out of sorts and stressed-out as well. One man said to me, "We've been in our comfort zone. We're men! We bring the money to the house! As soon as women start working, they're bursting our bubbles and basically doing our job. Doing it better, in some cases."

The men who were polled said that compared to their fathers, they're much more accepting of women working outside the home. But they're still looking for a playbook. Here's an exchange from Seattle:

> Maria: Is there a revolution going on about what it means to be a man, what are the rules of manhood today?
> Mike: Yes, but it wasn't started by us!

In fact, many Americans feel disoriented. The African American owner of an automotive parts company in Detroit told me, "Nothing in business school prepared me to deal with the problems I'm having." He said he has trouble sleeping at night. He's had to reduce his workforce by two-thirds, and employees are asking for pay cuts instead of layoffs. Female employees want help with child care or time off to tend to sick grandparents. "Men are conditioned to be problem-solvers," he explained to me. "I solve my own problems. Well, today, the problems that are out there are very difficult to solve."

And very difficult to adapt to, according to some men we met. One told me, "It used to be really easy. You'd go into all these kinds of arenas where there were just guys. The military, the firehouse, the police station, the law firm, everywhere you went. And the big change, of course, is that women are now in every one of those arenas. The dilemma for women has often been, 'How do I be those things that are called masculine, like confident and assertive and ambitious, and still be a woman?' And for men now, everywhere we go, there's women. And some guys sort of feel like, 'Oh my God, women have invaded!'"

And more and more often, a woman is the boss. One 55-year-old man told me, "In the olden days, women used their sexuality in the workplace, because they were looking for a husband to support them. Now the women have power." Intriguingly, though, the poll shows that women find it much harder to work for female bosses than men do.

And women often define that power differently from men. One woman who had made it to CEO chose to give up the corner office and downgrade to a lower-rung position. She told me, "I will admit, it was fun, it was power, and I was dealing with a bunch of top dogs. But now I get to hang out with my kids when they come home from school. For me the definition of success is not being a CEO and not being the biggest dog and frankly not making the most money. It's living a balanced life."

In fact, talk to women, and you hear a lot about the search for "a balanced life." More and more of them say if they could, they'd like to leave companies that are unresponsive and start their own businesses. Many of them do. In fact, the number of women working for themselves doubled between 1979 and 2003, so that women make up 35 percent of all self-employed people. Growth in the number of women-owned businesses is significantly higher than the growth in the overall business sector: The number of women-owned businesses is growing at a rate of almost 23 percent, 2½ times faster than the growth in the number of total businesses.[15]

One female corporate executive told me, "Women don't need equal pay. They actually need to be paid *more*, because the fact of the matter is that we typically are responsible for more within our families, and we have to pay to outsource more. Most of the men I have competed with for positions have had a stay-home wife at some point and many have had a wife throughout their entire marriage."

But other women countered that it's not up to employers to help with flex time or child care money. "If I'm doing the same amount of work as men, I want the same compensation. It's up to *me* figure out if I want to spend it on child care."

In 2009, these aren't just women's issues anymore. An overwhelming majority of both sexes believe the structure of the modern workplace isn't meeting people's needs. A preponderance of both men and women told the pollsters that if businesses fail to adapt to the needs of modern families, they risk losing good workers. Still, too many women *and* men who were polled said there were occasions when they wanted to take off from work to care for a child, but were unable to do so. In fact, women reported actually being afraid to ask for time off for caregiving. And large majorities of both sexes agreed that businesses should be required to provide paid family and medical leave for every worker who needs it.

Many of the highly successful women I spoke to worried about women who had made it big and then got beat up in the media. They talked about the outright sexism they've seen hurled at high-profile women such as Hillary Clinton and Sarah Palin, Katie Couric and Barbara Walters, Carly Fiorina and Martha Stewart. They question whether the climb all the way to the very top is even worth it.

Another hint that there's still plenty of underlying sexism: Women told me that male co-workers ask them all the time to give pep talks to their daughters, but never to their wives. They marveled, "They want us to inspire their girls to great achievement, but don't you go giving their wives any big ideas!"

In fact, the poll shows that a substantial majority of women feel that men resent women who have more power than they do. Yet wherever I went, I was surprised how open men were to sharing their bafflement about what women want—and their own insecurities about what's expected of them.

"All of us grew up thinking this was a man's world, that doors were just gonna open to us because we had a Y chromosome," a Seattle man told me. "And suddenly, we have to adjust to the fact that that's not the case. And the recession has made it even more intense for us. So every family is trying to figure out what does it mean that we're both working or that I'm laid off and you're working? We haven't thrown some switch to go from a man's world to a woman's world. It's more like we're finally, for the first time, in a position where it's no longer *only* a man's world. Now what does that mean?"

With all the change and insecurity, women told the pollsters they rely on faith-based institutions and spiritual practice in general for help getting through.

Good question. What does it mean, especially in families where wives are suddenly the primary providers? Those stories moved me. One man told me, "My wife makes about three times what I make, and that has been challenging to me. I was raised very traditionally. The masculine partner took the lead or was supposed to."

Some men talked about reinventing themselves. I met a stay-at-home father who says he's coming to terms with shuttling the kids around and being supported by his wife. "It's confusing. Am I turning into not enough of a man? It just all depends how it's defined in your own family. So if I'm enough of a man to them, that's all that matters."

Another father told me, "It's role reversal a little bit. I have dinner ready. I do the grocery shopping. I do laundry. She works harder than I ever did." And what about his wife? She's worried about their daughter, because "I feel like I'm not there as much for her as I ought to be. I do have some regrets." In fact, the men and women who were polled both said they're concerned about the effect of both parents working and raising children without a stay-at-home parent.

With all the change and insecurity, women overwhelmingly told the pollsters that religious faith is important to them in general for help getting through. And men report seeking connectedness through talking and listening to other men—on the Internet, on sports radio, in church groups.

Is there any group that doesn't feel like fish out of water? I was relieved to discover during my travels that many younger couples aren't so wedded to old stereotypes. When one twenty-something woman's live-in boyfriend lost his job in Detroit, she told me, "The expectation was that we would just pull together and figure it out. People from my generation just expect women to work." And I was glad that so many young men starting out today have a whole new sensibility about fatherhood. They told me they just expect to be active in their children's lives and help out at home, and they want it that way.

For some, of course, "woman as primary breadwinners" is old news, especially among Latinos and African Americans.

For some, of course, women as primary breadwinners is old news, especially among Latinos and African Americans. Said one black man, "When I see a strong woman, I'm actually more attracted to that, because that represents the women I was raised with." And a Hispanic single mother in Los Angeles said, "My mother taught me to work and be successful and not depend on a guy for all the things that I need." Gay couples aren't following old stereotypes either. One lesbian partner told us, "When we go to soccer and back-to-school night, usually we are the ones where both parents are there. We don't have gender rules, so we've always joked, 'Who's gonna be the husband tonight and take out the trash?' "

And marriages where the partners have adapted to the new realities seem to be stronger. As you'll read in this report, research shows that women are more sexually attracted to men who do more work around the house. And since a big predictor of a husband's satisfaction is how often he has sex, maybe all that kitchen-table negotiating and communicating about who does what around the house is having a good effect on the institution of marriage.

Within this huge shift, there will always be some who blame society's current ills on the very fact that so many women have gone to work and aren't staying at home with the children anymore. They point to high school dropout rates, teen pregnancies, and the millions of latchkey kids. They see those as women's issues. But most of the people we spoke to don't feel that way. They feel the care and nurturing of children isn't just a women's issue anymore. These are family issues, and they affect all of us. Families have moved beyond finger-pointing to figure out how to confront these problems together. A union man in Detroit put it this way: "I think the fact that our roles are changing is just another way of us adapting to get the job done. We will do whatever needs to be done. And we will do it well."

More than four decades after President Kennedy's Commission on the Status of Women, we've learned that while there's much to cheer about, we still have a long way to go. Women still don't make as much as men do for the same jobs. Women still don't make it to the top as often as men. Families too often can't get flex-time, child care, medical leave, or paid family leave. The United States still is the only major industrialized nation without comprehensive child care and family leave policies. Insurance companies still often charge women more than men for the exact same coverage. Women are still being punished by a tax code designed when men were the sole breadwinners and women the sole caregivers. Sexual violence against women remains a huge issue. Women still are disproportionately affected by lack of health care services. And lesbian couples and older women are among the poorest segment of our society.

But so much has changed. Homemaking is no longer, as Margaret Mead wrote back then, the "most generally approved" job for women. Women's expanding role in families, industry, the arts, government, politics, and other institutions is altering the American landscape. Women are learning they no longer have to shoehorn themselves into one stereotype or another, but they can do so if they choose—or they can make it up as they go along.

In 2009, women have more choices than they did 40 years ago. They can choose to have kids with a partner, in a traditional marriage or not. They can to stay childless, live as single parents, or choose a same-sex partner. They can be like the single mothers who raised a president of the United States and a brand-new Supreme Court justice. They can be like Hillary Clinton *and* Sarah Palin. They can be like Diane Sawyer, Michelle Obama, Sandra Day O'Connor, or like Nancy Pelosi, who spent the first half of her life staying home to raise five children and then went on to become the first female Speaker of the U.S. House of Representatives. Or anything else they can imagine.

It's in this new world that I'm raising four children. I'm trying to teach my boys to understand that the women in their lives will work and will have independent minds. I'm trying to teach them not just how to hold the door open, but how to do their own laundry and make their own mac and cheese. I'm also trying to teach my girls how to advocate for themselves, be smart about their finances—and to look not for a savior, but a loving, supportive, open-minded partner.

Which brings me back to my mother.

In so many articles after my mother's death, her brothers and pundits were quoted as saying, "If only Eunice had been a man, she could have been president!"

"If only." My mother learned from that. Her call to those who faced discrimination and the sting of rejection was to turn adversity into action. "Use adversity to give your life purpose and mission," she said. "Turn your adversity into advantage and opportunity." That's what she herself did, channeling her passion and outrage into changing the world for people with intellectual disabilities. She used her intelligence and her energy to improve the world—and that's why she's alongside so many other extraordinary women, all agents of change, who are immortalized in the Women's Hall of Fame in Seneca Falls, New York.

My mother figured out how to be true to herself in the man's world she was in—and I believe her solution makes her a real role model for today's American woman. She mothered five kids who adored her, shared the spotlight with her husband—and carved out a career for herself impacting millions of lives for the better. Her message to women was, "Don't let society tame you or contain you." Today, she *could* run for president. And I believe she would win.

I know for sure if she were alive today, she'd say about this report, "It's about time!" She'd get her hands on a hundred copies and send them to friends. She'd make bookstores put it in the window. She'd make sure every office on Capitol Hill had a copy, whether they wanted one or not. And when I'd say, "Mummy, calm down! This is just the first step," she'd say, "Well, when's the next step? Take that step, Maria, and take it now!"

And we shall. As we move into this phase we're calling a woman's nation, women can turn their pivotal role as wage-earners, as consumers, as bosses, as opinion-shapers, as co-equal partners in whatever we do into a potent force for change. Emergent economic power gives women a new seat at the table—at the head of the table.

As we move into this phase we're calling a woman's nation, women can turn their pivotal role as wage-earners, as consumers, as bosses, as opinion-shapers, as co-equal partners in whatever we do into a potent force for change.

Back in 1960, President Kennedy talked about the torch being passed to "a new generation." Well, five decades later, the torch *is* being passed . . . to a new gender. There's no doubt in my mind that we women will lift that torch. We will carry it. And we will light a new way forward.

ENDNOTES

1 President's Commission on the Status of Women, *American Women* (Washington: Government Printing Office, 1963), p. 18.

2 Ibid., p. 19.

3 See chapter by Boushey, Table 1, p. 38; Lawrence Mishel, Jared Bernstein, and Heidi Shierholz, *The State of Working America 2008/2009* (Ithaca, NY: Cornell University Press, 2009).

4 *American Women*, p. 4.

5 *American Women*, p. 204.

6 Betty Friedan, *The Feminine Mystique* (New York: Norton, 1963).

7 Heather Boushey, "Women Still Primary Breadwinners" (Washington: Center for American Progress, 2009). Institute for Women's Policy Research, "Unemployment Among Single Mother Families," IWPR Publication #C369 (2009). Ellen Galinsky, Kerstin Aumann and James T. Bond, "Times are Changing: Gender and Generation at Work and at Home" (New York: Family Work Institute, 2008), p. 8.

8 Boushey, "Women Still Primary Breadwinners."

9 Institute for Women's Policy Research, "Unemployment Among Single Mother Families," IWPR Publication #C369 (2009).

10 Galinsky, Aumann, and Bond, "Times are Changing," Figure 5.

11 Ibid, p. 6.

12 See chapter by Harrington and Ladge, p. 198.

13 Marti Barletta, *Marketing to Women: How to Understand, Reach, and Increase Your Share of the World's Largest Market Segment*, 2nd edition (Chicago: Dearborn Trade Publishing, 2006).

14 See chapter by Harrington and Ladge.

15 Darrene Hackler, Ellen Harpel, and Heike Mayer, "Human Capital and Women's Business Ownership" (Washington: Small Business Administration, 2008).

Executive Summary

By Heather Boushey and Ann O'Leary

This report describes how a woman's nation changes everything about how we live and work today. Now for the first time in our nation's history, women are half of all U.S. workers and mothers are the primary breadwinners or co-breadwinners in nearly two-thirds of American families. This is a dramatic shift from just a generation ago (in 1967 women made up only one-third of all workers). It changes how women spend their days and has a ripple effect that reverberates throughout our nation. It fundamentally changes how we all work and live, not just women but also their families, their co-workers, their bosses, their faith institutions, and their communities.

Quite simply, women as half of all workers changes everything.

Recognizing the importance of women's earnings to family well-being is the key piece to understanding why we are in a transformational moment. This social transformation is affecting nearly every aspect of our lives—from how we work to how we play to how we care for one another. Yet, we, as a nation, have not come to terms with what this means. In this report, we break new ground by taking a hard look at how women's changing roles affect our major societal institutions, from government and businesses to our faith communities. We outline how these institutions rely on outdated models of who works and who cares for our families. And we examine how our culture has responded to one of the greatest social transformations of our time.

FIGURE 1

The new normal

Changes in family structure and work, families with children under age 18, 1975 and 2008

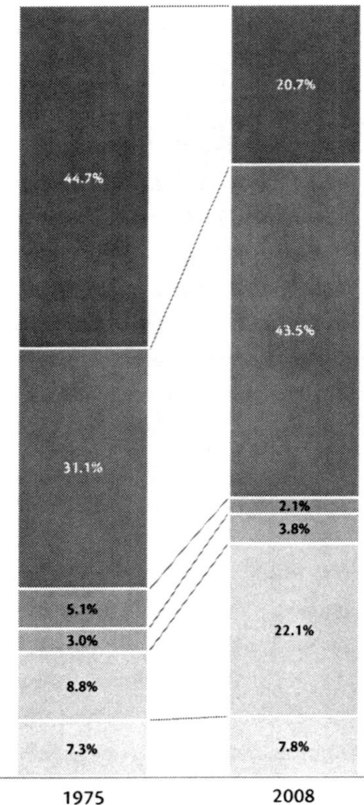

Source: Bureau of Labor Statistics, Economic News Release: Table 4. Families with own children: Employment status of parents by age of youngest child and family type, 2007-08 annual averages; Bureau of Labor Statistics, Indicator 18: Parent's Employment, Employment status of parents with own children under 18 years old, by type of family: 1975 to 1993.

Our findings should not be surprising to working men and women. Today, four-in-five families with children still at home are not the traditional male breadwinner, female homemaker. And women are increasingly becoming their family's breadwinner or co-breadwinner (see Figures 1 and 2). The deep economic downturn is amplifying and accelerating this trend. Men have lost three-out-of-four jobs so far since the Great Recession began in December 2007, leaving millions of wives to bring home the bacon while their husbands search for work. Women working outside the home, however, is not a short-term blip. This is a long-term trend that shows no signs of reversing.

Although our report is titled "A Woman's Nation Changes Everything," this is not just a woman's story. This is a report about how women becoming half of workers changes everything for men, women, and their families. The Rockefeller/*Time* nationwide poll, conducted in early September as the chapters of the report were being finalized, finds that the battle of the sexes is over and is replaced by negotiations between the sexes about work, family, household responsibilities, child care, and elder care. Yet, while men generally accept women working and making more money, men and women both express concern about kids left behind. Whose job is it? Men and women agree that government and business are out of

FIGURE 2

The new workforce

Share of mothers who are breadwinners or co-breadwinners, 1967 to 2008

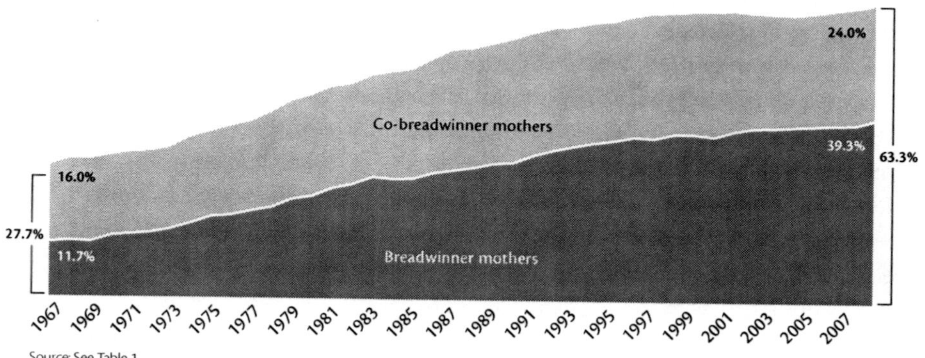

Source: See Table 1.

Notes: Breadwinner mothers include single mothers who work and married mothers who earn as much or more than their husbands. Co-breadwinners include all breadwinners as well as wives who bring home at least 25 percent of the couple's earnings. The data only include families with a mother who is between the ages of 18 and 60 and who has children under age 18 living with her.

touch with the realties of how most families live and work today. Families need more flexible work schedules, comprehensive child care policies, redesigned family and medical leave, and equal pay. The aim of this report is to take this conversation up to the national level, to engage men and women in thinking about what this new reality means for our vision of ourselves, our families, our communities, and the government, social, and religious institutions around us.

In short, this report lays the groundwork for how our society can better support the new American worker and the new American family.

The chapters in this report examine a host of ways in which our lives have changed forever because women have entered the labor force in ever greater numbers. The policy implications vary from issue to issue, but the conclusions are clear: We need to rethink our assumptions about families and about work and focus our policies—at all levels—to address this new reality.

Clearly we aren't going back to a time when women were available full time to be their families' unpaid caretakers, so we need to find another way forward. This report builds on the decades of work on these issues and aims to spark a national conversation and attract the attention of policymakers and political leaders to focus on the implications of this transformation for our society.

Maria Shriver opens our report with ***A Woman's Nation***. Her chapter describes the unique ways the Shriver and CAP teams approached this complex set of topics. She details how together we took a "deep dive" into how our culture and our society are responding to changes in women's dual roles in the workforce and in the family. Shriver takes a historical look at the transformation of the American woman since her uncle, President John F. Kennedy, asked Frist Lady Eleanor Roosevelt to chair the first Commission on the Status of Women in 1961. Shriver connects this overarching social shift to the most consistent roles of her life and of most women's lives—the roles of daughter and mother. As our country reshapes the face of its workforce, Shriver reminds us that the struggles of the women before us opened the doors for us to guide the next generation of young women through.

In her chapter, Shriver also describes the conversations she conducted with everyday Americans around the nation, discovering that men and women are indeed negotiating everything—from the daily struggle over whether the husband or wife will drop off their child at school in the morning to major life decisions about whether a family will relocate to further one spouse's career even if it hampers the other's. You'll find quotes from these conversations highlighted between the different chapters of this report—insights that bring to life the equally telling analysis of how we work and live today. And alongside our chapters is a collection of essays that Maria Shriver and her team gathered from an intriguing array of women and men, among them Oprah Winfrey, Billie Jean King, Suze Orman, Patricia Kempthorne, and Tammy Duckworth; less famous but equally insightful individuals such as Col. Maritza Sáenz Ryan, First Gentleman of Michigan Dan Mulhern and Accel Partners' Sukhinder Singh Cassidy; and everyday Americans at the forefront of these monumental changes in our society like Gianna Le, a young Vietnamese-American seeking to enter medical school this year. This chapter captures these insights and matches them to the analysis in the report to sharply define these personal experiences on the larger canvas of our changing nation.

The New Breadwinners, by **Heather Boushey**, Center for American Progress senior economist, explores the economic underpinnings of the transformation of women's work. This chapter homes in on who's gone to work, where women are working, why they are working, how well they are coping, and what this means for the economic well-being of women and their families. The chapter finds that while women are now half of workers and mothers are breadwinners or co-breadwinners in the majority of families, institutions have failed to catch up to this reality. Women have made great strides and are now more likely to be economically responsible for themselves and their families, but there is a still a long way to go. Equality in the workplace has not yet been achieved, even as families need women's equality now more than ever.

Family Friendly for All Families: Workers and caregivers need government policies that reflect today's realities, by **Ann O'Leary**, Center for American Progress senior fellow and executive director of the Berkeley Center for Health, Economic & Family Security at the University of California Berkeley School of Law, and **Karen Kornbluh**, former visiting fellow at the Center for American Progress, explores the implications of women in the workplace for government policy affecting workers and caregivers. O'Leary and Kornbluh argue that we need to reevaluate the values and assumptions underlying our nation's workplace policies and social insurance system to ensure that they reflect the actual—not outdated or imagined—ways that families work and care today.

Up until now, government policymakers largely focused on supporting women's entry into a male-oriented workforce on a par with men—a workplace where policies on hours, pay, benefits, and leave time were designed around male breadwinners who presumably had no family caregiving responsibilities. But allowing women to play by the same rules as a traditional male breadwinner worker is not enough. Too many workers—especially women and low-wage workers—today simply cannot work in the way traditional breadwinners once worked with a steady job and lifelong marriage with a wife at home.

O'Leary and Kornbluh suggest that a fruitful way for government to address this new economic and social reality would be to update our basic labor standards to include family-friendly employee benefits and reform our anti-discrimination laws so that employers cannot disproportionately exclude women from workplace benefits. Their chapter also argues that we need to modernize our social insurance system to account for varied families and new family responsibilities, including the need for paid family leave and social security retirement benefits that take into account time spent out of the workforce caring for children and other relatives. O'Leary and Kornbluh close with suggestions for increasing support to families for child care, early education, and elder care in order to help working parents cope with their dual responsibilities.

Next is a reflective essay, ***Invisible Yet Essential: Immigrant women in America,*** by **Maria Echaveste**, Center for American Progress senior fellow and senior distinguished fellow at the Warren Institute at University of California Berkeley School of Law. This chapter focuses in on how we often overlook the crucial work—child and parental care, home maintenance, food production, and cleaning—once done by the unpaid wives of male breadwinners but which is now the work of immigrant women. These hardworking immigrant women have helped make possible other women's mass entry into the workforce. Echaveste points out that our economy is increasingly based on a growing service-sector industry, which in turn challenges all of us to value the work of the millions of immigrant women performing these services. Indeed, she concludes that the work these women do will be necessary regardless of how high-tech our economy becomes. They can no longer be ignored.

Sick and Tired: Working women and their health, by **Jessica Arons**, director of the Women's Health and Rights Program at the Center for American Progress, and Northwestern University law professor **Dorothy Roberts**, explores the implications of women working and earning the family income on women's health, as well as women's access to employer-based and private health insurance. They find that women's breadwinning has not always come with greater access to health benefits and, too often, women's health is compromised as they combine work and family responsibilities. As more women work, the authors note that we are developing a greater understanding of the health implications for women and their families—everything from inequitable job conditions and workplace health hazards to the timing of when women become mothers. Further, they highlight how our current health insurance system, centered as it is on employer-sponsored insurance, fails women in a variety of ways.

Better Educating Our New Breadwinners: Creating opportunities for all women to succeed in the workforce, by professor and former dean of University of California Berkeley's graduate division **Mary Ann Mason**, explores the implications for our education system, focusing on post-secondary education. She finds that women have made great advances in educational attainment, yet there is still clear evidence that women face barriers within our educational institutions. Further, even when women receive the same degrees as men, they continue to face lower wages and fewer high-paying job prospects due to inflexible and unsupportive work environments.

Mason examines both sides of this gender coin. Women receive 52 percent of high school diplomas, 62 percent of associate's degrees, 57 percent of bachelor's degrees and 50 percent of doctoral degrees and professional degrees. But three problems persist. First, not all women have gained access to post-secondary education. Hispanic women, for example, lag far behind their counterparts. Second, women remain concentrated in the "helping" professions of health and education and are falling behind in entering the higher-paying fields of the future, including science, mathematics, engineering, and technology. Finally, more women with family responsibilities are attending all levels of post-secondary education, but they need family-friendly support to get their degrees (just as all workers need businesses to respond to the fact that our highly-educated workforce necessarily combines work and care). Mason recommends that policymakers focus on these three problems and offers some solutions to help them do so, including increasing family-friendly environments in our educational institutions and increasing compliance with Title IX with regard to science, engineering, mathematics, and technology at all post-secondary levels.

Got Talent? It Isn't Hard to Find: Recognizing and rewarding the value women create in the workplace, by **Brad Harrington**, professor of organization studies and executive director of the Center for Work & Family at the Carroll School of Management at Boston College, and **Jamie Ladge**, assistant professor of management and organizational development at Northeastern University, point out that women make up half the talent that is available to corporate America and small businesses. The authors argue that women's outstanding performance in educational institutions, especially in higher educational and professional schools, demands that employers create workplaces that attract, retain, develop, and exploit (in the best sense of the word) this tremendous resource. They detail, however, that the vast majority of employers need to let go of outdated models such as thinking that there is only one place that work gets done, one way to structure a workday, one model for the ideal career, and one leadership style that works in today's workplace.

Harrington and Ladge show that flexible work arrangements, flexible career paths, and new leadership styles better meet the needs of today's diverse workforce as well as today's flexible and fast-changing economic environment. They argue these new work policies should not be perks for only a chosen few. All workers need policies that meet the changed realities of work and family, not just elite workers. In short, the conversation is no longer about *whether* women will work, but rather about how businesses are dealing with the fact that their workforce is increasingly made up of women and most workers today—men and women—share in at least some care responsibilities.

The Challenge of Faith: Bringing spiritual sustenance to busy lives, by **Kimberly Morgan**, associate professor of political science and international affairs at The George Washington University, and **Sally Steenland**, senior policy advisor for the Faith and Progressive Policy project at the Center for American Progress, explore the ongoing role of religion and spirituality in women's lives. They ask how traditional faith communities and new organizational forms of spirituality have responded to women's increased employment outside the home. Their conclusion? Women are struggling to find the time for religious involvement amid the responsibilities of job and family, which in turn means religious institutions need to adapt to these new realities—especially as the support and services that organized religion provides become more important than ever.

Morgan and Steenland note that some congregations have actively engaged with today's new realities, providing increased services that address the challenges for families that no longer have an adult who remains outside the labor force. Yet others have not, and in many cases while women have entered boardrooms and are leading companies, faith institutions have been slow to incorporate women into their leadership. Morgan and Steenland suggest several ways for faith and spiritual communities to better engage with today's busy women.

University of Michigan communications professor **Susan Douglas** then shows us in ***Where Have You Gone, Roseanne Barr?*** how the media that we're surrounded by every day have in some ways overshot reality and in many ways not caught up on the way women work and live in our society today. The mainstream media outlets often suggest that women have "made it," portraying women as successful executives at the top of every profession, yet in real life there are far too few women among the highest ranks of the professions, and millions of everyday women struggle to make ends meet and to juggle work and family. Douglas suggests women need to challenge these misleading portraits with facts, vigor, and humor.

Douglas's provocative chapter is accompanied by an essay titled ***Sexy Socialization: Today's media and the next generation of women***, by **Stacy L. Smith**, a fellow at the Center for Communication Leadership and Policy at the Annenberg School of Communications, and two of her colleagues, **Cynthia Kennard**, a senior fellow at the Center, and **Amy D. Granados**, a policy analyst at Annenberg. The three authors highlight what today's 8-to-19-year-olds are taking in about the role of men and women in the workplace and society through the lens of various media, focusing on how troubling male and female sexual stereotypes could affect the life and career choices of our next generation. The authors express concern about the future of women breadwinners in the coming decades because of these stereotypes, but hold out hope that the media industry itself will change as more women rise within its ranks or launch new media outlets on their own.

Our report then shifts focus to a series of chapters and essays that we hope will get people talking about all of our analytical research. In ***Has a Man's World Become a Woman's Nation?***, **Michael Kimmel**, sociology professor at the State University of New York, Stonybrook, surveys the varied responses that men have had to women's entry into the workforce and to losing the title of sole breadwinner. He finds that most men have chosen the path toward acceptance of greater gender equality and often relish the extra earnings women bring into the family—but that some groups of men continue to struggle with the idea of widespread employment of women and mothers as it has made them question their very notion of masculinity.

Above all, though, Kimmel finds that while both men and women want the kind of support that makes it possible to have a dual-earner, dual-caregiver family, these issues are more often misperceived as only "women's issues" in Washington and statehouses around the nation. Men need family-friendly policies so that they can have the sorts of family relationships they say they want to have, as well as careers that enable them to work and live better in our changing 21st-century economy. Kimmel closes his chapter with a call for men to rally behind efforts to make it better for women and men together to work and live in our changing economy and society, not rely on women alone to do so.

Next, we learn that negotiating around the kitchen table can be good for your marriage. In her reflective essay, ***Sharing the Load***, Evergreen State College sociologist **Stephanie Coontz** provides evidence that the most stable, high-quality marriages are those where men and women share both paid work and domestic work. This is a shift from generations ago when the most stable marriages were those where husbands specialized in paid work and wives did all the domestic work.

In this section we also include two concluding reflective essays, one by senior correspondent for *The American Prospect* **Courtney E. Martin** and the other by political strategist and media consultant **Jamal Simmons**. They explore what it all means for today's generations of women and men who grew up in a world that was less likely to question the desirability of the equality of women but understands that does not yet mean true equality.

Simmons focuses on how the woman you commit to today may have the same name and social security number as the woman you are with tomorrow, but she may want completely different things in her life at different times throughout your lives together. For him, the rules seem to be maddeningly flexible. Martin notes that the women (and men) of her generation have come of age at a time when feminist values are simply in the water. But she argues that we need comprehensive policy reform that reflects an accurate picture of the workers and families as we really are, not as we imagine ourselves to be. She closes by saying that "It's a good thing we've been so pumped up on post-gender idealism, because there are some big battles ahead."

To gauge just how representative these conversations and observations are of actual conditions in American homes and workplaces, we close the report with a hot-off-the-press landmark nationwide poll. This Rockefeller/*Time* poll of 3,413 people nationwide takes a broad and deep look at what men and women think of their changing roles in society and their attitudes toward each other as spouses, parents, bosses, and co-workers. Center for American Progress fellows **John Halpin** and **Ruy Texiera**, **Kelly Daley** with global research company Abt SRBI Inc., and former *Los Angeles Times* pollster **Susan Pinkus** conducted, analyzed, and then concisely summarized the poll findings for us in their chapter ***Battle of the Sexes Gives Way to Negotiations***.

The poll results reveal a truce in the battle of the sexes, demonstrating that men and women are in agreement on many of the day-to-day work and family issues. The old line in the sand separating them has largely washed away. Indeed, both men and women agree that women's movement into employment is good for the country. Virtually all married couples see negotiating about the rules of relationships, work, and family as key making things work at home and at work. The authors conclude that the one clear message emerging from this poll is that the lives of Americans have changed significantly in recent years, yet the parameters of their jobs have yet to change to meet new demands. They find that political and business leaders who fail to take steps to address the needs of modern families risk losing good workers and the support of men and women who are riding the crest of major social change in America with little or no support.

Rather than pining for family structures of an earlier generation, the authors report that the poll found that men and women agree that government and businesses have failed to adapt to the needs of modern families. Americans across the board desire more flexibility in work schedules, paid family leave, and increased child care support. Given the ongoing difficulties many people face in balancing work and family life, it is not surprising that large numbers of Americans—men and women alike—view the decline in the percentage of children growing up in a family with a stay-at-home parent as a negative development for society. Yet, ever practical and pragmatic, this poll demonstrates that Americans understand that everything has changed in their work and lives today and that consequently they are working things out as best they can while looking to their government and their employers to catch up.

The academic research, anecdotal evidence, personal reflections, and poll results that make up this unique report all confirm that recognizing women now constitute half of the workers in the United States is only the first step. The second is identifying what we need to do to reshape the institutions around us. We can then begin to take the necessary actions to readjust our policies and practices. When you finish reading our report, we're confident you'll agree that more than four decades after President Kennedy's Commission on the Status of Women, we've learned that while there's much to cheer about, we still have a long way to go. We as a people must transform the way our government, our businesses, our faith-based institutions, and our media deal with the realities of a woman's nation so that all of us can better cope with the transformation of how we work and live. The ultimate goal is a more prosperous future for all women and men in a nation that recognizes the unique value of each of us to contribute to the common good at work and at home. We believe that we can get there together, and that this report takes an important step along that path.

The Economic Setting

JIM MAHONEY, DALLAS MORNING NEWS, CORBIS

The New Breadwinners

Women now account for half of all jobs, with sweeping consequences for our nation's economy, society, and future prosperity

By Heather Boushey

For a brief moment in American history, women during World War II accounted for more than one-third of the U.S. workforce as men streamed into the armed forces to defeat our fascist enemies.[1] This phenomenal transformation of the U.S. economy was brief but its influence was enduring. So many Americans can share "Rosie the Riveter" stories akin to President Obama's memories of tales about his grandmother working in an arms manufacturing plant while his grandfather served in Europe with General George Patton.

Today, the movement of women into the labor force is not just enduring but certifiably revolutionary—perhaps the greatest social transformation of our time. Women are more likely to work outside the home and their earnings are more important to family well-being than ever before in our nation's history. This transformation changes everything. At the most profound level, it changes the rules of what it means to be a woman—and what it means to be a man. Women are now increasingly sharing the role of breadwinner, as well as the role of caregiver, with the men in their lives. Even so, we have yet to come to terms with what it means to live in a nation where both men and women typically work outside the home and what we need to do to make this new reality workable for families who have child care and elder care responsibilities through most of their working lives.

Indeed, the transformation in how women spend their days affects nearly every aspect of our daily lives. As women move into the labor force, their earnings are increasingly important to families and women more and more become the major breadwinner—even though women continue to be paid 23 cents less than men for every dollar earned in our economy.[2] Nearly 4 in 10 mothers (39.3 percent) are primary breadwinners, bringing home the majority of the family's earnings, and nearly two-thirds (62.8 percent) are breadwinners or co-breadwinners, bringing home at least a quarter of the family's earnings. What's more, women are now much more likely to head families on their own.

Most women today are providing for their families by working outside the home—and still earning less than men—while providing more than their fair share of caregiving responsibilities at home.

These gains are by no means an unqualified victory for women in the workforce and in society, or for their families. Most women today are providing for their families by working outside the home—and still earning less than men—while providing more than their fair share of caregiving responsibilities inside the home, an increasingly impossible task. At home, families cope with this day-to-day time squeeze in a variety of unsatisfactory ways. In most families today, there's no one who stays at home all day and so there's no one with the time to prepare dinner, be home when the kids get back from school, or deal with the little things of everyday life, such as accepting a UPS package or getting the refrigerator repaired. Instead of having Mom at home keeping her eye on the children after school, families face the challenge of watching over their latchkey kids from afar and worry about what their teenagers are doing after school.

Yet the flip side is this: The presence of women is now commonplace in all kinds of workplaces and many are in positions of authority. Millions of workers now have a female boss and the more collaborative management styles that many women bring to the workplace are improving the bottom line. Increasingly, businesses are recognizing that most of their labor force has some kind of family care responsibility, and therefore are creating flexible workplace policies to deal with this reality. Many of the fastest-growing jobs replace the work women used to do for free in the home. The demand for home health aides, child care workers, and food service workers, for instance, has increased sharply.

Social patterns also are changing, and rapidly so. With women now half of all workers on U.S. payrolls, there is no longer a standard timeline for marriage and raising a family—if women even choose to marry or have children. The assisted reproductive technologies industry has blossomed as women—especially professional women—invest in their careers and delay motherhood into their 30s and 40s. And the share of women who are unmarried has skyrocketed: 40 percent of women over age 25 are now unmarried and a record 40 percent of children born in 2007 had an unmarried mother.[3] While divorce rates have fallen, many women delay and some never even enter marriage.

This transformation also boasts profound implications for communities around the nation. In schools and religious and community organizations, women are now less available to volunteer during the work week and have less time to devote to leading community organizations. The transformation affects our health care system, too, since health care providers have to cope with the fact that there is not likely to be someone to provide free, at-home care for a recovering patient.

And it affects our quality of life. Many retail stores, restaurants, and consumer support lines are now open 24 hours a day, seven days a week, which meets the needs of families with 9-to-5 work hours. But this has meant that millions of other families—disproportionately immigrants and lower-income families—have workers employed during nonstandard hours, affecting their marriages and their ability to access child care and other supports not generally available at nonstandard times.

Quite simply, as women go to work, everything changes. Yet, we, as a nation, have not yet digested what this all means and what changes are still to be made. But change we must, especially as the current recession amplifies and accelerates these trends throughout our economy and society. The Great Recession led to massive job losses, especially within male-dominated industries. Since the recession began in December 2007, men have accounted for three out of every four jobs lost (73.6 percent)[4] and now 2 million wives are supporting their families while their unemployed husbands seek work.[5]

Women now, for the first time, make up half (49.9 percent as of July 2009) of all workers on U.S. payrolls. This is a dramatic change from just over a generation ago: In 1969, women made up only a third of the workforce (35.3 percent).[6]

WORKING THE NIGHT SHIFTS. Gloria Castillo is 22 years old, married, a mother of two, a Latina from the rough side of Dallas, pictured at work. This is her third drive-through job. It is becoming a career.
[STEPHEN CROWLEY/*THE NEW YORK TIMES*]

Many American women have always worked, of course, but as more women joined the ranks of the employed and laws prohibiting outright discrimination came into effect, a wider array of opportunities opened up to women. By 2008, a working mother is no longer revolutionary and is in fact now common: Only one in five families with children (20.7 percent) are the traditional male breadwinner, female homemaker, compared to 44.7 percent in 1975.[7] That year, 4 in 10 mothers with a child under age 6 (39.6 percent) worked outside the home, but by 2008, that share had risen to two-thirds (64.3 percent).[8]

To understand what it means for women to become breadwinners, this chapter focuses on who's gone to work, where women are working, why they are working, and what this means for the economic well-being of women and their families. While women have made great strides and are now more likely to be economically responsible for themselves and their families, there is still a long way to go. Equity in the workplace has not yet been achieved, even as families need women's equality now more than ever.

Women's earnings making all the difference

One thing is very clear: The added earnings of women have made all the difference for families. There are more women living alone and raising children on their own, and within married-couple families, women's earnings have become more important.

Consider first the dramatic rise in women raising children on their own. Between 1973 and 2006, the share of all families headed by an unmarried woman rose to one in five, or 18.4 percent, from 1 in 10 (10 percent).[9] These families rely almost exclusively on a woman's wage. Only 4 in 10 custodial mothers (41.7 percent) receive any child support and only half (47.3 percent) of those awarded child support actually receive their full award.[10] Further, the incomes of families headed by unmarried women have not kept pace with those of dual-earner families. Between 1973 and 2006, families headed by a single woman saw their incomes rise by 25.5 percent, while dual-earner families saw their incomes rise by 37.1 percent.[11]

While single women bring home the bacon for their families, wives' earnings are typically no longer ancillary to the family's budget. Since the early 1970s, it has been the earnings of wives that have made the difference between families seeing no income growth and some income growth (see Figure 1). Today, married-couple families with a wife who doesn't work have inflation-adjusted incomes that are no higher than similar families in the early 1970s. Researchers Katherine Bradbury and Jane Katz at the Federal Reserve Bank of Boston found that families in which wives worked, worked longer hours, or had higher pay compared to families without such wives were more likely to move up the income ladder or maintain their position rather than fall down the ladder.[12]

Compared to their parents and grandparents, today's families put in more hours at work, but see fewer gains. They increasingly need two incomes just to cover the basics—the mortgage, the car, and health insurance.[13] This is a sharp reversal from the period after World War II through the early 1970s when *both* families with a wife in paid employment and those without saw their incomes rise year after year and both at about the same pace.

FIGURE 1

Married working couples struggle to get ahead

Couples with and without a working wife saw income grow at about the same pace from 1949 to 1973, but only those with a working wife saw income growth after 1973

Average annual income growth by family type, inflation-adjusted, 1949–1973 and 1973–2008

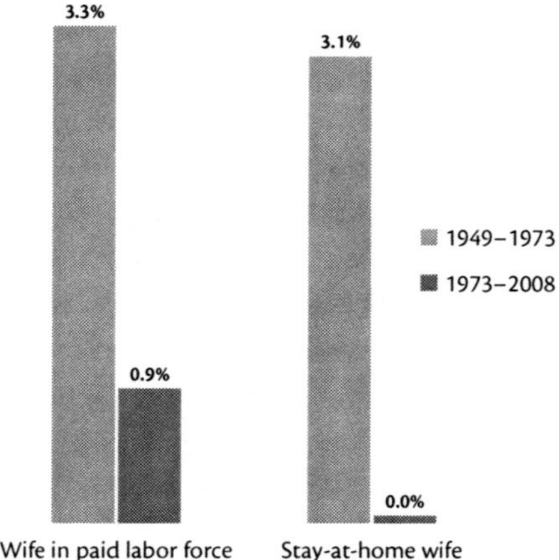

Source: Author's analysis of U.S. Census Bureau, Current Population Survey Annual Social and Economic Supplement.

Clearly, the days of Ozzie and Harriet are long gone. Within married-couple families, the typical working wife now brings home 42.2 percent of her family's earnings.[14] And women increasingly are the primary breadwinners. In 2008, nearly 4 in 10 mothers (39.3 percent) were the primary breadwinner in their family—either because they were a single, working parent or because they earned as much as or more than their spouse. An additional quarter (24.0 percent) of mothers are co-breadwinners—that is, a working wife bringing home at least 25 percent of her family's total earnings (see Figure 2 and Table 1).[15]

Women are becoming breadwinners among all kinds of married-couple families, by income, education, and race. Specifically:

FIGURE 2

The new workforce

Share of mothers who are breadwinners or co-breadwinners, 1967 to 2008

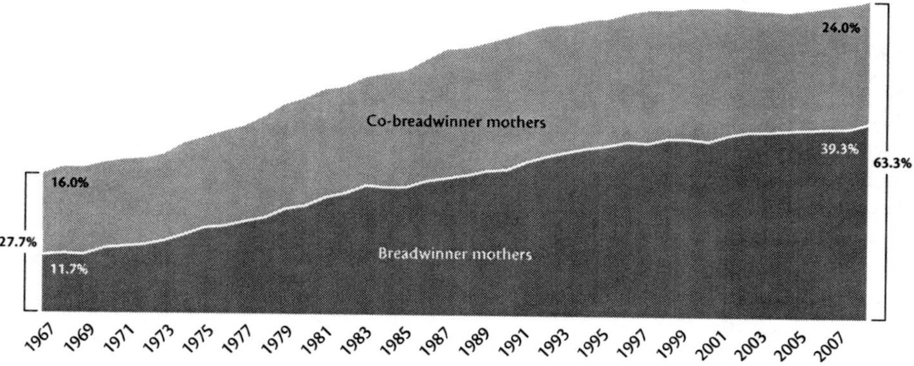

Source: See Table 1.

Notes: Breadwinner mothers include single mothers who work and married mothers who earn as much as or more than their husbands. Co-breadwinners include all breadwinners as well as wives who bring home at least 25 percent of the couple's earnings. The data only include families with a mother who is between the ages of 18 and 60 and who has children under age 18 living with her.

By income

- Just under a third (30.1 percent) of working wives in families with incomes in the top 20 percent of all families (not just married-couple families) brought home as much or more than their husbands did in 2008, compared to only one in eight (12.6 percent) in 1967. The trend is similar even among families with a child under age 6 in which nearly a third (28.0 percent) of working wives in the families in the top fifth bring home as much as or more than their husbands in 2008.

- In the bottom 20 percent of income distribution of all families, over two-thirds (67.7 percent) of working wives brought home as much as or more than their husbands in 2008, up from 44 percent in 1967, while in the next 20 percent of income distribution half (49.2 percent) of working wives now bring home as much or more than their husbands, up from 28.3 percent in 1967.

By education

- In families where the wife has only a high school diploma, the share of working wives earning as much as or more than their spouses stood at 36.6 percent in 2008 compared to 14.5 percent in 1967, while among working wives with a college degree 41.1 percent earned as much as or more than their spouses compared to 30.8 percent over the same period.

TABLE 1

Bringing home the bacon

Working wives bring home half or more of family earnings

	Share of working wives earning as much as or more than their husbands	
	1967	**2008**
All wives	18.7	38.1
With child under age 18	11.5	31.4
With child under age 6	9.3	31.0
Mother with high school diploma	7.5	27.8
Mother with some college	9.2	26.8
Mother with college degree	17.9	35.4
Mother under age 30	8.4	27.7
Mother aged 30 to 44	10.0	31.9
Women under age 30	14.8	30.3
Women 30 to 44	11.9	32.7
Women 45 to 60	24.1	40.0
Less than high school	20.3	35.3
High school	14.5	36.6
Some college	19.3	36.2
College	30.8	41.1

Source: Author and Jeff Chapman's analysis of Miriam King, Steven Ruggles, Trent Alexander, Donna Leicach, and Matthew Sobek. Integrated Public Use Microdata Series, Current Population Survey: Version 2.0. [Machine-readable database]. Minneapolis, MN: Minnesota Population Center [producer and distributor], 2009.

Note: Data include married couples with a wife over age 18. Data do not include gay or lesbian couples, regardless of marital status.

By race

- Among white families, over a third (36.9 percent) of working wives earned as much as or more than their husbands in 2008, compared to one in five (21.1 percent) in 1975. Over that same time period, among African American families, the share rose to 51.5 percent from 28.7 percent, and among Hispanic families, the share rose from 23.6 to 35.8 percent

And, of course, lesbian couples have always relied on the earnings of just women. Recent research shows that lesbian families are more likely than heterosexual couples to end up in poverty.[16] Since women on average earn less than men, lesbian couples have two lower-paid earners, and are doubly discriminated against because of continued heterosexist employment discrimination, on top of the discrimination that lesbians experience as women, mothers, or people of color.

A snapshot of today's working women

Three views of women's earnings power—percent of working wives earning as much as or more than their husbands

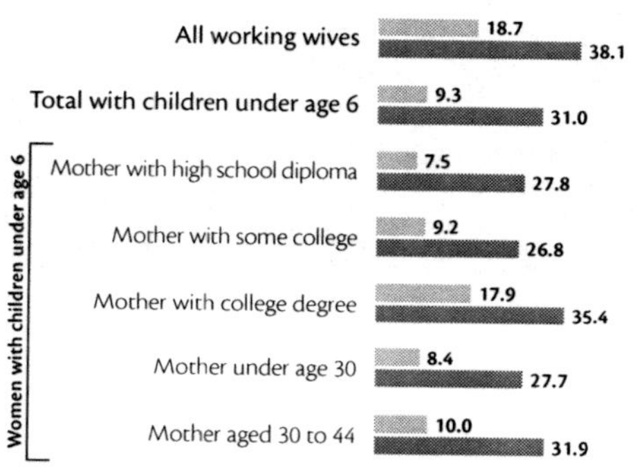

By wife's race/ethnicity

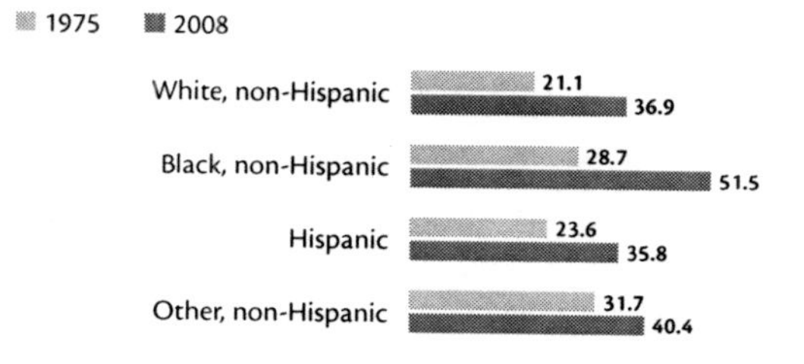

By family income quintile

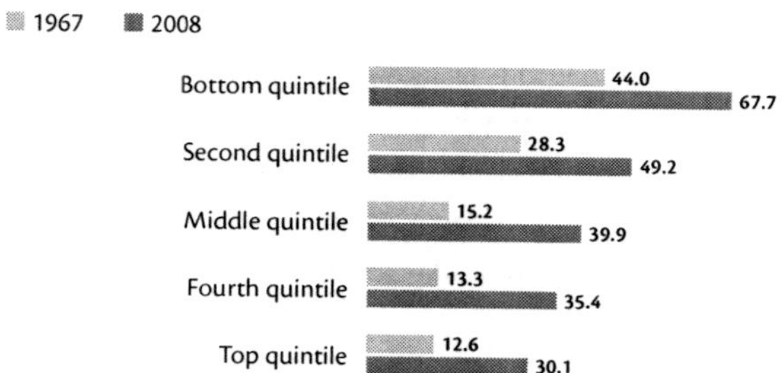

Source: See Table 1.

Note: Income quintiles are determined using all families, not only married-couple families.

Where women work matters

Part of the reason that women's earnings have become more important to family well-being is that women are now found in all kinds of jobs. Equal opportunity legislation made it possible for women to take nearly any job. But even though women now constitute half of all workers, they do not make up half of every kind of job. Continued sex segregation in employment is one of the primary factors explaining the wage gap between men and women.

Table 2 lists the top 20 occupations for men and women in 2008. The list tends to confirm gendered stereotypes about who does what and documents that many of the jobs most commonly held by women (and men!) require little or no higher education. The most common occupations for women are secretaries and administrative assistants, nurses, and schoolteachers. Of the top 20 jobs for women, only nurses and schoolteachers required advanced degrees. Men most commonly work as drivers, managers, and retail supervisors.

This table also confirms that men and women continue to work in highly segregated workplaces. There are only four occupations that appear on the list of the 20 most commonly held jobs for both men and women: retail salesperson (2.5 percent of women and 2.0 percent of men),

TWO SIDES OF A CAREER. The scheduling of deliveries remains largely a woman's job; the driving is still mostly in the hands of men. (ROBB KENDRICK, AURORA PHOTOS; PETER WYNN THOMPSON, *THE NEW YORK TIMES*)

first-line supervisors of retail stores (2.3 percent of women and 2.6 percent of men), all other managers (1.9 percent of women and 2.9 percent of men), and cooks (1.1 percent of women and 1.5 percent of men). This is only slight progress from a few generations ago. In 1979, half of women (51.7 percent) were employed in just 20 occupations, while the top 20 occupations employed 40.6 percent of men.[17]

Even though sex segregation continues to define the U.S. workplace, there has been some progress in women entering nontraditional fields. Women now constitute just over a third of engineers (35.9 percent in 2008) and lawyers and judges (36.5 percent), under a third of physicians and surgeons (31.8 percent), and nearly 4 in 10 managers (38.2 percent). Still, women remain the dominant workers in traditional female occupations, making up 97.8 percent of all preschool and kindergarten teachers, 97.3 percent of dental hygienists, 96.3 percent of all secretaries and administrative assistants, and 95.5 percent of all child care workers. And men still dominate in construction and building trades, making up 97.5 percent of all construction and extraction workers and 96.1 percent of all installation, repair, and maintenance jobs.[18]

TABLE 2

Who works where

Top 20 occupations for women and men, 2008

Occupation	Share of female workers	Occupation	Share of male workers
Secretaries and administrative assistants	4.7	Driver/sales workers and truck drivers	4.1
Registered nurses	3.8	**All other managers**	2.9
Elementary and middle school teachers	3.7	**First-line supervisors/managers of retail stores**	2.6
Cashiers	3.0	Construction laborers	2.1
Retail salespersons	2.5	Carpenters	2.1
Nursing, psychiatric, and home health aides	2.5	**Retail salespersons**	2.0
First-line supervisors/managers of retail stores	2.3	Laborers and freight, stock, and material movers, hand	2.0
Waiters and waitresses	2.1	Janitors and building cleaners	1.8
Bookkeeping, accounting, and auditing clerks	1.9	Chief executives	1.6
Receptionists and information clerks	1.9	**Cooks**	1.5
All other managers	1.9	Grounds maintenance workers	1.5
Customer service representatives	1.9	Construction managers	1.5
Maids and housekeeping cleaners	1.9	Sales representatives, wholesale and manufacturing	1.3
Child care workers	1.8	First-line supervisors/managers of non-retail sales workers	1.2
First-line supervisors/managers of office and administrative support workers	1.8	Stock clerks and order fillers	1.2
Accountants and auditors	1.6	Electricians	1.1
Office clerks, general	1.5	Automotive service technicians and mechanics	1.1
Teacher assistants	1.4	First-line supervisors/managers of construction trades and extraction workers	1.1
Cooks	1.1	Computer software engineers	1.1
Personal and home care aides	1.1	First-line supervisors/managers of production and operating workers	1.0
Share employed in the top 20 occupations			
Females	44.4	Males	34.8

Source: Author's analysis of the Center for Economic and Policy Research Extracts of the Current Population Survey Outgoing Rotation Group Files. Includes workers aged 18 to 64.

Note: Bold items appear on the list for both women and men.

Dual-income families are almost a staple now. So there has to be some sort of redefining of roles from that aspect strictly. That's been a challenge. My wife makes about three times what I make. I work in a world that says egalitarian values between men and women should be the norm. Even if they're not. And yet, I struggle personally with the fact that I'm not providing more to the household income.

Michael in Seattle

EDGEPLOT, FLICK

FIGURE 4

Future jobs

Projected job growth by occupation and gender, 2006–2016, in thousands of new jobs

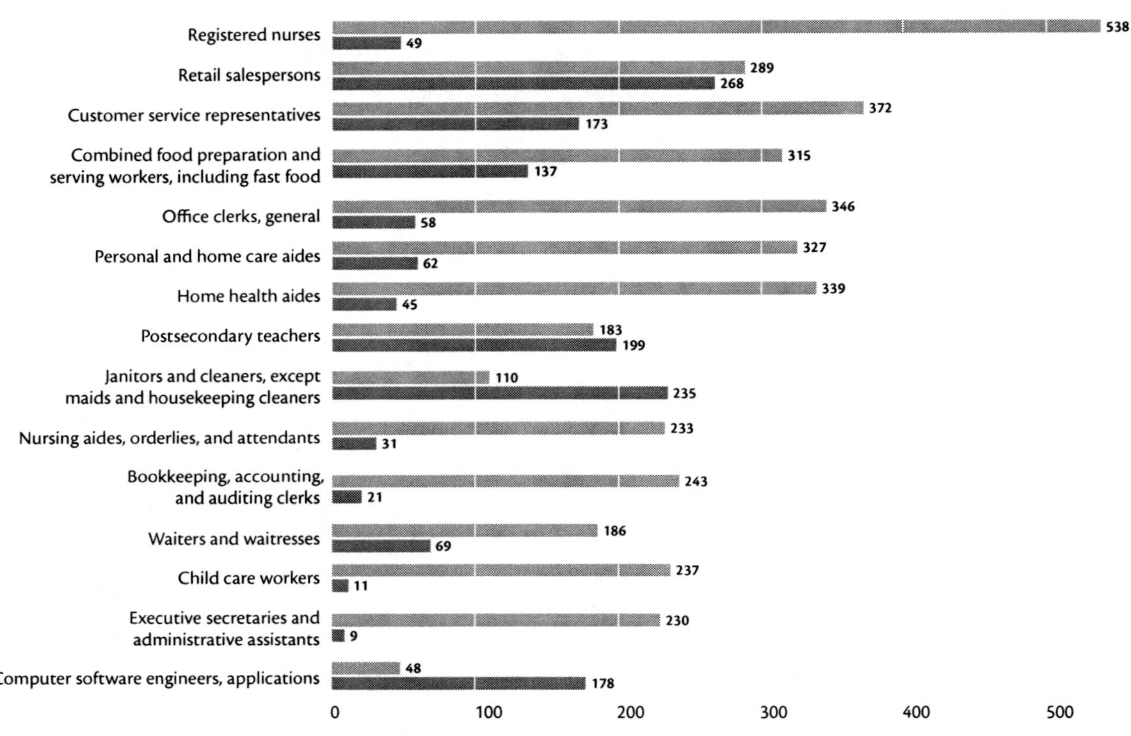

Source: See Table 1. Gender breakdown is based on the job occupants in 2008 by gender.

Looking forward, the Bureau of Labor Statistics' projection of future job growth shows a pattern that is similar to the jobs of today. Figure 4 shows that over the next decade, the occupations projected to have the largest number of new jobs are in services. Many have a caring aspect to them, such as nursing or home health aides, that replace the work that women historically did without pay in the home in the decades before women entered the labor force in great numbers. Most of these jobs require little higher education and most pay low wages (see Table 3). Currently, these occupations tend to be dominated by women, who make up more than two-thirds of the employees in all but five of the 15 occupations with largest projected job growth.

TABLE 3

Occupations with the largest projected new jobs, 2006–2016

Occupation	Employment		Quartile rank[1]	Most significant source of postsecondary education or training[2]	Share that is female, 2008[3]
	Thousands	Percent			
Registered nurses	587	23.5	VH	Associate degree	91.7
Retail salespersons	557	12.4	VL	Short-term on-the-job training	51.8
Customer service representatives	545	24.8	L	Moderate-term on-the-job training	68.2
Combined food preparation and serving workers, including fast food	452	18.1	VL	Short-term on-the-job training	69.8
Office clerks, general	404	12.6	L	Short-term on-the-job training	85.7
Personal and home care aides	389	50.6	VL	Short-term on-the-job training	84.1
Home health aides	384	48.7	VL	Short-term on-the-job training	88.2
Postsecondary teachers	382	22.9	VH	Doctoral degree	48.0
Janitors and cleaners, except maids and housekeeping cleaners	345	14.5	VL	Short-term on-the-job training	31.9
Nursing aides, orderlies, and attendants	264	18.2	L	Postsecondary vocational award	88.2
Bookkeeping, accounting, and auditing clerks	264	12.5	L	Moderate-term on-the-job training	92.1
Waiters and waitresses	255	10.8	VL	Short-term on-the-job training	73.0
Child care workers	248	17.8	VL	Short-term on-the-job training	95.5
Executive secretaries and administrative assistants	239	14.8	H	Work experience in a related occupation	96.3
Computer software engineers, applications	226	44.6	VH	Bachelor's degree	21.2

Source: Bureau of Labor Statistics, "Occupational employment projections to 2016," Monthly Labor Review, Vol. 130, No. 11, Table 3 (http://www.bls.gov/emp/emptab3.htm) and author's analysis of the Center for Economic and Policy Research Extracts of the Current Population Survey Outgoing Rotation Group Files (ORG), 2008.

Notes: 1. The quartile rankings of Occupational Employment Statistics Survey annual wages data are presented in the following categories: VH = very high ($46,360 or more), H = high ($30,630 to $46,300), L = low ($21,260 to $30,560), and VL = very low (up to $21,220). The rankings were based on quartiles, with one-fourth of total employment defining each quartile. Wages are for wage and salary workers. 2. An occupation is placed into 1 of 11 categories that best describes the postsecondary education or training needed by most workers to become fully qualified in that occupation. For more information about the categories, see Occupational Projections and Training Data, 2006-07 edition, Bulletin 2602 (Bureau of Labor Statistics, February 2006) and Occupational Projections and Training Data, 2008-09 edition, Bulletin 2702 (Bureau of Labor Statistics, forthcoming). 3. The ORG data combine home health aides and nursing aides into one category, "Nursing, psychiatric, and home health aides 31-1010," and we use the share of that workforce for both "Home health aides" and "Nursing aides, orderlies, and attendants."

Why women work

Women becoming breadwinners is the direct result of more women seeking employment in the first place. But as women became a larger share of those employed and took advantage of economic opportunities opening up to them, more of them have begun to be a family's lead earner. The trend toward more women working occurred among all kinds of women, although it is the women in the middle and top of income distribution in our country as well as mothers (both married and single) who have seen the starkest changes in their employment patterns over the past half-century.

But why did women enter employment in great numbers? Was it the desire to be a career woman that pulled so many women into the labor force? Was it the increase in women remaining (or becoming) unmarried that pushed women to believe that they needed to be bringing in their own incomes? The answer is a little of both. Women are in the labor force because they need to be, but also because many want to work and are taking advantage of expanded opportunities.

For starters, the world changed and technology marched forward in ways that freed women from work inside the home and from some of the constraints of biology. The post-World War II years saw technological improvements that reduced the time necessary for home production (although some research shows that this only upped the cleanliness standards).[19] And the introduction of the pill and, more importantly, its increased availability for single women, gave women the opportunity to invest in their education and their careers because they were able to plan when they would have their children.[20]

As a result of the women's movement—alongside structural changes in the economy away from manufacturing toward services that disproportionately employ women—women fanned out into a variety of occupations that had hitherto been closed to them.

At the same time, the rules changed. Even as late as the early 1970s, women were kept out of jobs by "marriage employment bans" or were fired upon telling their boss they were pregnant. Representative Carolyn Maloney of New York tells her story this way: In the early 1970s, when she asked her human resources office about its maternity leave policy, she was told there was no policy since "most women just leave."[21] The Civil Rights Act of 1964 made it illegal to fire a woman once she married and the Pregnancy Discrimination Act of 1978 made it illegal to fire a woman just because she was pregnant; but neither required that a women be granted maternity leave.

These rules didn't change on their own. The women's movement helped women pursue jobs outside the home and become economically independent, including

TRADING PLACES. Women are climbing the ladder on Wall Street but rarely reaching the top rungs. [NAJLAH FEANNY, CORBIS]

in "men's" jobs. They fought for—and won—landmark pieces of legislation that created real progress in reducing gender discrimination and helping millions of women break through the glass ceiling. As a result of their efforts—alongside structural changes in the economy away from manufacturing toward services that disproportionately employ women—women fanned out into a variety of occupations that had hitherto been closed to them.

During the 1980s, married middle-income and upper-income women rapidly entered the job market. This was at least partially attributable to the fact that for middle- and upper-income women, the career opportunities that opened up were more appealing than traditional female jobs. Furthermore, as women increased their educational attainment, they were able to enter jobs with higher career paths. Economists Chinhui Juhn and Kevin Murphy confirmed through econometric analysis that over the 1970s and 1980s changes in women's wages—that is, increases in women's own economic opportunities—led women into the labor market,[22] and economists Francine Blau and Lawrence Kahn found that this trend continued through 2000.[23]

On top of this, middle- and upper-income women's families could afford to replace their household labor by employing nannies, placing their children in high-quality child care, or hiring other household help, which lower-income families could not do. Without public support for working families, lower-income families continue to disproportionately rely on the unpaid work of women to address the problems of how to care for children, the aged, or infirm.

Without public support for working families, lower-income families continue to disproportionately rely on the unpaid work of women to address the problems of how to care for children, the aged, or infirm.

But it wasn't just these wealthier, better-educated women who entered the workforce in droves in recent decades. In the mid-1990s, policy changes also led more low-income women to seek employment. Welfare reform required low-income mothers to be employed, while other policies, such as the rise in the minimum wage, the expansion of the Earned Income Tax Credit, the increased funding for the Child Care Development Block Grant, and the introduction of the State Child Health Insurance Program, encouraged them to do so by boosting the take-home pay of those working at low-wage jobs. These pieces of legislation were passed in the middle of the strongest labor market in decades—especially for low-wage work—and were followed by sharp increases in the employment of unmarried mothers.

Today, women are likely to work outside the home regardless of their status as mothers. In the early 1980s, mothers had employment rates that were about 20 percentage points lower than non-mothers, all else equal. But the pull of children keeping women out of the workplace has grown weaker over time, leveling off

Many women have *always* worked

The news today is that women make up half of all workers, but it's always been the case that some women have worked outside the home. The remarkable changes in women's employment gloss over the reality that for some groups of women, becoming a breadwinner is nothing new.

African American women have historically been more likely than other racial and ethnic groups to work outside the home. In 1920, the labor force participation rate of black women was 38.9 percent, twice as large as any other racial or ethnic group except Japanese women, of whom 25.9 percent worked.[24] But as the 20th century marched forward, women of all racial groups began working in greater numbers. By 2007, labor force participation rates had risen to nearly 60 percent in all racial groups of women—African Americans the highest at 61.1 percent, white women next at 59 percent, followed by Asians at 58.6 percent and Hispanics at 56.5 percent.[25]

A century ago, a substantial percentage of employed women worked as domestics in other people's homes and this was fairly consistent across racial and ethnic groups. In 1900, among working women, about a third of Asians and whites and a higher share (43.5 percent) of African Americans held private household service jobs.[26] While many women have fanned out into a much larger array of occupations, recent immigrant women—mostly from Mexico and Central America—are now those most likely to do domestic labor.[27] These jobs tend not only to have low wages, but they are often "under the table" and do not provide workers with the same level of unemployment and Social Security benefits as other kinds of work.

in the 2000s at about 12 percentage points—just over half as large as just a few decades ago. This means that mothers are now about 12 percentage points less likely to work than nonmothers, all else equal.[28]

It is important to note, though, that not every woman has gone into paid employment and one in five families with children have a stay-at-home mother and breadwinner father. But even among women at home today, the overwhelming majority will work outside the home at some point in their lives.[29] Still, most workers do not have any workplace flexibility, nearly half do not have the right to a paid sick day to care for an ill child or family member, and most do not have access to paid family leave.

Which women work

Not all women seek to work in the same way or to the same degree over their working lives for obviously very different and very personal reasons. But there are patterns evident among different groups of working women, among them of course those women who have always worked (see box "Many women have *always* worked"). Let's examine several of those patterns.

THE LATEST FROM THE AMERICAN PEOPLE

Q: What share of your family's income do you personally earn?

Percent answering "half or more"

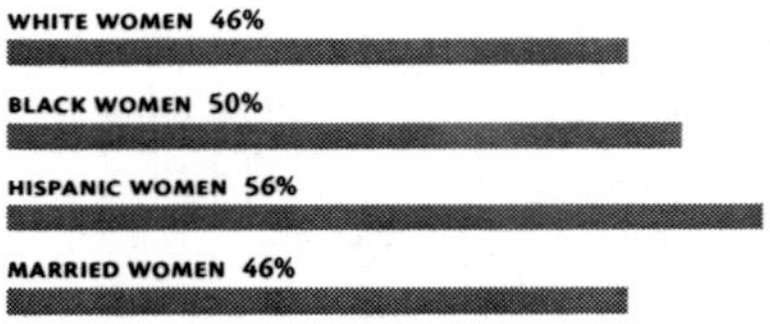

Group	Percent
WHITE WOMEN	46%
BLACK WOMEN	50%
HISPANIC WOMEN	56%
MARRIED WOMEN	46%

Source: Rockefeller/*Time* poll, 2009.

Historically, married women were less likely than unmarried women to work outside the home, not just because of tradition but also due to legally sanctioned discrimination by employers that kept wives out of the workplace. In 1963, 37 percent of wives were in the labor force, compared to 65.5 percent of unmarried women.[30] Since the mid- to late 1990s, however, labor force participation rates for married women have remained relatively stable, while rising for unmarried women: By 2008, 70.0 percent of wives and 72.5 percent of unmarried women were in the labor force during the year. The recession may lead more women—especially wives—to seek employment in 2009 and beyond as men face high numbers of layoffs and have difficulty finding new jobs.[31]

Mothers have typically been less likely than nonmothers to work outside the home. Since the late 1990s, the employment rates of unmarried mothers have begun to converge with those of women without children, but the employment rates of married mothers continue to be far below that of other women.[32]

Education also traditionally affects employment patterns. The highest educated women have always been more likely than other women to work, even once they became mothers. In 1963, 62.2 percent of college-educated women were in the labor force, compared to 46.5 percent of those with a high school degree. By 2008, among women with a college degree, 80.7 percent were in the labor force, compared to 73.2 percent of those with some college, 67.6 percent of those with a high school diploma, and 47.0 percent of those without. Highly educated women continue to have high labor-force participation rates even once they become mothers: 77.9 percent in 2008.[33]

The march toward greater employment has occurred at both ends of the age distribution. The recession is pulling older women into employment, either because their husbands have lost their jobs or because they are concerned about their retirement security. With falling home values alongside falling pension values and companies abdicating their responsibilities to their pensioners, many older women will need to work longer than in recent decades.[34] We are already seeing this in the data as the unemployment rate among workers 55 and over is at post-World War II historic highs.[35]

Historically, married women were less likely than unmarried women to work outside the home, not just because of tradition but also due to legally sanctioned discrimination by employers that kept wives out of the workplace.

As more women—especially professional and upper-middle-class women—have taken jobs outside the home in recent decades, the need for domestic labor both inside the home, as well as labor reproducing what women used to do, such as preparing meals, has increased.[36] Demand for domestic labor rose in the halcyon days of the late 1990s and 2000s, but as the Great Recession works its way through the economy, many middle-class and professional families will no longer be able to afford this luxury and we may see changes in the labor patterns of recent immigrant workers.

Should all women work?

The increase in women's labor force participation has made it near-impossible to say that particular groups of women *can't* work just because they're women or because they have children. Even so, there have been long-simmering debates over whether women *should* work outside the home—or even if they really want to. The

ACCEPTING THE NEW BREADWINNER IN THE HOUSE. Art Saxby and his wife, Linda, in their home in Cypress, Texas, earlier this year. Art's job was eliminated in May 2008, making his wife the main breadwinner in the family. Women today are poised to surpass men on the nation's payrolls, holding half of jobs for the first time in American history. {MICHAEL STRAVATO, *THE NEW YORK TIMES*}

reality is that mothers have taken up paid employment in great—and ever rising—numbers, yet the public discourse often remains mired in controversy over whether mothers should work, rarely appreciating the ship-has-sailed reality that most simply just go to work each day.

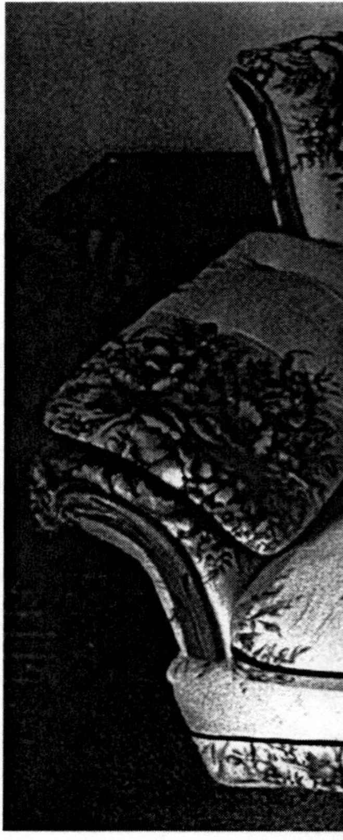

COPING SINGLE-HANDEDLY. Single mothers have to care for their kids and provide for their families, making for long days and nights. [MOFFY CASH, AP]

Two recent examples of this kind of discourse are the debate over welfare reform in the mid-1990s and the opt-out debate of the mid-2000s. The first pitted stay-at-home poor single mothers against employed mothers in blue-collar families by insisting that poor mothers should also be employed. The second was over whether professional women should stay home with their children and whether or not they were "opting out" in the early- to middle-2000s. Both debates helped define the cultural divides that the Great Recession may well put to rest simply because more and more women want to work and need to work. But both debates are worth a quick review for what they reveal about our society today.

The federal welfare program was established in 1935 as a part of the Social Security Act to provide cash assistance to widowed mothers. At that time, the expectation was that a widow could not support her family on her own. Fast forward to the early 1990s and we enter a world where a nearly a quarter of children were being raised by single mothers and most married-couple families were struggling to figure out how to have both mom and dad in the labor force and make it all work at home.[37] By the time President Clinton said in 1992 that he would "end welfare as we know it," there was no longer consensus that an unmarried mother should receive cash assistance.

Those pushing for the end of welfare often couched their arguments in ways that were designed to appeal to working middle-income and lower-middle-income families who were struggling to make ends meet and facing the stresses—the "time bind," the "second shift"—that accompany dual-earner families. Never mind that women in both types of families faced similar problems, among them the lack of affordable child care and low wages.

The rhetoric, though, had a perverse element of truth. Even though both groups needed assistance, only poor families could qualify for admittedly meager benefits and Medicaid or child care subsidies, while working families qualified for little to none of these kinds of benefits and were left to do it all on their own.[38] Of course, such rhetoric was also about marshaling resentment of the poor to push social policy down to the lowest (assistance-free) common denominator rather than appealing to a more aspirational and unifying higher standard for all families.

In the end, the 1996 welfare reform package included carrots and sticks designed to encourage single mothers to avoid cash assistance and instead rely on their earnings. But welfare reform did not address the more fundamental policy gap. Poor, working- and middle-class families alike are struggling to cope with the challenges of being unable to afford a stay-at-home parent yet are unable to afford decent alternatives to pay for care for their children or ailing family members. And this gap leaves them with little to no workplace flexibility to give their day-to-day lives some much-needed sanity. Welfare reform offered some of these kinds of benefits to very low-income families, but the low-income cut-offs—and five-year waiting periods for immigrant families—mean that millions of working families are ineligible, even though they cannot afford these kinds of services at market rates.[39]

A decade later, this culture debate over whether women should work turned to the other end of the income spectrum. Was it really possible—or desirable—for a woman to be both a professional and a mother? A spate of news articles claimed that professional women were opting out of employment in favor of motherhood. The message from this media maelstrom was that women couldn't be professionals and mothers, and what's more, they did not want to.

Mothers have taken up paid employment in great—and ever rising—numbers, yet the public discourse often remains mired in controversy over whether mothers should work, rarely appreciating the ship-has-sailed reality that most simply just go to work each day.

But just as with the welfare reform debates, reality did not confirm this tale. The overwhelming majority of professional mothers do work, more so than any other mothers, and there is no evidence that they were opting out in favor of motherhood.[40] There is evidence, however, that many have been pushed out by inflexible workplaces.

While the headlines were that highly educated women were choosing motherhood over work, the stories themselves told a tale of workplaces that were hostile toward working mothers and pushed them out of employment. In an analysis of the opt-out media maelstrom, Joan Williams, director of the Center for WorkLife Law, and her colleagues found that the claim that it's the "pull of family life" rather than the push of inflexible jobs is not even evident in the quotes journalists took from mothers who left their jobs to be full-time mothers.[41] Their findings are consistent with the research of sociologists Pamela Stone and Meg Lovejoy, who interviewed professional women who had left the labor force and found that nearly all—86 percent—reported workplace factors such as inflexible jobs as a critical reason they left their jobs.[42] This sounds more like pushed out, rather than opted out.

Just as importantly, there is absolutely no empirical evidence that women were increasingly not employed because they had children at home. The fact is that over the 2000s, the share of women—both mothers and nonmothers—and men with jobs flattened. But the evidence pointed toward the weak economic recovery of the early 2000s leading to a lack of job gains among all kinds of workers—moms and nonmoms alike—rather than a story of mothers increasingly dropping out because of the pull of motherhood.[43]

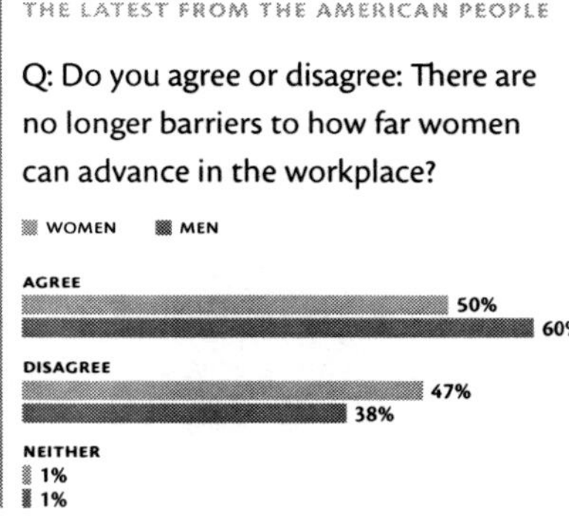

Source: Rockefeller/*Time* poll, 2009.

Quite simply, the opt-out trend was no trend at all. Like the debate over welfare reform, the opt-out story glossed over reality. Indeed, much of this hysteria seemed grounded in the neo-traditional romanticized yearnings such as those found in Judd Apatow's movie comedies, where women fulfill raunchy male sexual desires of the post-women's lib era while also being resigned to the economic status of the pre-women's lib era. Or conversely, in arch-feminist overreactions to these same yearnings, rather than a measured examination of empirical trends.

Equal opportunity, unequal outcomes

Although women may make up half of all workers, they have by no means achieved equality in the workplace. The typical full-time, full-year woman worker brings home 77 cents on the dollar, compared to her male colleagues. And, for specific groups of women—such as women of color or disabled workers—the gap with respect to the wages of white men is larger than for white women. And undocumented immigrant workers often fail to receive even minimum wage, as employment practices for these populations go under the radar.

Much of the gap is attributable to the fact that men and women work in different jobs, but a significant chunk (41.1 percent!) cannot be explained by characteristics of women or their jobs. Over time, the gender gap has narrowed—it was 59 cents on the dollar in the early 1970s—but the pace of convergence has slowed to a crawl in recent years.[44] The most significant compression in the gender pay gap occurred during the 1980s, but this was because men's wages fell, rather than because women's wages rose.

FIGURE 6

How women earn less

Breaking down the gender pay gap

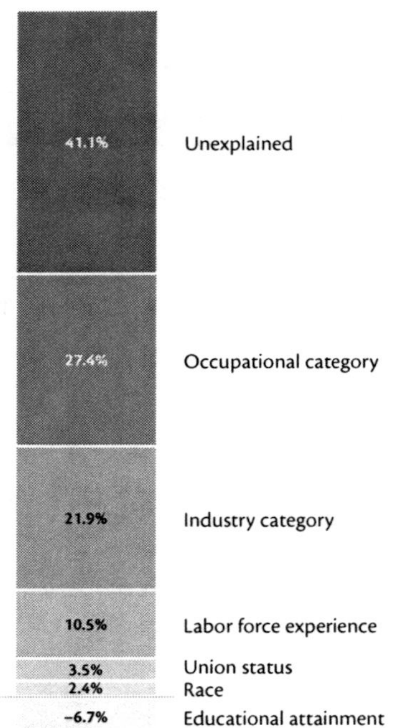

Source: Francine Blau and Lawrence Kahn, "The Gender Pay Gap: Have Women Gone as Far as They Can?" Academy of Management Perspectives, February 2007, pp. 7–23.

The upshot? Even though there may be 18 million cracks in the glass ceiling, it remains firmly in place for millions of U.S. women.

Economists Francine Blau and Lawrence Kahn do a detailed analysis of what accounts for the gender pay gap, which in their data is 20.3 percent. Figure 6 shows that of that gap, 10.5 percent can be explained by differences between men and women in their work experience, which captures time out of the labor force for caregiving or any other activity. Almost half of the gap (49.3 percent) can be explained by the kinds of jobs women and men hold in terms of industry and occupation, another 2.4 percent can be explained by race, and another 3.5 percent can be explained by men's greater likelihood of being in a union. When combined with the positive effects of women's educational attainment, which closes the gap by 6.7 percent, this leaves 41.1 percent of the wage gap as "unexplainable."

The segregation of men and women into different jobs explains the single-largest portion of the gender pay gap (49.3 percent). This may seem innocuous, but in reality, many jobs that women have historically held by women are underpaid, relative to men's jobs that require similar levels of skill. Bowling Green State University political scientist Ellen Frankel Paul, for example, points out that zookeepers—a traditionally male job—earn more than workers caring for children—a traditionally female job.[45] It's not that zookeepers have a much higher level of skills than child care workers, but that our society values these jobs differently and this is a choice we make. Women's jobs have been systemically undervalued for so long, we think it's natural, but in fact this is an ongoing legacy of past discrimination.

A woman who goes to the same kind of school, gets the same grades, has the same major, takes the same kind of job and has the same personal characteristics as her male colleague earns 5 percent less the first year out of school.

Differences in men's and women's work histories explain the second largest chunk—10.5 percent—of the gender wage gap. It's important to note, however, that the gender pay gap emerges as soon as women graduate, at a point in their lives when differences in work experience between them and their male colleagues should not play a large role in determining pay. The American Association of University Women examined the pay gap between college-educated men and women and found that a woman who goes to the same kind of school, gets the same grades, has the same major, takes the same kind of job with similar workplace flexibility perks, and has the same personal characteristics—such as marital status, race, and number of children—as her male colleague earns 5 percent less the *first year* out of school.[46] Ten years later, even if she keeps pace with the men around her, this research found that she'll earn 12 percent less. This gap is not about the "choices" a woman makes, as the model compares men and women who have made nearly identical choices.

How do we explain the "unexplained gap" to young women? After all, as women have taken their careers more seriously they have worked hard to get more education and that is paying off in terms of narrowing the gender pay gap, even if

UNFAIR OUTCOMES. Men still earn more than women straight out of college, as the female graduates at this job fair in Denver will soon learn. (JOHN MOORE, GETTY IMAGES)

it hasn't fully eliminated it. Women now are more likely than men to graduate from high school as well as college, even though among women ages 25 to 45, it remains the case that only a quarter have a college degree, and this is similar for men as well.[47]

Then there's the "maternal wall." New research focuses on the role of motherhood in accounting for at least some—if not most—of the unexplained pay gap. In groundbreaking work, Cornell University sociologists Shelley Correll, Stephen Benard, and In Paik used a laboratory experiment to find out whether being a mother means being paid less, all else equal. Study participants evaluated application materials for a pair of job candidates that were explicitly equally qualified—equal levels of education and work experience at similarly ranked schools—but one person was identified as a parent and the other was not.[48]

Their findings are astonishing: Even though the job candidates identified as mothers had the same credentials as the nonmothers, they were perceived to be less competent, less promotable, less likely to be recommended for management, less likely to be recommended for hire, and had lower recommended starting salaries. The job candidates identified as fathers were not penalized in the same way, and often saw a boost. Study participants also held mothers to higher standards than all men and women without children by requiring a higher score on a management exam and significantly fewer times of being late to work before being considered hirable or promotable.

Job candidates identified as mothers were perceived to be less competent, less promotable, less likely to be recommended for management, less likely to be recommended for hire, and had lower recommended starting salaries.

This research confirms prior work on the motherhood pay penalty. Sociologists Michele Budig at the University of Massachusetts, Amherst, and Paula England at Stanford University found that interruptions from work, working part time, and decreased seniority/experience explain no more than about one-third of the gap in pay between women with and without children, and that "mother-friendly" job characteristics explained very little of the gap. They conclude that two-thirds of the wage gap between mothers and nonmothers must be either because employed mothers are less productive at work or because of discrimination against mothers.[49]

What's more, the gender pay gap accumulates over time. The Institute for Women's Policy Research examined worker's employment and earnings data and found that, over a 15-year period, prime-age women workers earn 38 percent of what men earn.[50] Jessica Arons, director of the Women's Health and Rights program at the Center for American Progress, summed up the cumulative impact of the gender pay gap over a 40-year period—the "career wage gap"—and found that women lose an average of $434,000 in income. The pay gap accumulates for a variety of reasons, but chief among them are that pay raises are typically given as a percent of current salary, leaving women further behind each year, and an employer will typically ask a job applicant for a salary history when determining his or her starting salary, which limits women's upward mobility.[51]

But the pay gap is not entirely the fault of employers. Women make decisions that have an impact on how much they earn. The kinds of jobs women seek and what kinds of educational credentials they acquire affect future earnings. One study found that 95 percent of the gender differential in starting salaries can be explained by differences in college majors, with women continuing to be more likely to major in humanities.[52]

The pay gap accumulates for a variety of reasons, but chief among them are that pay raises are typically given as a percent of current salary, leaving women further behind each year.

Even so, within occupations, women are typically paid less than their male colleagues.[53] And, at least some of the wage gap between men and women, and between mothers and nonmothers, is attributable to women taking on greater parenting responsibilities and working fewer hours. Women are more than twice as likely as men to be employed part time and since few jobs offer part-time work, the part-time jobs available tend to pay less than comparable full-time jobs.[54] But the reality is that this cannot fully explain the gap in pay.

And if time away from employment for caregiving is important to explaining the gender pay gap, how do we as a society intend to deal with the new reality of working women? As more women work, more families do not have a stay-at-home caretaker, which means that both men and women workers are now more likely to balance a job with care responsibilities—either for a child or for an elderly or ill family member—and more are concerned about caregiver discrimination.

LILLY LEDBETTER. Lilly Ledbetter, a former Alabama Goodyear Tire & Rubber Co. worker who sued for wage discrimination, speaks during a news conference on Capitol Hill in Washington. Congress sent the White House its first legislation in Barack Obama's presidency, a bill that now allows women to sue retroactively for pay and other workplace discrimination that occurred years, even decades, in the past. [SUSAN WALSH, AP]

Takin' it to the max

One way, of course, is for families to keep on doing what they're doing. But is there a limit to how many hours women and men can put into the paid labor force and still maintain some sanity at home?

Women have gone to work in greater numbers, even as the world they worked in and lived in didn't change. The typical middle-class family puts in 568 more hours at work each year compared to the late 1970s,[55] which leaves less time to spend with children, clean the house, make a home-cooked meal, or plan a vacation. No wonder so many families report feeling stressed. And the recession only makes this worse as families increasingly worry about job losses or hour or wage cuts, on top of everything else.[56]

Inside the home, men continue to do less (usually much less) of the housework and care work than their wives—even though the number of hours they devote to work around the house has risen—and many businesses continue to act as though every worker has a stay-at-home spouse who can cope with all of life's little (and big) emergencies. Yet remarkably, amid this rising double duty mothers have not reduced their hours of parenting. Between 1985 and 2000, mothers spent an average of four more hours at a paid job and five more hours parenting. Mothers are spending less time on housework, volunteering, and on themselves. Fathers also are spending more time with their children: While fathers spent two more hours at their job, they spent four more hours parenting.[57]

Many families, especially those in lower-paid employment, have turned to "tag-team parenting" to make it all work. Parents work alternate shifts so that someone can always be home with the children. Lower-income families are more likely than higher-income families to have this kind of schedule. Some of it is driven by the kinds of jobs they have available to them—shift work is far less common among middle-class or professional jobs than in manufacturing and retail—and some of it is a way to keep child care costs low and care for their children themselves. And some professionals, such as academics or consultants, also "tag team," often for the very same reasons.[58]

But there may be a limit to how much more women can—or will be able to—work outside the home. Most important, the United States does not have a well-developed basket of policies to help families who have no one at home to provide care. And these are not just challenges for women. The 2008 National Study of the Changing Workforce reports that the majority of fathers (59 percent) in dual-earner couples report experiencing "some or a lot" of work/family conflict, as do 45 percent of mothers.[59] Clearly, we need to find a new way of addressing how families provide care.

Where do we go from here?

As men lose their jobs with frightening frequency amid the recession, women's employment is even more important to family well-being—in millions of families, women are now the "primary breadwinner." Recognizing this is the key piece to understanding how this social transformation is affecting nearly every aspect of our lives—from how we work to how we play to how we care for one another. Understanding that as women have gone to work, everything has changed is the first step. Identifying what we need to do to reshape the institutions around us is the next step. Then we can begin to take the necessary actions to readjust our policies and practices.

The policy implications vary from issue to issue, but the conclusions are clear: We need to rethink our assumptions about families and about work and focus our policies—at all levels—to address this new reality. Clearly, we aren't going back to a time when women were available full time to be their families' unpaid caretakers, so we need to find another way forward.

ENDNOTES

1 U.S. Census Bureau, Bureau of Labor Statistics, Current Population Survey, available at http://data.bls.gov/cgi-bin/srgate.

2 Here and throughout this report, we refer to overall gender pay gap as women earning 77 cents on the male dollar. This figure is the ratio of women's to men's median earnings for full-time, year-round workers as of 2008. This figure is the best way to show that women are paid less than men overall, but it does not include part-time workers, even though they are often paid less than their full-time colleagues for the same work. Further, the 77 cents figure does not get at difference in the skills that women and men bring to the job, nor does it address the fact that women and men tend to hold different jobs. U.S. Census Bureau, 2008, "Income, Poverty and Health Insurance in the United States: 2008," Current Population Survey, Table B-4, available at http://www.census.gov/hhes/www/income/incomestats.html#cps (September 4, 2009).

3 U.S. Census Bureau, DataFerrett, Current Population Survey, July 2009, available at http://dataferrett.census.gov; Stephanie Ventura, "Changing Patterns of Nonmarital Childbearing in the United States" (Hyattsville, MD: National Center for Health Statistics, May 2009), available at http://www.cdc.gov/nchs/data/databriefs/db18.htm.

4 U.S. Department of Labor, Bureau of Labor Statistics, 2009, *Current Establishment Survey*, Table B-4, available at ftp://ftp.bls.gov/pub/suppl/empsit.ceseeb4.txt (September 4, 2009).

5 Heather Boushey, "Women Breadwinners, Men Unemployed" (Washington: Center for American Progress, July 20, 2009), available at http://www.americanprogress.org/issues/2009/07/breadwin_women.html.

6 There are two surveys that the Bureau of Labor Statistics (BLS) conducts that track monthly employment in the United States. One is a survey of business establishments, the Current Establishment Survey, and the other is a survey of households, the Current Population Survey. The BLS reported that for July 2009, 49.9 percent of workers on U.S. payrolls were women, while women made up 46.7 percent of the total labor force, as reported by households. Throughout this report, we refer to the share of workers who are women, which is taken from the Establishment Survey.

7 Author's analysis of U.S. Census Bureau, Current Population Survey Annual Social and Economic Supplement.

8 Author and Jeff Chapman's analysis of Miriam King, Steven Ruggles, Trent Alexander, Donna Leicach, and Matthew Sobek. Integrated Public Use Microdata Series, Current Population Survey: Version 2.0 [Machine-readable database]. Minneapolis: Minnesota Population Center [producer and distributor], 2009.

9 These are families excluding single people. Lawrence Mishel, Jared Bernstein, and Heidi Shierholz, *The State of Working America 2008–2009* (Ithaca, NY: Cornell University Press, 2009).

10 Timothy S. Grall, "Custodial Mothers and Fathers and Their Child Support: 2005," (Washington: U.S. Census Bureau, 2007), available at www.census.gov/prod/2007pubs/p60-234.pdf.

11 Mishel, Bernstein, and Shierholz, *The State of Working America 2008–2009*.

12 Katharine Bradbury and Jane Katz, "Wives' Work and Family Income Mobility" (Boston: Federal Reserve Bank of Boston, 2004).

13 Elizabeth Warren and Amelia Warren Tyagi, *The Two-Income Trap: Why Middle-Class Mothers and Fathers Are Going Broke* (New York: Basic Books, 2003).

14 Author and Jeff Chapman's analysis of Miriam King, Steven Ruggles, Trent Alexander, Donna Leicach, and Matthew Sobek. Integrated Public Use Microdata Series, Current Population Survey: Version 2.0 [Machine-readable database]. Minneapolis: Minnesota Population Center [producer and distributor], 2009.

15 Ibid. Breadwinner mothers include single mothers who work and married mothers who earn as much or more than their husbands. Co-breadwinners include all breadwinners as well as wives who bring home at least 25 percent of the couple's earnings. The data only include families with a mother who is between the ages of 18 and 60 and who has children under age 18 living with her.

16 M.V. Lee Badgett, Randy Albelda, Alyssa Schneebaum, Gary J. Gates, "Poverty in the Lesbian, Gay, and Bisexual Community" (Los Angeles, CA: The Williams Institute, University of California Los Angeles School of Law, 2009).

17 Author's analysis of the Center for Economic and Policy Research Extracts of the Current Population Survey Outgoing Rotation Group Files.

18 Ibid.

19 Richard B. Freeman and Ronald Schettkat, "Marketization of Household Production and the EU-US Gap in Work," *Economic Policy Journal* 20, no. 41 (2005).

20 Claudia Goldin and Lawrence Katz, "The Power of the Pill: Oral Contraceptives and Women's Career and Marriage Decisions," *Journal of Political Economy* (2002), available at http://www.nber.org/papers/w7527.

21 Carolyn B. Maloney, *Rumors of Our Progress Have Been Greatly Exaggerated: Why Women's Lives Aren't Getting Any Easier—And How We Can Make Real Progress For Ourselves and Our Daughters* (New York: Modern Times, 2008).

22 Chinhui Juhn and Kevin M. Murphy, "Wage Inequality and Family Labor Supply" (Cambridge: National Bureau of Economic Research, 1996).

23 Francine D. Blau and Lawrence M. Kahn, "Changes in the Labor Supply Behavior of Married Women: 1980–2000" (Cambridge: NBER Working Paper No. W11230, 2005), available at http://www.nber.org/papers/w11230.

24 Teresa Amott and Julie Matthaei, *Race, Gender, and Work: A Multicultural Economic History of Women in the United States* (Boston: South End Press, 1991).

25 U.S. Department of Labor, U.S. Bureau of Labor Statistics, Current Population Survey.

26 Amott and Matthaei, *Race, Gender, and Work.*

27 Barbara Ehrenreich and Arlie Russell Hochschild, eds., *Global Women: Nannies, Maids, and Sex Workers in the New Economy* (Metropolitan/Holt Paperbacks Book, 2004).

28 Heather Boushey, "Opting Out? The Effect of Children on Women's Employment in the United States," *Feminist Economics* 14, no. 1 (2008).

29 Chad Newcomb, "Distribution of Zero-Earnings Years by Gender, Birth Cohort, and Level of Lifetime Earnings," Social Security Administration, Office of Policy, Office of Research, Evaluation, and Statistics. Note No 2000-02, November 2000, available at http://www.ssa.gov/policy/docs/rsnotes/rsn2000-02.html.

30 Author and Jeff Chapman's analysis of Miriam King, Steven Ruggles, Trent Alexander, Donna Leicach, and Matthew Sobek.

31 Boushey, "Women Breadwinners, Men Unemployed."

32 Author and Jeff Chapman's analysis of Miriam King, Steven Ruggles, Trent Alexander, Donna Leicach, and Matthew Sobek.

33 Ibid.

34 U.S. Department of Labor. 2009. Current Population Survey. Table A-6. Bureau of Labor Statistics (http://www.bls.gov/news.release/empsit.t06.htm [September 15, 2009]).

35 Nayla Kazzi and David Madland, "Mixed News for Older Workers" (Washington: Center for American Progress, September 4, 2009), available at http://www.americanprogress.org/issues/2009/09/older_worker.html.

36 Ehrenreich and Hochschild, *Global Women.*

37 Bureau of the Census, "Children with single parents—how they fare," Census Brief 97-1 (Department of Commerce, 1997), available at http://www.census.gov/prod/3/97pubs/cb-9701.pdf.

38 Randy Albelda and others, "Bridging the Gaps: A Picture of How Work Supports Work in Ten States" (Washington: Center for Economic and Policy Research, 2007), available at http://www.cepr.net/index.php/publications/reports/bridging-the-gaps-a-picture-of-how-work-supports-work-in-ten-states/.

39 Ibid.

40 Boushey, "Opting Out? The Effect of Children on Women's Employment in the United States."

41 Joan Williams, Jessica Manvell, and Stephanie Bornstein, *"Opt Out" or Pushed Out? How the Press Covers Work/Family Conflict: The Untold Story of Why Women Leave the Workforce* (San Francisco: The Center for WorkLife Law, University of California Hastings College of the Law, 2006).

42 Pamela Stone and Meg Lovejoy, "Fast-Track Women and the "Choice" to Stay Home," *Annals of the American Academy* 596 (2004), available at http://ann.sagepub.com/cgi/content/abstract/596/1/62.

43 Boushey, "Opting Out? The Effect of Children on Women's Employment in the United States."

44 Francine Blau and Lawrence Kahn, "Swimming Upstream: Trends in the Gender Wage Differential in the 1980s," Journal of Labor Economics, Vol. 15, No. 1, January 1997, available at http://papers.ssrn.com/sol3/papers.cfm?abstract_id=10786.

45 Ellen Frankel Paul, *Equity and Gender: The Comparable Worth Debate* (New Brunswick, N.J.: Transaction, 1988).

46 Judy Deyland and Catherine Hill, "Behind the Pay Gap" (Washington: American Association of University Women, 2007), available at http://www.aauw.org/research/upload/behindPayGap.pdf.

47 Author's analysis of the Center for Economic and Policy Research Extracts of the Current Population Survey Outgoing Rotation Group Files.

48 The differences were that one resume listed the applicant as "Parent-Teacher Association coordinator" and included phrase "Mother/father to Tom and Emily. Married to John/Karen," while the other listed "Fundraiser for his/her neighborhood association" and "Married to John/Karen." Shelly J. Correll, Stephen Benard, and In Paik, "Getting a Job: Is There a Motherhood Penalty," *The American Journal of Sociology* 112 (5)(2007): 1297–1338.

49 Michelle J. Budig and Paula England, "The Wage Penalty for Motherhood," *American Sociological Review* 66 (2)(2001): 204–225.

50 Heidi Hartmann and Stephen Rose, "Still a Man's Labor Market: The Long-Term Earnings Gap" (Washington: Institute for Women's Policy Research, 2004), available at www.iwpr.org/pdf/C366_RIB.pdf.

51 Jessica Arons, "Lifetime Losses: The Career Wage Gap" (Washington: Center for American Progress, 2007), available at http://www.americanprogressaction.org/issues/2008/pdf/equal_pay.pdf.

52 Judith A. McDonald and Robert J. Thornton, "Do New Male and Female College Graduates Receive Unequal Pay?," *Journal of Human Resources* XLII, no. 1 (2007), available at http://jhr.uwpress.org/cgi/content/abstract/XLII/1/32.

53 Ibid.

54 Jeffrey B. Wenger, "The Continuing Problem with Part-Time Jobs" (Washington: Economic Policy Institute, 2001), available at http://www.epi.org/Issuebriefs/ib155/ib155.pdf.

55 Mishel, Bernstein, and Shierholz, *The State of Working America 2008–2009*.

56 Madison Park, "Study: 8 Out of 10 Americans Stressed Because of Economy" (CNN.com, December 9, 2008), available at http://www.cnn.com/2008/HEALTH/conditions/10/06/economic.stress/index.html.

57 Suzanne M. Bianchi, John P. Robinson, and Melissa A. Milkie, *Changing Rhythms of American Family Life* (New York: Russell Sage Foundation, 2006).

58 Heather Boushey, "Family Friendly Policies: Helping Mothers Make Ends Meet," *Review of Social Economy* 66, no. 1 (2008).

59 Ellen Galinsky, Kerstin Aumann, and James T. Bond, "NCSW 2008: Times Are Changing: Gender and Generation at Work and Home," in *National Study of the Changing Workforce* (New York: Families and Work Institute, 2009).

When Will We Know?

By Heidi Hartmann, president, Institute for Women's Policy Research

We will have a woman's nation when women and men have equal opportunity to develop and use their skills and talents and equal responsibility to rear the next generation and sustain all generations. In such a nation, a newborn girl would have the same chances in life as a newborn boy—the same opportunity to strive to leave their mark on our collective human society and identity—by discovering a star, building a bridge, writing a play.

Too many women today still do not have these opportunities. Women still do the lion's share of the care for children and for adults. Women have subsidized the economy and subsidized the government for far too long. How? Well, for one, women's unpaid labor keeps families humming and keeps state budgets down. If women were not providing child care and long-term care to elderly family members at home then taxes and public spending would be much higher.

In the paid economy, women's lower wages keep profits high, too. Women earn less than men and women's jobs pay less than comparable men's jobs. If women were paid what they were worth, some of those profits would be redirected to women. Let's face it: Business owners and political leaders have been getting a free ride on the backs of women, taking advantage of their unpaid and underpaid labor.

In my view this is what the women's movement is all about—stopping the free ride and getting women their due by unleashing their talents, honing their skills, and enabling them to contribute to society far beyond their families.

Women have been voting with their feet, moving away from the family and into the marketplace. It is not that women do not want to raise children and nurture families. Of course they do. The human goal is about raising and providing for future generations and building a better place for all of us. But the reality is women today spend less time married, less time rearing children, and more time getting educations and job skills—more time working than earlier generations of women did.

They do so because women want more opportunities to contribute to the human endeavor in their wider communities and because, like men, many need to support themselves and their families. Women also want men to take more responsibility in the family arena, to share in the responsibility and joy of, for example, raising the next Einstein or Curie. So we will have a woman's nation when:

- Women have an equal share of the leadership positions in society: in business, in government, in religion, in the military, in the non-profit sector
- Men take an equal amount of time away from paid work to participate in hands-on care of family members
- Our laws, public policies, and social institutions make it possible for women and men to move readily between these two realms

Only then we will have a nation built on the principle that the work women have done for millennia is every bit as important to the survival and advancement of the human race as the work men have done.

This is the path our nation is on. This is the path that will provide more joy, more health, and more accomplishment to girls and boys, women and men, mothers and fathers, and their mothers and fathers.

We will have a woman's nation when women and men have equal opportunity to develop and use their skills and talents and equal responsibility to rear the next generation and sustain all generations.

That's Right, Women Are Wiser

By Giovanna Negretti, founding executive director of Oíste, a non-profit organization dedicated to advancing the political, social, and economic standing of Latinos and Latinas

What would a "wise Latina" think of "A Woman's Nation Changes Everything"? Since I couldn't get ahold of Justice Sotomayor, here's my perspective.

As a Latina, I am not surprised America has become a woman's nation. As far as I am concerned, we have been a woman's nation for a long time. Like many Latino families in this country led by single women, my family was no different. My mother was a single mom with three kids who worked full time. Same with my grandmother, who always said she had two full-time jobs—one at the office and one at home. Most of my friends growing up were the products of working mothers.

Recognizing we are a woman's nation offers a tremendous opportunity to embrace a new outlook on what women can bring to decision making and problem solving. The reality is that women solve problems differently. I joke all the time that with $20, Latinas can cook rice and beans for the entire block, take the kids to the movies at the local community center, get the tires fixed for free by one of their cousins down the street, get their hair done by their sister—and still have change left over. Latinas could be the perfect candidates to balance our nation's budget!

The differences I envision are that traditional roles are transformed and that the way women exercise leadership is nurtured and valued. In the book *Why Women Mean Business*, authors Aviva Wittenberg-Cox, CEO of consultancy 20-First, and former *Financial*

Times journalist Alison Maitland, an independent journalist and commentator, suggest that companies led by women or those that recognize the work-life realities faced by men and women today do better financially. But all institutions must be at the forefront of this critical reconfiguration.

Knowing that 50 percent of the workforce is women should drive home this message. Yet challenges still exist. Women are still underpaid, and are not seen enough in board rooms or in politics. Furthermore, the notion of a woman's nation raises expectations and gives room for what I like to call the "Sarah Palin complex," where women can (and should) be everything for everyone: attractive, outspoken, professional, sexy, sporty, and love to cook and watch soccer.

Recognizing we are a woman's nation offers a tremendous opportunity to embrace a new outlook on what women can bring to decision making and problem solving.

The reality, however, is that work-life balances are difficult, if not impossible. They create lots of stress for women and families. America needs to renegotiate its values to accommodate a new reality where a woman's way of exercising leadership paves the way to a better society.

There is hope, of course. At a press conference recently during the Louis Gates ordeal in Cambridge, Massachusetts, one of the Latino officers scheduled to be at the conference could not attend because he had child care duty. Hmm. Priority on family. What a wise Latino.

The Institutions

ANDREW HOLBROOKE, CORBIS

Family Friendly for All Families

Workers and caregivers need government policies that reflect today's realities

By Ann O'Leary and Karen Kornbluh

Four decades ago, President Richard Nixon famously declared that universal child care would have "family-weakening implications" that "would commit the vast moral authority of the federal government to the side of communal approaches to child rearing over the family-centered approach."[1] Wielding his veto pen, he blocked what became the last best chance for decades for the federal government to support working moms and dads trying to raise their children and earn a living at the same time.

Back in the early 1970s, Nixon and Congress looked at the 52 percent of so-called "traditional" families in the country (families with children still at home consisting of a married couple in which only the husband works outside the home) and saw decidedly different social and economic forces at work.[2] As women entered the workforce in droves during the 1970s, the number of "traditional" families immediately began to plummet—by 1975, it was already down to 45 percent of families with children.

Today, there's no mistaking the trend—only 21 percent of families with children at home are "traditional" families.[3] How do the other 79 percent of families working and raising children—the so-called "juggler families"—handle child care? How do these families cope with sick children and relatives or elderly parents in need of care?

FIGURE 1

Then and now

Changes in family structure and work, families with children under age 18, 1975 and 2008

- Married, traditional (only husband employed)
- Married, dual earner
- Married, both parents unemployed
- Married, nontraditional (only wife employed)
- Single parent, employed
- Single parent, unemployed

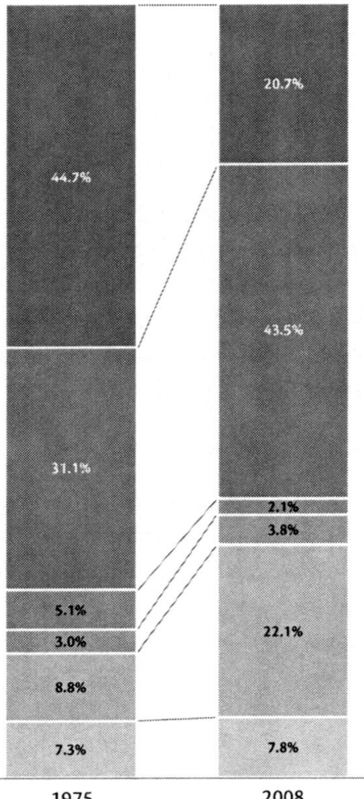

Source: Bureau of Labor Statistics, Economic News Release: Table 4. Families with own children: Employment status of parents by age of youngest child and family type, 2007-08 annual averages; Bureau of Labor Statistics, Indicator 18: Parent's Employment, Employment status of parents with own children under 18 years old, by type of family: 1975 to 1993.

Well, ask just about any mom or dad and they will tell you they mix and match caring and earning as best they can in workplaces designed decades ago around a worker who relied on a full-time homemaker to care for the young and the infirm and had no responsibility for caring for family members. This is no way to run an economy and to care for the next generation of Americans and those who built what our country is today.

Political leaders talk about "family values," but too often real reforms are set aside when it comes time to draw up the federal budget or do the heavy legislative lifting to ensure that women and men can raise their children, care for their elders, and continue to earn the incomes they need to survive and thrive in today's economy. Women, of course, are no longer the sole providers of care for the family, just as men are no longer the sole providers of the family income. Yet the federal government has not updated its policies to aid families in navigating this new reality.

Too many of our government policies—from our basic labor standards to our social insurance system—are still rooted in the fundamental assumption that families typically rely on a single breadwinner and that there is someone available to care for the young, the aged, and the infirm while the breadwinner is at work. But now that there are decidedly fewer "traditional families" and women comprise half of the workers on U.S. payrolls, we need to reevaluate the values and assumptions underlying our nation's workplace policies to ensure that they reflect the actual—not outdated or imagined—ways that families work and care today.

Up until now, government policymakers focused on supporting women's entry into a male-oriented workforce on par with men—a workplace where policies on hours, pay, benefits, and leave time were designed around male breadwinners with presumably no family caregiving responsibilities. Seeking equal opportunity in this workplace was critical, of course. Women could have never become half of all workers and entered previously male-dominated professions without Title VII of the Civil Rights Act of 1964, which prohibited sex discrimination in employment, and was amended by the Pregnancy Discrimination Act of 1978 to ensure that a woman couldn't be fired simply because she was having a child. And while women still have a long way to go to receive equal pay for equal work, the Equal Pay Act of 1963 certainly helped narrow the wage gap and increase women's economic stability.

Nearly all of our government policies—from our basic labor standards to our social insurance system—are still rooted in the fundamental assumption that families typically rely on a single breadwinner.

But allowing women to play by the same rules as the single male breadwinner worker of yore is not enough. Too many workers—especially women and low-wage workers—today simply cannot work in the way the breadwinner once worked with a steady job and lifelong marriage with a wife at home. Today, not only are half of all U.S. workers female, but our families are no longer static. The marriage rate is currently at the lowest point in its recorded history.[4] And while the divorce rate is down, it is still significant.[5] More than one in three families with children is headed by a single parent.[6] There are approximately 770,000 same-sex couples living in the United States, 20 percent of whom are raising children.[7] Yet there has been limited action at the federal level to update our workplace policies or create new policies to help working parents and their varied families—and not for lack of debate (see box "Plenty of study, few results").

Plenty of study, few results

Real family-friendly workplace reform is long overdue

A variety of federal commissions and conferences have supported efforts to encourage family-friendly workplace reforms, but with very little success in achieving new family-friendly benefits needed by today's workers. Cases in point:

- In 1963, President John F. Kennedy's Commission on the Status of Women delivered its report to the president. The report recommended that the federal government take the lead in creating legislation to establish cash maternity benefits for women when they were pregnant; that federal, state, and local governments partner to provide child care services with a priority for children of employed women; and that states help workers limit their hours at work by extending to men the state laws limiting the maximum hours employers could require women to work.[8] We still have no national policy of paid maternity or family leave and maximum-hour laws were never extended to all workers. Federal support for child care has been largely limited to low-income families.

- In 1980, delegates to President Jimmy Carter's White House Conference on Families called for "flextime, job-sharing programs, flexible leave policies for both sexes, part-time jobs with prorated pay and benefits, and dependent care options, including child care centers."[9] None of the flexibility options put forward by President Carter's commission was seriously considered by Congress or the Carter administration and a new push for universal child care fell apart in Congress during Carter's presidency.[10]

- In 1986, the White House Working Group on Families recommended to President Ronald Reagan that "without creating new entitlement programs, the federal government can assist parents with their child care needs by encouraging and endorsing employer efforts to adopt family-oriented policies which provide for flexibility in the workplace."[11] The Reagan administration spent the 1980s fighting Congressional efforts to pass federally funded child care and family leave and offered no legislation or executive action to "encourage or endorse employer efforts to promote flexibility."[12]

- And in 1991, the congressionally mandated bipartisan National Commission on Children recommended that "government and all private sector employers adopt family-oriented policies and practices—including family and medical leave policies, flexible work scheduling, and career sequencing—to enable employed mothers and fathers to meet their work and family responsibilities [and] government, communities and employers continue to improve the availability, affordability, and quality of child care services for all children and families that need them."[13] Congress passed and President Bill Clinton signed the Family and Medical Leave Act in 1993, but it offered only unpaid leave to about half of workers in the United States.[14] Child care funding increased, but again was limited almost entirely to lower-income families. And no serious effort was made to get private-sector employers to offer flexible work schedules and career sequencing.

Thus time and again we have heard the right words, but we have seen very limited action.

The notable exception is the Family and Medical Leave Act of 1993, but even it only allows 12 weeks of unpaid job-protected family or medical leave to approximately half of all workers in the United States.[15] Our federal government does not require employers to offer a minimum number of paid days off. Nor does it require or even incentivize employers to provide flexible work arrangements. Our child care assistance is mostly aimed at the poor and even that assistance reaches too few families.[16] Both our basic labor standards and our social insurance system are still based on supporting "traditional" workers and families and so do not accord protection to workers who must cut back on work to care for family members.

Tackling these challenges isn't going to be easy. For some, acknowledging that most women work challenges deeply held beliefs about what it means to be family and the "appropriate" roles for men and women. In a recent congressional debate over whether the federal government should provide paid parental leave to all new parents, Representative Darrell Issa (R-CA) implied that men do not need additional paid time off for family leave and that only mothers do immediately after the birth of a child,[17] even though fathers report that they want to spend more time with their children and that they are experiencing high levels of work-family conflict.[18]

This report demonstrates that women becoming half of all workers and mothers becoming breadwinners is not a woman's issue—it's an issue that affects our entire society. This chapter suggests that a fruitful way for government to address this new economic and social reality would be to reform our existing laws by:

- Updating our basic labor standards to include family-friendly employee benefits

- Reforming our anti-discrimination laws so that employers cannot discriminate against or disproportionately exclude women when offering workplace benefits

- Updating our social insurance system to the reality of varied families and new family responsibilities, including the need for paid family leave and social security retirement benefits that take into account time spent out of the workforce caring for children and other relatives

- Increasing support to families for child care, early education, and elder care to help working parents cope with their dual responsibilities

Updating these government policies so that they account for the reality of the overwhelming majority of today's workers and families is the challenge we address in the pages that follow.

Needed: Family time

Helping employers provide 21st-century family-friendly benefits

The United States is the only industrialized country without any requirement that employers provide paid family leave and without nationwide government-sponsored paid family leave. The U.S. government offers no federal subsidy for employers who provide family and medical leave—unlike existing government tax subsidies for employer-provided health care and pension savings programs.[19] As a result, 74 percent of all civilian workers have access to health benefits and 71 percent have access to retirement benefits, but only 9 percent of all civilian workers have access to dedicated paid family leave.[20]

PREGNANCY LEAVE. All women should have it. {HARAZ N. GHANBARI, AP}

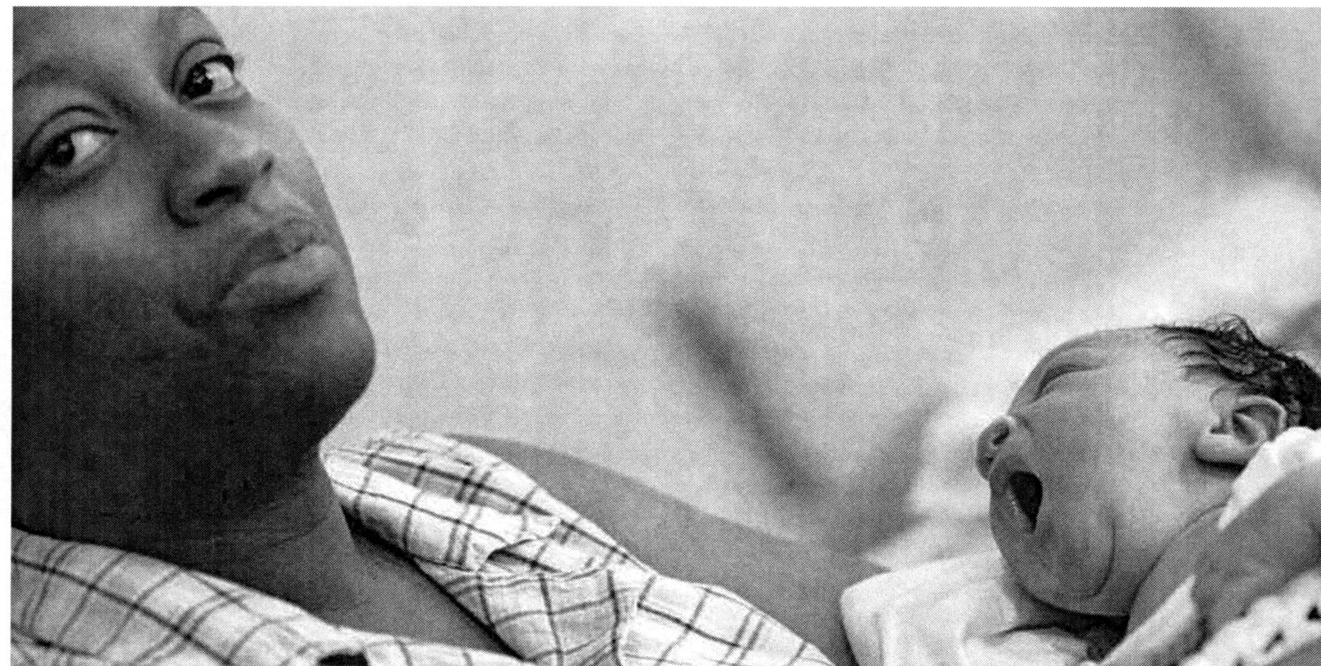

To a limited degree, the government has used the tax code to incentivize employers to provide assistance to employees for child care expenses and information, but these provisions do not come close to reaching the levels of support needed (the government also uses the tax code and subsidies to provide child care support directly to families, which we discuss below). The tax code allows employees to pay for health and dependent care expenses using pre-tax dollars if their employers offer Flexible Spending Accounts, but this allows working families to set aside only up to $5,000 per year for dependent care expenses.[21] This benefit is limited to workers whose employers choose to participate and it is worth far more to families at higher income levels. In 2006, only 30 percent of families had access to dependent care savings accounts.[22] And only 2 to 6 percent of all eligible employees are using flexible spending accounts to defray child care costs.[23]

The United States is the only industrialized country without any requirement that employers provide paid family leave.

Similarly, in 2001 the government began providing a federal employer tax credit for employers who either provide on-site child care, contribute to off-site care for their employees, or pay for resource and referral services that help employees locate quality child care in their community.[24] Despite this incentive, employers have not increased the child care subsidies or services offered to employees. From 2000 to 2008, the provision of assistance to employees for either on-site or off-site child care remained at 6 percent of all employees in the United States, and there has been a slight decrease in the provision of child care resource and referral services from 13.8 percent in June 2000 to 11 percent of employees in the United States receiving such support.[25]

In addition, the major government subsidized benefits—health care and pensions—disadvantage workers who take part-time or temp jobs or who start their own businesses so that they can pick up their kids from child care or have the flexibility to care for an aging parent. They often sacrifice employer-provided health and pension coverage—and the tax subsidy—as well. This is a seldom-mentioned argument for health care and pension reform.

To date, however, the federal government has failed to make a serious investment to encourage employers to offer new or update existing employee benefits to keep up with the changing face of the American worker and the American family structure.

Require employers to offer employer-sponsored benefits equally to all workers

Instead of providing incentives to employers to offer updated benefits aligned with the needs of today's families, the government has focused its effort on ensuring that all workers have "equal access" to the benefits that are provided by employers. The groundbreaking Title VII of the Civil Rights Act of 1964 is a central part of this story. Title VII made it unlawful for employers with more than 15 employees "to discriminate against any individual with respect to his compensation, terms, conditions, or privileges of employment, because of such individual's...sex."[26]

This is obviously important. Title VII is used today as a tool to combat discrimination against pregnant women and against men and women who are denied access to employment benefits because of gender stereotypes associated with caregiving. But Title VII is an extremely limited tool in helping employees take the leave and receive the flexibility they need to mix work with pregnancy or mix and match work and family responsibilities.

The reason: The law does not require employers to adjust to an employee's pregnancy or caregiving needs. Rather, it requires employers to offer benefits to all employees on the same terms, even if those benefits were not designed with pregnancy or caregiving in mind.

One major set of employer benefits voluntarily offered by some employers today is paid leave benefits—sick leave, vacation leave, holidays, disability leave, and family leave. Paid sick leave and disability benefits were traditionally offered by employers to provide a level of security for breadwinners and their families if the breadwinner was temporarily ill or disabled. Vacation and holiday pay were offered to provide workers with a period of restoration and revitalization. Because there is no federal requirement that employers offer vacation, sick, or holiday leave, paid or unpaid, access to paid time off is widely unequal across groups of workers.[27]

This means that the needs of women workers—whether for pregnancy or for family responsibilities—have to fit into leave benefits that were previously designed to serve male breadwinners. Because only 9 percent of all employees have access to dedicated paid family leave, the vast majority of workers have to fit their family leave needs into a patchwork of sick and vacation leave, where an employer offers the time and allows it to be used for this purpose, and then forfeit the true purposes of those days off, for healing or relaxing. Pregnant workers often have to take either disability or sick leave if their employer offers it in order to receive pay while on leave to give birth. Male workers who now have more caregiving responsibilities than ever before face the same inflexible access to employer-provided leave benefits.

Male workers who now have more caregiving responsibilities than ever before face the same inflexible access to employer-provided leave benefits.

This access to existing leave benefits may be equal but it is outdated, for it fails to match benefits with workers' new roles in the family or our society. Let's consider the limitations of the law with regard to pregnancy and caregiving.

Pregnancy leave

Upon passage and implementation of Title VII, one of the first questions for pregnant women in the workplace was whether private employers violated Title VII if they offered health insurance or disability leave that did not include pregnancy. Early on, the Equal Employment Opportunity Commission took the position that excluding maternity coverage was not discrimination.[28] But in the 1970s the EEOC reversed course.[29]

The Supreme Court, however, in 1976 ruled in *Gilbert v. General Electric Co.* that an employer's disability plan covering nonwork-related disabilities was not in violation of Title VII's prohibition against sex discrimination just because it did not cover disabilities arising from pregnancy.[30] Congress swiftly reacted, passing the Pregnancy Discrimination Act of 1978, which amended Title VII to clarify that the prohibition against sex discrimination in private employment included a prohibition against discrimination on the basis of pregnancy, childbirth, or related medical conditions.

The Pregnancy Discrimination Act had a tremendous impact on professional women employed in workplaces that already had disability or robust sick-leave policies on the book. The PDA meant these women would have equal access to those policies for the purposes of pregnancy and childbirth. But if a worker's employer did not offer disability or sick-leave benefits to any workers, then the PDA would not help them gain access to these benefits. Thus, the new law disproportionately benefited workers in high-waged occupations.

For women with a college education or more, access to paid maternity leave rose from 14 percent in 1961 to 59 percent in 1981 after the passage of the PDA and continued to climb, settling at 60 percent in 2003, the last year for which complete data are available. Women with less than a high school diploma, however, experienced only a 3 percentage point increase in access to paid maternity leave over that same period, from 19 percent in 1961 to 22 percent in 2003 (see Figure 2).[31] One of the only reasons that less-educated workers have any access to pregnancy leave is because labor unions historically and continuously have negotiated for such leave in collective bargaining agreements covering low-wage workers.

Most Americans believe it is illegal today for employers to fire a pregnant worker, but that is not the case. Unfortunately, there are many lawful reasons an

FIGURE 2

Want paid maternity leave? Then get an education or join a union

Percentage of women who received paid leave before or after their first birth by educational attainment: Selected years, 1961–1965 to 2001–2003

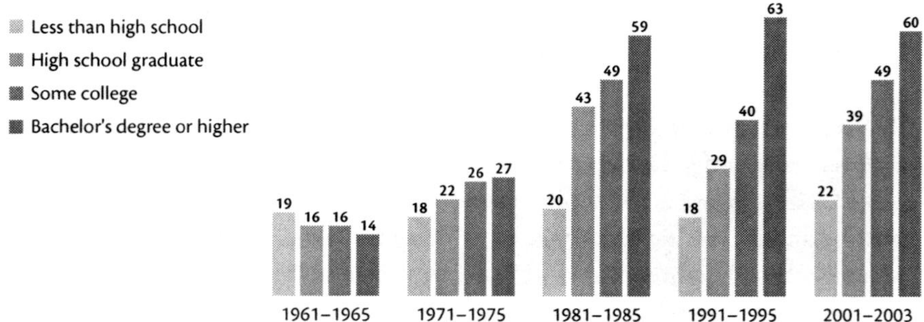

Note: Paid leave includes all paid maternity, sick, and vacation leave and other paid leave used before the birth and up to 12 weeks after the birth.

Source: 1961–1965 to 1971–1975: Bureau of the Census, Current Population Reports, Series P23-165 (*Work and Family Patterns of American Women*), Table B-9; 1981–1985 to 1991–1995: P70-79 (*Maternity Leave and Employment Patterns: 1961–1995*), Figure 4; and 2001–2003: Survey of Income and Program Participation, 2004 Panel, Wave 2.

employer in the United States can fire a pregnant worker and these reasons often disproportionately harm lower-wage workers. First, employers with fewer than 15 employees are not covered by Title VII and the Pregnancy Discrimination Act and are therefore under no obligation to treat all workers equally. This means 15 percent of the workforce is automatically excluded.[32]

> Most Americans believe it is illegal today for employers to fire a pregnant worker, but that is not the case.

Second, a number of federal courts have interpreted the PDA to mean that employers that do not allow workers any leave or extremely limited leave to recover from an illness or a disability are under no obligation to provide leave to pregnant workers.[33] This prohibition mainly affects low-wage workers who work for companies that offer no or limited leave to their employees for any reason. Nearly 80 percent of private-sector workers in the lowest quartile have no access to short-term paid disability leave; two-thirds have no access to paid sick days and nearly half receive no paid vacation days.[34] With no access to leave, women who by necessity must be away from work to give birth may lose their jobs.

Third, if a pregnant worker is told by her doctor that she should not lift heavy weights or needs to stay off her feet in order to avoid negative health consequences for herself or her baby, then her employer is under no obligation to transfer her to work to accommodate these restrictions. Instead, the employer can legally fire the pregnant worker. Sound heartless and improbable? Tell that to Amanda Reeves, a truck driver who asked to be switched to light-duty work upon instruction of her physician, only to find that her employer's policy of giving light-duty assignments only to workers injured on the job didn't violate the Pregnancy Discrimination Act.[35]

Finally, women who are pregnant or on maternity leave certainly have no greater right to keep their jobs when layoffs occur, although if they are targeted because they are pregnant or on maternity leave that is unlawful.[36] In recent recessions, claims of pregnancy discrimination have consistently gone up, meaning women are filing claims at a greater rate, suggesting that they are being fired because

Well, I'm pretty sure it took two people to make each one of those kids so it's interesting to me to hear all this progress we've made and yet child care remains a uniquely female issue.

Heidi in Silicon Valley

ED KASHI

they are pregnant. These women aren't just imagining discrimination—the percentage of these cases to be found to have merit remains at approximately 50 percent during highs and lows—so more women are found to have valid pregnancy discrimination claims in recessions than at other times.[37]

For women breadwinners, these gaps in the coverage of the Pregnancy Discrimination Act leave them vulnerable in a way that male breadwinners never were and never will be.

THE LATEST FROM THE AMERICAN PEOPLE

Q: Has there ever been a time when you wanted to take time off from work to care for your child or elderly parents but were unable to do so?

Percent answering "yes"

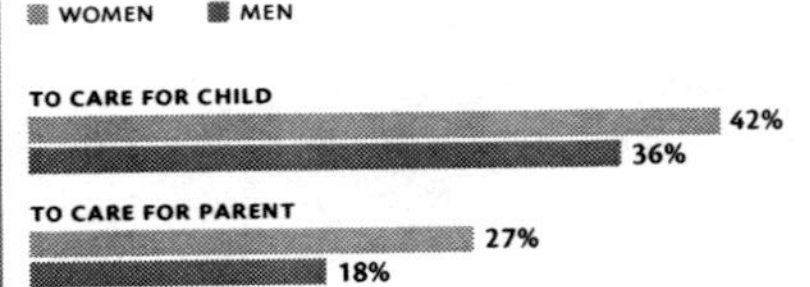

Source: Rockefeller/*Time* poll, 2009.

Protecting those with family responsibilities

Title VII also is used to combat workplace policies that treat men and women differently based on their marital status or their status as a parent or caregiver. In fact, the first Title VII case ever to reach the Supreme Court was a case in which a woman was denied a job because the employer had a blanket policy that women (but not men) with preschool-age children were prohibited from applying.[38] The Supreme Court ruled that such a policy was illegal, opening up the doors for women with children who were faced with such blatant and stark prohibitions against their participation in work.

The use of Title VII to combat caregiver discrimination in more subtle forms has increased in recent years because of the work of Joan Williams at the Center for WorkLife Law. Williams coined the phrase "family responsibility discrimination" to describe differential treatment of men or women because of their caregiving responsibilities for children, elderly parents, or sick relatives. In 2007, the Equal Employment Opportunity Commission issued guidance to employers on caregiver discrimination[39] that focused on the prohibition against gender stereotypes related to caregiving.

But using Title VII, including the Pregnancy Discrimination Act, to create policies to aid workers in combining work and family responsibilities has serious limitations. Equal protection laws are only as good as the nature and quantity of benefits the employer provides to other workers. Too often, most low- and many moderate-wage workers cannot access even the minimum benefits provided to more highly paid workers—paid sick days and paid maternity leave, for example.

Setting a minimum floor for employer-sponsored family leave

Congress passed the Family and Medical Leave Act of 1993 in response to the failures of the Pregnancy Discrimination Act to provide full protection to pregnant workers and the inability of both men and women to access needed leave for family responsibilities.[40] Congress recognized at the time that providing access to equitable employment benefits was not enough to ensure that workers had the right to take leave from their jobs for the birth or adoption of a new child, family caregiving, or even one's own ill health. This was an important step by Congress, but as we'll demonstrate, more is needed to provide economic security to dual-income, dual-caregiving parents or single parents—especially in low- and middle-income families.

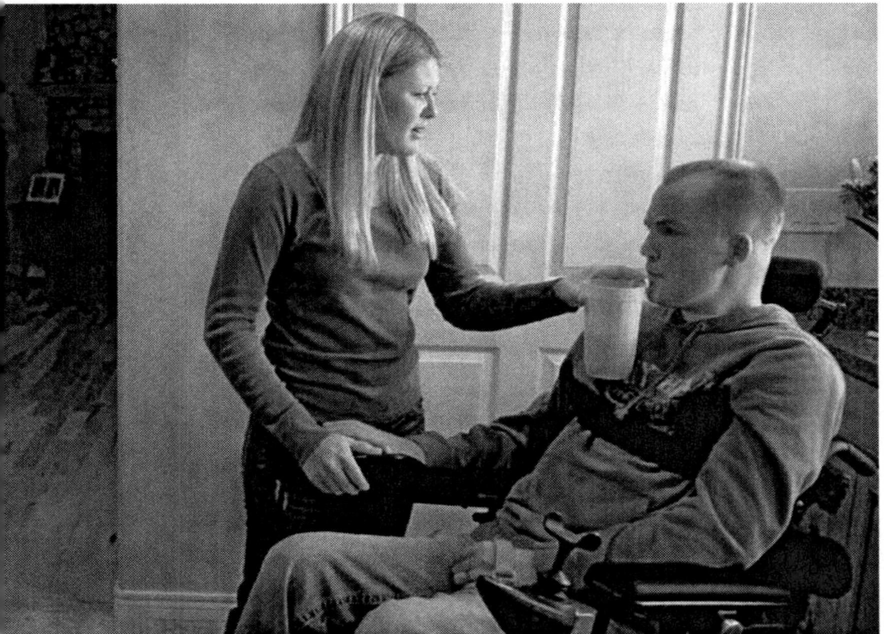

CAREGIVING FOR VETERANS COULD BE A CAREER. Tracy Keil and her husband, Matt, at home in Parker, Colorado. Staff Sgt. Keil was shot in the neck while on patrol in Ramadi, Iraq, and rendered a quadriplegic. While there is no program in place to pay family caregivers of wounded soldiers, the Family and Medical Leave Act was expanded in 2008 to provide greater job-protected leave for military family members. {KEVIN MOLONEY, *THE NEW YORK TIMES*}

The Family and Medical Leave Act amended the Fair Labor Standards Act to guarantee unpaid leave for at least some workers, regardless of gender, to care for family or medical needs. FMLA provides qualified employees with the right to take up to 12 weeks each year of job-protected unpaid leave for the birth or care of the employee's child, care of an immediate family member with a serious health condition, or for an employee's own serious health condition.[41]

Thanks to FMLA, millions of workers now have legal protections ensuring that they no longer have to fear losing their jobs and employer-provided health insurance during family or medical leave.

This law was the first of its kind—a law providing accommodation to workers based on the real needs of workers as caregivers regardless of gender. Thanks to FMLA, millions of workers now have legal protections ensuring that they no longer have to fear losing their jobs and employer-provided health insurance during family or medical leave. A low-wage pregnant woman who is covered by FMLA but cannot afford to take 12 weeks of leave can at least be assured that if she needs to take leave from work to give birth, she will still have her job when she is able to return.[42] The same can be said of a man or woman who needs time away to care for a seriously ill family member.

While applicable only to employers with 50 or more employees, an increasing number of employers not covered by FMLA have changed their practices to provide family and medical leave to their employees.[43] What's more, the new law provides guaranteed unpaid leave to men who wish to take paternity leave, a job benefit often not provided to men prior to the passage of FMLA.[44]

Despite these positive changes, about half of all workers are not covered by FMLA because they work for a small business with fewer than 50 employees, haven't worked for their employer for a year, or haven't worked enough hours to qualify for protection under the act.[45] These exemptions disproportionately exclude low-wage and younger workers who are less likely to remain employed by the same employer for a year, who are more likely to work for a small business, and who are more likely to work part time.[46]

But the biggest problem, of course, is that any leave granted under FMLA is unpaid, which means many workers cannot afford to take advantage of it because they cannot afford the loss of family income. In practice, the law favors families with one parent who makes less money (still more often the woman) providing care while the other higher-paid parent continues to support the family at work.

FMLA was a step in the right direction, but workers in our country today have extremely limited protections against the day-to-day stresses and strains of combining work with family care.

Needed: Flexibility and compensation

Workers' time and overtime should reflect caregiving needs

Our federal and state labor-law requirements on employers' ability to dictate their employees' working hours have not been updated to allow workers to effectively combine work and care. Many Americans may presume that workers are protected from being overworked by their employers because of 40-hour workweeks and overtime pay requirements. The Fair Labor Standards Act requires employers to pay covered workers one and a half times their regular pay for hours worked in excess of 40 hours,[47] but the law does not put an actual limit on the number of hours an employer can require an employee to work. Nor does it prohibit mandatory overtime or unpredictable, constantly changing workplace schedules.

Americans are not protected from being overworked by their employers because of 40-hour workweeks and overtime pay requirements.

To be sure, premium pay for overtime provides greater economic security to workers able to work overtime, but even the existing requirement leaves out many workers. First, the law excludes a disproportionate number of women of color who provide care to the "aged or infirm" or who work as a live-in domestic workers.[48] Second, salaried workers are exempt from the overtime provisions and, in 2004, federal regulatory changes greatly expanded the definition of "executive, administrative, and professional" workers. At the time, analysts estimated this

OVERWORKED, UNDERPAID. Hospitals often require the nurses they employ to work mandatory overtime—never mind whether those workers have caregiving responsibilities at home. (ED KASHI, AURORA)

redefinition would remove an added 8 million workers (about 6 percent of the total employed workforce) from eligibility for overtime pay.[49]

The upshot: While they do provide some added economic security, our wage and hour laws leave workers with little control over how many hours they can be required to work and when they can be required to put in those hours.

In addition, mandatory overtime is a problem for workers with family responsibilities, particularly for registered nurses (92 percent of whom are women), and, more recently, for state and local government workers (more than 50 percent of whom are women).[50] Registered nurses are in short supply, which prompts employers to require the nurses they employ to work mandatory overtime—never mind whether these workers have caregiving responsibilities at home.[51]

Similarly, state and local governments today are instituting widespread hiring freezes to cope with falling tax revenues due to the Great Recession and falling real estate values, which means existing workers are being required to make up the work through mandatory overtime.[52] Labor unions have had some success in passing state laws (12 to date) restricting mandatory overtime for nurses, and bills continue to be introduced in Congress to address the impact on the nursing profession, but there has been no broader push for restrictions on mandatory (and often unscheduled) overtime for government employees or private-sector workers.[53]

A majority of workers have no ability to control the time that they start and end their workdays, no ability to work from a different location, and no ability to reduce the hours they work.

The Fair Labor Standards Act also does not address flexible, predictable work schedules. The law currently allows for flexibility within the context of a 40-hour workweek, such as a compressed workweek or daily schedules with differing work hours, but this flexibility is left at the discretion and is in the sole control of the employer.[54] The result is that a majority of workers have no ability to control the time that they start and end their workdays, no ability to work from a different location, and no ability to reduce the hours they work.[55]

Only about a quarter of employees report that they have some kind of flexibility, though a much larger share of employers, anywhere from about half to most of them, report offering some kind of flexibility.[56] Whatever the case, workers with the least access to flexible and predictable work schedules are low-wage workers.[57] One study found that higher-earning employees have access to flexible daily schedules at more than double the rate of low-wage workers.[58] And as Heather Boushey points out in her chapter, the weight of the 24-hour economy often falls on the backs of our low-skilled, immigrant workers who have the least control over their schedules.

Needed: Social insurance that protects caregivers

"We can never insure one hundred percent of the population against one hundred percent of the hazards and vicissitudes of life, but we have tried to frame a law which will give some measure of protection to the average citizen and to his family against the loss of a job and against poverty-stricken old age."

- President Franklin D. Roosevelt, August 14, 1935, upon signing the Social Security Act of 1935

In the first half of the 20th century, the government created the backbone of the U.S. social insurance system by enacting the Social Security Act of 1935, which included retirement benefits, unemployment insurance, and aid to dependent children. Over the years it was expanded to include disability insurance, as well as Medicare and Medicaid. The aim of the combined programs in the Social Security Act is to protect workers and families against drops in family income resulting from old age, disability resulting in the inability to work, death of the breadwinner, or cyclical downturns in the economy.

The problem: Our national system of social insurance has never been updated to provide financial support to families who have a drop in income because a worker cuts back on work or needs to temporarily leave the workforce to provide care to a child or a sick or elderly relative. In recent years, there have been positive steps to update state social insurance systems to meet the needs of today's workers: California and New Jersey have enacted paid family leave as part of their state's temporary disability insurance program.[59]

But at the national level, social insurance reform is needed. We are in the process of debating health insurance reform—and the president has proposed pension reform—which would increase family economic security. With only 21 percent of families consisting of mothers still at home,[60] additional reform is needed to meet the needs of today's families.

Take basic Social Security, the retirement benefits that workers and their spouses receive in old age. Eligibility for Social Security benefits is based on an individual's work history, specifically how many "credits" a worker earns over his or her lifetime. Workers can earn a maximum of four credits per year; in 2009 a worker earned one credit for each $1,090 of earnings.[61] To qualify for retirement benefits, workers need at least 40 credits (10 years of work) over their lifetimes, meaning that any workers with 10 years in which they earned at least $4,360 qualify for retirement benefits in their own names.[62]

Back in the 1930s, however, President Franklin D. Roosevelt insisted that the Social Security Act protect the worker *and his family*. As a result, wives and widows were granted the right to collect retirement benefits based on their husbands' earnings. Spousal benefits allow dependent spouses (now wives or husbands) to collect 50 percent of the retirement benefits earned by the breadwinning spouse—on top of his benefit—so that married couples receive 150 percent of the benefits of a single worker with the same earnings. If both spouses work, then the lower-earning spouse can choose between receiving her own benefit based on her own work history or the spousal benefit, whichever is higher.

THE LATEST FROM THE AMERICAN PEOPLE

Q: Are you the primary breadwinner in your household?

Percent answering "yes"

WOMEN 40%

MEN 70%

Source: Rockefeller/*Time* poll, 2009.

In 2005, 51 percent of women received benefits based on their husbands' earnings (nearly 36 percent of women in retirement choose receipt of their spousal benefit over their own earnings record and another 15 percent qualified only for a spousal benefit, having no earnings record of their own).[63] Even with an increasing percentage of women currently carrying the title of breadwinner in their family, in 2008, an overwhelming 98 percent of spousal benefits were collected by women.[64]

These family-friendly provisions of Social Security are clearly laudable, but as the portion of traditional families has diminished the inequities in the system have become more apparent. When most families were married-for-life couples with a breadwinner and homemaker, basing benefits on one earner's employment history but providing benefits to the

THE SANDWICH GENERATION. Herbert Winokur, 83, suffers from dementia and has recently moved into his daughter's house in Montclair, NJ. His daughter, Julie Winokur, moved with her husband, Ed Kashi, and their two children, Eli, 11, and Isabel, 8, from San Francisco to help care for him. (ED KASHI)

breadwinner's "dependents" might have made sense. But today the basic structure of the Social Security retirement program leads certain families to lose out. These are usually "juggler families" in which both workers combine work and caregiving—with women more likely to dip in and out of the labor market depending on family needs—and families headed by single parents (most often single mothers, whether never married or divorced).

Workers who take time out of the workplace to care for family members not only sacrifice earnings and job security, but also Social Security retirement savings.

In short, workers who take time out of the workplace to care for family members not only sacrifice earnings and job security, but also Social Security retirement savings.

There are three main problems with Social Security's underlying design for today's varied families. First, a worker is expected to have a continuous record of full-time employment throughout his or her life, which is just not the case for all workers that combine work and caregiving. Many will take extended time off—while others will work part time or turn down a full-time job, sacrificing earnings and future benefits.

Second, there is no minimum retirement benefit that all Americans receive based on reaching retirement. It is all tied to work history—either your own or your spouse's. This means that there is no basic level of security for all individuals regardless of marriage or work history.

Third, the spousal benefit is based purely on marriage, not on an individual's caregiving responsibilities. This means caregivers who take time out of the workplace or limit their hours (and therefore earnings) to care for family members get no credit toward retirement for their caregiving directly but only as a derivative of their spouse's earnings. This is not only demeaning, it means they lose out if they divorce, are widowed before age 60, or are otherwise single parents. These rules play out differently for varying family types.

Even for traditional families, the benefits are not all that they seem. If the breadwinning spouse dies after the children are grown but before the wife reaches age 60, then the homemaker receives no survivors' benefits until she turns 60, and then she receives only partial benefits until she reaches the full retirement age of 66.[65] This "widow's gap" leaves homemakers, who often have few labor market skills, with little support in the intervening years before they reach retirement age.

Divorce—so common in our country today, even if the rate is falling—reveals the problem with making caregivers' benefits derivative of a spouse's benefits. If a couple divorces before 10 years of marriage, then the lower earner is entitled to no spousal benefits. This predominantly affects women since they are far more likely to be earning less in those first 10 years due to pregnancy and child-raising, and may certainly earn less as single parents. If a couple divorces after 10 years of marriage, then the lower-earning spouse (if she needs to elect to take a spousal benefit because her own earnings were so low) receives only the incremental spousal benefit, or half of what her former spouse receives.

Divorce—so common in our country today, even if the rate is falling—reveals the problem with making caregivers' benefits derivative of a spouse's benefits.

The structure of benefits is not entirely an accident; they reflect the realities and the biases of the time in which the program was created. Participants in the debate at the time argued that a woman living alone could survive on less than a man, with one participant declaring that a woman could do her own housekeeping while a man would have to eat in restaurants.[66] Sadly, this outdated notion remains in today's payout of benefits. Consider what these rules mean for dual-earner families. Both spouses must pay payroll taxes, yet the combination of the two benefits may be less than what a single-earner family receives. Eugene Steuerle, vice president of the Peter G. Peterson Foundation and one of the nation's foremost Social Security and tax experts, estimates that a couple with a single earner who earns twice the average wage would take home $100,000 more in Social Security benefits over a lifetime than a couple with dual earners who both earn the average wage.[67]

PARTNERS FOR LIFE, NO BENEFITS. For same-sex couples, Social Security provides no benefit at all to the family unit, only to each individual as though they were single. {MATT HOUSTON, AP}

For same-sex couples, Social Security provides no benefit at all to the family unit, only to each individual as though he or she were single. The Defense of Marriage Act of 1996 explicitly prohibits the recognition of same-sex couples as married for the purposes of Social Security even if states recognize the marriage.[68] Thus a lesbian mother who dedicates several years to care for her child not only forgoes building up credits to her own Social Security, but also will receive no spousal benefit for the work her breadwinning partner contributes to the family.

For unmarried women, the difficulty is twofold. Single women with children have the lowest annual earnings in our country and thus can save less for retirement. In addition, they earn less in Social Security benefits. For single moms, this double whammy at retirement threatens a life of poverty in old age.

Half of today's workers are female, divorce is common, more than one in three families with children is headed by a single mother, and more than a quarter of a million children are being raised by gay or lesbian parents who have no legal right to marry under the law of the federal government. How do we structure a system that is fair to all of these family types? How do we revise and update our Social Security system to value and reward taking time away from paid employment to rear children and care for aging parents, and still recognize that women are in the workforce to stay?

Changing the rules is more complicated than it seems. While the Social Security spousal benefit is overly broad in assuming that all spouses are mothers and overly narrow in assuming that all mothers are spouses, it keeps millions of women out of poverty in their retirement years and does act as a proxy, albeit a far from perfect proxy, for the unpaid work many married women invest in their families and our economy. Today, more than half of all female beneficiaries still receive retirement benefits on the basis of the spousal benefit.

But with more women as breadwinners, fewer women will collect spousal benefits in the future, relying instead on their own earnings. With more women in the labor force and more women as breadwinners, some may say that the simple answer would be to eliminate the spousal benefit and transform the benefit to one solely based on workforce attachment. But this cannot be done without addressing the different ways men and women work.

Needed: Time to care

Direct support to families for child care and elder care

This chapter focuses primarily on the government's role in encouraging or requiring employers to offer some basic labor standards, and in updating our social insurance system. But the government has other critical roles to play—providing direct subsidies to families to hire child care and elder care providers, and encouraging equity not only in the workplace, but also in the home.

Child care and elder care expenses take both an emotional and economic toll on today's single-parent and dual-earner families. Child care represents the second greatest expense after housing for married-couple families with children between ages 3 and 5.[69] Families providing informal care to aging parents or other sick relatives spend on average $200 per month and must make adjustments to their work schedules, which often means forgoing income.[70] The emotional and financial toll can be even greater for adult children who are helping a parent or other loved one suffering from Alzheimer's disease. Of those providing support to a relative with Alzheimer's, the vast majority (88 percent) provide emotional support, while more than half (52 percent) provide caregiving, averaging 16 hours a month, and more than 1 in 10 caregivers (14 percent) is providing financial support.[71]

The federal government has played only a modest role in supporting families with child care expenses and almost no role at all in supporting families with elder care responsibilities.

Yet the federal government has played only a modest role in supporting families with child care expenses and almost no role at all in supporting families with elder care responsibilities. The government provides some relief on child care expenses through the Dependent Care Tax Credit, which allows taxpayers to take a credit for employment-related child care expenses, but only up to $3,000 per year for one child and $6,000 per year for two. With child care expenses often averaging more than the tuition at a state college, this relief is incredibly modest.

And the tax relief, while designed to aid lower-income families by allowing them to cover a greater percentage of their child care expenses, doesn't reach our lowest-income families because it is not available to low-income families who owe no federal taxes because they make so little income. The government supports our lowest-income families by providing direct child care aid through welfare funding, the Child Care and Development Block Grant, and through publicly funded early education and preschool programs such as Head Start. But even these investments reach only a fraction of those eligible for the assistance.

President Obama's economic recovery package included a serious investment in child care and early education, targeting funding to low-income families. It provided more than $5 billion in child care and early-education funding that went directly into the hands of families to purchase child care, and directly to communities to improve their child care and preschool programs. Nonetheless, child care and early-education funding are still far from universally available, even to the families who need it the most. To meet the needs of all low- and middle-income families, the government would have to invest even more and rededicate itself to solving the child care problem that Nixon swept under the rug with the stroke of a pen back in 1971.

THE LATEST FROM THE AMERICAN PEOPLE

Q: Do your children currently receive supervised care by someone other than you and/or your spouse?

Percent answering "yes"

HOUSEHOLD EARNING <$40,000 PER YEAR 35%

HOUSEHOLD EARNING $40,000–$60,000 PER YEAR 44%

HOUSEHOLD EARNING >$60,000 PER YEAR 48%

Source: Rockefeller/*Time* poll, 2009.

Finally, there are no dedicated federal programs to help working families deal with care for the elderly. States offer some support in the form of in-home caregivers, but recent state budget cuts have seen these programs take massive hits. Once again, the main problem is a lack of recognition that there is no longer anyone at home who can care for free for our children, our ill family members, and our elders.

In addition, we as a nation must address the fact that reducing the penalty workers pay (in lost salary, benefits, child care costs, and government payments) for caregiving would not only increase women's economic security but also reduce the disincentive on men to take on more of the caregiving responsibilities. Updating government programs can help encourage more equitable sharing of responsibility at home—which is necessary if women and men are going to successfully mix and match work and family responsibilities.

Where do we go from here?

Our current laws and government programs are woefully out of date to help families cope with the rapidly changing economic and social realities of the 21st century. Programs that seem "neutral" between men and women actually cater to traditional male working patterns, which today are represented in the overwhelming minority of today's families. With women as half of workers in the United States and making vital contributions to the family income, the government needs to reform its incentives for employers to help their employees cope with work and family responsibilities as well as the requirements employers must meet in support of their employees in these dual responsibilities.

To do so, government policymakers should start a national conversation on how best to:

- **Update our basic labor standards to include family-friendly employee benefits.** It is possible to spur businesses to update their social benefits to support the new workforce without increasing burdens on them. Requiring paid sick days would ensure a healthy and productive workforce. Expanding the percentage of the workforce covered by the Family and Medical Leave Act would help employers reduce expensive turnover rates. And a "Right to Request Flexibility" law would help spark conversations in workplaces across the country about how employers and employees can better meet each other's needs.[72]

- **Reform our antidiscrimination laws so that employers cannot discriminate or disproportionately exclude women when offering workplace benefits.** Our antidiscrimination laws are long overdue for an overhaul to ensure that policies that disproportionately exclude women are considered illegal, including policies allowing employers to have a no-leave policy even when that means pregnant women will surely lose their jobs. There is still no way to be at work when you are in labor.

- **Update our social insurance system to reflect the reality of varied families and new family responsibilities.** In addition to health insurance and pension reform, this update should include the need for paid family leave and social security retirement benefits that take into account time spent out of the workforce caring for children and other relatives. If Social Security reform is debated, it will be essential that the reforms account for the new realities of a workplace and a nation in which women are now breadwinners.

- **Increase support to families for child care, early education and elder care to help working parents cope with their multiple responsibilities.** The efforts in the 1970s to enact universal child care should not be forgotten. All families need real support when there is no longer a wife at home to provide these services free of charge. And our government should not stop at solving the child care crisis: Families also need real support and aid in providing elder care.

- **Ensure that workforce and child care policies fully include men and respect their desire to be more involved in family life.** More and more, men are expressing a frustration with a lack of support of work-life demands on men. Our policies should be structured to fully support men's abilities to take time away from the labor force to provide care and support for their families.

Understanding that men and women work differently when women—and men—are breadwinners as well as caregivers requires a shift in thinking. But such a shift is necessary if policies, business practices, and community attitudes are to be changed. In fact, it is necessary in the daily negotiations among workers and employers, between spouses, and among parents and community institutions.

Public leaders can help increase understanding as well as respond to it. In addition to speeches and events, they can take a number of steps, including ensuring government serves as a role model. It can do this by improving its own policies and the policies of federal contractors, working with private sector leaders to encourage a new appreciation of the new challenges facing the workforce, and collecting and disseminating relevant data to highlight just how different the American workforce is today. It's time for family-friendly policies that meet the challenges of the 21st century.

ENDNOTES

1 President Richard Nixon, "Veto of the Economic Opportunity Amendments of 1971" (December 9, 1971), available at http://www.presidency.ucsb.edu/ws/index.php?pid=3251.

2 Bureau of Labor Statistics, "Number and Percent of Households Headed by a Married Couple with One or More Own Kids, in Which the Husband is in the Labor Force but the Wife is Not ('Traditional' Households), 1970–2002" (2003), available at http://www.prb.org/Source/a-MARR_Traditional_Families1.xls; U.S. Census Bureau, "Statistical Abstract of the United States: 1971" (1971), table 48, p. 39, available at http://www2.census.gov/prod2/statcomp/documents/1971-02.pdf.

3 Bureau of Labor Statistics, "Employment Characteristics of Families in 2008" (2009), available at http://www.bls.gov/news.release/pdf/famee.pdf.

4 Betsey Stevenson and Justin Wolfers, "Marriage and Divorce: Changes and their Driving Forces," *Journal of Economic Perspectives* 21(2) (2007): 29.

5 See chapter by Coontz, p. 370.

6 Bureau of Labor Statistics, "Employment Characteristics of Families in 2008" (2009), available at http://www.bls.gov/news.release/pdf/famee.pdf.

7 Adam Romero and others, "Census Snapshot, United States" (Los Angeles: The Williams Institute, December 2007), available at http://www.law.ucla.edu/williamsinstitute/publications/USCensusSnapshot.pdf.

8 President's Commission on the Status of Women, "American Women" (Washington: Government Printing Office, 1963).

9 White House Conference on Families, "Listening to America's Families: Action for the 80's" (October 1980), available at http://www.eric.ed.gov/ERICDocs/data/ericdocs2sql/content_storage_01/0000019b/80/37/b0/bf.pdf.

10 Steven K. Wisensale, "The White House and Congress on Child Care and Family Leave Policy: From Carter to Clinton," *Policy Studies Journal* 25 (1) (1997): 75–86.

11 White House Working Group on the Family, "The Family: Preserving America's Future, A Report to the President from the White House Working Group on the Family" (December 1986), p. 32, available at http://www.eric.ed.gov/ERICDocs/data/ericdocs2sql/content_storage_01/0000019b/80/20/03/b8.pdf.

12 Wisensale, "The White House and Congress on Child Care and Family Leave Policy," pp. 78–80.

13 National Commission on Children, "Beyond Rhetoric: A New American Agenda for Children and Families, Final Report of the National Commission on Children" (1991), available at http://www.eric.ed.gov/ERICDocs/data/ericdocs2sql/content_storage_01/0000019b/80/23/24/71.pdf.

14 Jane Waldfogel, "Family and Medical Leave: Evidence from the 2000 Surveys," *Monthly Labor Review* 124 (9) (2001): 19–20.

15 Ibid.

16 See Randy Albelda and Heather Boushey, "Bridging the Gaps: A Study of How Work Supports *Work* in Ten States" (Washington and Boston: Center for Economic Policy Research and Center for Social Policy, University of Massachusetts Boston, October 2007), p. 1, available at http://www.bridgingthegaps.org/publications/nationalreport.pdf. Fewer than 25 percent of those eligible for child care and housing assistance actually receive it.

17 *Congressional Record*, daily ed. June 4, 2009, pp. H6223–H6240.

18 Ellen Galinsky, Kerstin Aumann, and James T. Bond, "Times are Changing: Gender and Generation at Work and at Home" (New York: Families and Work Institute, 2008), pp. 18–20.

19 Rebecca Ray, Janet Gornick, and John Schmitt, "Parental Leave Policies in 21 Countries: Assessing Generosity and Gender Equality" (Washington: Center for Economic and Policy Research, September 2008), available at http://www.cepr.net/index.php/publications/reports/parental-leave-policies-in-21-countries-assessing-generosity-and-gender-equality.

20 U.S. Bureau of Labor Statistics, "Employee Benefits in the United States, March 2009," Tables 1 & 2, National Compensation Survey, U.S. Department of Labor (March 2009), available at http://www.bls.gov/news.release/pdf/ebs2.pdf; U.S. Bureau of Labor Statistics, "Employee Benefits Survey," Table 21, National Compensation Survey, U.S. Department of Labor (March 2008), available at http://www.bls.gov/ncs/ebs/benefits/2008/ownership/civilian/table21a.htm.

21 26 U.S.C. §§ 106, 125 (2006); "Information About Your FSAFEDS Choices," available at https://www.fsafeds.com/FSAFEDS/Popup/OpenSeason.asp.

22 Eli Stoltzfus, "Pretax Benefits: Access to Section 125 Cafeteria Benefits and Health Savings Accounts in the United States, Private Industry" (Washington: Bureau of Labor Statistics, March 2007), available at http://www.bls.gov/opub/cwc/cm20070321ar01p1.htm.

23 Paula A. Calimafde and Deborah A. Cohn, "Small Business and the Cafeteria Plan." In *New York University Review of Employee Benefits and Executive Compensation* (New York: New York University and Matthew Bender & Co., 2002).

24 U.S. Economic Growth and Reconciliation Act of 2001, 26 U.S.C. § 45F (2006).

25 Jerome E. King and Cathy A. Baker, "Childcare Benefits Continue to Evolve" (Washington: U.S. Bureau of Labor Statistics, 2001), table 1, available at http://www.bls.gov/opub/cwc/archive/summer2001art1.pdf; Bureau of Labor Statistics, "Quality of Life Benefits: Access, Civilian Workers" (March 2008), available at http://www.bls.gov/ncs/ebs/benefits/2008/ownership/civilian/table24a.pdf.

26 Civil Rights Act of 1964, 42 U.S.C. § 2000e–2 (2006).

27 Vicky Lovell, "No Time to Be Sick: Who Suffers When Workers Don't Have Sick Leave" (Washington: Institute for Women's Policy Research, 2004).

28 General Electric Company v. Gilbert, 429 U.S. 125, 142–43 (1976), which cites two opinion letters issued by the General Counsel of the Equal Employment Opportunity Commission in 1966 stating that pregnancy could be excluded from an employer's long-term salary continuation plan and that an insurance or other benefit may simply exclude pregnancy as a covered risk.

29 Ann O'Leary, "How Family Leave Laws Left Out Low-Wage Workers," *Berkeley Journal of Employment and Labor Law* 28 (1) (2007): 20–21 (citing EEOC opinions reversing course).

30 General Electric Company v. Gilbert, 429 U.S. 125 (1976).

31 Tallese D. Johnson, "Maternity Leave and Employment Patterns of First-Time Mothers: 1961–2003" (Washington: Department of Commerce, Census Bureau, 2008).

32 U.S. Small Business Administration, "Employer Firms, Establishments, Employment, and Annual Payroll, Small Firm Size Classes, 2006" (2006), available at http://www.sba.gov/advo/research/data_uspdf.xls.

33 For a description of courts' interpretation of the Pregnancy Discrimination Act and the circuit split on the issue of whether a no-leave policy creates a disparate impact, see Ann O'Leary, "How Family Leave Laws Left Out Low-Wage Workers," *Berkeley Journal of Employment and Labor Law* 28 (1) (2007): 30–35.

34 Bureau of Labor Statistics, "Life, Short-Term Disability, and Long-Term Disability Insurance Benefits, March 2008" (2008), table 12, available at http://www.bls.gov/ncs/ebs/benefits/2008/ownership/private/table12a.pdf; Bureau of Labor Statistics, "Selected Paid Leave Benefits: Access" (July 2009), available at http://www.bls.gov/news.release/ebs2.t06.htm.

35 Reeves v. Swift Transportation Co., 446 F. 3d 637 (6th Cir., 2006).

36 Lesley Alderman, "When the Stork Carries a Pink Slip," *The New York Times*, March 27, 2009, available at http://www.nytimes.com/2009/03/28/health/28patient.html.

37 U.S. Equal Employment Opportunity Commission, "Pregnancy Discrimination Charges EEOC & FEPAs Combined: FY 1997–FY 2008," available at http://www.eeoc.gov/stats/pregnanc.html.

38 Phillips v. Martin Marietta Corporation, 400 U.S. 542 (1971).

39 "Enforcement Guidance: Unlawful Disparate Treatment of Workers with Caregiving Responsibilities," available at http://www.eeoc.gov/policy/docs/caregiving.html.

40 Family and Medical Leave Act of 1993, 29 U.S.C. §§ 2601–2654 (2006).

41 Ibid.

42 See U.S. Department of Labor, "Balancing the Needs of Families and Employers: The Family and Medical Leave Surveys, 2000 Update" (2001), tables A2-2.6, A2-2.15. In fact, a significantly greater percentage of women (17.7 percent) with a family income of less than $20,000 reported that maternity leave was the primary reason they used the FMLA than did women in the higher income categories (8.8 percent of women with an annual family income of $75,000 to $100,000 reported maternity leave as the primary reason).

43 See U.S. Department of Labor, "Balancing the Needs of Families and Employers: The Family and Medical Leave Surveys, 2000 Update" (2001), section 5-5. The proportion of all establishments reporting policies consistent with the FMLA's leave provisions has increased from 27.9 percent in the 1995 survey to 39.1 percent in the 2000 survey.

44 See U.S. Department of Labor, "Balancing the Needs of Families and Employers: The Family and Medical Leave Surveys, 2000 Update" (2001), section 4-16. Approximately 34 percent of men with young children took leave under the FMLA, and of these male leave-takers, 75 percent took leave to care for a newborn or newly adopted child. Also see Nevada Department of Human Resources. v. Hibbs, 538 U.S. 721 (2003), which documents the gender gap in the provision of family leave prior to the passage of the FMLA.

45 Jane Waldfogel, "Family and Medical Leave: Evidence from the 2000 Surveys," *Monthly Labor Review* 124 (9) (2001): 19–20.

46 Ann O'Leary, "How Family Leave Laws Left Out Low-Wage Workers," *Berkeley Journal of Employment and Labor Law* 28 (1) (2007): 1–62.

47 Fair Labor Standards Act, 29 U.S.C. §207 (2006).

48 29 U.S.C. § 213(a)(15) (2006) *Long Island Care at Home, Ltd. v. Coke*, 551 U.S. 158, 162 (2007).

49 Heather Boushey and Chris Tilly, "The Limits of Work-Based Social Support in the United States," *Challenge* 52 (2) (March/April 2009), p. 90.

50 Bureau of Labor Statistics, "Employed Persons by Detailed Occupation and Sex, 2007 Annual Averages" (2008), available at http://www.bls.gov/cps/wlf-table11-2008.pdf; Bureau of Labor Statistics, "Table 16: Employed and Unemployed Full- and Part-time Workers by Class of Workers, Sex, Race, and Hispanic or Latino Ethnicity, Annual Average 2008" (2009), unpublished analysis, Current Population Survey 2008, Bureau of Labor Statistics, U.S. Department of Labor (available by request from author).

51 Katherine Kany, "Mandatory Overtime: New Developments in the Campaign," *American Journal of Nursing* 101 (5) (2001): 67–70, available at http://journals.lww.com/ajnonline/Fulltext/2001/05000/Mandatory_Overtime__New_developments_in_the.26.aspx.

52 Examples from Colorado and Illinois: Ed Sealover, "Colorado State Employees Make Pitch for Pay," *Denver Business Journal*, June 22, 2009, available at http://denver.bizjournals.com/denver/stories/2009/06/22/daily11.html; Dan Carden, "Would Massive State Layoffs Make Recession Worse?" *Daily Herald*, June 17, 2009, available at http://www.dailyherald.com/story/?id=300857.

53 Gregg Blesch, "Doing More with More? Hospitals Face Renewed Calls for Staffing Mandates While Dealing with Recession-Related Workforce Cuts," *Modern Healthcare* 39 (21) (May 2009): 26–7, 30.

54 William G. Whittaker, "The Fair Labor Standards Act: Overtime Pay Issues in the 108th Congress" (Washington: Congressional Research Service, 2005); Workplace Flexibility 2010, "Public Policy Platform on Flexible Work Arrangements" (2009), available at http://www.law.georgetown.edu/workplaceflexibility2010/definition/documents/PublicPolicyPlatformonFlexibleWorkArrangements.pdf.

55 Jodie Levin-Epstein, "Getting Punched: The Job and Family Clock ... It's Time for Flexible Work for Workers of All Wages" (Washington: Center for Law and Social Policy, 2006).

56 Lonnie Golden, "Flexibility Gaps: Differential Access to Flexible Work Schedules and Location in the U.S." Paper presented at: ISWT 2004. Proceedings of the 9th International Symposium on Working Time, 2004 Feb 26-28; Paris, France; Also see Ellen Galinsky, James T. Bond and E. Jeffrey Hill, "When Work Works: A Status Report on Workplace Flexibility" (New York: Families and Work Institute, 2004), p. 5.

57 Galinsky, Bond, and Hill, "When Work Works"; Urban Institute, "Lower-Wage Workers and Flexible Work Arrangements," available at http://www.law.georgetown.edu/workplaceflexibility2010/definition/documents/Lower-WageWorkersandFWAs.pdf.

58 James T. Bond and Ellen Galinsky, "What Workplace Flexibility is Available to Entry-Level, Hourly Employees?" Table 1, Research Brief No. 3 (New York: Families and Work Institute, 2006), available at http://familiesandwork.org/site/research/reports/brief3.pdf.

59 *California Paid Family Leave Act*, S.B. 1661, 2002 Cal. Stat. Ch. 901 (Cal. 2002) (effective July 1, 2004); New Jersey Family Leave Act, N.J.S.A. 34:11B-1, et seq. (law became effective January 1, 2009 and beneficiaries could begin collective benefits on July 1, 2009).

60 Bureau of Labor Statistics, "Employment Characteristics of Families in 2008" (May 27, 2009), available at http://www.bls.gov/news.release/pdf/famee.pdf.

61 Social Security Administration, "How You Earn Credits" (2009), available at http://www.ssa.gov/pubs/10072.pdf.

62 Ibid.

63 Institute for Women's Policy Research, "Women and Social Security: Benefit Types and Eligibility" (June 2005), available at http://www.iwpr.org/pdf/D463.pdf.

64 Social Security Administration, "Annual Statistical Supplement to the Social Security Bulletin, 2008," table 5.G1, (2009), available at http://www.ssa.gov/policy/docs/statcomps/supplement/2008/supplement08.pdf.

65 Goodwin Liu, "Social Security and the Treatment of Marriage: Spousal Benefits, Earnings Sharing, and The Challenge Of Reform," *Wisconsin Law Review* 1 (1999): 17–18.

66 Alice Kessler-Harris, *In Pursuit of Equity: Women, Men, and the Quest for Economic Citizenship in Twentieth-Century America* (New York: Oxford University Press, 2001), p. 137.

67 Eugene Steuerle, Christopher Spiro, and Adam Carasso, "Does Social Security Treat Spouses Fairly?" (Washington: Urban Institute, November 1999), available at http://www.urban.org/UploadedPDF/Straight12.pdf.

68 1 U.S.C § 7 (2006); 28 U.S.C § 1738C (2006).

69 Mark Lino, "Expenditures on Children by Families, 2006" (Department of Agriculture, Center for Nutrition Policy and Promotion, 2007), p.18, available at http://www.cnpp.usda.gov/Publications/CRC/crc2006.pdf.

70 The MetLife Foundation and Schmieding Center, "Caregiving in America" (2007), p. 21, available at http://www.schmiedingcenter.org/pdf/caregiving_in_america.pdf.

71 Harris Interactive, "HBO Alzheimer's Project/Harris Interactive Census: Examining the Impact of Alzheimer's Disease in America" (2009), p. 2, available at http://www.hbo.com/events/alzheimers/documents/Census.pdf.

72 Karen Kornbluh, "The Joy of Flex," *Washington Monthly*, December 2005, available at http://www.washingtonmonthly.com/features/2005/0512.kornbluh.html.

"In Blood and Spirit"

By Colonel Maritza Sáenz Ryan, professor and head of the Department of Law, United States Military Academy at West Point, which recently inaugurated the West Point Center for the Rule of Law

"*¡Si yo hubiese tenido la oportunidad, la hubiera aprovechado!*" ("If only I had had the opportunity, I would have taken it!") So averred my mother, who emigrated from Spain as a young woman in 1958, during a discussion we had about me attending West Point in the late 1970s.

My West Point classmates and I entered as members of the U.S. Military Academy class of 1982—the third year women were admitted, a milestone opportunity made possible by congressional statute, Public Law 94-106. The West Point name is inseparable from the tradition of Duty, Honor, Country, and every male who came here was seen as fulfilling that tradition. For a woman at that pivotal time in our nation's history, however, it seemed a revolutionary act.

Then again, "here in America," as Dwight Eisenhower once said, "we are descended in blood and in spirit from revolutionists and rebels—men and women who dared to dissent from accepted doctrine." One such "accepted doctrine" prevalent in the military as in society had long held that women can't fight and certainly couldn't lead in combat—this despite many women across various cultures, including our own, having done so successfully, if mostly anonymously, throughout history.

For over 30 years now, West Point and our sister academies have been educating, training, and inspiring women to lead—alongside men—a highly diverse, integrated force, the most powerful ever on earth. Our engagement in conflicts in distant places where the average woman's legal rights are often nil means that military women are proving themselves daily on the most dangerous battlefields. Already, the first female West Point graduate has made General Officer, followed by three more; two ROTC graduates have likewise set new marks as the first female General in the Judge Advocate General's Corps and the first woman to earn the Army's highest rank, four stars. Thanks to pioneering advocates such as Justice Ruth Bader Ginsburg, we can take for granted equal pay for equal work.

Still, daunting challenges—brass and glass ceilings—remain. Women continue to be underrepresented in the highest ranks. Anachronistic attitudes and policies persist, such as the Combat Exclusion Rule. And attaining and retaining critical mass is hindered by grinding redeployments. Likewise, despite the uptick in their numbers in the legal profession overall, women still fall heavily off the ladders of law firm leadership.

Our engagement in conflicts in distant places where the average woman's legal rights are often nil means that military women are proving themselves daily on the most dangerous battlefields.

As an Army officer, lawyer, and educator, and having personally benefited from the progress wrought by others, I remain optimistic. So long as military service, and the intangible attributes it implies—courage, tenacity, patriotism, and, yes, leadership—continues to be a hallmark of full membership in society as American citizens, and as long as our country needs leaders—smart, ethical, adaptive, and strong leaders—we will need women to lead alongside our male colleagues. And I am certain that, so long as a woman's nation remains one built upon the rule of law, we will have ever greater opportunities to serve our country equally and to the best of our abilities.

The views expressed in this essay are those of the author and do not reflect the official policy or position of the Department of the Army or the Department of Defense of the United States Government.

Tested and Proven

By Tammy Duckworth, an Iraq war veteran and assistant secretary of public and intergovernmental affairs for the U.S. Department of Veterans Affairs

In the military, rank has a wonderful way of leveling the playing field. A sergeant recognizes the gold oak leaf on my uniform, signifying my rank as a major in the Army National Guard. By virtue of that rank, I'm on par with every other major in the U.S. Army, female or male. Rank also commands respect in the military, no matter the gender.

I want to believe the recognition of my rank precedes the awareness of my gender—evident, of course, by the length of my hair and the sound of my voice. But recognizing rank over gender is not always the case today, and certainly not historically. Women like me who have served in the military for a few years can speak of the hardships and obstacles we've had to overcome to prove we were "just as good as the men." Many of us overcame them by trying to out-macho the men or join their "good ol' boys club."

In aviation, I made my way being as tough and gender-neutral as possible. But earlier in my career, I played tough and failed to realize (and failed to capitalize on) my strengths as a woman. In some cases, our strength is in our ability to encourage and engage others. For others, strength comes from the confidence gained through personal and career achievements. In the military, strength comes from the knowledge that women get equal pay for equal work; I earned exactly the same pay that my male counterparts did.

When my helicopter was shot down in Iraq in 2004, I didn't distinguish among the genders of my comrades who stayed by my side, determined not to leave me there, dying. And they didn't care about my gender. They cared about their fellow American, their fellow soldier, their buddy. Me.

In today's military, we have leveled the playing field in so many ways. Yet, sadly, much of American society lags behind. Each of us, men and women, has a wonderful opportunity to participate in this monumental shift in American society where women now equal the number of men in the workplace. We have a wonderful opportunity to transform our country so that each of us is an equal stakeholder in the American Dream.

It's time to stop thinking we can be "just as good as the men." We've already proven it.

Much remains to be done. There are glass ceilings that need to be shattered, sexual harassment that is still too common, and negative stereotypes that remain pervasive—that women are weaker, more emotional.

But it's a new day and age. We've just confirmed our third woman Supreme Court justice. We've doubled the number of women in the military in the last 30 years—350,000 are serving now. It's time to stop being surprised that America's daughters are fully capable of doing their jobs and fighting for freedom. It's time to stop thinking we can be "just as good as the men."

We've already proven it. More important, it's time to celebrate women taking part in the common goal of serving the greatest democracy the world has ever known.

MIKE DERER/AP

Invisible yet Essential

Immigrant women in America

By Maria Echaveste

The presence of immigrant men standing on street corners looking for work too often serves as the flashpoint for confrontation in communities across the country. Anti-immigrant groups, but also just concerned residents, focus on the perceived health and safety risks posed by the "eyesore" of day laborers and agitate for "controlling illegal immigration." Yet these very same people easily walk or drive by other immigrants (both documented and undocumented) who are present in public spaces: the nannies taking care of children and the elderly, maids entering families' homes, laborers working on farms, or cleaners working in office buildings at night.

Immigrant women are seen in communities across the country pushing strollers, feeding children, and playing in city playgrounds. An Asian face, a Caribbean accent, or the echo of Spanish reveals that millions of Americans entrust their most precious treasures—their children—to immigrants who are often undocumented.[1] Many Americans entrust these same women, who sometimes have limited training and difficult-to-understand accents, with the care of their aging parents.[2] They entrust their homes as well—thousands of housekeepers take public transportation across the country to dust, clean, and sweep for working individuals and families who are too exhausted to handle the burden of cleaning their own homes.

Immigrants also make up a substantial part of the countless workers who harvest fruits and vegetables across the country, who ensure a steady supply of milk and dairy products, and who slaughter chickens and cows for nightly dinner tables.[3]

A significant number of those workers are immigrant women, who often risk sexual harassment from male supervisors and endure arduous physical labor in an effort to provide for their own families.[4] Many are indigenous people, able to communicate more easily in Mixtec than in Spanish.[5] And then there are the countless office cleaners who descend upon downtown buildings in cities across the country, ensuring that all the crumbs from a lunch eaten over the keyboard are vacuumed up and the trash can is empty when office workers return in the morning.[6]

What is it about this work—child and parental care, home maintenance, food production, cleaning—that allows society to treat the workers in these occupations as invisible, or at least less important than the software developer, insurance adjustor, or any of the countless other occupations that have greater status in our society? If we measure status, or the lack thereof, by income, working conditions, benefits, and simple respect, then the above-described occupations clearly have very little.[7] Is it that nurturing children and maintaining homes has been undervalued for decades, if not centuries?

> *The critical role that child care providers and housekeepers play in maintaining or enhancing many middle-class families' quality of life has been greatly overlooked.*

In a society where knowledge workers are the most highly compensated, it is not surprising that those who work with their hands or engage in physical labor are undervalued. Or was the work once valued, but now easier to underappreciate or ignore since it is increasingly performed by immigrants, legal and otherwise? Such an attitude ignores their significant role in the American labor force—the increase in the American workforce over that past decade is due to the levels of immigration, legal and otherwise.[8]

Each of these occupations is essential to a well-functioning society. Take, for example, all those nannies. One area not fully explored in the raging economic debate over immigrants' cost and contributions to the U.S. economy, particularly of those not authorized to work in this country, is the extent to which the

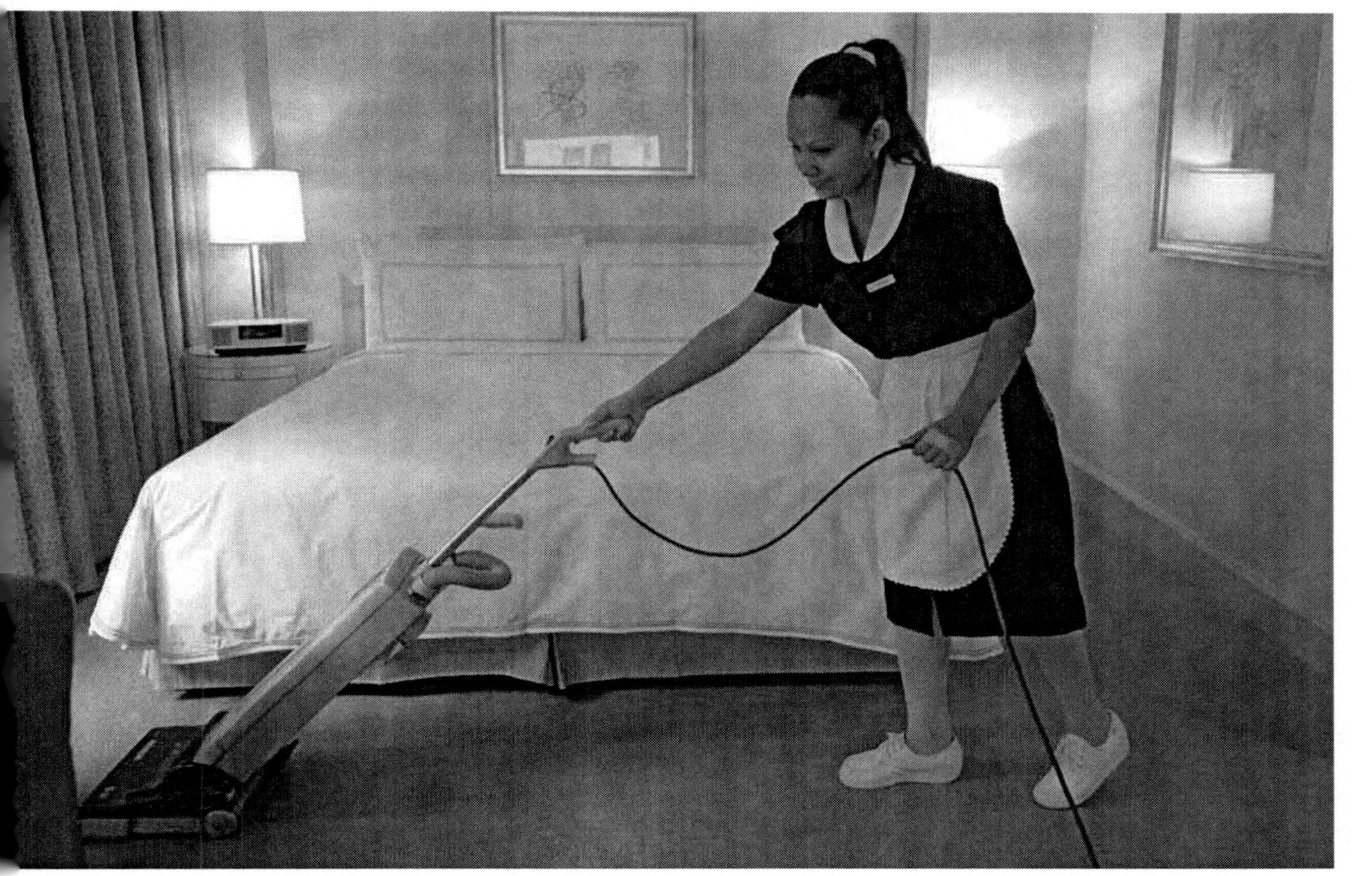

CLEANING UP BEHIND YOU. Housekeepers, many of whom are immigrants, invisibly power our service economy. [MARK PETERSON]

availability of low-cost child care and housekeeping services has allowed middle- and upper-middle-income people, especially women, to participate in the workforce. Women today, including married women with children, have the highest workforce participation in our nation's history.[9] That is possible only because of invisible workers.

The critical role that child care providers and housekeepers play in maintaining or enhancing many middle-class families' quality of life has been greatly overlooked. Why is it that work as critical as the care of children should be so undervalued?

We should also consider that these workers are mothers, wives, and working women themselves. The lack of affordable child care impacts these families as well. Immigrant women are on average both younger than the native born and have higher birth rates.[10] Who is minding their children? The lack of health insurance for these women and their families, for example, means that critical preventative care is being delayed or ignored, and when problems occur, the local emergency room becomes the family's health care provider, at greater cost to taxpayers and local communities.

Our 21st-century economy is increasingly based on a growing service sector economy, which is why we need to challenge ourselves to value the work of women, and especially the work of immigrant women.

Even now, in the debate over health care reform, many lawmakers propose excluding both documented and undocumented immigrants from any government subsidies. Their exclusion from national health care reform, if enacted, will make it that much harder to reduce health care costs, including those stemming from preventable diseases.

The U.S. economy over the past several decades has experienced the flight of millions of manufacturing jobs with good benefit packages overseas—many of which are unlikely to come back. Our 21st-century economy is increasingly based on a growing service sector economy, which is why we need to challenge ourselves to value the work of women, and especially the work of immigrant women. Such work will still be necessary regardless of how high tech our economy becomes. It must not remain invisible.

ENDNOTES

1 Delia Furtado and Heinrich Hoch, "Immigrant Labor, Child Care Services, and the Work-Fertility Trade Off in the United States" (Bonn, Germany: Institute for the Study of Labor, 2008), available at http://ftp.iza.org/dp3506.pdf.

2 See, for example, MetLife Foundation and Schmieding Center, "Caregiving in America" (2007). This study describes a "caregiving crisis" in the growing need for elder and other long-term care in the United States. More than 12 million people in the United States, including 6 million people over 65, need long-term care; the need for long-term care is expected to grow as much as 56 percent between 2004 and 2014. Low-wage workers, almost always women and often immigrants, are filling this gap in caregiving. Ninety percent of nursing home aides and home care aides are women. Immigrants officially account for 21.8 percent of home care aides and just over 12 percent each for home care aides and hospital aides. These numbers exclude undocumented immigrants and so are undoubtedly artificially low, especially for home care aides.

3 Seventy-eight percent of hired farm workers in the United States are foreign-born. See Department of Labor, "National Agricultural Workers Survey" (2002), available at http://www.doleta.gov/agworker/report9/toc.cfm.

4 Ninety percent of farm worker women in California cite sexual harassment as a major work problem. See "Harvesting Justice: The Bandana Project" (2009), available at http://www.harvestingjustice.org/index.php/farmworkers-in-the-us (last accessed August 2009).

5 Department of Labor, "National Agricultural Workers Survey" (2002), available at http://www.doleta.gov/agworker/report9/toc.cfm.

6 Seventeen percent of all workers employed in cleaning and 22 percent of maids and other household workers are unauthorized migrants. However, this does not account for authorized migrant laborers in these professions. See Jeffery Passel, "The Size and Characteristics of the Unauthorized Migrant Population in the U.S." (Washington: Pew Hispanic Center, 2006), available at http://pewhispanic.org/files/reports/61.pdf.

7 For agricultural workers, the average income in 2002 was between \$10,000 and \$12,500 per year. See Department of Labor, "National Agricultural Workers Survey" (2002). For careworkers, the 2004 median wage for home care aides, not including undocumented workers, was between \$8.18 and \$8.92 per hour. See MetLife Foundation and Schmieding Center, "Caregiving in America" (2007), p. 28, available at http://ww.ilcusa.org/media/pdfs/Caregivingi-nAmerica-Final.pdf.

8 New immigrants accounted for 60 percent of the growth in the U.S. labor force between 2000 and 2004 and half of the growth in the 1990s. "Employment and Workforce," available at http://www.migrationinformation.org/integration/workforce.cfm (last accessed August 2009).

9 Heather Boushey, "Women Breadwinners More Important Than Ever" (Washington: Center for American Progress, 2009), available at http://www.americanprogress.org/issues/2009/06/breadwinners_interactive.html. For further information, see Bureau of Labor Statistics, "Women in the Labor Force: A Databook" (December 2008), available at http://www.bls.gov/cps/wlf-databook-2008.pdf.

10 U.S. Census Bureau, "Fertility of American Women, 2006" (2006), available at http://www.census.gov/prod/2008pubs/p20-558.pdf; Pew Hispanic Center, "Statistical Portrait of the Foreign-Born Population in the United States, 2007" (2007), available at http://pewhispanic.org/factsheets/factsheet.php?factsheetID=45; Felisa Gonzales, "Hispanic Women in the United States, 2007" (Washington: Pew Hispanic Center, 2008), available at http://pewhispanic.org/files/factsheets/42.pdf.

"Con là trứng của Mẹ" ("I am my mother's daughter")

By Gianna Le, a young community health advocate who is applying to medical school

Sometimes, I imagine what kind of person my mother would have been had Saigon not fallen. But I dare not change the course of her history. I am not sure if I would know how to love, to forgive, to believe, and to be strong had my mother not experienced the trials and tragedies that taught her the values I learned to mirror.

Although I was born in America, I don't consider myself removed from the legacy of war, displacement, poverty, and determination that constituted my family's history. When my mother felt brave enough to relive the years after the Vietnam War, she'd tell me stories of becoming a refugee in her own land, escaping with her seven younger siblings boat by boat across turbulent seas, spending long months in refugee camps, and somehow surviving long enough to reach the "Land of the Free."

I consider her survival a miracle, a washing of the canvas, a sort of rebirth. For those who left Vietnam, the war and immigration experience did liberate (to an extent) our nation's then-newest immigrant enclaves from traditionally held gender roles. The experience wrung out previous patriarchal notions and offered new opportunities to Vietnamese-American women. But with those opportunities came both deep pain and hardship.

Culturally removed from the feminist movements that swept America in the previous decades, my mother defined her womanhood on her own terms—a delicate balance of strength and compassion. Unlike my grandmother, who held the traditional role of solely caring for her nine children, my mother juggled her role in the household while working every day of her life to secure a livelihood for her family. She did not miss any opportunity to get her family ahead.

Her first job in America, like many other Vietnamese immigrant women, was at a nail salon. She endured many years working in that environment—even through the pregnancy of my younger sister—until the chemical fumes proved to be too harmful to bear. I've even heard some of my aunts regretfully whisper that my sister was born mentally and physically disabled because of my mother's persistence in working there.

My mother eventually obtained a real estate license and years later, through her tenacity, resourcefulness, and strength, she lifted us into the middle class. And because my mother embraced opportunities that set her apart from the roles expected of the women from the generation before her, I, too, am offered the opportunities that will set me apart from the generation before me.

My generation lives in a society and an era where gender roles are becoming less rigidly defined. As my generation steps up to the plate, I hope we commit ourselves in the ideals that remind us to love, to forgive, to believe, and to be strong. Like my mother, I will stay determined amid hardships, humble amid success, and grateful for every opportunity to shape my own destiny. I cannot deny these words my mother still whispers, "Con là trứng của Mẹ" ("I am my mother's daughter").

Like my mother, I will stay determined amid hardships, humble amid success, and grateful for every opportunity to shape my own destiny.

ANDREW LICHTENSTEIN, CORBIS

Sick and Tired

Working women and their health

By Jessica Arons and Dorothy Roberts

"I am sick and tired of being sick and tired."
- *Fannie Lou Hamer, civil rights leader*

Waiting tables is not easy when six months pregnant, yet Mindy had no choice but to work the busy shifts at a local diner because she needed to contribute to the family income, and save for her new baby. She and her husband, a fellow restaurant worker with two jobs, had no health insurance through their employers, but luckily Mindy received pregnancy-specific insurance coverage through a state program.

Being on her feet most of the day, however, soon took its toll on Mindy's health and the health of her baby. The hard work and stress of the job—many patrons don't realize that restaurants are one of the most demanding service industries in the country—resulted in fatigue that complicated her pregnancy. Her doctor provided a note saying she needed regular breaks because Mindy's body was stressed and her baby was showing signs of that stress, growing erratically instead of steadily in size. But that's not how restaurants operate.

Mindy was forced to take early maternity leave because of her health problems but it was too little too late; she still needed a Caesarean section. Ultimately she had to quit her job to care for her own health and her new child and because the family couldn't afford to pay child care costs. Without her income, the new family struggled to get by on her husband's wages and tips, seeking government assistance to help purchase food.

Mindy's experience, as told to MomsRising.org co-founders Joan Blades and Kristin Rowe-Finkbeiner in their book, *The Motherhood Manifesto: What America's Moms Want—and What To Do About It*,[1] is far too common in America today. As our country stands on the precipice of two historic societal shifts—women becoming half of U.S. workers for the first time in our history and the potential of extending affordable health care coverage to everyone living in America—we need to revisit old assumptions about how best to create access to health care and healthy working conditions.

The crux of the problem is this—women have taken on a greater share of breadwinning while maintaining their responsibilities as primary caregivers.

The crux of the problem is simply this—women have taken on a greater share of breadwinning while maintaining their responsibilities as primary caregivers. But breadwinning has not always come with greater access to health benefits, and too often, women's health has been compromised as women try to combine work and family responsibilities.

As with so many of our institutions, employer-sponsored health insurance was developed around the assumption that men are the breadwinners, women are the caregivers, everyone gets married, and all families are nuclear. For this reason alone, our health insurance system fails women in significant ways—a full quarter of women still receive health insurance through their husbands' jobs, which makes them more vulnerable to losing coverage should something happen to him (he gets fired) or the relationship (they divorce). This is especially true now in the midst of the current recession. With men losing 73.6 percent of the jobs since the Great Recession began in December 2007, it should come as little surprise that 14,000 men, women, and children are losing their health insurance *each day*.[2] And, when women seek to buy health insurance on the private market, too often they find that they are charged more than men and cannot get the essential health benefits they need, including maternity and reproductive health coverage.

Of particular importance to the complex work-health relationship, women are the most fertile in their 20s and therefore most likely to start their families while building their careers. Because women can postpone starting their families, it is now more common and easier for them to work than in the past. And because more women now work, they are more likely to have their children at older ages than they previously did.

The presence or absence of workplace policies that support women's childbearing and child-rearing decisions can have multiple consequences for the health of working women, especially their reproductive health. For instance, a two-tier system that accommodates breastfeeding for professional mothers but ignores working-class moms can lead to health problems for the less-affluent women and their children.

A woman's physical and social work environment can have a tremendous impact on her health and well-being. While this is true for men too, inequitable working conditions related to sexism and sex stereotyping create heightened risks to women's health that have been overlooked for too long. For instance, whether working with hazardous chemicals in a hospital, a salon, or a laundry, women are regularly exposed to skin irritants, endocrine disruptors that interfere with fertility and reproduction, and even carcinogens.

Many of these jobs are just as or more risky than traditionally male jobs in sectors such as construction and mining, but they are rarely viewed in this light. And where women have tried to enter those male bastions, they often have been met with sexual harassment—itself a source of occupational stress—or protectionist policies that try to exclude them because of conditions that might threaten their fertility instead of efforts to make the workplace safer for everyone. The workplace also has failed to be a safe haven for employees who are dealing with domestic violence.

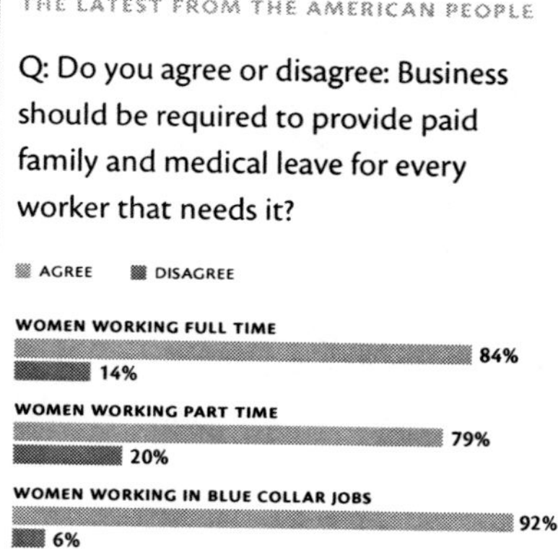

Source: Rockefeller/*Time* poll, 2009.

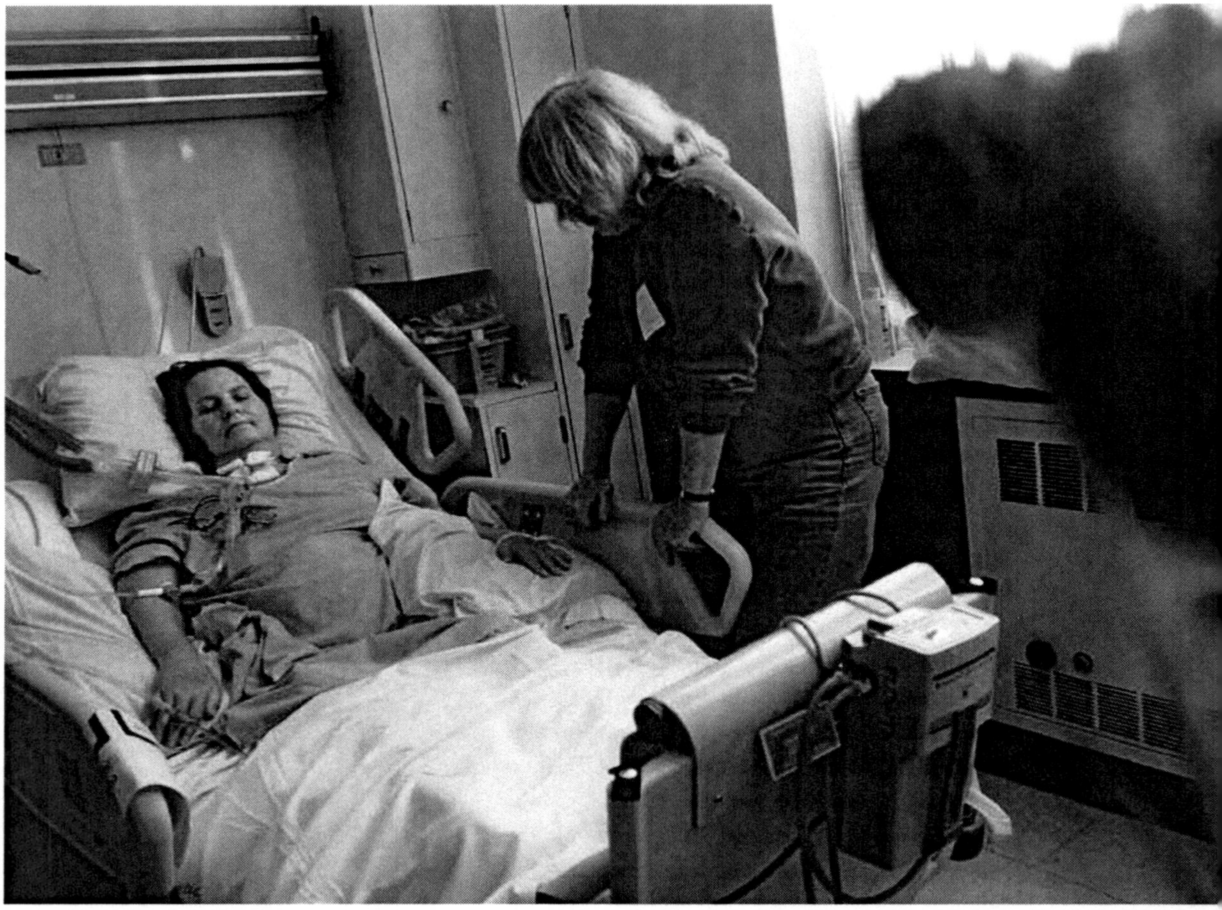

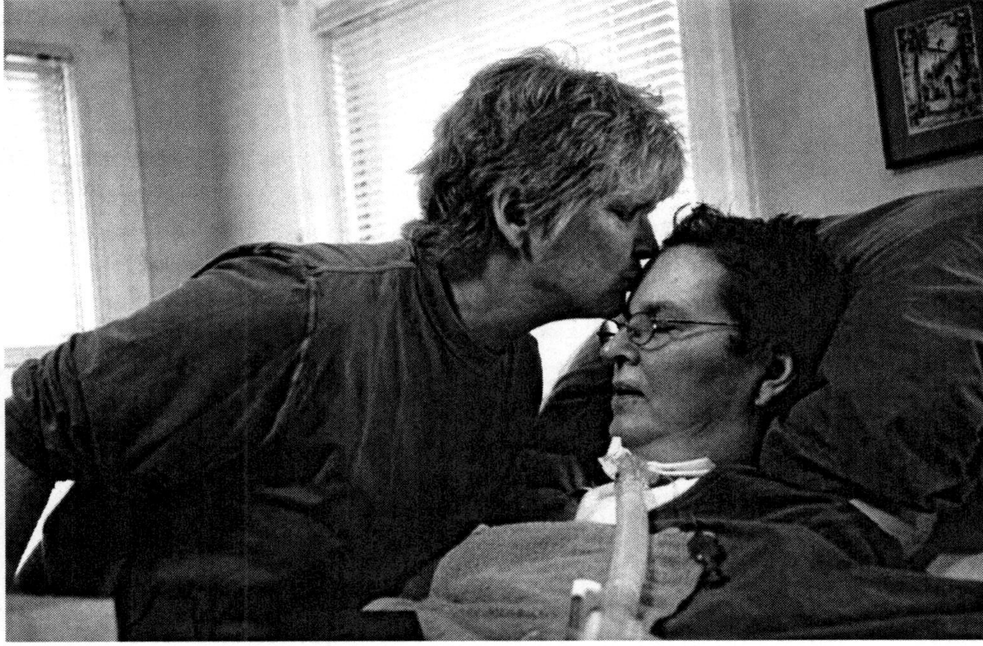

THE COST OF CARING FOR HER PARTNER. Karen Jorgensen and Karen Toloui, as they lived through five years of loss and love, while Jorgensen succumbed to Amyotrophic Lateral Sclerosis, or Lou Gehrig's Disease. There are serious consequences for the caregiver—they are almost twice as likely to report having chronic conditions such as heart disease, cancer, diabetes, or arthritis. [PHOTOS BY ERIN LUBIN]

This complex relationship between work and health is magnified by social obstacles based on race, disability, and sexual orientation. It is especially poor and low-income women, women of color, and immigrant women who are driven into the most hazardous and low-status jobs, who are given the least amount of flexibility in their schedules, and who are least likely to receive employer-provided benefits such as health care, sick leave, or family leave.

In addition, the competing demands of work and home often have greater adverse health effects on women than on men. Caregivers, the majority of whom are women, are almost twice as likely to report having chronic conditions such as heart disease, cancer, diabetes, or arthritis.[3] Women also are more likely to suffer chronic stress that can lead to headaches, sleeplessness, irritability, and depression. Indeed, a recent poll showed that women are more likely than men to feel the psychological effects of the Great Recession and to report physical symptoms of stress.[4]

Women are more likely than men to feel the psychological effects of the Great Recession and to report physical symptoms of stress.

In this chapter we will examine specific shortcomings in our current health insurance system, followed by an exploration of the relationship between women's reproductive health needs and their job opportunities. We then turn to the inequitable job conditions faced by women and the effects those conditions have on their physical and mental health. Sexual harassment, occupational segregation, sexism and racism, inadequate support for caregivers, and an atmosphere unresponsive to the ripple effects of domestic violence on the workplace all threaten the health and well-being of female employees.

We close out our chapter with three key suggestions on how we can redefine the relationship between health and work and restructure the workplace to recognize employees as whole human beings who have much to contribute to both economic and social life.

System failure

Employer-based health insurance leaves women vulnerable and the private market discriminates against women

Starla Darling was nearing the end of her pregnancy when she learned that the plant she worked for was shutting down. She was about to lose her job, and with it, her health insurance. She rushed to the hospital, had labor induced, and ended up needing a Caesarean section—all in the hope that giving birth while covered meant her insurance company would pay the bills. Even so, her insurance company denied the claim and left her with $17,000 in debt.[5]

Our health care system discriminates against women in numerous ways. While women are more likely than men to have health care because of government programs, employer-based coverage is structured in ways that commonly leave women out, make them more vulnerable to losing coverage, or fail to cover all of their health costs. When unregulated in the private market, insurers routinely charge women higher premiums than men and refuse to cover such basic care needs as contraception, Pap tests, and even maternity care. This discriminatory treatment and women's heightened need for medical services mean that women spend more on health care than men, despite the fact that women typically earn less than men for the same work.

The employer-sponsored system, modeled as it is on outmoded notions of family structure and workforce participation, currently leaves out too many women and must be strengthened through reform. Because so few jobs offer the flexibility needed for the unpaid caregiving duties women often perform for their families, many women must reduce their working hours or stop working completely, making it hard for them to obtain or maintain health insurance. Women are more likely to work in the types of jobs that do not offer benefits—low-wage (think fast food), part-time (a department store), or for small businesses (a hair salon).[6] Part-time jobs pay less than comparable full-time jobs, are concentrated in sectors that tend to be low-paying, and are often ineligible for the employer's health insurance plan.[7]

The quarter of women who receive health insurance through their husbands are especially at risk of losing coverage as men's jobs become less and less stable in our economy and with divorce rates remaining high.[8] And receiving benefits through a spouse is not an option for unmarried women.

When we combine uninsured women with those who have purchased private insurance on the individual market, we find that almost one out of every four women is subject to the whims of this deeply inequitable marketplace. Here, insurance companies routinely charge women higher premiums than men of the same age and health status, a practice known as "gender rating." Private policies also often deny coverage or increase premiums due to preexisting conditions that are either specific to women or disproportionately affect women. For instance, women may be excluded from general or specific coverage because they had a Caesarean section or are survivors of domestic violence.[9] What's more, private plans rarely include comprehensive maternity benefits, leaving women and their families to pick up the tab (an uncomplicated vaginal birth in a hospital averages approximately $7,500; Caesarean sections cost even more).[10]

The quarter of women who receive health insurance through their husbands are especially at risk of losing coverage as men's jobs become less and less stable in our economy and with divorce rates remaining high.

Women who have insurance do not always have sufficient coverage for all of their health care needs. They typically have higher out-of-pocket costs than men with insurance, due to co-pays, deductibles, or other cost-sharing for chronic conditions, prescription medication, and routine gynecological care.[11] Women ages 19 to 64 are more likely than their male counterparts to spend more than 10 percent of their income on out-of-pocket costs—an amount that officially classifies them as underinsured—and spend 68 percent more on their health care than men during their reproductive years.[12] And women who suffer physical abuse spend 42 percent more on health care than non-abused women.[13]

Not surprisingly, more women than men skip seeking medical care or filling a prescription due to cost. In fact, according to a recent study, more than half of women surveyed had problems getting care because of costs, including forgoing tests, medicine, or other treatment.[14] And this was before the recession began. In addition to cost barriers, women face workplace barriers to seeking care: Almost one in five women report delaying medical care because they could not get time off from work.[15] For women of color in particular, distrust of the medical system because of historic medical abuse, different cultural mores, or limited English proficiency can create additional barriers to accessing appropriate medical care.[16]

Because women are paid less than men on average, their medical expenses eat up a greater share of their income and they are less able to afford premium hikes, larger co-pays, or supplemental coverage.[17] Women also are less likely

"NOT A BUM. I'M A MOM. PLEASE HELP." Bob Wessenberg stands with his family in the backyard, counting the money his wife, Sheila, received by panhandling. Due to the economic downturn and a battle with breast cancer, the Wessenberg family has been struggling with bankruptcy and the lack of medical insurance. [ED KASHI, AURORA]

to be able to take advantage of employer benefits such as Health Savings Accounts, which are pretax medical savings accounts, and receive smaller contributions from their employers to such plans if contributions are pegged to their lower salaries.[18]

Moreover, the disparity in women's earnings, savings, and benefits while working often leaves women with insufficient funds to meet their health care needs in their elder years. They have a greater need for long-term care, but are less likely to be able to afford it. Women over 65 are 7 percent less likely than men to have employer-sponsored insurance as a supplement to Medicare coverage. And they are twice as likely as men to receive supplemental insurance through Medicaid as a result of their higher rates of poverty.[19]

THE LATEST FROM THE AMERICAN PEOPLE

Q: Do you agree or disagree: Businesses that fail to adapt to the needs of modern families risk losing good workers?

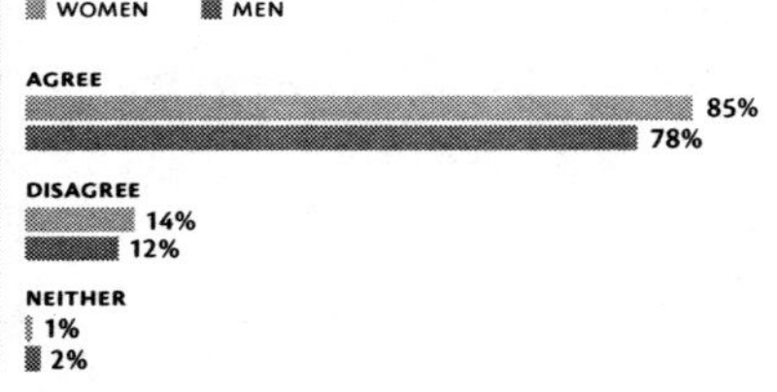

Source: Rockefeller/*Time* poll, 2009.

Higher medical costs combined with lower earnings add up to more medical bankruptcies for women.[20] Although no data are currently available on lesbians who file for medical bankruptcy, it is likely that they are hit even harder. Gays and lesbians are almost twice as likely to be uninsured as heterosexuals[21] because they have few employment protections and are less likely to qualify for coverage from a partner's job. And lesbian couples have a higher poverty rate (6.9 percent) than heterosexual married couples (5.4 percent) and gay male couples (4.0 percent),[22] possibly because they effectively face a double gender wage gap as well as multiple forms of discrimination.

The great irony is that women are the biggest consumers of health care. Women are more likely to suffer from chronic illnesses and disabilities than men, experience higher rates of mental health problems, and are 40 percent more likely to take prescription medication than men.[23] And women tend to make most of the health care decisions for their families, which means they must access the health care system on behalf of others as well as themselves.

Production and reproduction

Reproductive health care contributes to workforce productivity and workplace policies affect women's reproductive health and options

Women have always participated in formal and informal economies, but a fundamental shift occurred in the second half of the 20th century. The introduction of a relatively safe, low-cost, and effective method of birth control, bolstered by the civil rights and women's movements, paved the way for women to enter and stay in the workforce as they never had before. Yet 50 years later, we still haven't figured out what to do with female employees who want to protect their fertility from workplace hazards or raise a family while working.

The powerful pill

In ways that differ significantly from men, a woman's reproductive life is critically intertwined with her work life. To begin with, having the ability to control the timing and spacing of pregnancy and childbirth is essential for women to be able to participate fully in education and paid employment.

Perhaps one of the most significant factors facilitating women's large-scale entry into the workforce (and especially professional careers) was the advent of modern contraception. As any mother knows, caring for a child can make up-front, time-intensive career investments extremely challenging. Greater access to an almost infallible, convenient, painless, and female-controlled contraceptive method in the form of the birth control pill provided women with much greater certainty about pregnancy and directly reduced the economic and social costs of making long-term career investments and delaying marriage.[24]

In "The Power of the Pill," Harvard University economists Claudia Goldin and Lawrence Katz chronicle how the greater availability of the birth control pill to young, unmarried women in the 1960s coincided with increased female college graduation, increased female professional school matriculation rates, and increased age at first marriage rates.[25] Interestingly, the pill's uptake also altered

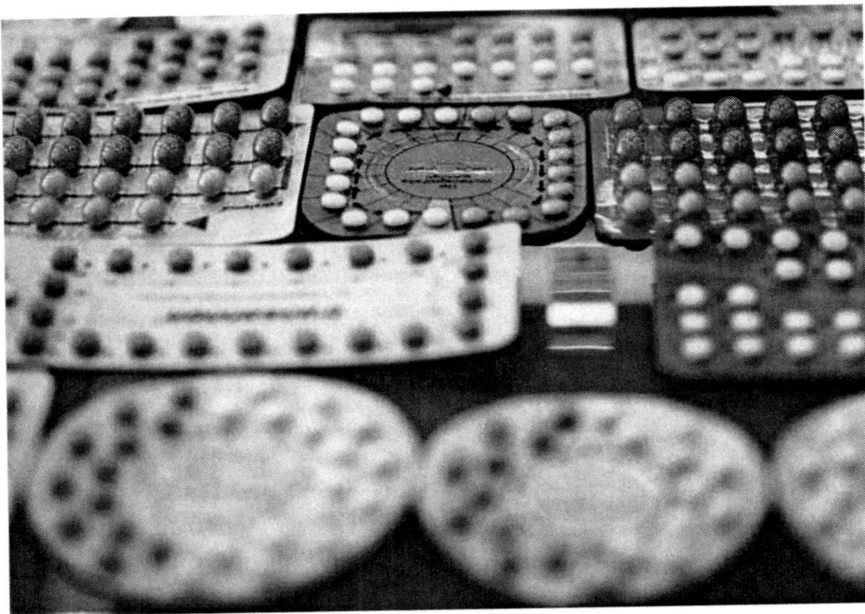

THE POWER OF THE PILL. Reproductive choice is demonstrably liberating. [GLAESCHER, LAIF, AURORA PHOTOS]

the marriage "market" by making marriage delay more acceptable and less costly for *all* women. Thus, the pill had the indirect effect of encouraging career investments even for women not using it.[26]

These factors, along with the feminist movement, the legalization of abortion, and sex discrimination legislation, resulted in seismic shifts in societal norms,[27] the effects of which are still reverberating today. Indeed, women becoming primary breadwinners and half of all workers quite simply could not have occurred in the absence of pervasive access to modern contraception.

Fallowed ground

At the same time that more affluent women started filling up college classrooms and moving onto boardrooms, a small number of working-class women slowly began to move into male bastions such as construction, mining, and manufacturing. Unfortunately, these traditionally male occupations failed to consider and protect against the effects of workplace exposures to hazardous chemicals on human reproductive systems. What's more, female-dominated occupations such as nursing and cosmetology do no better.

Many of the chemicals, toxins, and other harmful agents to which women workers are exposed are hazards that affect their reproductive system, their fertility, and fetal development.[28] Women employed in the health services profession are especially vulnerable owing to their contact with radiation, anesthetic gases, drugs, and viruses. But women working in shoe and textile manufacturing, printing, and facilities that produce pesticides and synthetic materials also absorb reproductive toxins daily. In addition, lead has long been known to cause infertility, reduced fertility, miscarriages, low birth weight, and developmental disorders.

At the same time that more affluent women started filling up college classrooms and moving onto boardrooms, a small number of working-class women slowly began to move into male bastions such as construction, mining, and manufacturing.

Employers sometimes respond to these reproductive hazards by excluding women from worksites deemed unsafe for them. Although male exposure to lead, radioactive sources, and other toxins can cause sterility and mutagenic effects, women have been the focus of exclusionary policies and men have been left unprotected.

A notorious example: Johnson Controls, Inc., a Wisconsin battery manufacturer, began to employ women in the 1970s, but because exposure to lead, a primary ingredient in battery manufacturing, is risky to workers' health and to the health of a fetus, the company first instituted a policy requiring women job applicants to sign a statement that they had been advised of the risk of becoming pregnant while exposed to lead and later shifted to a policy of outright exclusion. The company barred all "women who are pregnant or who are capable of bearing children" from jobs involving lead exposure and required medical documentation of sterility from women who wanted these jobs.

The plaintiffs in a class action lawsuit challenging the fetal-protection policy as sex discrimination included a woman who was sterilized in order to keep her job, a divorced worker who lost wages when she was transferred from a position with lead exposure, and a man who was denied a leave of absence to lower his lead level when he intended to become a father. In the end, the U.S. Supreme Court held that the remedy for reproductive hazards is not to restrict women's employment opportunities but to make the workplace safe for all workers.[29]

Not having it all

From a biological perspective, optimal fertility for women occurs between ages 20 and 35.[30] Despite trends showing an increase in maternal age in this country, especially for professional women, the average age at which American women have their first child is 25.[31] Thus, the age range for fertility happens to coincide with the period of time when employees are most likely to develop their educational and career skills and obtain greater responsibilities in their jobs. Yet most employers have not adjusted to this reality, which has ramifications for workplace equality, reproductive options, and the health and well-being of women and their families.

Workplace accommodations for pregnancy and childbearing affect women's health and that of their newborn children. Sylvia Guendelman, a professor at the University of California Berkeley's School of Public Health, shows that taking maternity leave before delivery can reduce Caesarean section rates fourfold and extended leave after childbirth can increase the successful establishment of breastfeeding among working mothers.[32] Such improvements result, respectively, in a decrease of complications and recovery time for the mother and the risk of allergies, obesity, and sudden infant death syndrome for the child.[33]

While professional women are increasingly enjoying workplace accommodations for breastfeeding, few working-class women receive such flexibility or support.[34] And pregnancy leave before childbirth is still rare in our society—it is used mostly for health problems, coping with stress and fatigue, or to mother young children rather than for health-promoting behavior. The failure to utilize such leave is likely due to economic deterrents and the desire to store up leave for the postnatal period.[35]

Take, for instance, what happened to Laura Walker, who worked at a Red Lobster restaurant. Instead of accommodating her need to pump breast milk on breaks, her managers responded to her nurse's note by cutting her hours, assigning her the worst tables, and harassing her with milk-related teasing. Denied an environment where she could regularly pump, her milk ducts clogged and she contracted mastitis, a painful breast infection.[36]

This differential system where working-class moms have fewer breastfeeding options than their professional sisters (contrast Walker's experience with that of Sarah Palin, who famously breastfed her son Trig while on conference calls) means that while 53 percent of college graduates still breastfeed their newborns after six months, only 29 percent of high school graduates do so.[37] In the case of breastfeeding, such decisions have long-term consequences on children's health as well.[38]

Given the continued obstacles for working mothers, some women, mostly with professional jobs, have followed traditional (read: male) workplace norms and tried to establish their careers before embarking on motherhood. From 1991 to 2001, the number of women becoming mothers for the first time between the ages of 35 and 39 jumped 36 percent and first-time mothers aged 40 to 44 spiked 70 percent.[39]

The age range for fertility happens to coincide with the period of time when employees are most likely to develop their educational and career skills and obtain greater responsibilities in their jobs.

But there are important health consequences to delayed childbearing. "Advanced maternal age," as women are described when they become pregnant past age 35, increases health risks for women and children, including a heightened chance of Down's Syndrome and other chromosomal disorders, high blood pressure, gestational diabetes, preterm birth, low birth weight, and miscarriage and stillbirth.[40]

Women over 35 also have lower fertility than women under 35 and may have trouble becoming pregnant in the first place. Some women have turned to fertility treatments, which carry their own health risks. Most notably, egg stimulation and retrieval for in vitro fertilization can trigger ovarian hyperstimulation syndrome,

RICHARD PASLEY, DOCTOR STOCK, SCIENCEFACTION, CORBIS

So I finally decided, my daughter is not going to grow up seeing her mother get beat down, she's not going to see her mother literally have to fight a man, literally, physically fight a man. So I left that relationship and I ended up moving to Washington to do a little soul-searching, you know as they say, and I had to figure out who I was as not only a Latina, but as a woman, as a mother, with two failed relationships under my belt. I said, who is the common denominator here, it's me. So what can I do different to attract somebody, something like my parents had.

Lily in Seattle

the symptoms of which include nausea and vomiting, abdominal discomfort, shortness of breath, labored breathing, clotting disorders, renal failure, ovarian twisting, and occasionally death.[41]

Researchers Mary Ann Mason and Marc Goulden of the University of California Berkeley found that tenure-track and tenured faculty women at UC Berkeley were most likely to have their first biological child between the ages of 38 and 40—due in large part to career track pressures and what is known as the "time bind" (the phenomenon that women with children spend significantly more time engaged in professional, housework, and caregiving activities than men with children and than men and women without children).[42] Given the increased health risks that come with advanced maternal age, this means that a failure to establish adequate "on and off ramps" and other policies that build flexibility into the academic career track can directly result in poorer health outcomes for mothers and babies.

Popular culture tends to blame women for "selfishly" focusing on their careers when they delay having children, but a complex set of incentives pressures white, affluent women to reproduce more and work less—among them the "opt-out" myth, the "mommy wars" debate, and the celebration of multiple births by white, married women—while pressuring low- and middle-income women and women of color to reproduce less and work more.[43] Women of color in particular are concentrated in low-wage occupations at the bottom end of the labor market that intensify the work-family tension. The low-skilled jobs most commonly occupied by women offer few benefits, irregular hours, and minimal time off, rendering them the least conducive for caregiving.[44]

THE LATEST FROM THE AMERICAN PEOPLE

Q: Do you agree or disagree: In households where both partners have jobs, women take on more responsibilities for the home and family than their male partners?

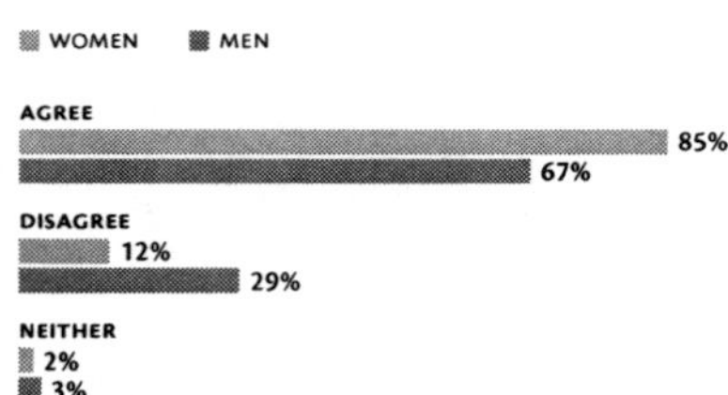

Source: Rockefeller/*Time* poll, 2009.

Hazardous to your health

The segregated workplace and inequitable job conditions pose physical and social risks to women's health

Fannie Lou Hamer's famous quotation about being sick and tired no doubt was a reference to her years toiling in the cotton fields while struggling to take care of her family.[45] Most American women no longer work under the conditions experienced by Hamer, but the workplace still leaves many women sick and tired.

The interaction of both physical and social hazards created by inequitable job conditions makes employment especially dangerous for women. Women's vulnerability does not result from biological difference so much as from occupational discrimination, including sex and race segregation.[46]

In addition, too many employers still treat matters of the home as private affairs with no bearing on the workplace. Ignoring the burdens of caregiving and the injury of domestic violence only serves to exacerbate threats to women's health, safety, and well-being.

Separate and unequal

In her bestselling expose, *Nickel and Dimed: On (Not) Getting By in America*, Barbara Ehrenreich goes undercover to investigate the impact of welfare reform on "unskilled" women workers.[47] She takes jobs in low-wage occupations that are typically reserved for women—waitress, hotel maid, nursing home aide, house cleaner, and sales clerk—and discovers that all of them are risky and none of them pay enough to live on.

While working as a house cleaner for a large franchise, Ehrenreich's co-worker Holly trips because of a hole in the ground, falling while carrying buckets, and screams in pain, "Something snapped." But Holly, who can't afford to miss a day of work, refuses to go to the emergency room and is soon cleaning the bathroom in the next customer's house with a bad limp. Only after Ehrenreich pleads with their boss does he give Holly one day off.[48]

Employment in the United States has historically been segregated by race and gender. Women are concentrated in a relatively small number of occupations, such as teaching, clerical services, nursing, and domestic work. These jobs pay less, are less prestigious, and often have less favorable working conditions than those in male-dominated sectors.[49]

Longstanding racial discrimination in employment intersects with sex segregation to relegate women of color to the bottom of the occupational ladder.[50] Only a tiny percentage of women of color occupy low health-risk professions such as professors, doctors, and corporate executives; most are employed in low-skilled clerical, manual, or service jobs.[51] Some cases in point:

PICKING PEPPERS WITH THE FAMILY. Female field workers, many of whom are immigrants, often take their small children to the fields with them because there is no affordable day care available. [PAT SULLIVAN, AP]

- Women are increasingly hired as migrant farm workers, an occupation dominated by people of color and immigrants and characterized by very low wages, few legal protections, and high exposure to pesticides[52]

- A majority of dry-cleaning employees are women, and over half of these women belong to minority or immigrant groups[53]

- Forty-two percent of all nail salon technicians nationwide are Asian and an estimated 80 percent of those in California are Vietnamese immigrant women[54]

A SURPRISING DANGER. Exposure to chemicals in nail salons is extremely dangerous to workers, many of whom are immigrant women. (OKAROL, FLICKR)

HEALTH CARE HAZARDS. Exposure to x-rays and other medical risks in hospitals aflict nurses in this female-dominated industry. (JOHN MOORE, GETTY IMAGES)

Although inadequately studied, their disproportionate exposure to workplace hazards plays a major role in the many health disparities experienced by women of color, who suffer higher death rates from childbirth, hypertension, diabetes, cancer, and other illnesses.[55]

The huge increase in women's employment has lessened, but certainly not eliminated, job segregation, especially in female-dominated professions. The failure of men to integrate into women's professions reflects the socially perceived inferior status and typically lower pay and benefits of these jobs.

DANGER AT THE DRY CLEANERS. Repetitive tasks amid hot and hazy working conditions make this a risky job. (JUSTIN SULLIVAN, GETTY IMAGES)

Even though we think of the kinds of jobs that men tend to hold—such as construction worker, machinist, or firefighter—as more dangerous or onerous than the jobs that women tend to hold, this isn't necessarily the case. Those women most at risk are typically the least informed about dangers and solutions and have the least resources to challenge hazards on the job. The underreporting of women's injuries and health problems creates the false impression that women are in "safer" industries and that only male-dominated occupations such as construction, mining, and environmental cleanup involve high-risk work.

Women's jobs carry particular health and safety risks because their working conditions are associated with stereotypically female personality traits and domestic roles.[56] For example, women typically carry out tasks requiring less strength but more precise, repetitive, and speedy movements (though some jobs, such as nursing and home health aides, do require the lifting of heavy patients and equipment). Women are more likely to work as typists than construction workers, but typing rapidly all day can lead to carpal tunnel syndrome and other repetitive strain injuries that inflame nerves and muscles.[57] Despite this, skeptics originally claimed such problems were the result of "psychosocial" problems and poor personal habits and successfully blocked ergonomics regulations in the mid-1990s.[58]

> The failure of men to integrate into women's professions reflects the socially perceived inferior status and typically lower pay and benefits of these jobs.

Women also are more likely than men to have jobs that mirror their roles as primary caregivers at home. Because they engage directly with children, kindergarten teachers and child care workers, who are almost all women, are exposed to more viruses, infections, and accidents than elementary school principals, who are more likely to be men. Caregiving jobs also tend to be less regulated and lack safety standard enforcement, in part because they are less likely to be unionized and thus have less bargaining and lobbying power. In addition, private employers who hire domestic workers to clean their homes, do their laundry, and care for their children and elderly parents often are not subject to safety regulations.

And consider the hospital working environment, which presents inherent risks despite regulation. More than three-quarters of hospital workers are women, with nursing, record processing, and food services dominated by women. A large share of hospital injuries result from puncture wounds and musculoskeletal problems caused by handling of heavy loads and equipment. Women working in health care are exposed to harmful ionizing radiation from X-rays, laboratories, and radioactive drugs, as well as chemical hazards from anesthetic waste gases, drugs, and sanitation procedures.[59] Nurses and aides spend far more time than doctors directly caring for patients, which exposes them to infectious diseases such as tuberculosis, hepatitis B, and HIV and painful injuries from lifting incapacitated patients.

The cosmetology industry, including hairdressers and nail salon workers, also employs mostly women. The products they use daily in poorly ventilated salons expose them to numerous dangerous chemicals and toxins that have been linked to cancer, asthma and other respiratory ailments, skin allergies, and dermatitis. Indeed, the cosmetology industry uses more than 10,000 chemicals in its products such as nail polish, dyes, and hair sprays, most of which have not been tested for safety by any independent agency.[60] Many workers also report carpal tunnel syndrome, vascular problems, and back pain from long hours of standing or uncomfortable body postures. So, too, women employed as cleaning or laundry workers are routinely exposed to harmful chemicals that cause burns and dermatitis from direct skin contact with irritating substances or respiratory problems from inhaling vapors and airborne micro-particles.

Women also have been entering professions previously closed to them in increasing numbers, but the workplace has been slow to respond to this change. Many traditionally male occupations have retained machinery, chemical safety levels, and protective wear that were designed with an all-male workforce in mind.[61] Gender differences in workforce participation exacerbate these hazards to women's health. Because women engage in more part-time and shift work, fewer are able to use employer safety services or engage in safety precautions and trainings.

Fear and loathing

In addition to physical injuries and risks, workplace inequities produce "social hazards" that also jeopardize women's health.[62] Women can experience intense psychological stress and related disorders from occupying lower status positions in the workforce—from the devaluation of their work to lacking control over their working conditions, from strenuous tasks to hostility they often encounter when they break through gender barriers. Moreover, the shift work women often perform can cause disturbance of regular circadian-metabolic rhythm, which intensifies occupational stress. And another major source of occupational stress for women is sexual harassment.

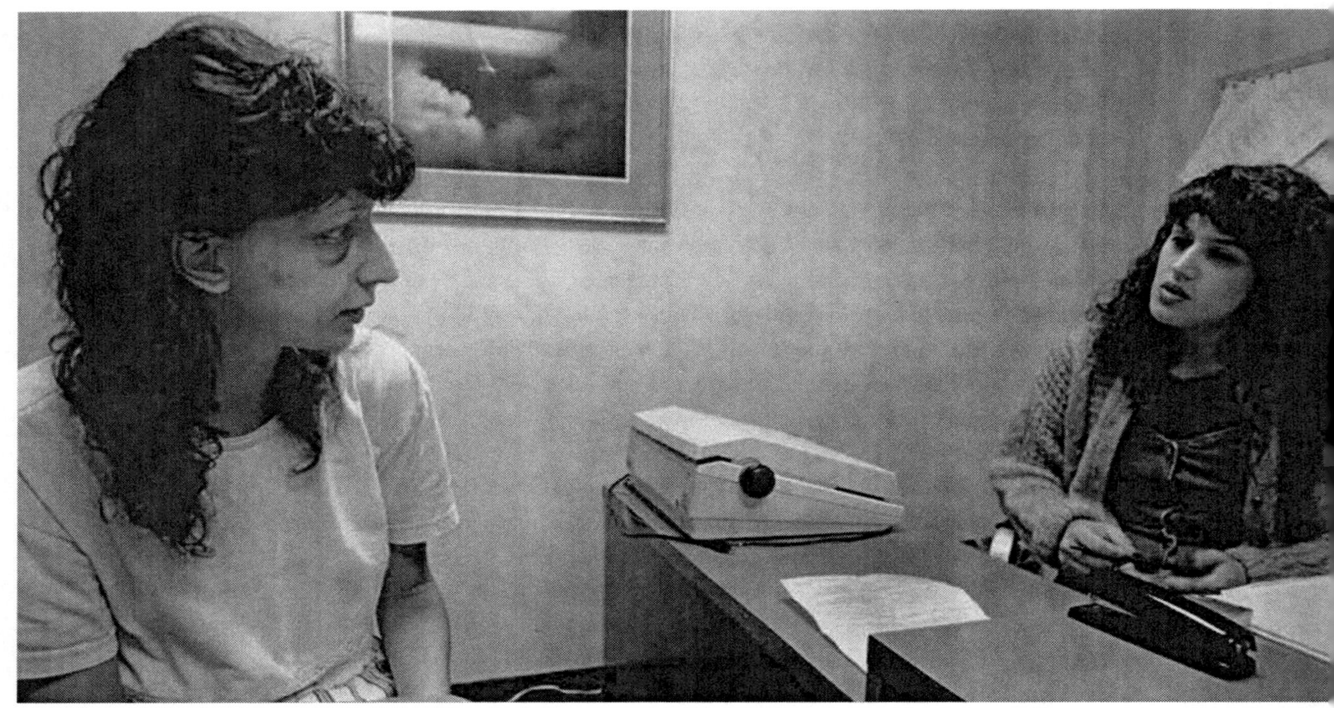

SEEN BUT UNSEEN. Domestic violence has many unacknowledged effects on the workplace. {VIVIANE MOOS, CORBIS}

Just about all of these hazards plagued women at Eveleth Mines in Minnesota. For its first 10 years of operation, the iron-ore mining and processing company employed only men in its hourly workforce.[63] In the 1980s, women began to get jobs formerly reserved for men but made up less than 5 percent of the hourly employees. No woman had ever been promoted to foreman. Women workers earned much less than men because they were confined to the lower job classifications and worked fewer overtime hours.

Eveleth Mines was male-dominated not only in terms of who was in charge but also in terms of the sexualized atmosphere. Men plastered the walls and equipment with graphic graffiti, photos, and cartoons that depicted women as sex objects. They referred to women by their body parts and called their female co-workers degrading epithets, commented on the women's sex lives, and openly described their own sexual exploits.

Some women were also subjected to sexual assault such as feigned sex acts and unwanted touching. The judge who presided over the class-action lawsuit against Eveleth Mines found that the sexualized workplace told the women in no uncertain terms "that they were perceived primarily as sexual objects and inferior to men, rather than as co-workers."[64] Ultimately, Eveleth settled with 15 women for $3.5 million.[65]

Unfortunately, sexual harassment persists today. In 2008, 13,867 charges of sexual harassment were reported to the Equal Employment Opportunity Commission, with 15.9 percent filed by men.[66] The pioneering work of legal scholar Catharine MacKinnon and others led to the recognition of sexual harassment in the workplace as a form of sex discrimination rather than "office romance."[67] Sexual harassment, however, is typically not considered an occupational health hazard. Yet numerous studies reveal that harassment on the job causes stress-related illness, lowers productivity, and increases absenteeism and job turnover, impeding women's opportunities for advancement.[68]

Racial discrimination and racist sexual stereotypes compound the workplace harassment experienced by women of color.[69] Heterosexism and homophobia also pervade the workplace. Women who have traditionally male jobs are often taunted as being lesbians and lesbians are often subjected to harassment on the basis of their sexual orientation.

A woman's work is never done

According to the World Health Organization, depression is twice as prevalent in women as in men. Disproportionate caregiving responsibilities are among the gender-specific risk factors for common mental health disorders such as depression and anxiety (other factors include gender-based violence, socioeconomic disadvantage, income inequality and poverty, and subordinate social status).[70]

Caregivers are nearly twice as likely as non-caregivers to report a chronic condition, but they are less likely to have health insurance because they have had to reduce their working hours or leave the workforce altogether.[71] Their lack of access to health care combined with the time they spend on caregiving means that they often fall behind in self-care. Caregivers are less likely to fill prescriptions for themselves or visit the doctor.[72] In one study, 21 percent of female caregivers reported receiving mammograms less often than they did before they were caregivers.[73]

Studies have shown women's disproportionate caregiving results in adverse mental health effects as well, especially chronic stress. Additional negative effects of caregiving include depression, feelings of helplessness, poor eating habits, disturbed sleep, strained relationships, anger and hostility, dissatisfaction, anxiety, and alcoholism.[74] In a study of those providing care for stroke survivors, the ones who were employed full-time were at higher risk of depressive symptoms than those who were not working.[75]

Then there are the emotional costs of trying to work around the lack of institutional support for dual-career/dual-carer families. A more common solution among lower-income families is "tag-team" parenting, where parents work alternating schedules so that one parent watches the children while the other one works.[76] It solves the problem of finding adequate and affordable child care but limits parents' ability to spend time together or with the whole family.[77]

No safe space

Domestic violence is the number one cause of injury to women. Once thought of as a purely private matter, intimate violence is now recognized to have far-reaching public health and financial consequences that extend to the workplace. Perpetrators often try to threaten the stability of a survivor's job, in order to further control her and make her more financially dependent on the perpetrator. Domestic violence contributes to a job loss for a quarter to half of all survivors.[78]

Perpetrators often carry out acts of violence at a survivor's workplace because that is where they know they can find her. This places the survivors, their co-workers, and their customers or clients at heightened risk. Colleagues also must sometimes cover for an affected employee and protect that employee from harassing calls or visits.[79]

Each year, women suffer approximately 2 million injuries from intimate partner violence.[80] As a result of this violence, employers lose $3 billion to $5 billion annually from the lost productivity of survivors, perpetrators, and colleagues.[81] In addition, employers suffer the costs of covering absent employees on short notice, training replacement employees, property damage, medical costs, and insurance premiums, and occasionally public relations problems. Survivors also have sued employers for failing to keep the workplace safe or for firing them because of the abuse.[82]

Despite the devastating effects of domestic violence on the workplace and the apparent increase in intimate violence during this recession, few preventive workplace approaches have been implemented.[83]

Where do we go from here?

Women need to be healthy in order to participate as equal and productive members of the workforce, but too often the workplace itself poses a hazard to women's health and well-being. Although the barriers to health and equality outlined above may seem too numerous to tackle, the solutions are available, starting with engaging creative approaches from every sector of society.

Our social mores have changed so significantly we now take it for granted that most women will work in paid employment for at least some portion of their lives, often while raising young children at the same time. Imagine the cultural shifts yet to come if we are able to reform our health care system, implement workplace flexibility, and clean up our physical working environment.

Working together, we can find ways to meet the needs of our changing workforce, such as:

- Making affordable, quality, comprehensive health care coverage available regardless of gender, employment status, or health
- Removing the many employment barriers to building a family and a career at the same time
- Addressing inequitable and unsafe working conditions to improve the work environment for everyone

As women's work becomes more important than ever, it is incumbent on each of us to develop new ways to both value their labor *and* protect their health. Transforming our workforce from sick and tired to healthy and productive is a job we all must share.

ENDNOTES

1 Joan Blades and Kristin Rowe-Finkbeiner, *The Motherhood Manifesto: What America's Moms Want—and What To Do About It* (New York: Nation Books, 2006).

2 Center for American Progress Action Fund, "Health Care in Crisis: 14,000 Losing Coverage Each Day" (2009), available at http://www.americanprogressaction.org/issues/2009/02/pdf/health_care_crisis.pdf.

3 Alice Ho and others, "*A Look at Working-Age Caregivers' Roles, Health Concerns, and Need for Support*" (New York: The Commonwealth Fund, August 2005), available at http://www.commonwealthfund.org/~/media/Files/Publications/Issue%20Brief/2005/Aug/A%20Look%20at%20Working%20Age%20Caregivers%20Roles%20%20Health%20Concerns%20%20and%20Need%20for%20Support/854_Ho_lookatworkingcaregiversroles_IB%20pdf.pdf; Family Caregiver Alliance, National Center on Caregiving, "Fact Sheet: Caregiver Health" (2006), available at http://www.caregiver.org/caregiver/jsp/content_node.jsp?nodeid=1822#52.

4 American Psychological Association, "APA Poll Finds Women Bear Brunt of Nation's Stress, Financial Downturn" (October 2008), available at http://www.apa.org/releases/women-stress1008.html.

5 Robert Pear, "When a Job Disappears, So Does the Health Care," *The New York Times*, December 6, 2008, available at http://www.nytimes.com/2008/12/07/us/07uninsured.html?pagewanted=1&_r=5&sq=When%20a%20job%20disappears,%20so%20does%20th.

6 Heather Boushey and Joseph Wright, "Workers Receiving Employer-Provided Health Insurance" (Washington: Center for Economic and Policy Research, 2004), available at http://www.cepr.net/documents/publications/health_insurance_3_2004_04.pdf.

7 Lawrence Mishel, Jared Bernstein, and Heidi Shierholz, *The State of Working America 2008/2009* (Washington: Economic Policy Institute, 2008).

8 The flip side to this is that while women are more vulnerable to losing coverage they have through their spouse, they are less likely to lose their own employer-sponsored insurance when they have it. Because men have lost more jobs recently and were more likely to have insurance through their own job, four times as many men as women have lost their employer-provided coverage in this recession. See Nayla Kazzi, "More Americans Losing Health Insurance Every Day" (Washington: Center for American Progress, 2009), available at http://www.americanprogress.org/issues/2009/05/insurance_loss.html.

9 National Women's Law Center, "Nowhere to Turn: How the Individual Health Insurance Market Fails Women" (September 2008), available at http://action.nwlc.org/site/PageNavigator/nowheretoturn_Report.

10 Ibid.

11 National Women's Law Center, "Fact Sheet: Addressing the Health Care Crisis" (August 2008), available at http://www.nwlc.org/pdf/AddressingtheHealthCareCrisisAug08.pdf.

12 Ibid.

13 Ohio State University, "Physical Abuse Raises Women's Health Costs over 40 Percent," *Science Daily*, March 24, 2009, available at http://www.sciencedaily.com/releases/2009/03/090323110454.htm.

14 Kathleen Doheny, "Most Women Struggle With Rising Health Care Costs," *U.S. News & World Report*, May 11, 2009, available at http://health.usnews.com/articles/health/healthday/2009/05/11/most-women-struggle-with-rising-health care-costs.html.

15 Henry J. Kaiser Family Foundation, "Women and Health Care: A National Profile" (2005), available at http://www.kff.org/womenshealth/7336.cfm.

16 Courtney Chappell, "Reclaiming Choice, Broadening the Movement" (Washington: National Asian Pacific American Women's Forum, 2005), available at www.napawf.org/file/issues/RJPolicy_Agenda.pdf; Office on Women's Health, "Minorities Distrust Medical System More" (Department of Health and Human Services, 2009), available at http://www.womanshealth.gov/news/english/623856.htm; Dorothy Roberts, *Killing the Black Body: Race, Reproduction, and the Meaning of Liberty* (New York: Vintage Books, 1998).

17 National Women's Law Center, "Addressing the Health Care Crisis."

18 Center for American Progress Action Fund and Planned Parenthood Action Fund, "Worse for Women" (2008), available at http://www.americanprogressaction.org/issues/2008/womens_health_mccain.html.

19 Alina Salganicoff, "Health Coverage and Concerns Facing Older Women" (Washington: Kaiser Family Foundation, 2009), available at http://nwlc.org/reformmatters/pdf/HealthCoverageandConcernsFacingOlderWomen.pdf.

20 Brigette Courtot, "Health Reform Can't Come Soon Enough: New Findings on Medical Bankruptcy," available at http://www.womenstake.org/2009/06/health-reform-cant-come-soon-enough-new-findings-on-medical-bankruptcy.html.

21 "Nearly One in Four Gay and Lesbian Adults Lack Health Insurance," available at http://www.harrisinteractive.com/NEWS/allnewsbydate.asp?NewsID=1307.

22 Randy Albelda and others, "Poverty in the Lesbian, Gay, and Bisexual Community" (Los Angeles: The Williams Institute, March 2009), available at http://www.law.ucla.edu/williamsinstitute/pdf/LGBPovertyReport.pdf.

23 National Women's Law Center, "Addressing the Health Care Crisis."

24 Claudia Goldin and Lawrence Katz, "The Power of the Pill: Oral Contraceptives and Women's Career and Marriage Decisions," *Journal of Political Economy* 110 (4) (2002): 730–770.

25 Ibid.

26 Ibid.

27 Ibid.

28 National Institute for Occupational Safety and Health and Centers for Disease Control, "The Effects of Workplace Hazards on Female Reproductive Health" (1999), available at http://www.cdc.gov/niosh/docs/99-104/.

29 International Union v. Johnson Controls, 499 U.S. 187 (1991); See also International Labour Organization, "Gender Issues in Occupational Safety and Health" (1999), § 3, available at http://actrav.itcilo.org/english/calendar/2001/a3_2387/resource/Gender_and_OSH.htm.

30 Jeremy Laurance, "The Big Question: So Is There an Optimum Age for a Woman to Have a Baby?" *The Independent*, October 26, 2006, available at http://www.independent.co.uk/news/science/the-big-question-so-is-there-an-optimum-age-for-a-woman-to-have-a-baby-421597.html.

31 Tallese D. Johnson, "Maternity Leave and Employment Patterns of First-Time Mothers: 1961–2003" (Washington: Department of Commerce, Census Bureau, 2008), available at http://www.census.gov/prod/2008pubs/p70-113.pdf.

32 Sylvia Guendelman and others, "Maternity Leave in the Ninth Month of Pregnancy and Birth Outcomes Among Working Women," *Women's Health Issues* 19 (1) (2009): 30–37, available at http://www.ijgo.org/article/S1049-3867%2808%2900102-3/abstract; Sylvia Guendelman and others, "Juggling Work and Breastfeeding: Effects of Maternity Leave and Occupational Characteristics," *Pediatrics* 123 (1) (2009): e38–46, available at http://pediatrics.aappublications.org/cgi/content/abstract/123/1/e38.

33 Guendelman and others, "Maternity Leave"; Guendelman and others, "Juggling Work"; Jill Tucker, "Pre-birth maternity leave aids babies, moms," *San Francisco Chronicle*, January 8, 2009, p. B1, available at http://www.sfgate.com/cgi-bin/article.cgi?f=/c/a/2009/01/08/BAC51540IG.DTL.

34 Jodi Kantor, "On the Job, Nursing Mothers Find a 2-Class System," *The New York Times*, September 1, 2006, available at http://www.nytimes.com/2006/09/01/health/01nurse.html?pagewanted=print.

35 Sylvia Guendelman and others, "Utilization of Pay in Antenatal Leave among Working Women in Southern California," *Maternal and Child Health Journal* 10 (1) (2006): 63–73; Tucker, "Pre-birth maternity leave."

36 Kantor, "On the Job."

37 Ibid.

38 Ibid.

39 Linda J. Heffner, "Advanced Maternal Age—How Old Is Too Old?" *New England Journal of Medicine* 351 (19) (2004): 1927–1929, available at http://content.nejm.org/cgi/content/short/351/19/1927.

40 March of Dimes, "Quick Reference: Pregnancy After 35," available at http://www.marchofdimes.com/professionals/14332_1155.asp.

41 Reproductive Health Technologies Project, "Ovarian Stimulation and Egg Retrieval: Overview and Issues to Consider" (Washington, 2009), available at http://www.rhtp.org/documents/RHTP-OvarianStimulationandEggRetrievalPaperUpdated.pdf.

42 Mary Ann Mason and Marc Goulden, "Marriage and Baby Blues: Redefining Gender Equity in the Academy," *Annals of the American Academy of Political and Social Science* 596 (1) (2004): 86–103, available at http://ucfamilyedge.berkeley.edu/marriagebabyblues.pdf.

43 Roberts, *Killing the Black Body*, pp. 269–70.

44 Dorothy E. Roberts, "Welfare Reform and Economic Freedom: Low-Income Mothers' Decisions about Work at Home and in the Market," *Santa Clara Law Review* 44 (4) (2004): 1029–1063.

45 Kay Mills, *This Little Light of Mine: The Life of Fannie Lou Hamer* (New York: Plume, 1993).

46 Alice Abel Kemp and Pamela Jenkins, "Gender and Technological Hazards: Women at Risk in Hospital Settings," *Industrial Crisis Quarterly* 6 (2) (1992): 137–152; International Labour Organization, "Gender Issues," §§ 2-3.

47 Barbara Ehrenreich, *Nickel and Dimed: On (Not) Getting By in America* (New York: Metropolitan, 2001).

48 Ibid.

49 Paula England, "Gender Inequality in Labor Markets: The Role of Motherhood and Segregation," *Social Politics* 12 (2) (2005): 264–288, at 266.

50 Jacqueline Jones, *Labor of Love, Labor of Sorrow: Black Women, Work, and the Family, from Slavery to the Present* (New York: Basic Books, 1985); Evelyn Nakano Glenn, *Unequal Freedom: How Race and Gender Shaped American Citizenship and Labor* (Cambridge: Harvard University Press, 2002).

51 Annette Dula, S. Kurtz, and M.L. Samper, "Occupational and Environmental Reproductive Hazards Education and Resources for Communities of Color," *Environmental Health Perspectives Supplements* 101 (2) (1993): 181–189, available at http://www.pubmedcentral.nih.gov/articlerender.fcgi?artid=1519960.

52 "Migrant Tomato Workers Face Chronic Abuses," available at http://www.splcenter.org/news/item.jps?aid=308.

53 Centers for Disease Control and National Institute for Occupational Safety and Health, "Occupational Health Disparities: Outcomes" (2009), available at http://www.cdc.gov/niosh/programs/ohd/outcomes.html.

54 National Asian Pacific American Women's Forum, "Issue Brief: The Nail Salon Industry: The Impact of Environmental Toxins on API Women's Reproductive Health" (2006), available at www.napawf.org/file/issues/issues-Nail_Salon.pdf.

55 Kemp and Jenkins, "Gender and Technological Hazards"; Dula, Kurtz, and Samper, "Reproductive Hazards."

56 International Labour Organization, "Gender Issues," § 2; International Labour Organization, "Gender Equality at the Heart of Decent Work" (2009), § 5.1.3, available at http://www.ilo.org/wcmsp5/groups/public/---ed_norm/---re/conf/documents/meetingdocument/5S]partl:wcms_105119.pdf; European Agency for Safety and Health at Work, "Gender Issues in Safety and Health at Work–A Review" (2003), pp. 32–34, available at http://osha.europa.eu/en/publications/reports/209.

57 Maurits van Tulder, Antti Malmivaara, and Bart Koes, "Repetitive Strain Injury," *Lancet* 369 (9575) (2007): 1815–22.

58 Barnaby J. Feder, "A Spreading Pain, and Cries for Justice," *The New York Times*, June 5, 1994, available at http://www.nytimes.com/1994/06/05/business/a-spreading-pain-and-cries-for-justice.html; Steve Lohr, "Administration Balks at New Job Standards on Repetitive Strain," *The New York Times*, June 12, 1995, available at http://www.nytimes.com/1995/06/12/business/administration-balks-at-new-job-standards-on-repetitive-strain.html.

59 Kemp and Jenkins, "Gender and Technological Hazards."

60 National Asian Pacific American Women's Forum, "The Nail Salon Industry"; United States Environmental Protection Agency, "Protecting the Health of Nail Salon Workers" (2007), available at www.epa.gov/dfe/pubs/projects/salon/nailsalonguide.pdf; Sian Wu, "Health Risks to Vietnamese Nail Salon Workers: Are They Being Glossed Over?" *International Examiner* 34 (7) (2007), available at http://www.modernsolutionsinc.com/archives291.

61 International Labour Organization, "Gender Issues," § 2; International Labour Organization, "Providing Safe and Healthy Workplaces for Both Women and Men" (2009), p. 4, available at http://www.ilo.org/wcmsp5/groups/public/---dgreports/---gender/documents/publication/wcms_105060.pdf.

62 Kemp and Jenkins, "Gender and Technological Hazards," pp. 143–44.

63 Jenson v. Eveleth Taconite Co., 824 F. Supp. 847 (D. Minn. 1993).

64 Ibid. at 885.

65 Sexual Harassment Support, "Jenson vs. Eveleth Mines Timeline," available at http://www.sexualharassmentsupport.org/JensonVsEvelethTimeline.html.

66 U.S. Equal Employment Opportunity Commission, "Sexual Harassment," available at www.eeoc.gov/types/sexual_harassment.html.

67 Catharine A. MacKinnon, *Sexual Harassment of Working Women* (New Haven: Yale University Press, 1979).

68 Kemp and Jenkins, "Gender and Technological Hazards," p. 144; "Effects of Sexual Harassment," available at www.stopvaw.org/Effects_of_Sexual_Harassment.html (last accessed June 2009).

69 Tanya Kateri Hernandez, "The Racism of Sexual Harassment." In Catharine A. MacKinnon and Reva B. Siegel, eds., *Directions in Sexual Harassment Law* (New Haven: Yale University Press, 2003).

70 World Health Organization, "Gender Disparities and Mental Health: The Facts," available at http://www.who.int/mental_health/prevention/genderwomen/en.

71 Family Caregiver Alliance, "Caregiver Health."

72 Ibid.

73 Evercare and National Alliance for Caregiving, "Evercare® Study of Caregivers in Decline: A Close-up Look at the Health Risks of Caring for a Loved One" (2006), available at http://www.caregiving.org/data/Caregivers%20in%20Decline%20Study-FINAL_lowres.pdf.

74 "Women's Unpaid Caregiving and Stress," available at http://findarticles.com/p/articles/mi_qu4118/is_200604/ai_n17174924/; Evercare and National Alliance for Caregiving, "Caregivers in Decline."

75 Jean Y. Ko, Dawn M. Aycock, and Patricia C. Clark, "A Comparison of Working Versus Nonworking Family Caregivers of Stroke Survivors," *Journal of Neuroscience Nursing* 39 (4) (August 2007): 217–225, available at http://www.entrepreneur.com/tradejournals/article/167894726.html.

76 Heather Boushey, "Tag-Team Parenting" (Washington: Center for Economic and Policy Research, 2006), available at http://www.cepr.net/documents/work_schedules_2006_08.pdf.

77 Arlie Russell Hochschild, *The Time Bind: When Work Becomes Home and Home Becomes Work* (New York: Metropolitan Books, 1997); Arlie Russell Hochschild and Anne Machung, *The Second Shift* (New York: Penguin USA, 2003); Blanche Grosswald, "The Effects of Shift Work on Family Satisfaction," *Families in Society: The Journal of Contemporary Social Services* 85 (3) (2004): 413–423.

78 Marcy L. Karin, "Changing Federal Statutory Proposals to Address Domestic Violence at Work," *Brooklyn Law Review* 74 (2) (2009): 377–428, available at www.brooklaw.edu/students/journals/blr/74.2%2003Karin.pdf.

79 Ibid.

80 Family Violence Prevention Fund, "Get the Facts: The Facts on Domestic, Dating and Sexual Violence," available at http://endabuse.org/content/action_center/detail/754.

81 Karin, "Domestic Violence at Work."

82 Ibid.

83 Ibid.; Associated Press, "Domestic Abuse on the Rise as Economy Sinks," April 10, 2009, available at http://www.msnbc.msn.com/id/30156918.

Women's Sports, Women's Health

By Billie Jean King, 2009 recipient of the Presidential Medal of Freedom

I am a big believer that if you help others, you help yourself.

For the last 35 years, I have been working with the Women's Sports Foundation to create programs and opportunities for young girls and women. We currently have an initiative called GoGirlGo!, which seeks to get more inactive girls active and to improve their overall health and quality of life. Since its inception, we reached almost 1 million girls at more than 14,000 organizations in cities across the nation. And we hope to reach several million before too long.

This is just another example of how health lies at the true core of our future—especially the future of women and our families. Few things illustrate this point better than the progress we are making toward the financial health and independence of women in this country and around the world. It is simply at the very core of our future.

If you have not already done so, I urge you to read Muhammad Yunus' book, "Banker to the Poor." Professor Yunus' concept of teamwork and free enterprise is changing the face of our future. By providing financial resources to women through low-cost loans arranged through The Grameen Bank—now operating both here as Grameen America and abroad—he gives them much more than money. These women gain status in their own communities, confidence in themselves, and become better caregivers for their families. By thinking globally and acting locally, we can—and will—create change in our lives, our communities, and in our homes.

Financial independence provides women with mobility, choices, and new experiences. We are seeing the roots of financial independence create new opportunities. Many of our children are becoming the first in their family to attend college. Women are seeking leadership positions in public government and overall we are reaching higher and feeling more fulfilled with our life's work.

Beginning in 1968 and continuing until 2007, it took 39 years of patient, hard work for professional women tennis players to obtain equal prize money for women and men at the four major tennis tournaments. And while it was an important milestone, it was not only about the money, it was also about the message. That historic moment is symbolic of what financial independence can do for us as women and for you as a person. If I learned one thing from our experience in securing equal prize money in tennis, it is that we recognized we had a voice and we understood how important it was to use our voice effectively.

The 21st century is the century of and for women. We need to take full advantage of what lies ahead of us.

While I am so proud of the progress women have made over the years and feel strongly we should celebrate our advancements, we still have a long way to go. With the privilege of being part of a movement come challenges, experiences, and connections that not only fulfill us as individuals but help us make a difference in the lives of others.

So how do we get there? We do it by actively listening to and learning from others. We do it by respecting others (regardless of their position). And we do it by remaining strong in our own beliefs. We do have a voice and it's up to us how we use it.

The 21st century is the century of and for women. We need to take full advantage of what lies ahead of us. Financial independence will give us the tools to be strong, the power to believe, and the right to belong.

Go For It!

Making Choices

By Lynn Rosenthal, White House adviser on violence against women

Women today are moving in ever expanding circles. We can't look at a day's headlines without reading about incredible women breaking new glass ceilings in sports, politics, science, and the corporate world. Yet as a long-time advocate for victims of domestic violence and sexual assault, I have met far too many women whose potential to achieve their own dreams was radically changed when they became victims of violence. Our nation has suffered from this lost potential.

I was the director of a battered women's shelter when I read the 1991 report by then Senator Joseph Biden called "A Week in the Life of American Women." Describing incidents of rape and battering that women were experiencing around the country, this report provided the momentum needed to pass the Violence Against Women Act in 1994. Since then we have made great strides. There is no doubt that domestic violence and sexual assault are no longer the hidden crimes they once were, and that victims now have a place to turn rather than suffer in isolation. Still, violence today is all too common and takes a tremendous toll on women and their families.

Domestic violence and sexual assault affect victims physically, emotionally, financially, and spiritually. For victims of domestic violence, every day is a struggle to keep themselves and their children safe. It is an exhausting world of trying to work while someone is sabotaging you, trying to care for your children while someone is threatening them, trying to live while someone may be trying to kill you. Sexual violence also takes its toll on women and girls. While we imagine the stranger in a dark alley, most women who are sexually assaulted are attacked when they least expect it, usually by someone they know and often by someone they trust. Young women are at the greatest risk of such violence, and the aftermath can be devastating.

We have an opportunity to make sure that all girls grow up without the scars of violence and abuse, and that all women are free to reach their true potential.

Despite the challenges we face, I am more optimistic than ever about our future. Earlier this summer, I was named White House adviser on Violence Against Women, a newly created position, dedicated specifically to advising the president and vice president on domestic violence and sexual assault. I believe that we now have a rare opportunity to change the future. We have an opportunity to make sure that all girls grow up without the scars of violence and abuse, and that all women are free to reach their true potential. When we accomplish this, we will truly have a woman's nation.

ADAN GARCIA, FLICKR

Better Educating Our New Breadwinners

Creating opportunities for all women to succeed in the workforce

By Mary Ann Mason

More and more American women are taking on the role of breadwinner, both for themselves and for their families, with many of them looking to education as a bridge to opportunity and to a heftier paycheck. The good news is that women's overall participation in postsecondary education today is remarkable. Consider these facts: Women today receive 62 percent of college associate's degrees, 57 percent of bachelor's degrees, 60 percent of all master's degrees, half of all professional degrees, and just under half of all Ph.D.s.[1] That's a stunning advance. In 1970, women received fewer than half of undergraduate degrees, fewer than 40 percent of all graduate degrees, and fewer than 10 percent of all professional degrees and doctoral degrees.[2]

But here's the not-so-good news. While these overall numbers are inspiring, once we dig a little deeper it becomes clear that many women receiving post-secondary education are not investing in degrees that will lead to society's highest-paying jobs. Women throughout the educational system either choose or are steered toward traditionally female careers. Even though the fastest growing careers are in traditionally female-dominated fields such as health care, the highest paying careers remain in male-dominated fields, including engineering, technology and other science-related industries and services—all fields in which women still lag very far behind men in educational degrees.

THE LATEST FROM THE AMERICAN PEOPLE

Q: Which of these things, in particular, would need to change in order for working parents to balance evenly their job, their marriage, and their children?

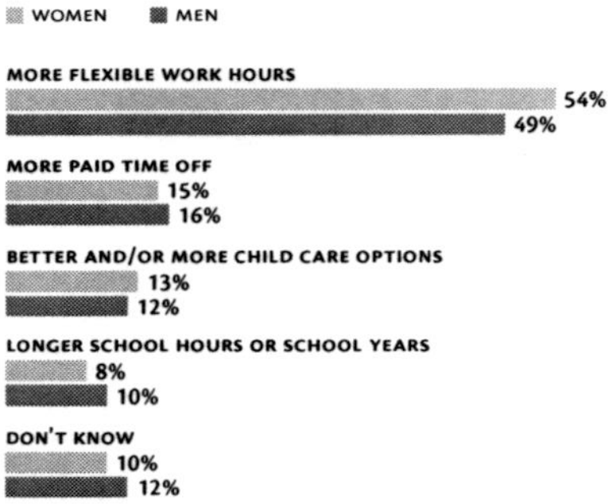

WOMEN MEN

MORE FLEXIBLE WORK HOURS
54%
49%

MORE PAID TIME OFF
15%
16%

BETTER AND/OR MORE CHILD CARE OPTIONS
13%
12%

LONGER SCHOOL HOURS OR SCHOOL YEARS
8%
10%

DON'T KNOW
10%
12%

Source: Rockefeller/*Time* poll, 2009.

As more women take on breadwinning roles, the educational system must prepare women for jobs that can support a family rather than the jobs our grandmothers were allowed to hold. This means our postsecondary educational institutions—community colleges, four-year colleges and universities and their many graduate school programs alike—will need to take further proactive steps to ensure women pursue and complete degrees that allow them to bring home the same-size paychecks and benefits from the same array of professions as men. For this to happen, these educational institutions must seek parity between the genders in all majors and concentrations from first-year postsecondary education to post-doctoral research. But this is not enough. They also need to provide family-friendly support and child care as well flexible class scheduling so that women (and men) can attain successive levels of education in order to boost their earnings in today's economy while juggling shared responsibilities in life.

Here's why. Despite reaching college in greater numbers, women still cluster largely in traditional female majors when they choose their course of study. They receive 86 percent of the bachelor's degrees in the health professions, which includes nursing, 79 percent in education, and 78 percent in psychology.[3] These professions, often called the "helping professions" or "women's professions," have always attracted women and were once the only professions open to them. Men, in the era when they were typically the sole breadwinners of their families, were less attracted to these professions in large part because they offered lower wages and less career advancement, as they do today.

There are encouraging signs this dynamic is shifting in some academic arenas. The significant trend in college toward business degrees, the most popular major for both men and women over the past 20 years, means that women now receive 50 percent of all undergraduate business degrees. Similarly, 62 percent of biological and medical science undergraduate degrees are awarded to women, doubling their participation over the past 20 years.[4] But the distribution among the doctoral disciplines is not even close to parity in most fields. While women now receive 49 percent of the doctorates in the biological sciences, in the physical sciences women are still struggling to enter a male bastion. In 2006, women received 30 percent of the doctorates awarded in the fields of physical science and math, and only 22 percent of computer science degrees and 20 percent of engineering degrees.[5]

Women with the same degrees still lag behind men's pay and almost never catch up. Education raises women's pay, but the gender gap remains at all educational levels.

Consider the impact of women's education degree choices on their jobs and their wages. Women with degrees remain segregated in lower-paying occupations. Nearly all registered nurses (91.7 percent), elementary and middle school teachers (81.6 percent), and preschool and kindergarten teachers (97.8 percent) are women, but women comprise smaller percentages of the highest-paying occupations, such as lawyers and judges (36.5 percent), physicians and surgeons (31.8 percent), dentists (25.4 percent), civil engineers (11.8 percent), electrical and electronics engineers (7.8 percent), aircraft pilots and flight engineers (3.4 percent).[6]

What's more, women with the same degrees still lag behind men's pay and almost never catch up. Education raises women's pay, but the gender gap remains at all educational levels. In 2008, the ratio of women's to men's median hourly wages was about 77 cents on the dollar for those with college degrees as well as those with only high school degrees. Women who make significant investments in college educations earn more than they would otherwise, but they don't earn as much as men, often because they remain in lower-paying female-dominated occupations. While the gap has narrowed in recent decades, we still have a long way to go to get to earnings parity (see Figures 1 and 2).

It is not new news that women do not receive equal pay for equal work, but what is depressing is that education, the much-touted engine for economic opportunity, fails to provide gender equality. Even with the increased numbers of women in higher education and in the workforce, the wage and power gaps remain large and stagnant at all educational levels. Women who are breadwinners simply cannot bring home a family income equal to a man with the same educational background (see Figures 1 and 2).

One reason that women may be encouraged or even choose not to enter male-dominated educational fields and occupations is that once female graduates enter the workforce, they find inflexible workplace policies that can exacerbate gender inequalities (policies that are often inflexible across the board, but may be exacerbated in male-dominated fields). Knowing this, students choose jobs they perceive to be more family friendly.

Most workplaces still maintain the structure established in the late 19th century, when husbands worked full time to support their families and never needed to consider taking time off to care for their a family member because most had a wife at home to attend to such matters. In this environment, workers are penalized for working less than full time, or for taking a break from their jobs to care for their family. In short, simply opening the door to higher education does not necessarily allow women to achieve true equality in the workforce.

FIGURE 1

Equal education, unequal pay

Median hourly wages by gender and educational attainment, 2008

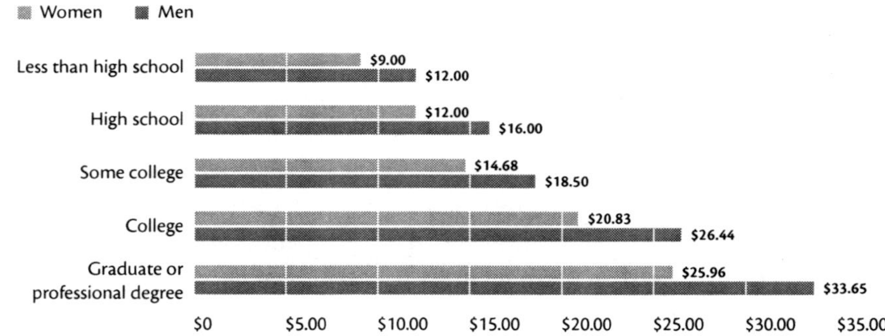

Source: Center for American Progress analysis of the Center for Economic and Policy Research Extracts of the Current Population Survey Outgoing Rotation Group Files.

Notes: Data include all workers ages 25 to 64. Wages are adjusted for top-coding and do not include overtime.

Still, the educational system may finally be poised for change. First, women are now half of U.S. workers. As women become equal in numbers and take more leadership positions, traditional workplace policies may be revised to allow for alternate career ladders. Second, our existing gender equity laws, particularly Title IX of the Education Amendments of 1972, which prohibits discrimination based on sex in educational programs and activities that receive federal financial assistance,[7] are being looked at in new ways to level the playing field for women in science, technology, math and engineering much as it has done successfully in sports.[8]

This chapter will first describe the current state of the U.S. educational system for women and girls, with special emphasis on how education often thwarts rather than advances the economic opportunities of women, beginning with community colleges, then four-year educational institutions, then graduate and post-graduate programs (see box "The forgotten third" that examines gender stereotypes in career training programs for young women and men without college degrees). We will then explore the achievements nonetheless made by women despite these obstacles. We will then conclude with several suggestions for how American post-secondary education can be reformed to ensure that women are able to function as equal partners in the future workplace.

FIGURE 2

Gaining ground

Gender pay ratio, by education, 1979 and 2008

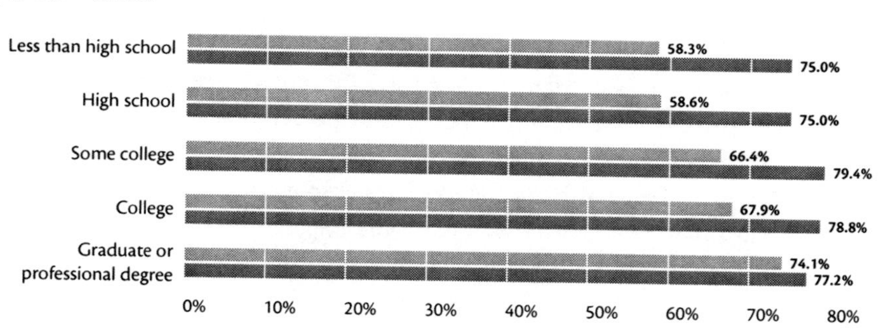

Source: Center for American Progress analysis of the Center for Economic and Policy Research Extracts of the Current Population Survey Outgoing Rotation Group Files.

Notes: Data include all workers ages 25 to 64. Wages are adjusted for top-coding and do not include overtime.

The first career gateway: Community colleges

Community colleges provide opportunities for women to earn educational credentials that can help them increase their earnings potential through accessible, flexible, and low-cost academic programs. Today, community colleges are serving 37 percent of all students enrolled in postsecondary education.[9] And the majority of these students are women: 62 percent.[10] What's more, our community colleges educate single parents at nearly three times the rate of four-year colleges.[11] And community college students are more likely to be older and independent of their parents—61 percent are not claimed as dependents by their parents compared to only 34 percent of students at public four-year colleges.[12]

Originally, these educational institutions were structured to provide high school seniors an affordable first two years of college before they transferred into a baccalaureate program. Today, however, many community colleges have expanded their mission in order to accommodate the economy's increased demand for graduates with specific career skills in disciplines such as information technology and home health care.

Community colleges offer nearly everyone a chance—95 percent of community colleges offer an open admissions policy and the annual tuition and fees are less than half that at private four-year institutions and one-tenth those at private four-year colleges and universities. For many older students they offer a second or third chance. Nearly half of all students at community colleges are over 25. Because of their accessibility and low cost, community colleges enroll a diverse group of students, including larger percentages of nontraditional, low-income, and minority students than four-year colleges.

Clearly, a community college degree is a good step forward for women, both to gain higher earnings and as a step toward a four-year degree. However, women often start, but fail to complete their degrees at community colleges.[13] At community colleges, women were less likely to complete a degree or transfer to a four-year college within six years than men—41 percent of women compared to 48 percent of men.[14]

The influx of students with significant family responsibilities presents new challenges not traditionally faced by younger students. Community colleges and universities found that mothers especially needed additional help to be successful at

NEW OPPORTUNITIES FOR CAREGIVERS. Community colleges increasingly offer flexible schedules for working moms. {TYRONE TURNER *THE NEW YORK TIMES*}

school, whether for financial aid, counseling, or esteem building. They also often needed child care on campus.[15] All major educational institutions offer some type of program for students with families, but the role of integrating students with families into the mainstream of educational programs has traditionally fallen predominantly to two-year community colleges.[16]

In the past decade, however, more colleges have taken inspiration from the type of opportunity offered by community colleges and sought to integrate low-income students with families into their educational programs. One case in point is Hamilton College's ACCESS project, which creates a pathway to educational

Excluding poor women

Some states make it hard to attend community college

Often, very poor women are excluded from attending community college. In 1996, national welfare reform included a provision requiring recipients to receive no more than five years of aid and to work or attend school while receiving aid. Only two states, Maine and Wyoming, allow recipients to pursue postsecondary education and receive welfare without exhausting their five-year lifetime limit on welfare. Although studies consistently show that postsecondary education is instrumental in helping people leave welfare, education has been treated as a luxury in the work-or-else approach to welfare reform.[17]

A few other states give work credit for postsecondary education, but it must take place within the five-year lifetime limits of federal law. Still other states provide educational support for those who work part time. In Pennsylvania, for example, women can now receive some scholarship support while working for pay half time and attending classes. The New Choices/New Options programs are designed to help low-income women and other nontraditional students get training for careers in well-paying jobs. For these students and most others around the country, the federal time limits still apply.

In most states, according to advocates, students are pushed into short-term training programs and discouraged from choosing their own course of study.[18] However, innovative new programs are trying to reach low-income women. The Center for Women and Work at Rutgers University, for example, has spearheaded an effort to introduce Internet-based distance learning into community colleges, aimed especially at low-income mothers. Their program, the Sloan Center for Innovative Training and Workforce Development, works to advance online training programs for the working poor. The access to training matters. In a New Jersey pilot program, 92 percent of participants completed the training and they achieved a 14 percent wage increase through the program.[19]

opportunity for very low-income parents in New York. The project provides academic supports for a liberal arts education in conjunction with comprehensive social services.[20] Within the first three years of operation, the ACCESS project achieved a 95 percent retention rate and movement of participating students from being 98 percent dependent on social services and income supports to being less than 10 percent dependent on social services.[21] The project attributes its successful student retention and outcomes to the integration of liberal arts educational opportunities with basic services such as child care and transportation, supports for domestic violence survivors, and interventions to ameliorate homelessness and hunger.[22]

Despite the openness and flexibility of community colleges, traditionally gendered career choices remain the norm. Women predominate in traditional female majors such as education (80.2 percent) and health sciences (83.4 percent all students), which includes nursing, while men predominate in computer and information sciences (73.1 percent) and manufacturing construction, repair and transportation (92.3 percent).[23] These choices certainly influence potential earning power, but there are also fundamental concerns about how much earning power an associate's degree from a community college will bring.

Indeed, community colleges often aren't doing enough to get women on the path toward the highest-paying careers. Increasingly, many of the popular career choices pursued by community college students are requiring a four-year bachelor's degree or specialized training. This is true for both men and women as more careers, including computer technology and science, education, and health, rely on higher-educated workers.

Community colleges often aren't doing enough to get women on the path toward the highest-paying careers.

In the high-tech occupations that are growing most rapidly—computer engineering, computer science, and systems analysis—workers must have four-year degrees and women are severely underrepresented.[24] In the health field, most workers have a job that requires less than a four-year degree, though the profession is highly divided in that the higher ranks of health care professions include some of the most highly educated workers in the country. Lacking a four-year degree, and even more so, lacking any sort of postsecondary specialized training, severely limits the advancement and income potential of health care workers, most of whom are women.[25]

All other things equal, however, an associate's degree generally provides workers with a wage boost of about 20 percent to 30 percent over a high school diploma and the returns are generally higher for women (even though the wage gap persists). The boost is much higher for workers who pursue a career track rather than a technical track. In the few studies that have been done on certificate holders who do not attain an associate's degree, few positive wage effects were found.[26]

WOMEN TEACHING WOMEN. It happens all the time in traditional female occupations such as nursing, but not enough in all technical fields. [TOM GANNAM, AP]

Despite the more accessible environment of community colleges, large strides still need to be made toward assisting nontraditional students with degree and certificate persistence. Unfortunately, most of our educational institutions are not set up to offer the flexibility that is required in order to deal with the challenges presented by students who are older, more likely to work while attending school, and often have family obligations as well. According to a report by the Center for American Progress, budget cuts, when combined with antiquated regulations and systems that were designed to meet the needs of a different era's students, have created institutions of higher education that cannot adequately deal with today's students. According to the CAP report, "as suppliers, postsecondary institutions are not fully ready to deliver quality, flexible education that leads to college and career success."[27]

But barriers to advancement beyond community college remain.[28] Thirty-nine percent of students come from minority backgrounds, compared to only 24 percent at the four-year college level. The difference is particularly strong for Hispanic students: They represent only 7 percent of four-year college students, but 16 percent of community college students.[29] Poor women, especially poor minority women, face particular challenges (see box "Excluding poor women").

Reclaiming the American Dream through colleges and universities

One of the most significant social phenomena of the last third of the 20th century and the beginning years of the new millennium is the steady rise of women in undergraduate, and more spectacularly, in graduate and professional education. Many factors, including gender equity laws, birth control, and recognition that women are now important players in the economy all contributed to this trend.

Much has been made of the fact that women now receive about 57 percent of all college degrees, and indeed across all ethnic and racial groups women significantly outpace men in receiving degrees. Closer inspection, however, reveals a more complex story. What is not usually acknowledged is that men and women enter college after high school at about the same rate. But it is the latecomers—the independents not sent by their parents, 2-to-1 of whom are women, some already with families—that tilt the final degree count. One-third of African American women who eventually graduate from college enroll when they are age 25 or older.[30]

These so called re-entry women, many of them single mothers and some of whom are welfare recipients, realize that a college degree is necessary to support their

FIGURE 3

Closing the degree gap

Percentage of bachelor's degrees deferred by gender, race, and ethnicity between the 1976–77 and 2004–05 school years

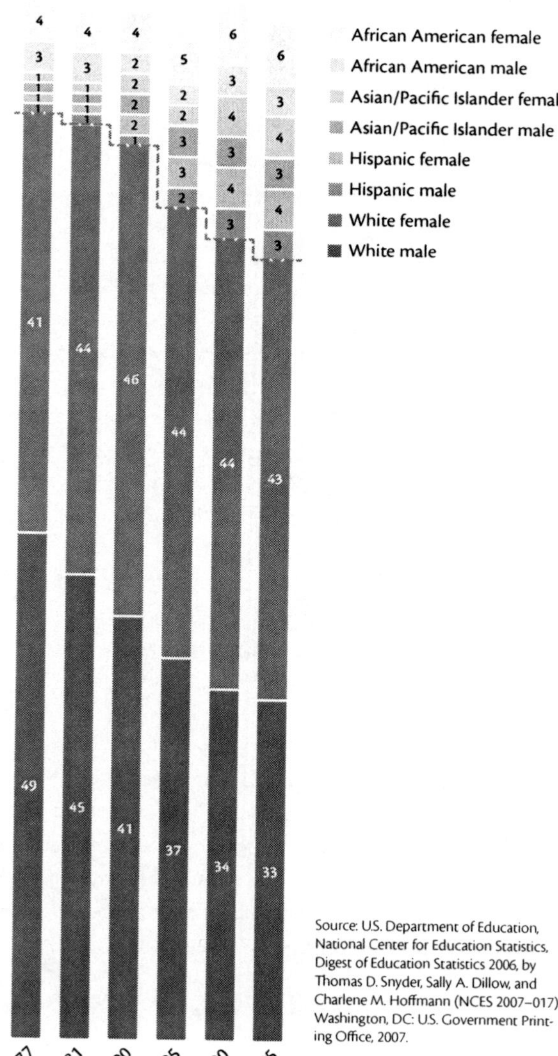

Source: U.S. Department of Education, National Center for Education Statistics, Digest of Education Statistics 2006, by Thomas D. Snyder, Sally A. Dillow, and Charlene M. Hoffmann (NCES 2007–017). Washington, DC: U.S. Government Printing Office, 2007.

The forgotten third

Many young adults never go to college, and training programs to help them favor men

Many young adults never go on to a community college, a university, or even a technical training program. Who are they and what are their prospects for thriving in a 21st-century economy that relies on women and men to be the main breadwinners?

In 1988, two groundbreaking studies on young people in the United States called attention to the dismal economic prospects of the nearly one-half of American young people who did not go on to any postsecondary education following high school, the "Forgotten Half."[31] In 2008, the American Youth Policy Forum revisited the Forgotten Half to update statistics on key indicators of the condition of young people in the United States.[32] Importantly, the "Forgotten Half" is now more accurately the "Forgotten Third," with high school dropout rates falling and greater numbers of high school graduates beginning postsecondary education and training programs.[33] This represents a major achievement for community and school reforms.

Yet for those left behind the future is bleak because their economic prospects have grown dimmer in the past 20 years. Employment rates among those not continuing on to postsecondary education are lower for the current generation than in 1989, and full-time employment rates for minority youth are 20 percent to 30 percent lower than for their white peers.[34] Those among the Forgotten Third who are employed are earning less money. For male high school graduates, inflation-adjusted earnings have fallen 16 percent over the past three decades; for their female counterparts, earnings actually grew by 4 percent.[35] Of course, women started well below men, so while their wages have not fallen in recent decades the ratio of women's to men's pay among those with only a high school degree still remains at 75 percent.[36]

For the Forgotten Third, training matters. Whether training comes through career pathway programs, community college degree curriculums, or four-year colleges, new educational opportunities can meet the needs of these young adults, but for women gender stereotypes need to be addressed. Research shows that the benefits of some types of career transition programs accrue disproportionately to young men, and may actually be harmful to young women due to their tendency to reinforce gender stereotypes.[37]

A career pathway program is a series of connected education and training programs and support services that enable individuals to secure employment within a specific industry or occupational sector, and to advance over time to successively higher levels of education and employment in that sector. Each step on a career pathway is designed explicitly to prepare the participant for the next level of employment and education. Career pathways target jobs in industries of importance to local economies. They are designed to create both avenues of advancement for current workers, job seekers and new and future labor market entrants, as well as a supply of qualified workers for local employers.[38]

Career pathway programs can include job shadowing (observing particular occupations in the workplace), mentoring (matching students with an individual in their chosen occupation), internships, and apprenticeships. But nearly all of the programs have a greater positive impact for male participants than female. Research shows that men who participate in a career-focused program are likely to have higher employment rates overall and shorter periods of idleness when unemployed.[39] For women who participate, there is less evidence that the programs are effective. One national study of Career Academies (a popular high school reform that combines academic instruction in core subjects such as math with career development opportunities) found that labor market success was concentrated among young men.[40]

Why is this? The most common career pathway programs often reinforce negative gender stereotypes about "women's work" and "men's work," which may well be why participation has a negative effect on employment outcomes for some groups of young women. One study found that career pathway programs do reduce the risk of unemployment, but that white men receive the majority of the benefit compared to black females, who are more likely to be persistently unemployed than their counterparts without this education. The same study found that Hispanic and Asian females who participate "are more likely to be persistently unemployed than their White counterparts."[41]

These poor results may be because of persistent gender stereotypes, which career pathway programs often reinforce. Girls are significantly more likely to take courses focused on low-wage service sector work where women have typically been overrepresented.[42] Indeed, in high school technical training programs that often lead to career pathway programs, the National Women's Law Center found that girls were most likely to take courses in fields like cosmetology, child care, and health professions, while boys were much more likely to be in traditional male fields of construction, automotive repair, and engineering.[43]

This persistent channeling of young women into traditionally female career paths can be an insidious barrier for women trying to attain high-paying jobs to support their families over the course of their careers.

families. Some colleges and universities provide special services and support for re-entry students. But this important trend has not received the attention and support it deserves (see Figure 3).

Still, women have advanced in both numbers and in proportion over the whole college degree-holding population in every racial and ethnic group over the past thirty years. This is good news, but more for some groups than others. The distribution of college degrees can be explained in large part by the size of the group in the general population. Many of these groups, Hispanics and Asians in particular, have swelled on the new immigration wave. But are the new immigrants receiving their fair share of the degrees? No. Smaller percentages of Hispanic women and men earn degrees according to their population. This corresponds with the group's disproportionate share of high school dropouts—there are fewer Hispanics prepared to enter the college pipeline.

Like their counterparts at community colleges, women pursuing bachelor's degrees still cluster largely in traditional female majors when they choose their course of study.

In contrast, white and Asian women are overrepresented in college compared to their respective percentages in the population. African American women and white men earn bachelor's degrees in approximate proportion to their representation in the general population. African American men are seriously underrepresented, and have not increased their participation in 30 years.[44]

Like their counterparts at community colleges, women pursuing bachelor's degrees still cluster largely in traditional female majors when they choose their course of study. In 2006, women received 86 percent of the degrees in education, and 79 percent of the degrees in the health professions, which includes nursing, and 78 percent of the degrees in psychology.[45]

Yet there also are very positive signs, including the increase of women majoring in business and in the biological sciences. Women now receive 50 percent of all undergraduate business degrees. The biological sciences have captured the imagination of the public and the pocketbooks of drug companies and the government, creating many new jobs. Today, 62 percent of biological and biomedical science undergraduates degrees go to women—women now earn twice the number of degrees in these fields that they did 20 years ago.[46]

The door not open: Physical sciences and technologies

The discouraging news is that women are still a small presence among those receiving degrees in engineering, where a large percentage of high-paying jobs have been and are predicted to increase in the future. In 2006, women earned 18 percent of engineering degrees, only a minor improvement over the dismal 14 percent they earned in 1990.[47] Distressingly, among computer sciences graduates, women are a declining share, falling from 29 percent to 21 percent over the past 15 years.[48]

Yet these are the areas of technological innovation where a large percentage of high-paying jobs are predicted to increase in the future. Even in math and statistics, where women once represented close to half of the undergraduates, the past two decades have shown a decline in female participation.[49] There is no easy explanation for this trend, but it rings an alarm bell, which calls for investigation.

Women are still a small presence among those receiving degrees in engineering, where a large percentage of high-paying jobs have been and are predicted to increase in the future.

The only bright spot is a positive trend in the share of women in the physical sciences and science technologies, up from 32 percent to 42 percent over 15 years.[50] Again, there is no easy explanation, but there has been a concerted move by professional societies, in particular federal agencies to attract and retain women in this field. While too many women are taking themselves out of the high-tech pipeline at the undergraduate level, the women who graduate from college are more likely to begin graduate studies than they once were. Among computer science doctoral candidates, the percentage of women has increased in

STILL TEACHING, STILL EARNING LESS. Women continue to dominate primary and high school classrooms and are still dedicated to their profession even though society doesn't pay equitably for their efforts. (BRENDAN HOFFMAN, AP)

the past two decades, from 14 percent to 22 percent. Slightly larger changes can be seen among engineering doctoral students, where female participation has increased from 9 percent to 20 percent over the same period.[51]

Despite these gains, women remain far less likely than men to pursue the highest graduate degrees and ultimately careers in cutting edge scientific research—careers that bring status power and higher salaries. This lack of women scholars at the top of the science and technologies pyramid boasts enormous implications for future generations of women.

Missing at the top: Women as role models

The presence of a successful role model to inspire a career in any field is critical. In law and medicine there are a substantial number of women professionals working in the field, and a steady diet of popular media featuring women characters

BREAKING INTO THE LABORATORY. Women are now entering traditionally male-dominated fields such as chemistry in record numbers. {NINA BERMAN, REDUX}

litigating in the courtroom or curing patients of deadly diseases. But there are many fewer role models for women in engineering or the computer sciences.

Overall, women make up less than 30 percent of full professors at four-year educational institutions.[52] In engineering and the physical sciences the numbers are far smaller; in 2005, the American Institute of Physics found that only 10 percent of faculty members in physics were women.[53] There are many physics departments in this country where women faculty number in single digits or are not present at all.

There are some innovative success stories of programs to attract and retain women in the sciences. In 2009, the fourth annual Conference for the Undergraduate Women in Physics sponsored by NASA, the Department of Energy, and three participating research universities attracted more than 350 young female students from across the country. They came to network and to hear the dazzling

DAVID MCNEW

I don't know how many of you around the table are first-generation college graduates but that's my reality, and so I don't have those networks or the mom or dad who maybe are an attorney, right, who can pull in a special partner favor for us. We don't have the moms and dads who can get us those great internships every summer.

Delores in Los Angeles

research talks of distinguished female physicists from places such as NASA's Jet Propulsion Laboratory and the University of California Berkeley.[54] Many of these students were from small colleges where there were no women on the faculty. Preliminary results from the early years indicate that the conferences were influential in encouraging young women physicists to continue in graduate school.

Professorial gains—graduate and professional degrees

Gender parity in graduate and professional education is one of the most remarkable accomplishments of the last third of the 20th century. In 1966, only 10 percent of all American doctorates were awarded to women. By 2008 that number had soared to about 50 percent. The same story holds for the professions, particularly law and medicine, which began with an even lower proportion of women students.[55]

Minority students, particularly women, are also earning doctorates at a historic pace, though the numbers do not match their proportionate representation in the U.S. population. Today, minority students represent 24 percent of all graduate students, more than doubling their representation over the past 30 years. Female students of color have made the most significant gains.[56]

But once again, the distribution among the doctoral disciplines is not even. Women now receive half of the doctorates in the biological sciences but in the physical sciences, women are still struggling to enter a male bastion. In 2006, women received 30 percent of the doctorates awarded in the fields of physical science and math, and only 22 percent of computer science degrees and 20 percent of engineering degrees.[57]

Science and engineering: Still a man's world

The most troubling numbers show that while women earned 30 percent of the doctorates in the physical sciences in 2006, women still make up just 16.1 percent of the assistant professors on campuses, 14.2 percent of the associate professors and only 6.4 percent of the full professors. A 2009 survey by the National Research Council of the National Academy of Sciences found that women who receive Ph.D.s in the sciences, including the very popular biological sciences, are far less likely than men to seek academic research positions—the path to cutting-edge discovery—and are more likely to drop out early if they do take on a faculty post.[58]

Unfortunately, the National Research Council report says its survey could not shed light on why women drop out at these critical transitions, but other new research clearly makes the connection between women's concerns about the lack of family accommodation in scientific careers and the decision to leave. Data collected by the National Science Foundation, for example, show that family formation—most importantly marriage and childbirth—account for the largest leaks in the pipeline between receiving a Ph.D. and the acquisition of tenure for women in the sciences.[59] Women who are married with children in the sciences have 37 percent lower odds of entering a tenure track position after receipt of their Ph.D. than married men with children. And they are 27 percent less likely than their counterparts to achieve tenure upon entering a tenure-track job (see Figure 4).[60]

In contrast, single women without children are about as likely to attain a tenure track position as men. These findings illustrate that family formation, particularly marriage and childbirth together, is the most important reason why women with Ph.D.s in the sciences do not begin academic careers with tenure-track jobs. What is surprising is that while marriage and childbirth often derail the tenure plans of women, they actually have a positive effect on the tenure of men. Close to 80 percent of men who have a child within five years of receiving their Ph.D. receive tenure within 14 years, compared with about 70 percent of tenure-track faculty overall.[61]

The decision not to continue in a research science career often begins in graduate school. Family balance weighs heavily on the minds of students in considering their career choices. In a survey of 8,000 University of California graduate students in all fields, 84 percent of women and 74 percent

THE LATEST FROM THE AMERICAN PEOPLE

Q: Who in your household has the most responsibility for caring for your elderly parents?

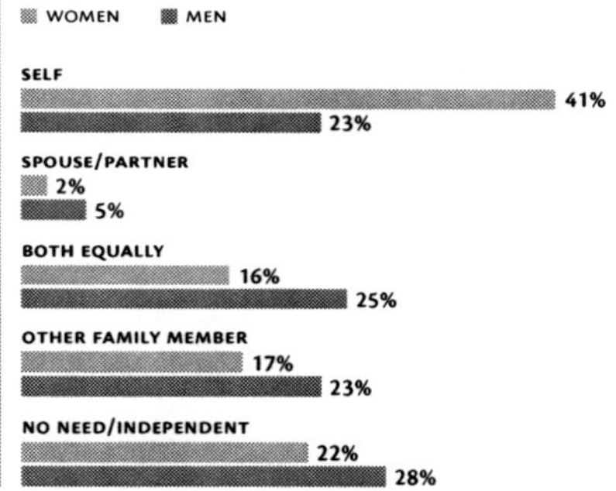

Source: Rockefeller/*Time* poll, 2009.

of men registered the family friendliness of their future workplace as a serious concern. But they do not see their own universities meeting that goal. More than 70 percent of women in the survey, and more than half of the men, did not consider research universities to be family friendly.[62]

The number of young women who want to pursue careers in academic science decreases by 34 percent over the course of their doctoral study, and the number of men decreases by 20 percent.[63] Most women offer family balance concerns as a major component of their decision-making process. Graduate student women in all disciplines indicate that having a female role model in their department is critical in how they perceive the university as a family-friendly workplace. In the sciences, there are generally few women faculty, and even fewer who have children. Role

FIGURE 4

Falling off the tenure track

In academia, women Ph.D.s struggle to gain tenured positions at colleges and universities

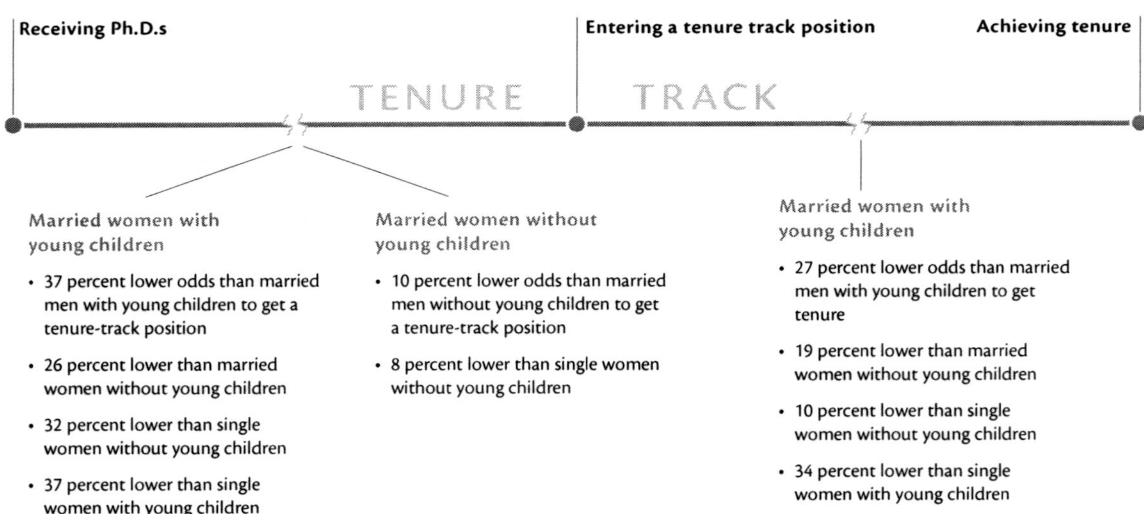

Results are based on Survival Analysis of the Survey of Doctorate Recipients (a national biennial longitudinal data set funded by the National Science Foundation and others, 1979 to 1999) in all sciences, including social sciences. The analysis takes into account disciplinary, age, ethnicity, Ph.D. calendar year, time-to-Ph.D. degree, and National Research Council academic reputation rankings of Ph.D. program effects. For each event (Ph.D. to TT job procurement, or TT job to Tenure), data are limited to maximum of 16 years.

Note: The use of NSF data does not imply the endorsement of research methods or conclusions.

models affect life decisions. In departments where women faculty with children are common, 46 percent of female respondents agreed that research universities were family friendly. Where they were uncommon, only 12 percent of women agreed.[64]

Women scientists who do have children in graduate school are very unlikely to continue. The competitive race to achieve scientific breakthroughs and prove oneself offers little respite for childbirth or child-rearing. The effect of parenthood on the choices of female doctoral students supported by federal grants (the source of support for most students in the sciences) is undeniable. Only a fraction of universities provide paid maternity leave or any other family accommodation for graduate students. They must often return to work in a very few weeks.[65]

Women scientists who do have children in graduate school are very unlikely to continue. The competitive race to achieve scientific breakthroughs and prove oneself offers little respite for childbirth or child-rearing.

The consequences are telling. Forty-six percent of female respondents began their graduate studies working toward a faculty position in a research university, but babies changed that, resulting in only 11 percent of new mothers saying they now want to continue on that path.[66] And once again, fatherhood for men similarly situated in graduate studies appears to have less impact. Fifty-nine percent began their doctoral programs planning to pursue a research-intensive academic career and 45 percent still plan to do so.[67]

Men and women scientists who wish to pursue a scientific research career are usually expected to spend from one to five years as a postdoctoral fellow to enhance their research skills and number of publications following the receipt of the Ph.D. before they take a professorial position. The women who have taken this step are usually already in their thirties and are serious about their research careers. This also is the optimal age for childbearing in the United States and many will have children during their post doctoral years.

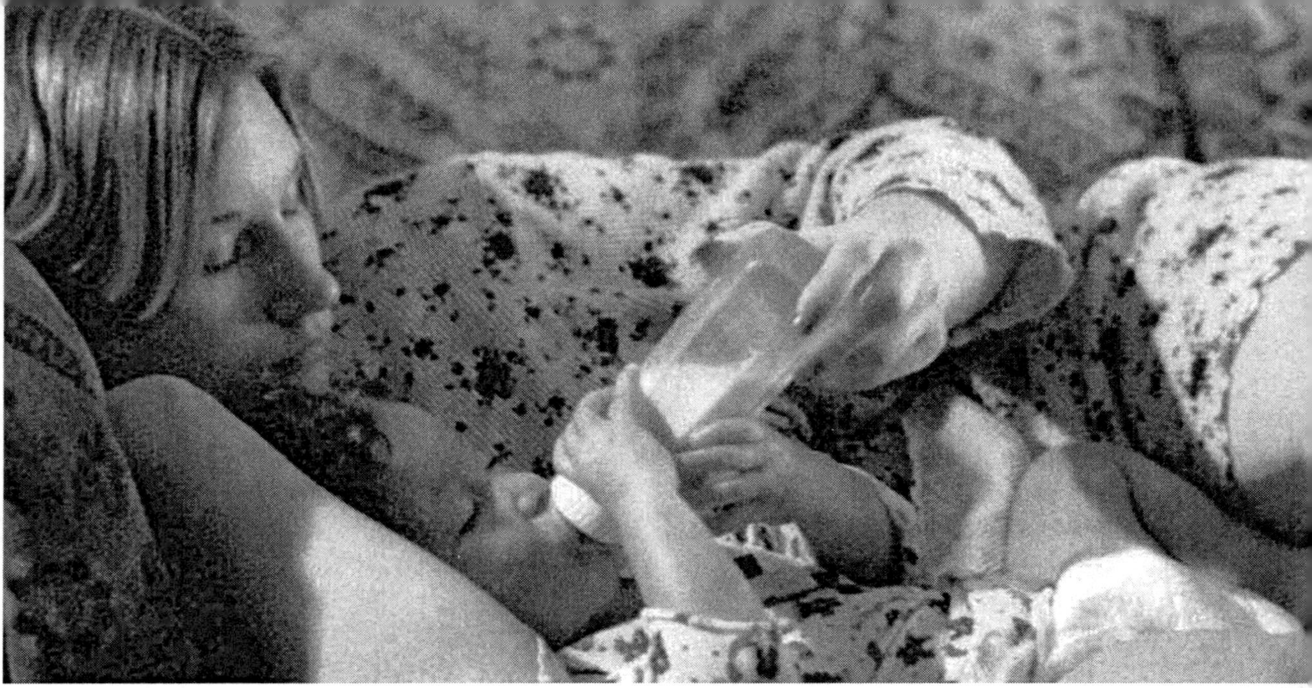

LEARNING AND CARING. Juggling children and the quest for a college degree is difficult but rewarding, as this young woman would tell you. {OLIVIA BARRIONUEVO}

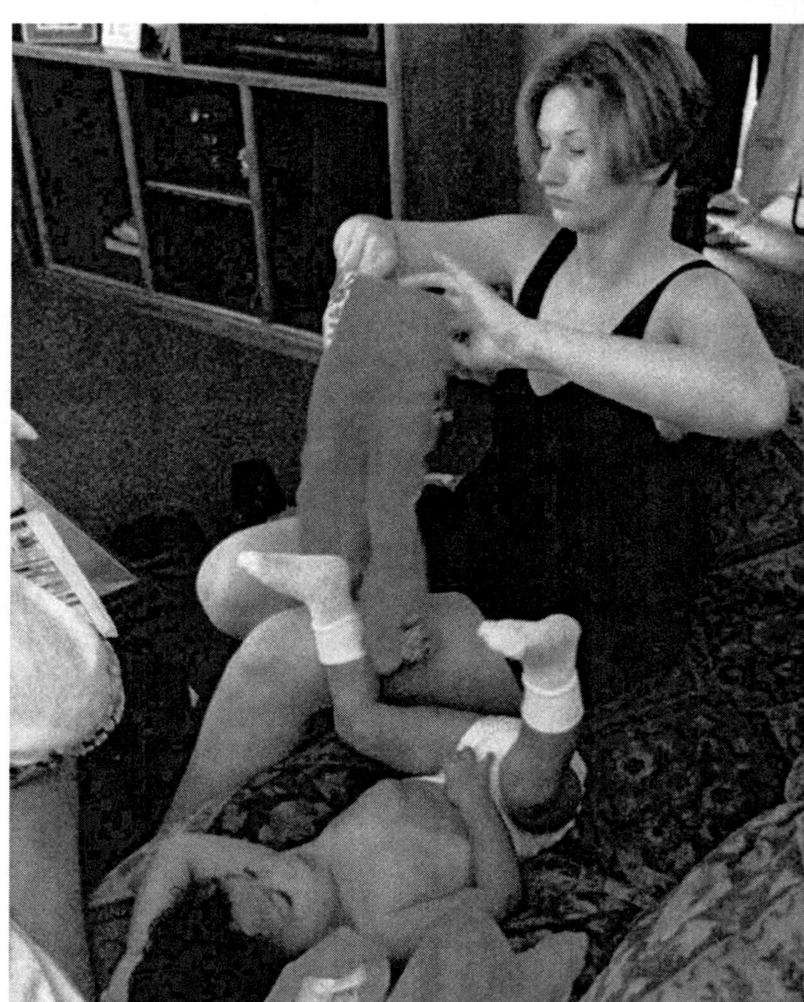

MUIR HIGH SCHOOL

But, as with graduate students, childbirth often derails the scientific ambition of postdoctoral students. Forty-one percent of women graduate student scientists who have babies in the University of California system while working in a post doctoral position decide not to pursue an academic research career.[68] This drastic shift by mothers away from a research science career following childbirth may be explained in part by the fact that only a handful of the major research universities offer any paid leave for graduate students and postdocs, and some have no leave policy at all.[69] Unfortunately, students and postdocs are also sometimes openly discouraged from having children by their mentors, who explain that, as mothers, they will not be considered "serious scientists."

Only a handful of the major research universities offer any paid leave for graduate students and postdocs, and some have no leave policy at all.

This story is not just true for women scientists. It appears to be true across the board for highly educated women who prepare for careers that were previously dominated by men. Law and medicine are the most populous and, one might argue, the most esteemed of the male-dominated professions. Women now attend law school and medical school in fairly equal numbers to men. They train for and enter these male enclaves of power and privilege in large numbers, but, like women scientists, most are not reaching leadership positions and lag behind men in salary.

All male-dominated fields show a similar pattern. Based on a male workplace model, they are most demanding of their new employees during the first years when they must prove that they have the "right stuff." These testing years usually involve focused commitment and grueling hours. Since these professions require a fairly long training period after colleges, women are usually in their thirties, their prime child-bearing years during these same trial years. Without support from their employer and the culture, they are far more likely than men to drop out or drop down to a less demanding level in the profession. For those who remain in the profession, their salaries are significantly lower: Female lawyers make 77 cents on the dollar of their male counterpoint, female doctors 59 cents.[70]

Where do we go from here?

While women have made tremendous progress in gaining access to all levels of education in the past 30 years, there remain several persistent problems that policymakers need to focus on in order to ensure that women have full access to all fields within education and to ensure that their education degrees will pay off:

- While women overall have dramatically increased their access to education, there are still some groups of women that lag far behind. Too few Hispanics, for example, are entering our four-year colleges. Hispanics represent only 7 percent of four-year college students compared to 16 percent of community college students.

- At all levels of postsecondary education, women are still highly concentrated in the low-paying "helping" professions of health and education and not encouraged to enter the high-paying fields of the future, including mathematics, engineering, and computer science.

- When women do receive degrees in fields that could lead to high-paying professions such as academia, law, or business, they face inflexible workplaces that do not allow them to combine work with family responsibilities, and thus too many of our highly educated women dropoff the career track for which they trained. When they do stay, they often earn less than their male counterparts because they are in less "prestigious" positions—they are primary care physicians instead of surgeons, biologists instead of physicists, and government attorneys instead of corporate law partners.

What can be done about these three persistent problems? Our government has already started to tackle the first two problems, which is heartening. Initiatives that work to address the high rate of high school dropouts and the lack of academic preparation for women who are underrepresented in education, particularly Hispanics, will go a long way. And our government has begun to focus real attention on increasing representation of women in all fields, particularly science, engineering, mathematics, and technology. Congress has been investigating the problem and holding hearings on potential solutions. President Obama and others have urged equitable enforcement of Title IX as a tool to level the playing field for women in the sciences, just as it has done successfully for sports.[71]

Title IX of the Education Amendments Act of 1972 prohibits discrimination based on sex in educational programs and activities that receive federal financial assistance.[72] Congress modeled Title IX based on Title VI of the Civil Rights Act of 1964, which prohibits discrimination on the basis of race, color, or national origin in programs or activities that receive federal funds.[73] The law conditions federal funding "on a promise by the recipient not to discriminate, in what is essentially a contract between the government and the recipient of funds."[74]

Title IX has been used with great success to attract and retain women in athletic pursuits. Forty years ago it was assumed that more men participated in sports because women were disinterested. With the passage of Title IX, the number of women in high school sports grew 904 percent as these women saw an opportunity to participate competitively at the college level and perhaps even at a pro level. Of course, not all high school athletes achieve success in college, but even still, the number of women participating in sports at the college level increased 456 percent over the same period.[75]

A Title IX strategy could be applied to the currently sex-segregated and sex-stereotyped patterns of education, beginning with high school education and continuing through community colleges all the way to advanced degrees. Title IX makes clear that gender stereotyping is prohibited, yet too few schools have the know-how or the resources to break down these historic patterns. And our government is only just beginning a serious effort to look at whether postsecondary education institutions are complying with Title IX when it comes to the science, technology, and math fields.[76]

But Title IX isn't the only answer. Women with family responsibilities need to be supported at all levels of education and once they enter the workforce. To support women scientists, federal agencies providing research grants, for example, could offer financial incentives to universities and colleges to include family accommodations, among them child care to attend conferences and paid family leave to encourage young graduate students in particular to continue their scientific careers. Similarly, more should be done to replicate the good work of community colleges and four-year colleges providing family-friendly support and child care as well as flexible class scheduling so that women (and their partners) can attain successive levels of education to boost their earnings in today's economy.

GETTING DOWN TO BUSINESS. Women now match men in the pursuit of business degrees.
{EDLABDESIGNER, FLICKR}

But the real answer may lay in the next chapter authored by Brad Harrington and Jamie Ladge on how businesses have and should respond to women's entry into the workplace. Without businesses to support women's rise to the top and support the everyday struggle of combining work and care, receiving a good education will never be enough.

ENDNOTES

1 National Center for Education Statistics, "Digest of Education Statistics 2007" (2007), Table 177.

2 Catherine Freeman, "Trends in Educational Equity of Girls and Women: 2004" (Washington: National Center for Education Statistics, 2004).

3 Michael Planty and others, "The Condition of Education 2008" (Washington: National Center for Education Statistics, 2008), Table 27-1.

4 Ibid.

5 Ibid.

6 Center for American Progress analysis of Center for Economic and Policy Research Extracts of the Current Population Survey Outgoing Rotation Group files (2008).

7 20 U.S.C. § 1681, et seq.

8 The White House, Office of the Press Secretary, "Valerie Jarrett and Education Secretary Arne Duncan Hold White House Roundtable on Title IX" (June 23, 2009), available at http://www.whitehouse.gov/the_press_office/Valerie-Jarrett-and-Education-Secretary-Arne-Duncan-Hold-White-House-Roundtable-on-Title-IX/. See also Association for Women and Science and Society of Women Engineers, "Campaign Responses to Questions from the Association of Women in Science and the Society of Women Engineers" (October 13, 2008), available at http://www.researchresearch.com/media/pdf/Obama-McCain3080.pdf.

9 Laura Horn and Thomas Weko, "On Track to Complete? A Taxonomy of Beginning Community College Students and Their Outcomes 3 Years After Enrolling: 2003–04 Through 2006," (Washington: National Center for Education Statistics, 2009).

10 Mary Lufkin, Mary Wiberg and others, "Gender Equity in Career and Technical Education." In Susan Klein, ed., Handbook for Achieving Gender Equity Through Education, Second Edition (Mahway, NJ: Lawrence Erlbaum, 2007).

11 National Center for Education Statistics, "Special Analysis 2008: Community Colleges" (Washington: 2008) p. 40.

12 Ibid.

13 Lutz Berkner, Shirley He, and Emily Forrest Cataldi, "Descriptive Summary of 1995–96 Beginning Postsecondary Students: Six Years Later" (Washington: National Center for Education Statistics, 2002).

14 Ibid at Table 2.1-C.

15 Linda M. Erickson, "Historical Dictionary of Women's Education in the United States" (New York: Greenwood Press, 1998), p. 342.

16 Miriam K. Chamberlain, "Women in Academe" (New York: Russell Sage Foundation, 1991), p. 366.

17 Marie Tessier, "Welfare + Education Leads to Jobs, Higher Pay," *Women's eNews*, September 17, 2009, available at http://www.womensenews.org/article.cfm/dyn/aid/592.

18 Ibid.

19 Mary Gatta and Kevin McCabe, "The Poor Need Training that Works for Them," *The Star-Ledger*, January 24, 2006, available at http://www.itwd.rutgers.edu/news/poor_need_training.htm.

20 Nolita Clark, Shannon Stanfield, and Vivyan Adair, "Remarkable Journeys: Poor, Single Mothers Accessing Higher Education," On Campus With Women 33 (3–4) (Spring/Summer 2004), available at http://www.aacu.org/ocww/volume33_3/fromwhereisit.cfm?section=1.

21 Vivyan Adair, "The ACCESS Project at Hamilton College 2003 Year End Report" (Clinton, NY: Hamilton College, 2003).

22 Ibid.

23 National Center for Education Statistics, "Career/Technical Education Statistics" (2003–2004), Table P51.

24 U.S. Department of Labor, Women's Bureau, "Facts on Working Women: Women in High-Tech Jobs," (2002), available at http://www.dol.gov/wb/factsheets/hitech02.htm.

25 Bureau of Labor Statistics, "Career Guide to Industries, Health Care, 2008–09 Edition" (2008), available at http://www.bls.gov/oco/cg/cgs035.htm.

26 Anthony P. Carnevale and Donna M. Desrochers, "Help Wanted...Credentials Required: Community Colleges in the Knowledge Economy" (Annapolis, MD: Community College Press, 2001), p. 57.

27 Louis Soares and Christopher Mazzeo, "College Ready Students, Student Ready Colleges" (Washington: Center for American Progress, 2008).

28 National Center for Education Statistics, "Special Analysis 2008: Community Colleges" (2008).

29 Christianne Corbett, Catherine Hill, and Andresse St. Rose, "Where the Girls Are: The Facts about Gender Equity in Education" (Washington: American Association of University Women Educational Foundation, 2008), p. 62.

30 Ibid., p. 60.

31 William T. Grant Foundation Commission on Work, Family and Citizenship, "The Forgotten Half: Non-College-Bound Youth in America" (1988); William T. Grant Foundation Commission on Work, Family and Citizenship, "The Forgotten Half: Pathway to Success for America's Youth and Young Families" (1988).

32 Samuel Halperin, "The Forgotten Half Revisited: American Youth and Families, 1988–2008" (Washington: American Youth Policy Forum, 1998).

33 Ibid.

34 Ibid.

35 Bureau of Labor Statistics, "Highlights of Women's Earnings in 2007" (Department of Labor, 2008) p. 5, chart 3.

36 Bureau of the Census, "Income, Earnings and Poverty Data from the 2007 American Communities Survey" (Department of Commerce, 2008), p. 15, table 7.

37 David Neumark and Donna Rothstein, "Do School-to-Work Programs Help the 'Forgotten Half'?" Working Paper 11636 (National Bureau of Economic Research, 2005).

38 Davis Jenkins, "Career Pathways: Aligning Public Resources to Support Individual and Regional Economic Advancement in the Knowledge Economy" (New York: Workforce Strategy Center, 2006), available at http://www.workforcestrategy.org/publications/WSC_pathways8.17.06.pdf.

39 James W. Ainsworth and Vincent J. Roscigno, "Stratification, School-Work Linkages and Vocational Education," Social Forces, 84 (1) (2005): 257–284.

40 James Kemple and Cynthia J. Willner, "Career Academies: Long-Term Impacts on Labor Market Outcomes, Educational Attainment, and Transitions to Adulthood" (New York: MDCR, 2008).

41 For example, for "low service students" where all ethnic/gender parings except Asian males are sufficiently represented, the persistent unemployment rate among the women students was 20.3 percent for white women, 45.8 percent for black women, 27.7 percent for Hispanic women, and 47.3 percent for Asian women. See Ainsworth and Roscigno, "Stratification, School-Work Linkages and Vocational Education."

42 Ainsworth and Roscigno, "Stratification, School-Work Linkages and Vocational Education."

43 National Women's Law Center, "Title IX and Equal Opportunity in Vocational and Technical Education: A Promise Still Owed to the Nation's Young Women" (2002).

44 Corbett, Hill and St. Rose, "Where the Girls Are," p.62.

45 Michael Planty and others, "The Condition of Education 2008," (Washington: National Center for Education Statistics, 2008), Table 27-1.

46 Ibid.

47 Ibid.

48 Ibid.

49 Ibid.

50 Ibid.

51 Ibid.

52 Martha West, John Curtis, "AAUP Faculty Gender Equity Indicators 2006," (Washington: American Association of University Professors, 2006), p. 10.

53 American Institute of Physics, "New Report on Women in Physics and Astronomy" (2005), available at http://www.aip.org/fyi/2005/035.html.

54 American Institute of Physics, "New Report on Women in Physics and Astronomy" (2005), available at http://www.aip.org/statistics/trends/reports/women05.pdf.

55 National Center for Education Statistics, "Integrated Postsecondary Education Data System, Completions Survey" (2008); Freeman, "Trends in Educational Equity of Girls and Women: 2004."

56 National Center for Education Statistics, "Table A-11-2: Graduate and Professional Education," available at http://nces.ed.gov/programs/coe/2009/section1/table-gre-2.asp (last accessed September 2009).

57 Michael Planty and others, "The Condition of Education 2008," (Washington: National Center for Education Statistics, 2008), Table 27-1.

58 The National Academies, "Gender Differences at Critical Transitions in the Careers of Science, Engineering, and Mathematics Faculty" (2009), p. 24.

59 Mary Ann Mason and Marc Goulden, "Do Babies Matter: The Effect of Family Formation on the Lifelong Careers of Academic Men and Women," Academe 88 (6) (November–December 2002).

60 Marc Goulden, Karie Frasch, and Mary Ann Mason, "Staying Competitive: Patching America's Leaky Pipeline in the Sciences" (University of California Berkeley Center on Health, Economic, and Family Security, forthcoming), p. 5.

61 Mary Ann Mason and Marc Goulden, "Do Babies Matter?"

62 Mary Ann Mason, Marc Goulden, and Karie Frasch, "Why Graduate Students Reject the Fast-Track," *Academe* 95 (1) (January–February 2009), available at http://ucfamilyedge.berkeley.edu/Why%20Graduate%20Students%20Reject%20the%20Fast%20Track.pdf/.

63 Results from Mary Ann Mason, Marc Goulden, and Karie Frasch, "UC Postdoctoral Career Life Survey" (2008), available at http://ucfamilyedge.berkeley.edu/grad%20life%20survey.html.

64 Mason, Goulden, and Frasch, "Why Graduate Students Reject the Fast-Track."

65 Goulden, Frasch and Mason, "Staying Competitive," p. 7.

66 Goulden, Frasch and Mason, "Staying Competitive," p. 25.

67 Goulden, Frasch and Mason, "Staying Competitive," p. 25.

68 Mary Ann Mason, "Do Babies Matter in Science?" (2008), p. 20, available at http://sdbonline.org/Re-BootCamp09/Mason_ReBootSDB09.pdf.

69 Mason, "Do Babies Matter in Science?" p. 23, figure 11.

70 U.S. Bureau of Labor Statistics, "Highlights of Women's Earnings in 2007" (October 2008), table 2, available at http://www.bls.gov/cps/cpswom2007.pdf.

71 The White House, Office of the Press Secretary, "Valerie Jarrett and Education Secretary Arne Duncan Hold White House Roundtable on Title IX" (June 23, 2009), available at http://www.whitehouse.gov/the_press_office/Valerie-Jarrett-and-Education-Secretary-Arne-Duncan-Hold-White-House-Roundtable-on-Title-IX/. See also Association for Women and Science and Society of Women Engineers, "Campaign Responses to Questions from the Association of Women in Science and the Society of Women Engineers" (October 13, 2008), available at http://www.researchresearch.com/media/pdf/Obama-McCain3080.pdf.

72 Title IX of the Education Amendments of 1972, 20 U.S.C. §§ 1681-88 (2006).

73 "Title IX Legal Manual," available at http://www.usdoj.gov/crt/cor/coord/ixlegal.php#I.%20Overview%20of%20Title%20IX:%20Interplay%20with%20Title%20VI,%20Section%20504,%20Title%20VII,%20and%20the%20Fourteenth%20Amendment (last accessed March 20, 2009).

74 Ibid.

75 Women's Sports Foundation. "2008 Statistics- Gender Equity in High School and College Athletics: Most Recent Participation & Budget Statistics," available at http://www.womenssportsfoundation.org/Content/Articles/Issues/General/123/2008-Statistics--Gender%20Equity-in-High-School-and-College-Athletics-Most-Recent-Participation--Budge.aspx (last accessed August 2009).

76 United States Government Accountability Office, "Gender Issues: Women's Participation in the Sciences has Increased, but Agencies Need to do More to Ensure Compliance with Title IX" (July 2004).

Must Jill Come Tumbling After?

By Delaine Eastin, California superintendent of public instruction, 1995-2003

When we observe the Taliban burning down girls' schools, we intuitively sense what's at work. Cultures that stubbornly refuse to harness half their brainpower also happen to be the poorest places on earth. The two are directly connected. Now go to Los Angeles or New York. Early marriage, early motherhood, single motherhood, divorce—these don't burn down girls' schools, they burn down girls' dreams. The net effect on our society is tragically similar to what has been wrought in a third-world country.

Today the education of our children, particularly our girls, is not positioning our nation to lead the world in terms of our democracy or our economy. In science and mathematics education today, some nations do a better job for girls than does the United States. Within a few years, Indian and Chinese children may well be better positioned as scientists, mathematicians, and engineers than our children.

Despite some progress, we know there is less access to math and science for girls. And while more young women are getting college degrees in some of the sciences, they remain flat in engineering, computer science, and mathematics. Why? "Study after study has shown that adults, both teachers and parents, underestimate the intelligence of girls," observe education scholars Myra and David Sadker in their 1994 book *Failing at Fairness*.[1] "Teachers' beliefs that boys are smarter in mathematics and science begin in the earliest school years, at the very time when girls are getting better grades and equal scores on standardized tests."

Nor has this situation improved markedly since then. The American Association of University Women provides some important data in its series of studies on gender equity in schools in the 1990s. It points out girls make up a small percentage of students in computer science classes and that the gender gap widens between 8th and 11th grade. To the extent that girls enter computer courses, they are more likely to take clerical courses, and less likely to enroll in advanced science and graphics courses. And to the extent that vocational and technical educational training exists in high schools, there is an institutionalization of sexist cultural norms that tends to stereotype by gender.[2]

Forty years ago it was assumed that more men participated in sports because women were uninterested. With the passage of Title IX of the Education Act of 1972, the number of women in high school sports grew 904 percent.[3] It turns out the girls were interested, as Barbara Richardson and Pamela Sandoval note in their 2007 study "Impact of Education on Gender Equity in Employment."[4] What other things are we that sure of that just aren't so?

Education is the best path to liberty and justice for all.

Today's children must be educated to the reality that virtually all of them will work 30 to 40 years outside the home—and there will be scant opportunities to go back later and try it again unless they have a good education foundation, argue Richardson and Sandoval. They're right, of course. Every child must know it's now or never. Education is the best path to liberty and justice for all. Jack and Jill must ascend the path on the same footing or America will stumble.

ENDNOTES

1 Myra Sadker and David Sadker, *Failing at Fairness: How Our Schools Cheat Girls* (New York: Touchstone, 1994).

2 American Association of University Women, "Tech Savvy: Educating Girls in the New Computer Age" (2000), available at http://www.aauw.org/research/upload/techsavvy.pdf.

3 Women's Sports Foundation, "2008 Statistics – Gender Equity in High School and College Athletics: Most Recent Participation and Budget Statistics" (2008), available at http://www.womenssportsfoundation.org/Content/Articles/Issues/General/123/2008-Statistics--Gender%20Equity-in-High-School-and-College-Athletics-Most-Recent-Participation--Budge.aspx.

4 Barbara Richardson and Pamela Sandoval, "Impact of Education on Gender Equity in Employment." In Susan Klein, ed., *Handbook for Achieving Gender Equity Through Education*, Second Edition (Mahwah, NJ: Lawrence Erlbaum, 2007).

Don't Make This Bridge Our Back

By Malika Sada Saar, founder and executive director of the Rebecca Project for Human Rights

For those of us who come from low- and medium-income communities of color, women working as the only or primary breadwinner in the family is not a new phenomenon. In many of our families, there is rarely an economic choice between staying home and raising our children. Indeed, for decades, black, Latina and Asian women have been leaving their own families to cook, clean, and do the child-rearing in the homes of other families.

This role as primary breadwinner is not necessarily a place of power. I am reminded of the image evoked by Cherrie Moraga in the title of her groundbreaking collection of essays "This Bridge Called My Back," which told the tale of mothers of color journeying into the job market to bridge the worlds of their families with the majority culture's need for low-wage workers. So often that bridging between home—the barrio, the hood, and other places in America where the poor reside—and the workplace in order to feed one's family has been a brutal burden.

Sometimes that burden includes violence, derision, and marginalization. There is the undeniable physical and sexual victimization women of color suffer by men to remind them of their place—men who are either their spouses or their employers, or perhaps their ex-husbands or boyfriends. Or sometimes the imperative of work denies mothers of color full engagement with their children. They are absent in the evenings, unable to make PTA meetings, too busy to go over homework assignments, and too tired to simply enjoy their children's laughter.

Many mothers who are primary or sole breadwinners for their families, especially African Americans, also are derided for emasculating their men, and hence held responsible for the overall pathologies of black America. Rarely are low-income, African American mothers honored for the endless sacrifices they make for their families' health and economic well-being.

The question, then, at this transformative moment in American history, when most women—regardless of race, class, or ethnicity—are poised to become the primary breadwinners in their families, is how we ensure our economic ascent as a place of power, not injury, for all of us? On a policy level, it means passing legislation on health care reform, affordable child care, and comprehensive Early Start and Head Start programs. And it means paid maternity and paternity leave, expanded access to higher education for low-income women, and flexible work hours for low-wage workers.

Claiming our place of power requires that we demand public policies that protect and support all mothers in our capacity as primary breadwinners.

But we cannot surrender the process of transforming the lives of women and families to government alone. There are the organic networks that ought to be nurtured. It is about the emergence of co-madre—"the mothering with," or "co-mothering"—that we as women across race and income must commit ourselves to. The creation of co-madre communities can be places where mothers help each other out and raise up the sacredness of our mothering.

Claiming our place of power requires that we demand public policies that protect and support all mothers in our capacity as primary breadwinners, and that we turn to each other as women, across the divides of race, ethnicity, and income, to be co-madres. If we can do that, then we will truly transform the United States into a woman's nation—a pro-family nation.

NICOLE BENGIVENO, *THE NEW YORK TIMES*

BUSINESS

Got Talent? It Isn't Hard to Find

Recognizing and rewarding the value women create in the workplace

By Brad Harrington and Jamie J. Ladge

"The company that finds the right formula to get the most out of the talent base? That's the company that's going to win. That's the company that will be distinctive. And nowhere is that more true than with women," argues Samuel DiPiazza, Global CEO of accounting giant PricewaterhouseCoopers. "And in PwC, where we have so many talented women in our team, how do we get more of them into leadership of the organization? To me, that's the critical question."[1]

DiPiazza has put his insights into action: His firm is ranked one of the top five global companies to work for by DiversityInc, a leading publishing, research, and consulting firm on diversity and business. But his words and deeds aren't simply about "doing the right thing" by promoting diversity, they are also smart business. By sheer numbers, women are now on half of U.S. payrolls and they are granted more degrees than men. Women represent the fastest-growing segment of small-business owners, are responsible for making 80 percent of consumer buying decisions, and are inevitably becoming the driving force fueling economic growth.[2] These numbers indicate that change for businesses large and small is inevitable, ready or not.

Indeed, there is now such a strong business case for hiring, retaining, and promoting women that increasingly companies of all sizes are beginning to rethink their structures, hiring practices, and human resources strategies to respond to the workplace needs and expectations of women. These new efforts to bring women more fully into the American workforce at all levels benefit women and men alike. New research demonstrates that companies that consistently promote women to positions of power and leadership over time and across their operations have greater financial success across a variety of measures.

Yet most companies haven't done enough to incorporate women into their business models. Nor have they made great strides in addressing the work-life conflicts that most workers, but especially women, face. The vast majority of companies in the United States still seem to be reluctant to embrace practices that will most effectively manage, promote, and retain women.[3] Yet, for all workers, conflict between what their families need and what their employers need can make it difficult to be both good workers and good family members. Since the bulk of care responsibilities continue to fall on women (although this has been slowly changing), women bear the brunt of the costs of not addressing these issues.

New research demonstrates that companies that consistently promote women to positions of power and leadership over time and across their operations have greater financial success across a variety of measures.

Women across the income spectrum are struggling to cope with work-family conflict because of these important gains in women's participation in the workforce. For hourly workers, work-life conflict can have particularly dire consequences. Many hourly workers have very little control over their schedules and can be fired for being late or missing a day's work due to a schedule conflict. For middle- and higher-income workers these same conflicts may be the reason that women don't reach the upper echelons of their organizations as fast as men, and also the reason that some leave the workforce altogether.[4]

We contend in this chapter that those employers who have made the adjustments swiftly are reaping the benefits while those who have not are continuing to embrace management practices that are out of step with the needs and desires of today's workforce. The problem for most companies is that deeply entrenched corporate cultures often value people's time over their efforts, which impedes the retention and promotion of women and others who demand greater flexibility over their schedules.

The reality for all U.S. businesses, though, is clear: This change is unavoidable and organizations will need to change with it in order to thrive. The movement of women into the labor force has fundamentally altered the environment in which businesses function.

The conversation is no longer about whether women will work, but rather how businesses are dealing with both women workers and most workers sharing in at least some home-and-family care responsibilities.

This chapter juxtaposes the gains women have made with the barriers and challenges they continue to face. We then identify the changes in the way businesses operate that will allow women in the labor force to be successful. We conclude with a set of recommendations for both organizations and society as a whole to address the concerns and opportunities for women in business.

Where are the women?

What are women doing today? In spite of the much-heralded progress women have made in building careers, there is still a long way to go before women reach parity, especially in senior-level management positions. While it is encouraging to note that 38 percent of working women are employed in managerial, professional, and related occupations, a great many women in the United States remain employed in what might be seen as traditionally female occupations, such as secretarial, nursing, or teaching.

In terms of specific professions, women have obviously made progress across a broad spectrum of careers. For instance, more than half of accounting graduates are women and women make up about 54 percent of all accountants in the United States. Women of color represent nearly 30 percent of all female accountants.[5] Women also represent 45 percent of all associates in law firms and are generally equally represented in industries such as banking and insurance.

THE CORNER OFFICE. Many women lawyers have risen in the ranks of law firms but few occupy the coveted corner office. (MARC ASNIN, REDUX)

The professional area where women continue to have low representation is in engineering and science. In engineering for example, women earn only about 20 percent of the degrees awarded in the United States, with the highest percentages of those being in chemical and industrial engineering (earning 30 percent or more.) The lowest percentages are in some of the largest disciplines such as mechanical and electrical engineering, in which women are representated at or below 18 percent, according to the National Science Foundation.[6]

In 2008, 68 million women were employed in the United States. Seventy-five percent worked full time. Twenty-five percent worked part time (35 hours or less). Women are more likely than men to work part time and not surprisingly, those with young children are the most likely to seek reduced work hours. The result for women is a still-pervasive wage gap, as Heather Boushey amply demonstrates in her chapter of this report.

Advancing toward the C-Suite

Despite the progress women have made, as of July 2009, only 15 companies on the Fortune 500 list were run by female chief executives, and 14 of the next 501 to 1,000 companies, according to Catalyst, the leading women's nonprofit research organization.[7] That's less than 3 percent. Further, only 15.7 percent of corporate officer positions in Fortune 500 companies were held by women—and this number has not increased at all since 2002.[8] These low numbers and the lack of progress in recent years suggest that it is not simply a time lag that results in the low number of women in senior management. It is also the effects of the so-called "leaky pipeline," as women drop out of organizations' talent management systems before they reach senior management positions.

Despite low representation of women in senior-level roles, the proposition that corporate bottom lines are improved if women are full participants at every level in companies is now bolstered by a number of studies. Several recent studies conducted both in the United States and abroad show that when women are at the helm of major corporations, those companies enjoy greater financial success. Among them:

- A 2001 Pepperdine University study led by the late marketing professor Roy Adler found that the 25 best corporations for women within the Fortune 500 list of companies (those that aggressively promoted women) had 34 percent higher profits compared to industry medians.[9]

- A 2007 study conducted by Catalyst found that Fortune 500 companies with more female board members were more profitable than those with fewer or no women when using financial measures such as return on equity, return on sales, and return on invested capital. The top 25 percent of companies in terms of number of women on their boards of directors yielded a 13.9 percent return on equity compared to a 9.1 percent yield for companies in the bottom 25 percent in terms of number of women on their boards.[10]

These are just a few examples of a range of recent studies that focus on the relationship between female executive leadership and corporate financial performance. While we would not suggest that these studies provide indisputable evidence that women are better leaders than men, they do suggest that the ways women lead can yield positive organizational outcomes.

In their recent report "'Girl Power': Female Participation in Top Management and Firm Performance," University of Maryland business professor Cristian Dezso and Columbia Business School professor David Gaddis Ross examined more than 1,500 U.S. companies from 1992 to 2006 and found strong indications that when women exert influence in positions of leadership and power, they get more beneficial results. This is due in part to their participatory and democratic style of leading, which tends to foster both creativity and teamwork.[11] The benefits of having women in these positions is now evident in the movement of more and more women into positions of leadership and influence outside the C-suite.

THE LATEST FROM THE AMERICAN PEOPLE

Q: Do you agree or disagree: There would be fewer problems in the world if women had a more equal position in government and business?

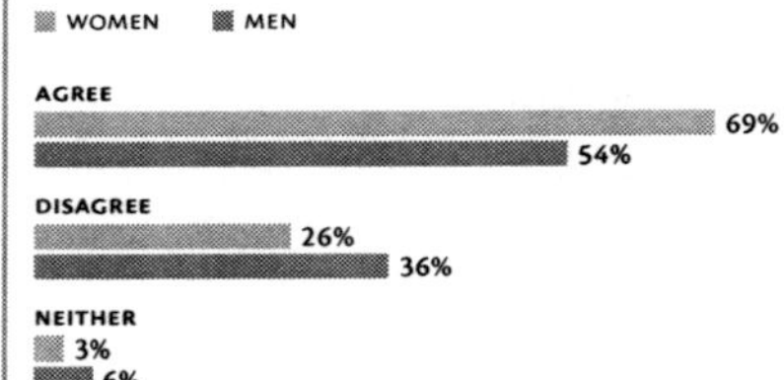

Source: Rockefeller/*Time* poll, 2009.

Hopping off the ladder

For the vast majority of women (and men for that matter), reaching a C-suite level position is not very likely (or perhaps even desirable). The statistics on educated women entering the workforce and the early but encouraging research we have outlined suggesting that women are highly effective in senior-level positions would lead one to ask:

- Why aren't women more equally represented at senior levels of the business organizations?
- Why is the number of women at the top still so small?
- Why are there so many leaks in the pipeline of women into leadership in corporate America?

Later, we will discuss the underlying reasons that are thwarting women's advancement, but first we consider the alternative career paths of the professional women who are not pursuing the C-suite, and examine how business supports (or fails to support, as the case may be) the vast majority of women who are working in occupations with little prospect of career advancement.

Among the many reasons women hop off the career ladder is work-life conflict. Two options that many women pursue to address these conflicts are: "opting out" (or downshifting) and pursuing entrepreneurial careers.

Off the career track

The term "opting out" was coined by Lisa Belkin in a 2003 *New York Times Magazine* article.[12] While the piece was controversial and empirical research contradicted the hypothesis that this is a widespread phenomenon, Belkin did rightly point out that many highly educated women leave their employers prematurely due to the barriers they encounter in the workplace and the challenge of integrating work and family.[13]

But opting out is not simply a response to inflexible schedules and problems rectifying work-family conflict. In their 2006 book *The Opt-Out Revolt*, Lisa Mainiero and Sherry Sullivan point out that women are more likely to leave the workforce because their jobs are not satisfying or lack meaning. Many women, especially those at midlife, opt out because they do not feel valued.[14]

A second option for women is to take on a reduced work schedule, working part time or job sharing. This approach, like opting out, is viable only for those families that can afford to live on less earnings. Women are far more likely than men to pursue reduced-hours arrangements in order to accommodate their caregiving demands. Unfortunately, employers appear to have an almost inexplicably high level of resistance to establishing part-time professional positions.

Many highly skilled women seek professional part-time roles where they can contribute in meaningful ways, only to find that such roles pay poorly, are marginalized, and often do not include benefits (not even on a pro-rated basis). The result is a serious talent drain that would be very easily remedied by employers simply letting go of an outdated belief that professionals and managers work full time.

Overall, a quarter of women workers are employed part time (fewer than 35 hours per week), and most are employed in a relatively small number of occupations, with cashiers (6.3 percent), waitresses (5.1 percent), and retail sales (5.1 percent)

being the most common. As stated earlier, much of the overall gender wage gap is due to women's propensity to work part-time schedules or take time out of the workforce to care for their children.[15] Unfortunately, for many employees, part-time work often carries with it a stigma, a serious lack of "good" opportunities, and a wage-and-benefits penalty that limits career growth.

The entrepreneurial call

Another option that is an increasingly attractive alternative for many women has been to start their own companies. Data from 2008-09 indicate that women are running more than 10 million businesses with combined sales of $1.1 trillion.[16] Women are starting these new companies mostly in industries where they have traditionally been well-represented as employees and line managers but not so often as owners and leaders.

Researchers at the Small Business Administration in 2008 took a deep dive into the data behind all this female entrepreneurial activity. They discovered that between 1997 and 2006, the number of women-owned businesses grew in number by 69 percent in service industries, 82.7 percent in professional services, 116.8 percent in arts and recreation services, 130 percent in retailing, 116.8 percent in real estate and 130 percent in the health care sector.[17]

The challenge, however, is that many women-owned businesses make very little money: Forty-six percent of women-owned companies earn $10,000 or less and about 80 percent have annual revenues of less than $50,000.[18] Despite the growing number of women entrepreneurs, only 3 percent of women-owned businesses have revenues of $1 million or more compared with 6 percent of men-owned businesses.[19]

Pink-collar workers

The vast majority of women are not working in jobs that could take them high up the career ladder in a traditional, private-sector business. Most women are working as secretaries and administrative

STARTING A NEW COMPANY. Many women are starting their own companies in industries they have traditionally dominated, such as child care. (NAJLAH FEANNY, CORBIS SABA)

assistants in these businesses, as registered nurses in our hospitals, as teachers in our public schools, and as retail salespeople or cashiers. Table 1 shows the 10 most prevalent occupations for employed women in the United States.

The story of how businesses support these women is quite different from the stories about professional women. One of the most common characteristics of many

TABLE 1

Top 10 occupations for women

Women still work mostly in traditionally female jobs

Occupation	Millions of women	Share of women workers
Secretaries and administrative assistants	3.0	4.7
Registered nurses	2.5	3.8
Elementary and middle school teachers	2.4	3.7
Cashiers	1.9	3.0
Retail salespersons	1.6	2.5
Nursing, psychiatric, and home health aides	1.6	2.5
First-line supervisors/managers of retail	1.4	2.3
Waitresses	1.3	2.1
Bookkeeping, accounting, and auditing clerks	1.3	1.9
Receptionists and information clerks	1.2	1.9

Source: Center for American Progress analysis of the Center for Economic and Policy Research Extracts of the Current Population Survey Outgoing Rotation Group Files. Includes workers aged 18 to 64.

Note: Number of women differs slightly from published BLS data due to rounding errors.

of the jobs listed in Table 1 is that they are in the service sector and that many are hourly, not salaried. They may be subject to regular (or unexpected) shift changes, too many or too few hours, and wages that are low relative to comparably skilled male-dominated occupations. They struggle with work-family conflicts just as professional workers do, but they earn much less, cannot afford to pay for high-quality child care or elder care, and often have far less control over their workdays. Since nonprofessional women make up the majority of women in the workplace, employers need to include them in their thinking about how to retain female talent overall.

The barriers women face in corporate America

While women have come a long way in corporate America, progress, as we point out—especially at the highest echelons—is still slow. What are the major barriers that help explain these numbers and why do women continue to trail their male counterparts?

The most common barriers women face as they navigate organizational life in corporate America are hardly new. They include the persistence of traditional gender-based caregiving roles, exclusion from informal corporate networks, and gender differences embedded in male-dominated organizational cultures—all of which can lead to "organizational invisibility" for women and for women's issues. We will explore each of these barriers in more detail to set the stage for what can and is being done in some leading organizations to create an environment that fosters the engagement and development of key talent—and most especially women.

The (perceived) problem with moms

When it comes to challenges women continue to face, nothing compares to the issue of balancing (or integrating) their caregiving responsibilities with their work. In spite of the dramatic increase in the amount of time women spend in paid employment, the time mothers spend with children has declined very little over the past 30 years. This dual work-family role was termed the "second shift" by Arlie Hochschild in 1989 to describe women overloaded from working two full-time shifts—at work and then at home.[20]

When it comes to challenges women continue to face, nothing compares to the issue of balancing their caregiving responsibilities with their work.

The second-shift problem is still alive and well for most women today. Many studies have shown that men have increased their commitment to domestic tasks and child-rearing. In fact, according to Suzanne Bianchi, one of the country's leading work-family scholars, men have more than doubled the time engaged in domestic tasks and child-rearing over the past 40 years (from seven hours a week in 1965 to 16.3 hours a week in 2005).[21] But this represents only about half the time women with children dedicate to these roles—31.8 hours a week in 2005.

Single and childless women seem to enjoy steady gains in organizational advancement, but their progress very often slows when they become mothers. The so-called "maternal wall," a term coined by Deborah Swiss and Judith Walker in their 1993 book *Women and the Work/Family Dilemma*, describes the frustration of many women in the upper echelons of corporations who found their workplaces less receptive to them when they became mothers.[22] These women felt they were more

A lot of companies right now are so focused on cost cutting that they are really forgetting about benefits, whether it's flexibility benefits, good internal communications—you know, the whole notion of mentoring employees and motivating them and reaching out to people. This is all stuff that five years ago I thought was finally beginning to happen in American business.

Esther in Silicon Valley

MARK J. SEBASTIAN, FLICKR

likely to be turned down for promotions, receive negative performance appraisals, be passed up for important assignments, and be viewed as less committed to their employers as a result of becoming mothers.

Hitting the "maternal wall" often results in wage gaps and career discrimination. While childless women working in corporations earn nearly the same pay as their male counterparts, mothers earn 15 percent less on average than men and single mothers earn 40 percent less.[23] The gender gap has narrowed over the last 30 years, but it clearly remains substantial. What is particularly problematic is that most mothers across all wage levels rely on their incomes to support their families. The reason: Flat wage growth for most Americans over the past two decades, in tandem with most layoffs—especially in this Great Recession—occurring in traditionally male-dominated industries, have left women as key and sometimes the sole breadwinners.

While childless women working in corporations earn nearly the same pay as their male counterparts, mothers earn 15 percent less on average than men and single mothers earn 40 percent less.

It is critical to point out that these dual responsibilities do not apply only to parenting. In the 2002 National Study of the Changing Workforce, 35 percent of female and male employees said they had significant elder care responsibilities—a trend that continues to persist as Americans live longer and require greater care. Elder care is an enormous looming problem that will profoundly impact the U.S. labor force and businesses in coming years.

Unlike child care, where physical care gets easier over a relatively predictable time frame, elder care has a far less predictable time frame and increases in difficulty as the health of the person being cared for worsens. Caring for a child can also be uplifting and can offer many psychological benefits; caring for elders is often psychologically debilitating. And elder care costs are significantly higher than child care, involving private care and nursing homes for families who can afford it and lengthy time off or careers deferred or upended for those who cannot.

While men's roles in elder care tend to be more equal with women's than in child care, these caregiving roles occur at significant times in women's careers.

No "old girl" networks

The second major problem faced by working women pertains to all women, not just those with significant dependent care issues. The famed "old boy" network doesn't really exist for women in most companies. Such networks are critical to forging relationships with mentors, sponsors, and other important social connections that facilitate work effectiveness and career development. Informal networking also fosters collaboration and social support and enhances relationships.[24] Yet many women, and African American women in particular, have difficulty networking with individuals at higher levels of the organization, particularly if those individuals are predominantly white and male (which, most of the time, they are).[25]

In their study of black and white professional women, University of South Africa Professor Stella Nkomo and Dartmouth Professor Ella Bell found that only 59 percent of African American women in the United States reported having white men in their professional networks. The women in their study explained that informal networking is the key to visibility in the workplace and that without access there are limited opportunities for growth and advancement.

White women also struggle to navigate informal networks in organizations that are particularly male-dominated. Without formal mechanisms for women and minorities to become a part of the network, this can remain a significant impediment to progress. Exclusion from informal aspects of the organization can often leave women feeling isolated and disconnected from their peers, work, and institutions. Seemingly simple things such as joining colleagues for happy hour are often impossible for caregiving women, while single women face barriers to socializing with their married male colleagues or supervisors because of misconceptions that may arise, or due to the fact that these are often couples-only events.

The invisible woman in a male-dominated culture

Finally, women face the challenge of working in organizations whose character and culture have largely been forged by males. While discussions of culture are often more amorphous and organizational responses and solutions are frequently less clear, it would be a mistake to ignore this critical impediment to women's success.

Studies show that men and women communicate, lead, and negotiate differently, with serious implications for women.[26] Georgetown Professor Deborah Tannen's work from the mid-1990s showed stark differences in how men and women communicate and the implications for women in the workplace.[27] Tannen found that men communicate to preserve status in group settings while women use communication as a means to gain intimacy and closeness with others.

Several other studies show differences in how men and women negotiate for resources in the workplace. While managers try to give employees equal access to resources, women often get shortchanged because they don't ask for resources as frequently as men.[28] Women, it seems, ask for less due to gendered behavioral expectations—they don't want to appear too aggressive.[29] As a result, women give the appearance that they lack the skills to negotiate and claim authority in the workplace.

Women often get shortchanged because they don't ask for resources as frequently as men. Women, it seems, ask for less due to gendered behavioral expectations—they don't want to appear too aggressive.

Scholars have also looked at potential differences in leadership styles between men and women. In *Ways Women Lead*, University of California at Irvine Professor Judy Rosener found that men tend to use more delegating, transactional leadership whereas women use a more transformational style by sharing their power and information in a participative approach.[30] This is in line with other research that supports the notion that transformational leaders inspire others to be more engaged, committed, and creative, which can lead to improved overall organizational effectiveness.[31]

But other studies find those differences are more of a myth based on gendered expectation of differences rather than actual behavioral differences.[32] In their recent book *Through the Labyrinth: The Truth About How Women Become Leaders*, Northwestern University and Wellesley College faculty members Alice Eagly and Linda

Carli posit, "There is no defensible argument that men are naturally, inherently, or actually better suited to leadership than women are."[33]

These invisible assumptions are the foundation of most organizational cultures. They are forged in male-dominated senior management meetings and in informal networks that often exclude women. Consequently, the ways women instinctively respond to business situations may not conform to the widely accepted, and yet untested, cultural norms of organizations.[34] This can create significant problems for working women.[35]

Regardless of whether these differences are real or perceived, they often leave women at a disadvantage in traditionally male-dominated environments where masculine styles are expected and rewarded. Business organizations often cling to one interpretation of what effective leadership is rather than capitalizing on the strength of diverse styles of leadership. That may explain why we have yet to see a woman at the helm of a major company in male-dominated industries such as automotives, construction, and manufacturing.

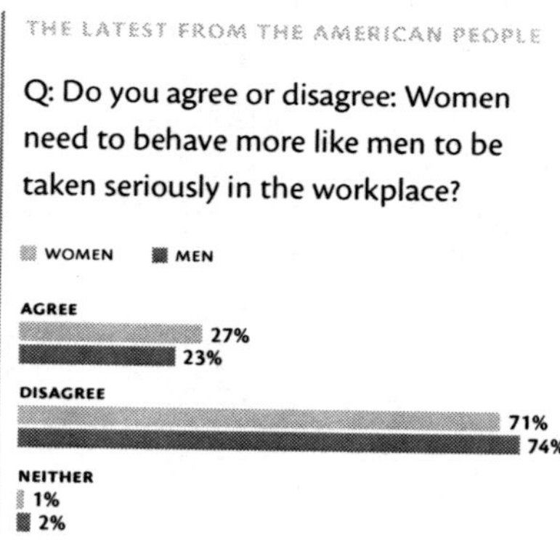

Source: Rockefeller/*Time* poll, 2009.

The result is that women are faced with a double bind in many organizations—either staying true to their core values or adopting the masculine values and traits that are dominant in their organizations. When they enact the former approach they may be seen as too feminine, and when they enact the latter they can be viewed as trying to be something they are not.[36] Likewise, when women take advantage of programs such as flexible work arrangements they are viewed as less committed or ambitious because doing so runs counter to "ideal worker" norms, which assume workers have no lives outside of their organizations.[37]

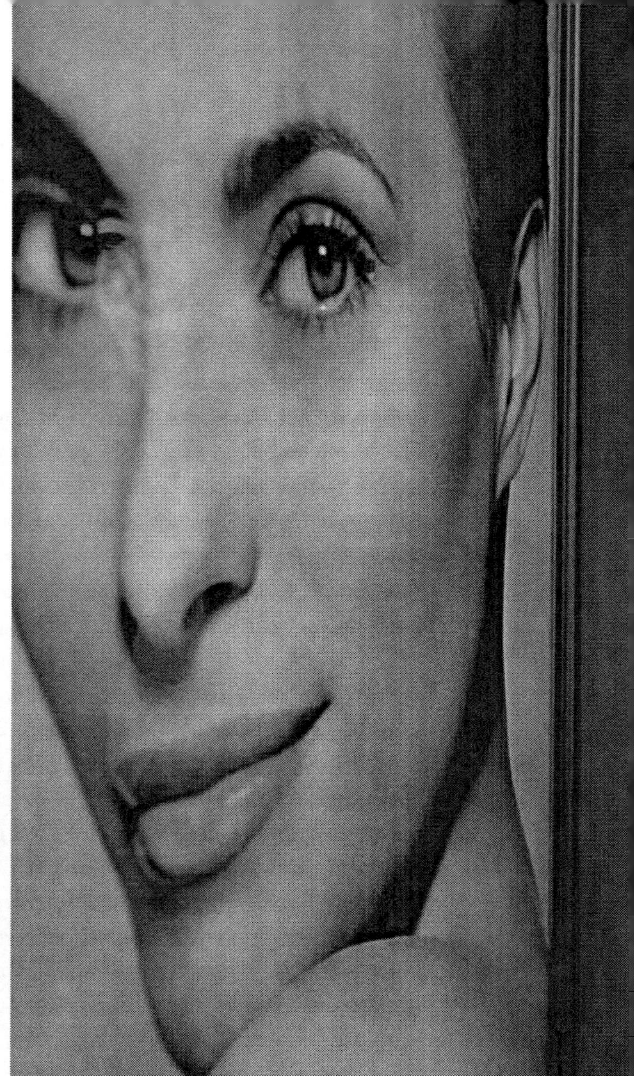

NEW TYPES OF BUSINESS LEADERS. Chairman and CEO of Avon Products Inc. Andrea Jung at the celebration of International Women's Day with the Virtue Foundation at the Global Summit for a Better Tomorrow at The United Nations.

At far left, actress and Avon Global Ambassador Reese Witherspoon speaks as Jung listens at a press conference before announcing the United Nations Development Fund for Women partnership with Avon to promote an end to violence against women through economic empowerment at the United Nations.

{PHOTO CREDITS CLOCKWISE FROM FAR LEFT: FOESTER AXEL, CORBIS; BEN BAKER; GETTY IMAGES FOR BRAGMAN NYMAN CAFARELLI; MICHAEL NAGLE, GETTY IMAGES}

Indeed, women fare better in newer industries such as high technology that recognize and reward differences rather than old-line companies that value masculine ways of knowing and doing.[38] And it is these innovation-led companies that will be the driving force of the U.S. economy in the 21st century—not just big high-tech companies but the many small- and medium-sized businesses. Women will do well in these companies and the companies will do well in turn as more and more women take more and more positions of responsibility throughout their ranks of these businesses amid changing workplace structures in the coming years.

How companies are responding

Some leading companies have rethought some of their core principles and have been willing to alter longstanding management practices—embracing a more flexible approach to doing business that recognizes the new realities facing workers and their families. But most U.S. companies have not. There is ample evidence that those who have embraced change are reaping significant benefits and that there are three primary needs of women in business that employers need to address:

- Work-life and flexibility programs that enable women to adjust their everyday work schedules, especially women in low- and middle-salary ranges where these types of programs are noticeably absent

> *Women are faced with a double bind in organizations—staying true to their core values or adopting the masculine values and traits that are dominant in their organizations.*

- Career development programs that take into account the fundamental changes in the relationship between workers and their employers and that recognize that career development should not assume a "one-size-fits-all" human resource development strategy

- Inclusive work environments in which women's diversity of inputs into company decision making reap the best benefits for businesses

These three sets of workplace initiatives are clearly interrelated, but each needs to be examined separately to underscore their importance and the overall benefits to companies, women, and their families alike.

Work-life and flexibility programs

Since the mid-1980s, leading-edge organizations have been exploring ways to help their workforces minimize the conflict inherent in successfully integrating the work and family domains. Offerings can run a very broad spectrum, from on-site child care to flexible work schedules to telecommuting. The need for these organizational policies became more prominent due to the rise in professional working women and dual-career couples, but it would be a mistake to assume that such initiatives are only valued by women. A 2005 *Fortune* magazine article, "Get a Life!", for example, reported the results of a study of Fortune 500 male executives. These men made the case in no uncertain terms that flexibility is critically important for them, too. For instance, 84 percent of the participants in the *Fortune* study said they would like job options that allow them to realize their professional aspirations while having more time for things outside of work. And 87 percent said companies that do so will have a competitive advantage attracting talent.[39]

The good news is that there are proven benefits for both employers and employees when companies institute flexible work schedules. A 2002 study by the Families and Work Institute, for example, found that when employees have greater access to flexible work arrangements, they are more committed and loyal to their employers and are willing to work harder than required to help their employers be successful.[40] Other studies have found significant cost savings and other benefits as a result of offering flexible work arrangements. Case in point: The professional services consultancy Deloitte Touche Tohmatsu estimates a savings of $41.5 million in 2003 in reduced turnover costs by retaining employees who would have left if they did not have a flexible work arrangement.[41]

Workplace flexibility also improves the productivity of workers and can reduce the level of employee stress, which is a leading cause of unscheduled absences.[42] Furthermore, worker flexibility facilitates commitment to the job.[43] Examples of these programs abound. Hewlett-Packard Co., one of the world's leading technology companies, has offered flexible hours to virtually all employees since the early 1970s. Or consider International Business Machines Corp., which designates 40 percent of its 330,000-person workforce as virtual workers—meaning they work from client sites or from home, not IBM offices.

Other companies boast compressed workweeks for all of their employees in specific business units, among them Raytheon Co.'s missile systems business. Under this arrangement, every employee can work nine days over two weeks, not

THE TRADEOFFS WORKING MOTHERS MAKE. This businesswoman works at her home office while her elder son does his homework. Millions of working mothers—and fathers—have to make often difficult trade-offs when it comes to work and family. (ROLF OESER, *THE NEW YORK TIMES*)

including weekends, allowing them every other Friday off to take care of personal or family issues. And some highly successful companies, among them Intel Corp., follow traditional maternity leaves with a "new parent reintegration process," which allows up to one year of integration time following leave for new parents. During this time, an employee might work part time for 6 to 12 months and get access to a variety of forms of scheduling flexibility.[44]

Phased retirement programs also are growing in popularity and seem particularly appropriate in light of the aging workforce population. Phased retirement programs allow employees to "ease" into retirement in stages by gradually decreasing hours worked over a period of months or years. This allows a smoother transition to retirement or into a new role during traditional retirement years and minimizes the adverse impacts of going from full-time work to an unstructured retirement. Businesses that utilize these kinds of flexible work arrangements have experienced dramatic improvements in productivity, loyalty, employee retention, and cost reduction.[45]

> Workplace flexibility improves the productivity of workers and can reduce the level of employee stress, which is a leading cause of unscheduled absences.

But offering these programs alone often is not enough to address the needs of working women. Indeed, many women (and men) are highly reluctant to utilize flexible work arrangements for fear they will be perceived by their employers as less committed. Women and men need to feel supported and respected for their flexible work choices and the benefits of offering these programs, for the employer and the employee, need to be highlighted.[46]

Moreover, such flexibility should not be limited to white-collar workers. Hourly workers benefit greatly from flexible work options. Studies conducted by the Boston College Center for Work & Family[47] and Corporate Voices for Working Families[48] found that flexibility programs for hourly employees are just as successful as those created for professional employees. Companies in a wide range of industries, including hotel giant Marriott and the national drugstore chain CVS, have invested heavily in addressing the work-life challenges of their hourly employees. The benefits of such programs for companies are similar to those experienced by companies offering these programs to their white-collar workforces—savings in recruitment and retention costs, improved productivity, and much greater employee engagement.

But too few companies are offering these kinds of programs to hourly or low-wage workers. While some hourly workers face rigid work schedules, with very little ability to alter their work hours, others must deal with constantly fluctuating work schedules, including the precise work hours and amount of work hours, both of which may vary dramatically from week to week. The most effective dimension for improvement depends on the type of work schedule the worker faces. For workers on rigid work schedules, meaningful input into work schedules is key. For workers on unpredictable work schedules, predictability is key. For workers whose hours fluctuate, stable work schedules are key. And for those workers subject to challenging work schedules that are resistant to change, such as those who work overnight, strategies to mitigate the negative effects of those challenges will be key.

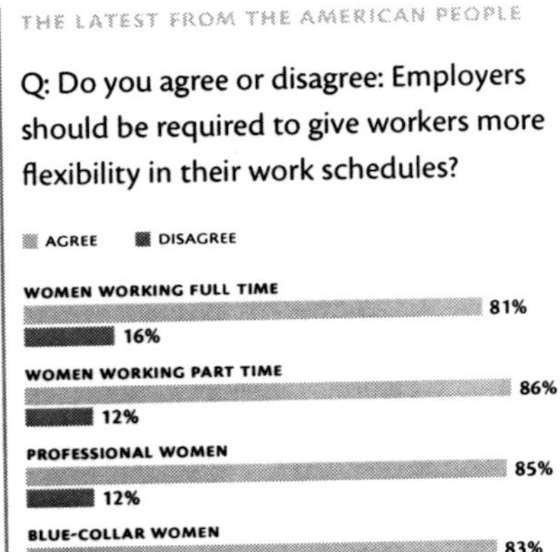

Source: Rockefeller/*Time* poll, 2009.

Career development

In addition to flexibility, women also need investment in their development. Companies need to help women thrive in the workplace to reap long-term benefits. Increasingly, the need to navigate careers while maintaining work-life integration has become an enormous challenge for all working people and their employers. Organizational careers within one company are increasingly a thing of the past and families' structures are very different today than they were 20 to 30 years ago. Today, employers and employees alike are fast moving toward a self-directed career model that noted career scholar Douglas T. Hall of Boston University has termed the "protean career."[49]

A protean career puts individuals squarely in charge of steering their own career development, but supporting greater flexibility, creating customized careers, and ensuring that individuals have the competence to navigate the myriad of career options cannot be left to chance. It requires a coordinated effort that modifies organizational human resource policies and stresses shared responsibility between organizational leaders and individual contributors to create win-win solutions for the organization and its members.[50]

Women and men need to feel supported and respected for their flexible work choices and the benefits of offering these programs, for the employer and the employee, need to be highlighted.

Deloitte Touche Tohmatsu provides an excellent example of an employer that has taken an aggressive leadership position in protean career approaches. Its program, "Mass Career Customization," enables employees to create individualized career goals that take into consideration obligations outside of work. Deloitte's MCC program grew out of a women's initiative within the company, but it is now being used across the board for individuals regardless of level in the organization, age, or gender.

For career development programs to work effectively, companies also need organizational mentors.[51] Women and minority group members often struggle to find effective mentors within their organizations because these one-on-one relationships typically evolve informally. But the lack of mentors for minorities or female employees in the higher echelons of a company make this difficult.[52] There are two things that organizations can do to help foster effective mentoring for women in light of the small number of senior female executives.

First, companies can develop formal mentoring programs. Many large companies, including the accounting and consulting firm KPMG, assign all new interns and employees a formal mentor. The formality of the arrangement is sometimes challenging, as most mentoring relationships evolve in an informal manner. The existence of a mentoring culture within the organization can help to overcome some of the artificiality of the relationships inherent in formal mentor-mentee matching services. It also ensures access to mentors for diverse employees who may not otherwise have an easy time developing mentoring relationships through informal channels.

Second, companies need to recognize the importance and usefulness of employee networks. A woman's network, for example, which may be made up of peers,

THE IMPORTANCE OF MENTORING. Women in senior positions in some companies are taking their younger coworkers under their wings. [MARC ASNIN, REDUX]

subordinates, and managers, can provide others in the network with the psychosocial and career support they need. IBM and the pharmaceutical company Merck are examples of large, global organizations that have invested heavily in developing and supporting these employee groups.[53]

Inclusive work environments

Finally, women (and minorities) in the workforce need to be recognized and rewarded for their differences rather than being encouraged to fit outdated norms. Many organizations have developed diversity initiatives, but such programs can segment diverse groups by demographics rather than creating heterogeneous groups that would allow the members to explore and learn from their differences. Research shows that when diversity is viewed as strength and there is a high level of acceptance of distinct viewpoints, organizations benefit because it allows for a broader range of perspectives and unique contributions.[54]

What's more, when women and minorities feel respected for their differences, they will be more "retainable." Companies that offer diversity and inclusion programs can benefit handsomely for the effort. These efforts typically include:

- Management and employee diversity training programs
- Succession planning systems aimed at increasing the representation of underrepresented groups in higher-level roles
- Employee networks and affinity groups for women and minorities
- A wide menu of programs and policies crafted to respond to a variety of employee needs and family situations in different cultural contexts
- Access, recognition, and awards programs for nonwork obligations, such as leadership efforts in the community and volunteer work[55]

When differences are recognized and rewarded, women and other minority groups feel more comfortable raising issues that promote their well-being. Jane Dutton and her colleagues from the University of Michigan found in their 2002 study that women take cues from their environment that influence whether they are willing to raise gender-equity issues in their workplaces. Their study found that demographic patterns, qualities of top management, and qualities of the organizational culture each served as indicators as to whether women would feel comfortable voicing their concerns.[56]

PepsiCo has been one of the pioneer U.S. corporations in promoting and rewarding women and minorities. As we mentioned, while only 16 percent of Fortune 500 corporate officers are women, as of 2009, 33 percent of PepsiCo's executives and 30 percent of its board of directors are women. The organization has a long history of both developing and promoting women, which is a major part of the firm's overall business strategy and success.[57] Since 2006, when Indra Nooyi took the helm, revenues have increased by nearly 10 percent, despite slow economic growth. In addition, over the past decade, the company's share price has increased more than 50 percent while the Dow has gone down by nearly 18 percent during that same period.

More and more companies today recognize the advantages of promoting women throughout their organizational structures, yet there remain clear glass ceilings—organizational barriers to the advancement of women throughout their careers.

Where do we go from here?

The Great Recession may mark a turning point for women in the workplace. As some of the old icons of American industry struggle to survive, management practices that were seen as innovative in the early- to mid-20th century will be challenged because of new technologies, changing consumer needs, and contemporary workforce education, demographics, and values. Now is the ideal time to let go of outdated management frameworks that no longer foster employee engagement or facilitate desired organizational outcomes, given the increasing diversity of the American workforce.

For cultural shifts to occur across businesses and industries large and small, there needs to be a shift in U.S. policy around work-family issues, flexibility, and diversity. Despite its position as a global economic leader and a leader in the advancement of equality for women, our nation continues to show little appetite to address the needs of working women and families through government policy. In a study of the maternity policies of 168 countries, for example, the United States ranked at the bottom in terms of time and financial support provided for maternity leave.[58] And the lack of provision of medical insurance and caregiving all strongly suggest that the United States falls far below many less prosperous countries in the provision of the basic policies that would support families, specifically the U.S. working women who are primarily responsible for the care of these families.

AT THE HELM. PepsiCo CEO Indra Nooyi at a lunch meeting with other top executives at the company's headquarters in Purchase, New York. [MARK PETERSON, REDUX]

To summarize, there are five key points that need to be clearly understood:

1. Women make up more than half the talent that is available for corporate America, and their outstanding performance in educational institutions—especially higher education and professional schools—demands that employers create workplaces that attract, retain, develop, and exploit (in the best sense of the word) this tremendous resource.

2. While we have grown and changed as a society over the past 30 years and women have reached greater equality in the workplace, life outside the workplace still places enormous and highly unequal challenges and demands on women. This must be understood and addressed by corporations and society as a whole. Otherwise, the unparalleled talent that women bring to business will always be underutilized as disillusioned women play roles that are well beneath their abilities and become part of the so-called leaky talent pipeline as they leave their employers.

Despite its position as a global economic leader and a leader in the advancement of equality for women, our nation continues to show little appetite to address the needs of working women and families through government policy.

3. The highest impact actions employers can take to increase women's contributions and enhance their progress cost very little. Such actions involve letting go of outdated mental models such as the idea that there is only one place that work gets done, one way to structure a workday, one model for the ideal career, and one leadership style that works in today's workplace. Flexible work arrangements, flexible career paths, and new leadership styles better meet the needs of today's diverse workforce but also today's flexible and fast-changing economic environment.

4. Many companies are putting forward progressive workplace policies for women, but too few of these companies include policies that apply to workers who are at the low and middle end of the company pyramid. All workers need policies that meet the changed realities of work and family, not just high-end workers.

5. Too few businesses have taken the initiative to change workplaces on their own. Government has a real role to play in incentivizing businesses to update their employment policies.

In closing, the support that women need to be successful is not different from the support all working people need. Women's responsibilities for childbearing and caregiving, and their lack of access to positions of authority in business, simply make women's needs far more acute. If the United States is truly to be a successful economic engine and role model for the 21st-century global economy, it will be because we found a way to fully utilize the human potential that exists in this country. Now is the time to replace outmoded ways of operating with progressive and proven new models of leadership in organizations that will help us achieve that objective.

ENDNOTES

1 Samuel DiPiazza Jr., "Closing the Gender Gap: Challenges, Opportunities and the Future" (PricewaterhouseCoopers LLP video, 2008). Transcript available at http://www.pwc.com/en_GX/gx/women-at-pwc/assets/closing_the_gender_gap_full_film_transcript.pdf.

2 Marti Barletta, *Marketing to Women: How to Understand, Reach, and Increase Your Share of the World's Largest Market Segment, 2nd edition* (Chicago: Dearborn Trade Publishing, 2006).

3 Sylvia Hewlett and others, "The Hidden Brain Drain: Off-Ramps and On-Ramps in Women's Careers" (New York: Center for Work-Life Policy, 2005).

4 Avivah Wittenberg-Cox and Alison Maitland, *Why Women Mean Business: Understanding the Emergence of our Next Economic Revolution* (West Sussex, UK: John Wiley & Sons Ltd., 2008).

5 "2006 Equal Employment Opportunity Commission Aggregate Report, NAICS-5 Code 54121: Accounting/Tax Prep/Bookkeep/Payroll Services," available at http://www.eeoc.gov/stats/jobpat/2006/nac5/54121.html (last accessed August 2009).

6 National Science Foundation, "Bachelor's Degrees, by Field and Sex: 1997 – 2006" (2008), available at http://www.nsf.gov/statistics/wmpd/degrees.cfm#bachelor.

7 Catalyst Inc., "Women CEOs of the Fortune 1000" (2009), available at http://www.catalyst.org/publication/322/women-ceos-of-the-fortune-1000.

8 Catalyst Inc., "Women in U.S. Management" (2009), available at http://www.catalyst.org/file/192/qt_women_in_us_management.pdf.

9 Roy Adler, "Women and Profits," *Harvard Business Review* 79 (10) (2001): 30.

10 Catalyst Inc., "The Bottom Line: Corporate Performance and Women's Representation on Boards" (2007), available at http://www.catalyst.org/file/139/bottom%20line%202.pdf.

11 Christian Dezso and David Gaddis Ross, "'Girl Power': Female Participation in Top Management and Firm Performance." Working Paper (Social Science Research Network, 2008).

12 Lisa Belkin, "The Opt-Out Revolution," *The New York Times*, October 26, 2003, available at http://www.nytimes.com/2003/10/26/magazine/26WOMEN.html?pagewanted=all.

13 Pamela Stone, *Opting Out? Why Women Really Quit Careers and Head Home* (Berkeley, CA: University of California Press, 2007).

14 Lisa Mainiero and Sherry Sullivan, "The Opt-out Revolt: Why People are Leaving Companies to Create Kaleidoscope Careers" (Mountain View, CA.: Davies-Black Publishing, 2006).

15 Ellen Galinsky, Kerstin Aumann, and James T. Bond, "Times are Changing: Gender and Generation at Work and at Home" (New York: Families and Work Institute, 2008), available at familiesandwork.org/site/research/reports/Times_Are_Changing.pdf.

16 Center for Women's Business Research, "Key Facts about Women-Owned Businesses" (2009), available at http://www.womensbusinessresearchcenter.org/research/keyfacts.

17 Darrene Hackler, Ellen Harpel, and Heike Mayer, "Human Capital and Women's Business Ownership" (Washington: Small Business Administration, 2008).

18 Ying Lowrey, "Women in Business, 2006: A Demographic Review of Women's Business Ownership," Working Paper (Small Business Administration Office of Advocacy, August 2006), available at http://www.sba.gov/advo/research/rs280tot.pdf.

19 Center for Women's Business Research, "Key Facts about Women-Owned Businesses."

20 Arlie Hochschild, *The Second Shift: Working Parents and the Revolution at Home* (New York: Viking, 1989).

21 Suzanne M. Bianchi, John P. Robinson, and Melissa Milkie, *Changing Rhythm of American Family Life* (New York: Russell Sage Foundation, 2006).

22 Deborah Swiss and Judith Walker, *Women and the Work/Family Dilemma: How Today's Professional Women Are Finding Solutions*, (New York: John Wiley & Sons, 1994).

23 Dane Waldfogel, "Understanding the 'Family Gap' in Pay for Women with Children," *The Journal of Economic Perspectives* 12(1)(1998): 137–156.

24 Herminia Ibarra, "Personal Networks of Women and Minorities in Management: A Conceptual Framework," *Academy of Management Review*, 18 (1) (1993): 56–87.

25 Ella Edmonson Bell and Stella Nkomo, *Our Separate Ways* (Cambridge: Harvard Business School Press, 2001).

26 Deborah Tannen, *Talking from 9 to 5: How Women's and Men's Conversational Styles Affect Who Gets Heard, Who Gets Credit, and What Gets Done at Work* (London: Virago, 1994); Deborah Kolb, Judith Williams, and Carol Frohlinger, *Her Place at the Table: A Woman's Guide to Negotiating Five Key Challenges to Leadership Success* (San Francisco: Jossey-Bass, 2004); Judy Rosener, "Ways Women Lead," *Harvard Business Review* 68 (6) (November–December 1990): 119–125.

27 Tannen, *Talking from 9 to 5.*

28 Linda Babcock and others, "Nice Girls Don't Ask," *Harvard Business Review* 81 (10) (2003): 14–16.

29 Hannah Riley Bowles and Kathleen L. McGinn, "Claiming Authority: Negotiating Challenges for Women Leaders," in David M. Messick and Roderick M. Kramer, eds., *The Psychology of Leadership: New Perspectives and Research* (Mahwah, NJ, Lawrence Erlbaum Associates, 2005), pp. 191–208.

30 Rosener, "Ways Women Lead."

31 Alice Eagly and Linda Carli, "The Female Leadership Advantage: An Evaluation of the Evidence," *Leadership Quarterly* 14 (6) (2003):807–834; Alice Eagly and Blair Johnson, "Gender and Leadership Style: A Meta-Analysis," *Psychological Bulletin* 108 (2) (1990): 233–256.

32 Peter Glick and Susan Fiske, "An Ambivalent Alliance: Hostile and Benevolent Sexism as Complementary Justifications of Gender Inequality," *American Psychologist 56 (2)* (2001): 109–118.

33 Alice Eagly and Linda Carli, *Through the Labyrinth: The Truth About How Women Become Leaders* (Boston: Harvard University Business School Press, 2007).

34 Joyce K. Fletcher, *Disappearing Acts: Gender, Power, and Relational Power at Work* (Cambridge: MIT Press, 1999).

35 Ibid.

36 Robin J. Ely, "The Effects of Organizational Demographics and Social Identity on Relationships among Professional Women," *Administrative Science Quarterly* 39 (2) (1994): 203–238; Kathleen Hall Jamieson, *Beyond the Double Binds: Women and Leadership* (New York: Oxford University Press, 1995).

37 Joan Williams, *Unbending Gender: Why Work and Family Conflict and What to Do About It* (New York: Oxford University Press, 2000).

38 Eagly and Carli, *Through the Labyrinth*, p. 6.

39 Jody Miller, "Get a Life!" *Fortune*, November 28, 2005, available at http://money.cnn.com/magazines/fortune/fortune_archive/2005/11/28/8361955/index.htm.

40 Fredric Van Deusen and others, "Overcoming the Implementation Gap: How 20 Leading Companies are Making Flexibility Work" (Chestnut Hill, MA: Boston College Center for Work & Family, 2008).

41 Corporate Voices for Working Families, "Business Impacts of Flexibility: An Imperative for Expansion, (November 2005), available at http://www.cvworkingfamilies.org/system/files/Business%20Impacts%20of%20Flexibility.pdf.

42 Ibid, p. 14.

43 Ibid, p. 13.

44 Van Deusen and others, "Overcoming the Implementation Gap."

45 Van Deusen and others, "Overcoming the Implementation Gap"; Fredric Van Deusen and others, "Making the Business Case for Work-Life Programs" (Chestnut Hill, MA: Boston College Center for Work and Family, 2008).

46 Brad Harrington and Jamie J. Ladge, "Work-Life Integration: Present Dynamics and Future Directions for Organizations," *Organizational Dynamics* 38 (2) (2009):148–157.

47 Leon Litchfield, Jennifer Swanberg, and Catherine Sigworth, "Increasing the Visibility of the Invisible Workforce: Model Programs and Policies for Hourly and Lower Wage Employees" (Chestnut Hill, MA: Boston College Center for Work and Family, 2004), available at http://www.cvworkingfamilies.org/system/files/modelprogramsandpolicieforlower-wageemployees.pdf.

48 Corporate Voices for Working Families, "Innovative Workplace Flexibility Options for Hourly Workers" (May 2009), available at http://www.cvworkingfamilies.org/system/files/CVWF%20report-FINAL.pdf.

49 Brad Harrington and Douglas T. Hall, *Career Management & Work-Life Integration: Using Self-Assessment to Navigate Contemporary Careers* (Thousand Oaks, CA: Sage Publications, 2007).

50 Harrington and Ladge, "Work-Life Integration."

51 Kathy Kram, *Mentoring at Work: Developmental Relationships in Organizational Life* (Glenville, IL: Scott, Foresman and Co., 1985).

52 Kram, *Mentoring at Work*.

53 Boston College Center for Work and Family, "Partner Profile: Women's Advancement" (2008).

54 Jeffrey T. Polzer, Laurie P. Milton, and William B. Swann, Jr., "Capitalizing on Diversity: Interpersonal Congruence in Small Work Groups," *Administrative Sciences Quarterly* 47 (2) (2002): 296–324.

55 Harrington and Ladge, "Work-Life Integration."

56 Jane Dutton, "Red Light, Green Light: Making Sense of the Organizational Context for Issue Selling" *Organization Science* 13 (4) (2002): 355–369.

57 Molly Selvin, "PepsiCo Names Successor to CEO," *Los Angeles Times*, August 15, 2006, available at http://articles.latimes.com/2006/aug/15/business/fi-pepsi15.

58 Jody Heymann, Alison Earle, and Jeffrey Hayes, "The Work, Family, and Equity Index: How Does the United States Measure Up?" (Boston and Montreal: Project on Global Working Families and the Institute for Health and Social Policy, 2007), available http://www.mcgill.ca/files/ihsp/WFEI2007.pdf.

Money Matters

By Suze Orman, best-selling personal finance expert

We need to move money front and center in this conversation. Not later. Right now.

I am excited that "A Woman's Nation Changes Everything" is bringing such formidable intellectual power to bear on the vitally important topic of how women's evolving role in every facet of society can be better served by corporate and legislative policy. But all of our best efforts will be for naught if we don't focus on the real catalyst for change—altering the dysfunctional relationship many women have with money, especially women who are struggling to survive in abusive relationships but also including those many women who are now coming to terms with the "power of the purse" as the new breadwinners in American society.

It starts with basic financial literacy. In the recent Prudential study "Financial Experience & Behaviors Among Women," less than 25 percent of the women surveyed said they are "very well prepared" to make financial decisions.[1] Women are grappling with everyday spending, savings, and investment decisions, often after earning the lioness' share of the family income, yet they feel overwhelmed and underqualified to put that hard-earned money to work. How can we expect women who cannot understand or manage their own family finances to climb the ladder at a Fortune 500 company?

Until women accept the need to make themselves a priority, they will continue to struggle to find their way in the new world order. Women need to feel great about using their hard-earned money to fund a Roth IRA rather than using the money to buy more things their already cared-for kids don't really need. Women need to say no when asked to co-sign a loan because they know it may jeopardize their own credit score and financial security. To allay very real bag-lady fears,[2] women must see the value of paying down their mortgage to ensure a secure retirement rather than sending that money to a grown child with a full-time job and ample income to help pay down student loan debt.

The money disconnect is just as pervasive for stay-at-home mothers. Please let's not lose sight of this vitally important subset of our female population. I am talking about stay-at-home moms who come to me for advice on how to ask their partner for money since he is the one earning the money. I tell them: You don't ask. You share. A woman needs to understand her equal value to her family. She needs to respect herself. She needs to not put herself on sale.

Then there are the mothers, daughters, sisters, aunts, female employers, employees, and friends who spend every last penny they have helping everyone else without considering the personal impact it will have. I've learned in my career that when it comes to money, women feel as if the goal of their money is to take care of others before they use it to take care of themselves. Women fail to see how saying yes out of love, or out fear of what others will think or do to them, is so wrong and dangerous if it robs them of their own financial security.

Women are grappling with everyday spending, savings, and investment decisions, often after earning the lioness' share of the family income.

If you are a woman and are uncomfortable with what I just said, you are most likely living evidence of what I am talking about. You probably think it is crass or myopic to lay so much responsibility at money's feet, because you aren't comfortable with money in your own life. Please understand that I more than most know all about the breadwinner phenomenon. I know the stress that comes from making my own way in life, losing everything I had or could borrow, and then clawing my way back into the black to take control of my own life and my own business.

Men often reach for the metaphor "winning a ballgame" to describe negotiations, but women opted for the victim's metaphor of "going to the dentist." It's hard to thrive in the workplace with that mindset.

Whether the negotiation is a salary, a business deal, or a delicate bit of office politics, a woman can't succeed if she lets herself be pushed around rather than pushing her own agenda. I agree that there are very real cultural and corporate biases that hold women back. But I do not agree on any level with the notion that the main solutions to these challenges are solely institutional.

What needs to be fixed, first and foremost, is utterly personal. Women must own the power to control their destiny. They must want to own that power. They must feel it is okay to give to themselves as much as they give of themselves. I do not say this as an indictment. My message is not one of shortcoming or failure. I am inspired and awestruck by all that women are achieving today, at how far women have progressed professionally, personally, and culturally, compared to their mothers and grandmothers. I am asking that we focus on how we can push the amazing evolution of women's role in society into its next phase where women embrace their money and therefore their power.

Women must own the power to control their destiny.

The challenge is how do we make this happen? Don't expect or even want someone else to do it for you. Don't wait for someone else to legislate it for you. Don't ask someone else to manage it on your behalf. That's the definition of powerlessness, and too often it is exactly how women still navigate this new world of ours.

Until now. We can change this once and for all. We can chart a course that redefines a woman's relationship with money. Recognizing that women have the tools to embrace their role as a major economic force in our country means we are indeed a woman's nation. Now let's transform it into a powerful woman's nation. It all starts right here and right now.

ENDNOTES

1 Prudential, "Financial Experience and Behaviors Among Women" (2008), available at http://www.prudential.com/media/managed/2006WomenBrochure_FINAL.pdf.

2 Allianz, "Women, Money and Power" (2006), available at https://www.allianz.com/en/press/news/studies/archive/news6.html. Nearly half of respondents said they had thoughts of becoming a bag lady.

A Woman's Place Is in Her Union

By Arlene Holt Baker, executive vice president, AFL-CIO

I got my first job in high school in the 1960s because of President Lyndon Johnson's War on Poverty, working after school for the minimum wage of $1.40 an hour. That may not sound like much, but it was certainly more than the $6 a day my mother was earning as a full-time domestic worker.

My mom was and still is an inspiration to me. She refused to let my six siblings and me dwell on the fact that we didn't have a great deal. She would sacrifice to pay her poll tax in Texas, her church tithe, and her NAACP dues. And she deeply believed in volunteering for good causes. So early on, living and working—especially as a young woman of color and the daughter of Georgia Louise Leslie—meant struggle and determination and strength.

My outlook expanded and changed in 1972 when I joined the union movement. When I went to work for the American Federation of State, County and Municipal Employees, or AFSCME, in Los Angeles, I had the chance to work on behalf of equal pay for women who had joined together with their union sisters and brothers to seek higher wages, greater benefits, and a better life. That changed my life.

I'll never forget the women I met in those days. Years later, I went back to visit with them where they worked and to find out how they were doing. They told me that because of their union contracts they had the chance to buy their first homes or their first cars, or to send their kids to college. It was uplifting.

What I've discovered over the past 37 years is the same thing millions of other women know so very well. They can tell you that union membership isn't as important for women as it is for men—it is far more important for women. All too often, women are the first to be laid off, or denied a raise, or discriminated against, or passed by for promotions.

What I first witnessed with public-sector workers in California many years ago is still true all over our nation. I've seen that with a union, a telephone operator can own a home. An assembly line worker can have health insurance and a vacation. A service rep can have a secure pension.

According to the most recent statistics, full-time working women with union cards are paid 32 percent more than nonunionized sisters.[1] Moreover, women in unions are far more likely to have job-based health insurance (75 percent compared to 51 percent for nonunion women)[2] and defined-benefit pensions (a staggering 77 percent compared to 20 percent for nonunion women).[3]

There's a powerful lesson in all of this. Every generation has its own mission for justice. In the past it was demanding the right to vote, marching against the sweatshops where young women were kept in terrible poverty, and fighting in the courts and Congress for our civil rights. Some of those missions were successful. Other missions continue.

I deeply believe that our mission today in a woman's nation is to help our sisters and daughters achieve economic security and find a place in the middle class.

For our own generation, I deeply believe that our mission today in a woman's nation is to help our sisters and daughters achieve economic security and find a place in the middle class. And I know that the best way to do that is to enable millions more women to join the union movement and win a better life for themselves and their co-workers. I know the difference it can make. It's my dream, and I'll do everything I can for as long as I can to help make it come true.

ENDNOTES

1 AFL-CIO, "The Union Difference: Union Advantage by the Numbers" (January 2009), available at http://www.aflcio.org/joinaunion/why/uniondifference/upload/advantage_0109.pdf.

2 John Schmitt, "Unions and Upward Mobility for Women Workers" (Washington: Center for Economic and Policy Research, 2008), available at http://www.cepr.net/documents/publications/unions_and_upward_mobility_for_women_workers_2008_12.pdf.

3 AFL-CIO, "Union Workers Have Better Health Care and Pensions" (2009), available at http://www.aflcio.org/joinaunion/why/uniondifference/uniondiff6.cfm.

Moms Rising

By Kristin Rowe-Finkbeiner, executive director and co-founder, MomsRising.org

I wear a ring on my left hand next to my wedding ring every day. This ring was given to my grandmother by my great-grandmother, who was the first president of Rochester, New York's Planned Parenthood chapter in the time of Susan B. Anthony. My grandmother remembers her mother standing tall in the face of priests banging loudly at the door of her house, protesting that my great-grandmother was teaching women about birth control in a time when only "people of ill repute" considered such a thing.

Then the ring was passed down from my grandmother, who later became president of the Rochester Planned Parenthood chapter, to my mother, who is a strong feminist in her own right. She worked for many years as a social worker for Prince George's County Family Services in Maryland.

My mom passed the ring to me when I turned 16. For me, the ring is an ever-present historical anchor, reminding me that women in our nation only got the right to vote not so very long ago in 1920. Just 89 years ago.

The ring also reminds me every day that due to the hard work of the women before us, incredible battles have been won. One prime example is the landmark Civil Rights Act of 1964, Title VII, which banned employment discrimination based on race, sex, religion, or national origin, and was a pivotal gain for women in the workplace.

Today, one of the greatest barriers to gender equality is smack dab in the center of motherhood—the "maternal wall." A little known fact is that many women never even get to the glass ceiling because the maternal wall is standing in the way of ever reaching any rooms with glass in the first place. The maternal wall stands tall for the majority of women in our nation since more than 80 percent of women in the United States have children by the time they are 44.[1]

Here's what that maternal wall looks like: Women without children make about 90 cents to a man's dollar, which is outrageous enough, but mothers make only 73 cents to a man's dollar, and single moms make only about 60 cents per man's dollar.[2] To make matters worse, a recent study found that given equal resumes, women with children are 79 percent less likely to be hired than women without children.[3]

Many women never even get to the glass ceiling because the maternal wall is standing in the way of ever reaching any rooms with glass in the first place.

Women are now nearly half the entire paid labor force in our nation, and three-quarters of mothers are in the modern labor force, yet American workplaces are still stuck in the 1950s. Studies show that enacting family economic security policies such as paid family leave, health care, and access to early child care can help lower the gender wage gap and bring down the maternal wall.

Wearing my ring each day, I'm reminded that the work MomsRising.org does, and the successes we've had thus far helping to pass laws such as the Lilly Ledbetter Fair Pay Act, are the result of a continuum of work done both by those who are now fighting for women's rights, as well as by those whose shoulders we all stand upon.

Looking at my son and daughter (who is already lobbying to wear the ring at 10 years old), I'm inspired to continue the fight.

ENDNOTES

1 Jane Lawler Dye, "Fertility of American Women: 2006" (Washington: Department of the Census, 2008), available at http://www.census.gov/prod/2008pubs/p20-558.pdf.

2 Jane Waldfogel, "Understanding the 'Family Gap' in Pay for Women with Children," *Journal of Economic Perspectives* 12 (1) (1998): 137–156.

3 Shelley J. Correll, Stephen Benard, and In Paik, "Getting a Job: Is There a Motherhood Penalty?" *American Journal of Sociology* 112 (5) (2007): 1297-1338.

The Challenge of Faith

Bringing spiritual sustenance to busy lives

By Kimberly Morgan and Sally Steenland

[I wish church leaders could] spend a day with a typical working mom, single mother, or caregiver to see the stresses of women's jobs.[1]

[I'd love to] change the perception that a working woman is less of a mother and that her family suffers because she works.[2]

It's a fallacy to think women can do it all. Women can do what they're called to do.[3]

These women's voices, captured in a series of focus groups and conversations across the country, express a dilemma facing millions of women today: how to balance work, family, and faith. It is hard enough for women to find sufficient hours in the day for job and family. Finding time for religious involvement is harder still, even though the support and services that organized religion provides may be needed now more than ever.

Religious institutions today also face a dilemma. They exist in a competitive, mobile marketplace and must adapt to the changing roles and time constraints of women in order to grow—and even to survive.

Religion is important in the lives of many women who look to it for sustenance, community, inspiration, and guidance in their daily lives. Women also seek in religion a purpose larger than themselves and the opportunity to put their faith into action and work for a better world. For women whose lives are often fragmented and harried, religious communities provide a place where stresses can be unburdened and joys shared—where they can step back from the fray, connect with God and others, and prepare to re-enter the world.

As more and more demands have been placed on women, many religious institutions have attempted to respond, adapting their beliefs and practices to meet the needs of women and their families. Many have done so out of a sense of mission, connecting theological beliefs in human dignity, equality, and justice with practical support.

Some religious institutions maintain a firm belief in the spiritual superiority of the "traditional" family and primacy of women's domestic role, yet they offer programs to accommodate working mothers and blended families.

For some religious institutions, the reality of working women's lives has exposed a discrepancy between their beliefs and day-to-day practices. On the one hand, they maintain a firm belief in the spiritual superiority of the "traditional" family and primacy of women's domestic role, yet they offer programs to accommodate working mothers and blended families. Child care programs, especially, are growing across faith traditions, so that at least one-quarter of children in child care centers are in programs located in churches, synagogues, and other places of worship.

That is not the only discrepancy regarding women and religion today. Women say that religion matters a great deal to them, but the numbers show that as their workforce participation increases, their religious participation declines. Women today are also religiously mobile, moving from one faith tradition to another, and in and out of organized religion altogether. Spirituality is also on the rise. From meditation and yoga to contemplative walks and New Age self-help books, more and more women are seeking renewal in sources outside organized religion.

These changes—and the dynamic interactions among them—are highly significant for individuals and for society. The faith communities that women belong to exist within larger institutions with histories, doctrines, cultures, and influence. Over the centuries, these institutions have helped shape social morality and cultural norms, and in turn, have been influenced by them. In the private sphere, religious institutions shape how we find meaning, balance responsibility to others with self-fulfillment, and respond to the modern world. In the public sphere, religious institutions can be prophetic voices for justice, as well as rigid defenders of an unjust status quo. Their views on family and morality have helped form government policies, and their power to engage and inspire people to action remains a powerful force today.

This chapter examines many of these changes and challenges. We examine the role of religion in women's lives—how it helps to unify their different identities and navigate competing demands and stresses. We look at the ways religious institutions are responding to changes in their congregations. We also analyze the growth of spirituality and how it is shifting followers away from the traditions, teachings, and public witness that many religious institutions provide.

As women (and men) increasingly grapple with shifting gender roles and responsibilities, as families face greater economic stress, and as women juggle multiple tasks in days that are too short, religious institutions can provide sustenance and support. However, their budgets are shrinking as demands for their services are rising. Their volunteer pool of women has been greatly diminished. The challenges facing religious institutions today are significant. They need to provide for the spiritual and material needs of women and their families, while speaking out on behalf of a moral vision that values women and family in a way that is neither regressive nor nostalgic, but authentic and prophetic for today.

Religion matters to millions of women

A glance at polling data might lead one to think that as women have left the home for paid work, they have also left religion. There are many reasons for declining religious participation in this country, but the correlation between women's rising workforce participation and decreasing religious activity is real.[4] The opposite also tends to be true—the more religious women are, the less likely they are to work outside the home.

One obvious reason for women's declining religious participation is lack of time. As women cram into their day a host of work and family responsibilities, they

A current snapshot of women and religion: diverse and mobile

The picture of religion and women in America is varied and complex, filled with seeming contradictions and blank spaces where research is missing. For instance, as women's workforce participation has risen, their religious attendance has declined. And yet religion is important in women's lives—more so, according to research studies—than in men's. For instance, women are more likely than men to say they believe in a personal God,[5] to pray daily, and to attend weekly worship services.[6]

More than 82 percent of American women are Christian. Over 53 percent of all women belong to the Protestant tradition, nearly 27 percent are affiliated with evangelical churches, 19 percent with mainline churches, and 8 percent with historically black churches. Twenty-five percent of American women are Catholic. Other affiliations include Mormonism (1.8 percent), Judaism (1.6 percent), Buddhism (0.7 percent), Islam (0.4 percent), and Hinduism (0.3 percent). Thirteen percent of women claim no specific religious affiliation.[7] Although their numbers are lower, millions of women are not religious: 0.9 percent are atheists, and 1.7 percent are agnostics.[8]

Women outnumber men in virtually every Christian tradition (see Figure 1). The numbers are highest for African American women: 60 percent of those affiliated with historically black churches are women. In fact, African American women are the most religious of all Americans. More than eight in 10 say that religion is very important to them and about 6 in 10 attend worship services every week.[9] In non-Christian faiths, the numbers are reversed. For example, there are higher proportions of men than women affiliated with the Muslim, Jewish, and Hindu traditions.[10]

Hispanic women—both Catholic and Protestant—are also more religiously active than men, although Protestant Hispanics of both sexes are more active than those who are Catholic.[11] Asian Americans are most likely to be unaffiliated with a religious tradition. Nearly one in four have no religious affiliation. About 17 percent of Asians are evangelicals; another 17 percent are Catholic, and 14 percent are Hindu.[12]

None of these figures captures the extent to which women are involved in more informal religious practices. Studies of Latinas find that they are often leaders within their own communities in the practice of folk religion—activities not sanctioned by the Catholic Church but that are manifestations of popular religious beliefs.[13] Ignoring this role (what one scholar labels the "matriarchal core of Latino Catholicism"[14]) can lead researchers to underestimate the significance of religious commitment in this community, and the leadership roles of women within them. Similarly, an in-depth study of immigrant congregations including Hindus,

often find their tasks spilling into the next day and their energy stretched to its limits. This is what University of Minnesota sociologist Penny Edgell found in a study of working mothers who were religiously active—they felt drained in their family and work life. According to Edgell, managing work, family, and religious activities could be harder for women than men, partly because of the longer hours women spend on housework and home chores.[24]

Greek Orthodox, Zoroastrians, Buddhists, and Mexican Catholics found that women are often central to the practice of domestic religious rituals in these faiths.[15]

In terms of race and ethnicity, most religious traditions are majority white (see Figure 2). For instance, Protestant congregations are 74 percent white/non-Hispanic and the Catholic Church is 65 percent white/non-Hispanic. Islam is the only religion with no racial majority.[16]

Nonetheless, the growth in immigration from non-European nations since the 1950s has not only increased the population of non-Christians in American society, but has changed the face of many Christian congregations, a process of "de-Europeanization" of American Christianity, as one sociologist has put it.[17] Immigration from the Caribbean and African countries has altered the membership of historically black churches as well.

One notable change in recent years has been the frequency with which women, and men, switch religious affiliation, moving among different faith traditions—and in and out of organized religion altogether. A recent study by the Pew Forum on Religion & Public Life found that about half of all Americans change their faith at least once during their lives. People change faiths for widely different reasons, from marrying someone from another religion, to moving to a new community, to finding a faith they like more.[18] One example of large-scale mobility has been the movement of Hispanics out of the Catholic Church and into various Protestant churches—what sociologist of religion Andrew Greeley has called the "worst defection in the history of the Catholic Church in the United States."[19]

Given the competitive market facing religious congregations, many have shown considerable capacity for change. Case in point: the growth of mega-churches, usually defined as Protestant congregations with more than 2,000 members.[20] Another change is the development of "post-denominational" Christianity, in which churches shed denominational doctrines, hymns, liturgy, and organizational structures for a more fluid, generic style.[21] Some of these newer churches seem to be responding to popular demand for a less content-heavy, more emotional, and "user-friendly" religious experience. In fact, some analysts argue that being able to adapt to public tastes is what has kept religion current and helps explain why the United States has higher rates of religious practice and belief than other industrialized nations.[22]

It should be noted that many of those who leave one religious tradition do not join another. According to the Pew survey, "the group that has grown the most...due to religious change is the unaffiliated population."[23]

In fact, a study that Edgell conducted of pastors and lay leaders in upstate New York found that many cited lack of time as the main problem facing their congregations.[25] National data back this up, showing that "for both men and women, long hours spent at work is related to lower levels of church attendance, less involvement in other congregational ministries and a reduced sense of the importance of religion...these problems [may be] particularly acute for workers in

RETURNING TO THE FOLD. Young people often reconnect with or participate for the first time in organized religion when they get married and have children. (MONA REEDER, DALLAS MORNING NEWS, CORBIS)

lower-paying service and blue-collar jobs, who may not have resources to pay for services that help them cope with the time squeeze."[26]

Besides lack of time, another reason for declining religious attendance among women is generational. Young people often reconnect with or participate for the first time in organized religion when they get married and have children. Starting a family seems to trigger the desire to belong to a faith community, as new parents seek help giving their children a moral and spiritual foundation for growing up. New parents also look for others like themselves to find support and community.

Today, however, women are getting married and having children later in life. This means that most adults in their early 20s are now single, and not yet inclined in large numbers to join religious communities. It used to be that young people who went to worship services and those who did not were similar in terms of marriage and family. But that is no longer the case. Now those who are religiously active are far more likely to be married than those who are not.

Young women facing economic and work stresses, mobility among friends, relationship uncertainties, questions of identity, and more, are unlikely to seek out a faith community as a place of understanding and support.

There may be a confusion of cause and effect here, whereby the family orientation of many religious institutions discourages singles from attending. For young women, this means that at a time when they may be facing economic and work stresses, mobility among friends, relationship uncertainties, questions of identity, and more, they are unlikely to seek out a faith community as a place of understanding and support.[27]

This is not to say that religious institutions are not reaching out to singles. Indeed, many are. A participant in a conversation with faith leaders in Atlanta convened for this report described efforts of her synagogue to attract young singles and build community among them. In addition to holding regular activities and events, leaders make a practice of following up with attendees, inviting them to lunch or Shabbat dinner.

There are other, less easily explained, reasons for declining religious participation among women and men. At the conversation in Atlanta, a female pastor described "regular nonmembers" in her congregation—those who show up weekly for worship

FIGURE 1

Women outnumber men in virtually every Christian tradition, but not other faith traditions

Percent of gender distribution of major religious traditions

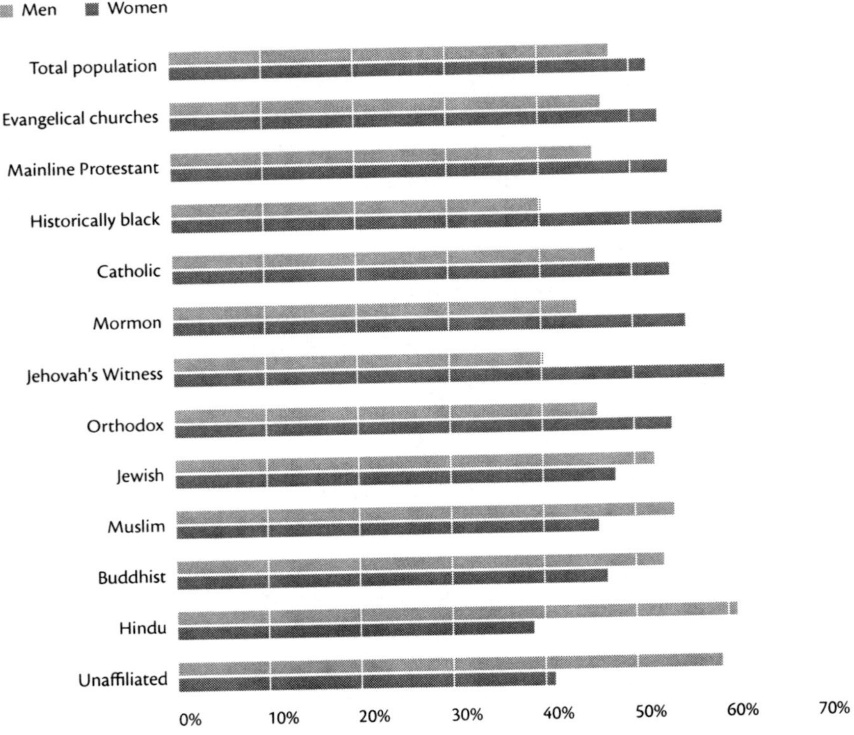

Source: Pew Forum on Religion & Public Life, *U.S. Landscape Survey* (2008): p. 63.

services and put money in the offering plate, but get no further involved. Some attend for a good sermon and music, but don't want the commitment of belonging. Others go "church hopping" because they like various aspects of each place and don't want to settle on one. The pastor said that these "regular nonmembers" have few demands. If they get sick, they don't expect a pastoral visit, nor do they expect services from the church community. The pastor described other parishioners who are active—but in specific, self-directed ways. They are not interested in serving on committees, but instead want to do projects that involve their families, such as working in a food bank or helping to build a house.

Millions of lesbian, bisexual, and transgender women are people of faith—and yet they are not welcomed as participants, members, or leaders in many religious institutions. A few denominations, such as the United Church of Christ and the Unitarian Universalist Association, are officially inclusive. Some religious institutions have no public position regarding gays, lesbians, bisexuals, and transsexuals participating and joining their congregations, while others declare homosexuality to be a sin. Increasingly, religious institutions are facing a challenge to their beliefs and practices when it comes to gays and lesbians who participate in worship services, offer their time and gifts as volunteers, contribute financially, and enrich the community in myriad ways. One participant in the Atlanta conversation with faith leaders told of her church welcoming those who'd been turned away from other churches. Her church expanded its capacity for compassion and deepened its sense of community through an AIDS ministry it created that eventually broadened its scope to care for the sick and deliver meals to those in need—programs and services that had not existed before.

TABLE 1

Women's religious affiliations

Christian	**82.4%**
Protestant	53.8%
Evangelical	26.9%
Mainline	19.0%
Historically black	8.0%
Catholic	25.0%
Mormon	1.8%
Jehovah's Witness	0.8%
Orthodox	0.6%
Other Christian	0.3%
Other religions	**4.2%**
Jewish	1.6%
Muslim	0.4%
Buddhist	0.7%
Hindu	0.3%
Other world religions	<0.3%
Other faiths	1.1%
Unaffiliated	**12.8%**
Atheist	0.9%
Agnostic	1.7%
Secular unaffiliated	4.8%
Religious unaffiliated	5.4%
Don't know/refused	**0.7%**

Source: Pew Forum on Religion & Public Life, *U.S. Religious Landscape Survey* (2008): p. 62.

Many women want to connect family, work, and faith

Despite a significant decline in women's religious participation, the fact remains that religion is central in the lives of millions of women. It offers them daily guidance and help in navigating life's complexities, as well as a way to unify their different roles. Sociologist Mary Ellen Konieczny at the University of Notre Dame discovered this in her ethnographic study of two Catholic parishes, one theologically conservative and the other more liberal. In both parishes, women said their faith helped them make decisions on a range of family issues, including the struggle over whether to leave their jobs to stay home and raise their children. Women said they were guided by the moral ideals of their faith, its practices, and by connecting with others in their church.[28]

Similar themes emerged from a series of focus groups conducted by the Catholic Church in 2002 that asked nearly 300 women in dioceses across the country about their spirituality and their work outside the home.[29] Despite geographic, racial-ethnic, and age differences, the women echoed one another in a number of areas. First, they refused to compartmentalize the different aspects of their lives, seeing spirituality as a "unifying factor" that connected work and family.

Women want the Catholic Church to see their paid work as valuable, and to recognize and utilize their skills.

In addition, women wanted the church to see their paid work as valuable, and to recognize and utilize their workplace skills. Women also wanted the church to acknowledge the time constraints they faced. When asked how the church could be of help to them, women offered a variety of suggestions, such as: Reach out to single mothers, provide support to unmarried women, invite older women to be mentors for younger women who are juggling home and work, and support legislation and policies that help working women, such as affordable child care, living wages, and more.[30]

The need to connect work, family, and faith was also echoed by Protestant women, both liberal and conservative, in interviews conducted by Emory University sociologist Tracy Scott. Conservative women saw motherhood as the most important "work" a woman could do—yet many were dissatisfied with its day-to-day realities. One young mother told Scott, "Being a mother is the largest part of my identity...but it's hard to raise kids; it's hard to be with them endless hours a day.... I know that when I work [at my paid job]... I come home and I have so much energy. If I spend all day home...by five-o'clock I'm like a wet rag."[31]

Conservative women interviewed in this survey valued the esteem, appreciation, and praise they got from working—and having their own paycheck. They liked feeling productive, contributing to the community and world, and having an identity apart from those of "wife" and "mother." When they talked about the "God-created differences between men and women," many felt that their churches encouraged domestic work as women's "real work" and family as their top priority.[32] Some women searched for biblical passages to give them guidance about "women's roles outside of 'family work.'" One woman began occasionally attending an evangelical church with fewer fundamentalist notions than her home church. It was at this new church that she heard a sermon proclaiming that there was nothing wrong with a woman having a paid job, as long as her priority remained the home. The woman told Scott: "I agree with that."[33]

Liberal women spoke of choices and struggles, too—especially choices made between job and family. Yet they did not speak of pressure "to live up to any prescribed roles" nor did they feel constrained by theological gender restrictions.[34]

Both conservative and liberal women discussed the religious notion of "calling"—in which work has spiritual meaning and purpose that provides fulfillment. The sense of being called to a vocation was stronger among conservative women, even though they were less committed than liberal women to paid work.[35] According to Scott, the notion of "calling" among conservative women was flexible, referring to any number of tasks or roles and included both paid and family work. For conservative women, the sense of being called by God justified the different choices they made and blessed their roles outside the home.[36] In contrast, liberal women spoke

FIGURE 2

Most religious traditions are majority white

The racial and ethnic composition of American religions

By percent

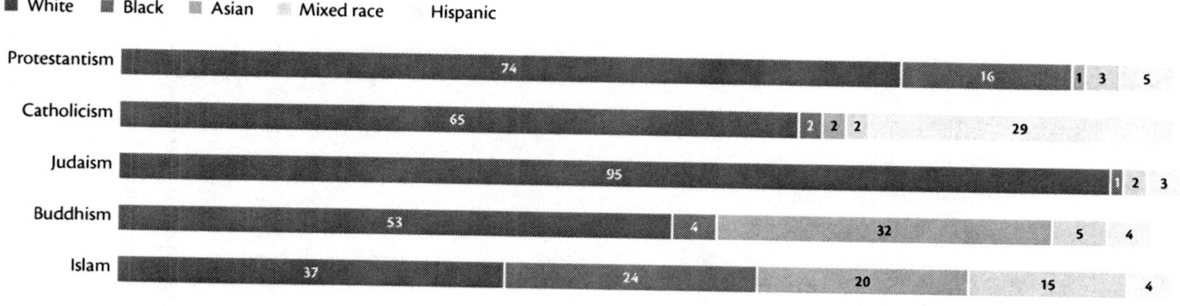

Source: Pew Forum on Religion & Public Life, U.S. *Landscape Survey* (2008): p. 44.

One of the ways churches and synagogues and faith communities have to be relevant is to reach out to the people who are in nontraditional kinds of settings. I find that my denomination has refugees from other churches and traditions that are not accepting of divorce, who are looked down upon, gays, lesbians, and people who are in any kind of nontraditional kind of family setting. The faith communities are going to be left in the dust because the world is changing. That doesn't mean we give up. We're not giving up anything. We're gaining something.

Kathy in Atlanta

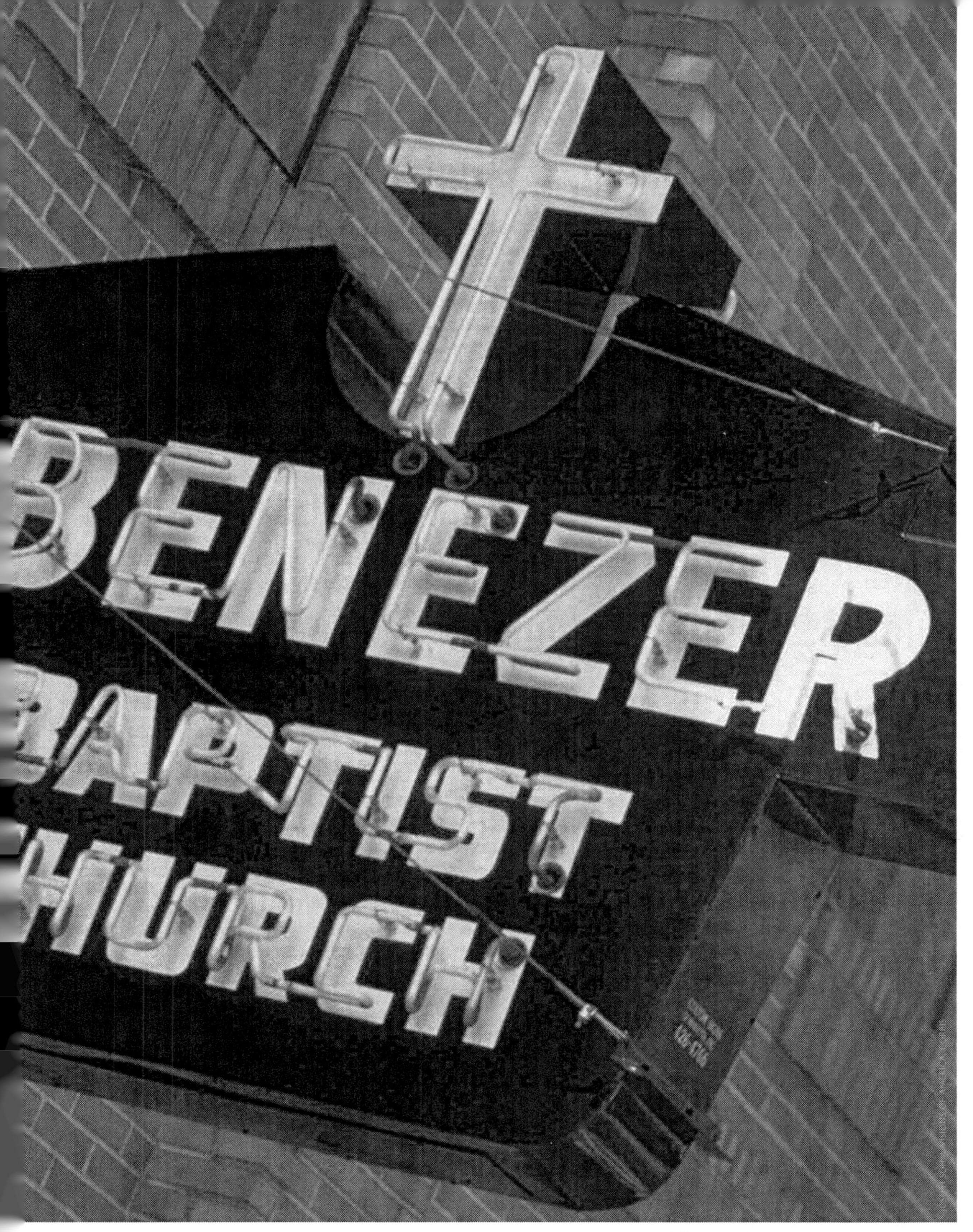
BENEZER
APTIST
HURCH

of "calling" in terms of paid work, not motherhood, and linked it to fulfillment and purpose in the world.

The centrality of religion in the lives of African American women cannot be overstated. Not only are women the backbone of many traditional black denominations, a number of which might not exist without their contributions, but faith is a basic pillar in many black women's lives. As Daphne Wiggins, associate pastor at the Union Baptist Church in Durham, North Carolina, found in her ethnographic study of two African American congregations in Georgia, spirituality and church membership not only provide practical assistance to women (help with family care, for instance) but also emotional sustenance and spiritual fortification that help them cope with the challenges of family and work. A nurse in the study who had a stressful job told Wiggins, "It's only my spirituality and my closeness with God [that] gives me that confidence. I feel confident when I'm at work, even with all the chaos going on."[37]

Not only are women the backbone of many traditional black denominations, a number of which might not exist without their contributions, but faith is a basic pillar in many black women's lives.

Religion is also a vital force in the lives of many Latinas. Although there is little research that directly speaks to the role of faith in helping Latinas grapple with paid work and family, scholars have remarked upon the active presence of religion in the lives of Hispanic men and women.[38] For women who struggle against discrimination, toil in low-wage jobs, and bear heavy domestic responsibilities, religion is often a daily source of sustenance and support. In the words of one author, "Latinas' God is a personal, living God with whom they converse daily—upon awakening, while driving to work, booting up a computer, reprimanding children, and wondering how they will possibly get through another day."[39]

One of the Jewish participants at the faith leaders' conversation in Atlanta spoke of the importance of religion in the home and of teaching religious values to one's children. "I wear the tallis in my family," she said, referring to a prayer shawl traditionally worn by males, adding that she felt women were "spiritually hard-wired" to transmit religious values. In addition to carrying out traditions in the home and contributing time and skills to synagogue, many Jewish women are leaders in faith-based organizations such as the National Council of Jewish Women, Jewish Women International, and other groups that have long and impressive histories of working on social justice issues, especially those involving women, children, and families.

Religious institutions are adapting to women's changing lives

Historically, religious institutions have held as a spiritual ideal the model of a two-parent family in which women cared for the children and home and men were the financial providers. Although many families never reflected this model—high numbers of African American, immigrant, and white working-class women were always in the workforce—the notion of a female caregiver and male breadwinner was often sanctified as the way God intended the world to be.

THE LATEST FROM THE AMERICAN PEOPLE

Q: Forty years ago just over one-third of all workers were women. Today about a half of all workers are women. Has this change been positive or negative for American society?

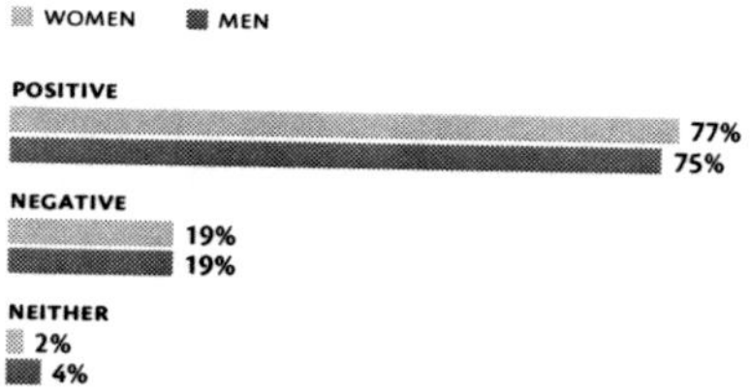

	WOMEN	MEN
POSITIVE	77%	75%
NEGATIVE	19%	19%
NEITHER	2%	4%

Source: Rockefeller/*Time* poll, 2009.

Religious institutions benefited greatly from the traditional nuclear family, especially in the post-war years. Women served as volunteers, teaching Sunday school, organizing charity efforts, devotional classes, and more. As one author wrote about synagogues, "Women emerged as the most powerful and sustaining force.... They dominated congregational activities, and their efforts made all religious functions possible."[40]

The concept of the nuclear family came crashing down in the 1960s. Divorce rates increased, women entered the workforce in record numbers, had fewer children, and challenged traditional gender norms.

"THE METHODIST FAMILY OF THE YEAR" OF 1951. Historically, religious institutions have held as a spiritual ideal the model of a traditional two-parent family, but the nuclear family became less common starting in the 1960s. [BETTMANN, CORBIS]

Religious institutions came under scrutiny as well. Women criticized male-dominated structures and fought to be ordained. They questioned patriarchal theology and created feminist doctrines of the divine. They looked for spiritual fulfillment outside religion. And they left the volunteer positions that had sustained religious institutions and led them to thrive.

In the 1980s, many conservative evangelical churches decried the dramatic transformation of the family. Blame often fell on women for "forsaking" their maternal nature and "deserting" their children for paid jobs, thus destroying the moral fabric of society. Policy issues such as child care and parental leave were caught in an ideological battle, as conservatives battled mainline Protestants, Jewish organizations, and others that supported federally funded child care.

Despite the inflammatory rhetoric that often surrounded such battles, the reality on the ground turned out to be somewhat different, as even evangelical churches had to adapt to increasing numbers of working mothers and divorced parents in their congregations. According to Penny Edgell, "as the proportion of the population who are most likely to attend church—two-parent families with children in the home—shrinks, the religious 'market' shrinks."[41]

Adapting their attitudes and beliefs

Given the traditional foundations and centuries-old beliefs of many religious institutions, it isn't surprising that there remains within them a residue of outdated views that have the veneer of truth. Often these views are unspoken, or even unconscious. But assumptions about the primacy of women's domestic responsibilities and related beliefs about the spiritual superiority of traditional families, motherhood, and restrictive sexuality can stymie religious institutions from being more creative and supportive in meeting the needs of women today.

Yet, religion exists in a spiritually competitive marketplace. Unlike ages past when the faith you were born into was likely to be the faith you died in, religious traditions today gain and lose members on an ongoing basis. And while people who shift allegiances claim a variety of reasons for doing so—from disagreeing with spiritual teachings to disapproving of the rigidity of religious institutions—the reality is that religious institutions must work to gain and retain their followers.

Many mainline Protestant denominations, such as Lutheran, Methodist, Presbyterian, and Episcopal, have shifted their views to support women's changing roles. In these churches today, there is broad acceptance of mothers' employment and diverse kinds of families—including, in some churches, same-sex couples and parents. These are also the denominations in which female clergy are most welcome and likely to be found.

Jewish faith traditions—Reform, Reconstructionist, Conservative, and Orthodox—have also changed their views toward women. Many synagogues have taken down the partition (mehitzah) that separates men and women during services, and women have taken on religious practices once exclusively controlled by men. Some researchers have found that feminism has had a beneficial impact on the Jewish community, increasing educational rates of women and raising their profile and leadership in the community. Since the early 1970s, Reform and Reconstructionist branches of Judaism have ordained women as rabbis, and women became rabbis in the Conservative branch in the 1980s.

RITES OF PASSAGE. For most Jewish women today, their bat mitzvahs happens at adolescence, but for decades this wasn't this case. That's why these 10 women close to or in their 90s who were denied this rite of passage in the 1950s and 1960s are preparing for it now. [DAVID AHNHOLTZ, *THE NEW YORK TIMES*]

The response of the Catholic Church to changes in gender roles, sexuality, and the family has been complex. Historically, Catholic churches have been somewhat more accepting of working mothers than mainline or evangelical denominations because many parishes served immigrant communities in which a number of women worked outside the home. In addition, an important dimension of

Catholic social teaching emphasizes providing for the needy and vulnerable. For many Catholics, this support has included government assistance for programs on poverty, health care, and more. Still, many Catholic leaders—all of them male and unmarried—maintain a rigidly conservative stance on abortion, contraception, sexual education, and divorce—all issues of elemental importance to women. Female leadership in the church remains constrained, since women are forbidden to be priests. However, Catholic women have shaped history as nuns, religious activists, and heads of faith-based institutions delivering much-needed services and fighting social and economic injustice.

An important dimension of Catholic social teaching emphasizes providing for the needy and vulnerable. This support has included government assistance for programs on poverty, health care, and more.

White evangelical churches have also found themselves forced to adapt to societal change. Despite their preaching and pronouncements, mothers in these congregations went to work, children went to child care, and husbands and wives got divorced. However, the adaptation by evangelicals was neither easy nor swift. Initial reaction to the feminist movement in the 1970s was harsh. Leaders criticized evangelical feminists who challenged claims that women's subordination to men within marriage was biblically ordained, and they criticized mothers for working outside the home. As recently as 1998, the Southern Baptist Convention adopted a statement declaring that "A wife is to submit herself graciously to the servant leadership of her husband, even as the church willingly submits to the headship of Christ."[42]

Despite such sexist statements by religious leaders, church communities have begun to speak in a different voice—one that emphasized marital partnerships and male and female complementarity[43] in which men and women were created differently but not unequally. A "pragmatic egalitarianism" took hold in many churches.[44] At the same time, many evangelical churches became less condemning of divorce, shifting from denouncement to silence. As congregations included more single parents and blended families, divorce became less decried as a spiritual and social ill. Evangelical leaders turned to other issues, such as abortion and same-sex marriage, to blame for threatening the soul of America.[45] The advantage of those two issues was that they were "external sins" that did not visibly affect most evangelicals, while an issue such as divorce was "too close for comfort."[46]

THE LATEST FROM THE AMERICAN PEOPLE

Q: Do you agree or disagree: Husbands and wives today are negotiating more than earlier generations about the rules on relationships, work , and family?

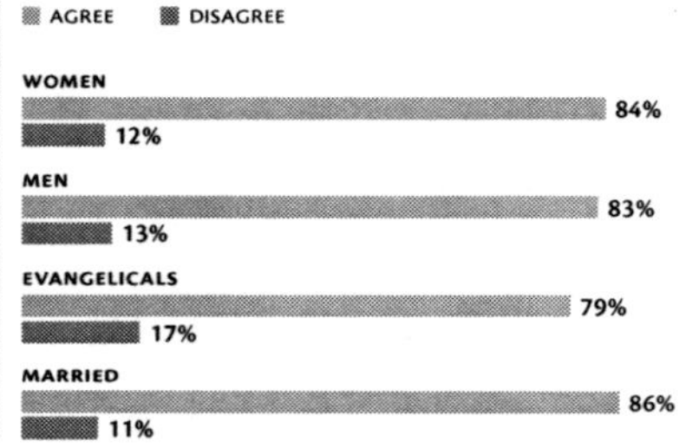

Source: Rockefeller/*Time* poll, 2009.

In reality today, many evangelical churches support men and women as equal decision-makers in the home, and evangelical men appear to be as engaged as other men, if not more so, in day-to-day parenting.[47] Moreover, although evangelical mothers have lower rates of workforce participation, their numbers since the 1990s have been rising.[48] As Penny Edgell observes, "Lived religion blunts the sharp edge of ideological zeal while new understandings of the good family evolve. This lived religion is what most Americans encounter and what shapes hearts and minds."[49]

Offering new programs and services

In addition to shifting their views, religious organizations have been adapting their programs and ministries to respond to the changing family. Typical shifts include moving the time of worship and other activities and offering new kinds of services. For instance, many activities for families are no longer offered during the daytime when most parents work, and many denominations now have programs for single parents.[50]

Child care is of particular importance to working parents. Although some religious institutions have long provided it, the growth in mothers' workforce participation since the 1970s prompted more religious institutions to move into this area.[51] Between 1992 and 2008, there was a 76.4 percent increase in child care provided in Protestant institutions, a

52.6 percent increase offered by Catholic institutions, and a 47.7 percent increase by Jewish institutions.[52] Today, one-quarter of children under the age of 5 who are in center-based child care are in programs located in churches, synagogues, and other places of worship.[53] This figure may even underestimate the proportion of children in religiously affiliated child care because many children are in "faith-affiliated" and "faith-infused programs" that are located outside places of worship.[54]

Conservative Protestant churches also are increasingly providing child care, driven in part by the desire to teach religious values through these programs.[55] In fact, one study has found that although liberal churches tend to be more symbolically accepting of diverse lifestyles and nonrestrictive gender roles, they offer fewer programs and services for women and their families than conservative churches do. Conservative churches have also been more likely to find innovative ways to adjust the schedules of their children's programs to attract kids amid the competition of secular activities.[56]

One point to highlight is that the Great Recession we're in has greatly increased the need for services provided by religious and faith-based institutions. These institutions are close to their communities, witnessing job losses, home foreclosures, and members of their congregations and communities going without health insurance and food. At a time when social-service programs can be out of reach or nonexistent for many people, religious and faith-based institutions are among the places that provide support.[57] Besides offering prayer and spiritual guidance, many religious organizations offer practical assistance through food and clothing banks, emergency loan programs, job retraining, and more—and doing

BREAKING STAINED GLASS BARRIERS. Katharine Jefferts Schori is the first female priest to lead a national church in the nearly 500-year-old Anglican Communion. [MATTHEW CAVANAUGH, EPA, CORBIS]

NEW REVIVALISTS. The Grand Opening of Lakewood Church's new Central Campus. Over 57,000 people packed the Sanctuary and video overflow rooms. Houston's Lakewood Baptist Church spent over $95 million to turn the former NBA sports arena into one of the largest churches in the country. {NINA BERMAN, REDUX PICTURES}

so at a time when their budgets are shrinking. Many religious institutions are also advocating for public policies such as universal health care as part of their mission.

"Churches are at the forefront of this recession," said a participant at the faith leaders' conversation in Atlanta. "People are reducing their tithes and offerings... yet more are coming to church with needs. The rent is due. The car broke down. Church is a refuge. How do we help them?"[58]

Religious institutions with immigrant congregations are often active providers of social services, despite the fact that in some disadvantaged communities they lack the resources to offer a wide array of programs.

In addition to responding to these urgent needs, religious institutions provide ongoing services, such as marriage and family counseling, programs for senior citizens, youth mentoring, and after-school programs.[59] A 2000 study of Islamic mosques found similar services for families. For instance, 74 percent offered marital or family counseling, 84 percent provided cash benefits to families or individuals, and 16 percent provided child care or preschool.[60] Educational programs were also important: 21 percent of mosques had a full-time Islamic school, while 71 percent provided a weekend school for either children or adults.

Religious institutions with immigrant congregations are often active providers of social services, despite the fact that they lack the resources in some disadvantaged communities to offer a wide array of programs.[61] In addition to youth groups and summer camp, many immigrant congregations, including those of non-Christian faiths, hold their own "Sunday school" as a way to teach children their religious beliefs.[62] One in-depth study of immigrant congregations found that a number sponsored women's groups to provide social services, especially to other immigrant women. A Muslim woman in the study said that their activities focused on areas "where women have always taken a leadership role behind the scenes," such as helping children, the sick, divorced women, and in other areas of need.[63]

Among religious institutions that offer the most programs and services are mega-churches. For many mega-churches, their sense of mission is intimately tied to an entrepreneurial business model whereby they aim to be responsive to their followers—or "clients." This spiritual-business model often relies on a sizeable budget that allows a dazzling variety of services and amenities, such as health clubs, cafes, and movie theaters, to attract and retain followers. For instance, Southeast Christian Church in Louisville, Kentucky, offers 16 basketball courts, a Cybex health club, a bank, a rock-climbing wall, eateries, and shops.[64] And Joel Osteen's Lakewood Church in Houston, Texas, offers drama, dance, and video workshops; finance and tax classes; activities for children of all ages; marriage-strengthening classes; programs for women including movie nights, autism support groups, and Bible study; service opportunities; and more. According to a 2002 *New York Times* article, "these churches are becoming civic in a way unimaginable since the 13th century and its cathedral towns. No longer simply places to worship, they have become part resort, part mall, part extended family and part town square."[65]

For many mega-churches, their sense of mission is intimately tied to an entrepreneurial business model whereby they aim to be responsive to their followers—or "clients."

Spirituality is growing fast

Spirituality in America is growingly rapidly, especially among women. Books, retreats, workshops, rituals, and meditation practices are gaining followers among women who are religious, and those who are not. At first glance, there might seem to be little commonality among spiritual practices that range from massage therapy and sweat lodges to Zen meditation, 12-step programs, feminist nature rituals, and fasting.[66] And it is true that many practices called "spiritual" are so simply because that is how their followers describe them. Yet among its varied expressions, spirituality is often thought to fall into three categories: spirituality that is separate and distinct from organized religion; spirituality that is in conflict with organized religion; and spirituality that complements, or is part of, organized religion.[67]

For many African American women, religiously inspired spirituality offers an effective way to respond to work-related stress. In one research study, 97 percent of black women said that spiritual practices helped them cope with stresses at work. Spirituality was the most frequently named coping mechanism, with many women saying they prayed "a great deal."[68] In addition to prayer, African American women relied upon their trust in God, in their hope for a miracle, and in the renewal of their faith as they faced difficulties on the job. For these women, major stresses included the overwhelming demands of their job, the need to make ends meet, and working with prejudiced co-workers.[69]

Spirituality was also important to the Catholic women in the focus groups discussed earlier. A number of them identified "nonreligious" activities as

RELIEVING STRESS, FINDING STRENGTH. For many women, spirituality is found in yoga and other exercise routines. {LAIF, REDUX PICTURES}

spiritually renewing, such as gardening, walking on the beach, yoga, poetry, music, and exercise.

Younger women are more likely to be involved in spirituality than older women. They are more likely to choose personal experience over church doctrine as the best way to understand God[70] and to create their own belief system from a variety of sources, such as friends, websites, magazine articles, TV shows, books, and movies. Because fewer of them are involved in organized religion, their spiritual beliefs and practices tend to be separate from religion.[71]

There are a number of reasons for the growth of spirituality among women. It is flexible and portable, able to fit into a busy schedule of work, chores, and travel.

For many women, doing yoga or meditating each morning can provide them with greater spiritual focus and energy than going to weekly worship services. This is especially true if worship services are scheduled at a time that competes with family activities and chores. Reading spiritual self-help books can provide specific methods and techniques for self enhancement—a toning up of the soul, just as the gym tones up the body.

> *There are a number of reasons for the growth of spirituality among women. It is flexible and portable, able to fit into a busy schedule of work, chores, and travel.*

Another reason for spirituality's appeal is that it doesn't claim a specific set of doctrines or beliefs to conflict with or supplant the beliefs of organized religion. The fluidity of spirituality seems appealing to increasing numbers of Americans, many of whom have "only a vague denominational identification" and are unclear about which religious group they belong to.[72] In addition, as people travel longer distances to reach houses of worship, spirituality can feel more convenient and efficient. Furthermore, the once-unique role of clergy in answering spiritual questions has been supplanted by a wide variety of sources, including the Internet, which can answer questions instantly and anonymously in the comfort of one's home. Finally, the community that women once found in religious institutions is now being found in the workplace, at the gym, and other places where women spend their days.

Not everyone thinks the growth of spirituality is a good thing. In his essay "Against Spirituality," the late Rabbi Arnold Jacob Wolf argues that the Kabbalah and other forms of Jewish spirituality are undermining the deep sense of social connectivity, mutual responsibility, self-criticism, historical roots, and intellectual rigor of Judaism.[73] Wolf quotes Reverend Donna Schoper, who warns of the "dangerous lure of spirituality" for all religions. She says, "Amateurish tai chi and yoga, quasi-Buddhist meditation, and New Age prayers are a far cry from the ancient practice of the Sabbath."[74] Schoper goes on to complain about highly personalized spirituality replacing organized religion. Spirituality can mire a person in the self, she says, and cause him or her to lose sight of the sacred. According to Schoper, "religion steeps people in its long history of reflection on ethics" and at its best "offers time and space for spiritual experience." In contrast, "spirituality gives us a quick fix that fits into our fast-paced insular lifestyle."[75]

Others are not so critical. Theologian Sandra Schneiders, emeritus professor at the Jesuit School of Theology, sees spirituality as an important vehicle for transcendence. The paradox of religious institutions, she says, is that they are culturally based and can be hypocritical, rigid, corrupt, and reflect the biases of the larger society.[76] However, she defends organized religion for its capacity to initiate people into "an authentic tradition of spirituality," giving them "companions on the journey and tested wisdom by which to live," as well as support in times of suffering.[77] Schneiders goes on to say that when people leave religious institutions to "find a small group of like-minded companions in exile, they are left without the corrective criticism of an historically tested community and the public scrutiny that any society focuses on recognized groups within it. And they also lose the leverage which would enable them to influence systemically either church or society."[78]

Source: Rockefeller/*Time* poll, 2009.

This last point is especially important for working women, since religious institutions can be strong allies and advocates for a social agenda and public policies that help women better fulfill their roles as parents and workers. Schneiders argues against a "privatized spirituality," which she likens to "social cocooning," claiming that it can be naive and narcissistic, and a private pursuit[79] rather than a disciplined and committed participation in community. It is important to be outward looking as well as inward looking, focusing on social, as well as personal, transformation.

Where do we go from here?

As more women become the breadwinners in their families and soon the majority of workers, the stresses and demands in their lives will grow. So will their need for support, sustenance, and services. It may be that women will continue to leave organized religion if institutions don't respond to their needs. Already, more and more women are patching together a crazy quilt of religious practices and spiritual activities in order to find a space for reflection and wholeness in their lives. However, they need something more. They need religious institutions to listen to their voices and pay attention to the complicated reality of their lives.

As women strive to integrate work, family, and faith, religious institutions must also do their part. They must put forth a moral vision of what it truly means to value women and families, and lay out steps for achieving that vision. This means working for public policies that tangibly support families and make it easier for women (and men) to be both good parents and employees. It means valuing women's leadership talents and skills—and eradicating outdated customs that value men above women. Finally, it means re-invigorating sacred teachings on compassion, dignity, justice, and equality to speak out forcefully on behalf of women and their families today.

ENDNOTES

1 "Laity, Marriage, Family Life and Youth: Diocesan Focus Groups (Part 3)," available at http://www.usccb.org/laity/women/focusgroups3.shtml (last accessed August 2009).

2 Ibid.

3 Kathy McDowell, conversation with faith leaders in Atlanta, GA, July 20, 2009. This conversation was part of a series convened by Maria Shriver to collect women's and men's views for this report.

4 There is dispute over this trend, with some scholars arguing that there has not been a decline. See Stanley Presser and Mark Chaves, "Is Religious Service Attendance Declining?" *Journal for the Scientific Study of Religion* 46 (3) (September 2007): 417–423. See also Holley Ulbrich and Myles Wallace, "Women's Work Force Status and Church Attendence," *Journal for the Scientific Study of Religion* 23 (4) (December 1984): 341–350, which argued that workforce participation alone would not account for long term projections of decline.

5 Pew Forum on Religion & Public Life, "U.S. Religious Landscape Survey: Religious Beliefs and Practices: Diverse and Politically Relevant" (June 2008), p. 29.

6 Ibid., p. 38.

7 Ibid., p. 8.

8 Pew Forum on Religion & Public Life, "U.S. Religious Landscape Survey: Religious Affiliation: Diverse and Dynamic," p. 62.

9 Pew Forum on Religion & Public Life, "A Religious Portrait of African-Americans" (Jan. 30, 2009), p. 4.

10 Pew Forum on Religion & Public Life, "A Religious Portrait of African-Americans," pp. 63–64.

11 Larry L. Hunt, "Religion, Gender, and the Hispanic Experience in the United States: Catholic/Protestant Differences in Religious Involvement, Social Status, and Gender-Role Attitudes," *Social Forces* 43 (2) (2001): 139–60.

12 Ibid., p. 41.

13 Milagros Peña and Lisa M. Frehill, "Latina Religious Practice: Analyzing Cultural Dimensions in Measures of Religiosity," *Journal for the Scientific Study of Religion* 37 (4) (1998): 620–635.

14 Ana María Díaz-Stevens, "The Saving Grace: The Matriarchal Core of Latino Catholicism," *Latino Studies Journal* 4:3 (1993): 60–78.

15 Helen Rose Ebaugh and Janet Saltzman Chafetz, "Agents for Cultural Reproduction and Structural Change: The Ironic Role of Women in Immigrant Religious Institutions," *Social Forces* 78 (2) (1999): 585–613.

16 Ibid., p. 44.

17 R. Stephen Warner, "The De-Europeanization of American Christianity," Paper presented at the annual meeting of the American Sociological Association, San Francisco, CA, Aug. 14, 2004.

18 Pew Forum on Religion & Public Life, "Faith in Flux: Change in Religious Affiliation in the U.S." (April 2009).

19 Andrew Greeley, "Defection Among Hispanics (Updated)," *America* 177 (8) (1997): 12–13.

20 Scott Thumma, Dave Travis, and Warren Bird, "Megachurches Today: Summary of Research Findings" (Hartford: Hartford Institute for Religion Research, 2001).

21 Donald E. Miller, "Postdenominational Christianity in the Twenty-First Century," *Annals of the American Academy of Political and Social Science* 558 (1) (1998): 196–210.

22 R. Stephen Warner, "Work in Progress Toward a New Paradigm for the Sociological Study of Religion in the United States," *American Journal of Sociology* 98 (5) (March 1993): 1044–93; For a contrary view, see Pippa Norris and Ronald Inglehart, *Sacred and Secular: Religion and Politics Worldwide* (Cambridge: Cambridge University Press, 2004).

23 Pew Forum on Religion & Public Life, "Faith in Flux: Change in Religious Affiliation in the U.S." (April 2009), p. 1.

24 Penny Edgell, *Religion and Family in a Changing Society* (Princeton: Princeton University Press 2006), pp. 64–65.

25 "It's a Matter of Time: Exploring the Relationship between Time Spent at Work and at Church," available at http://hirr.hartsem.edu/research/edgell-time.html (last accessed August 2009).

26 Ibid.

27 Robert Wuthnow, *After the Baby Boomers: How Twenty- and Thirty-Somethings Are Shaping the Future of American Religion* (Princeton: Princeton University Press, 2007), p. 49.

28 Mary Ellen Konieczny, *The Spirit's Tether: Family, Work, and Religion among American Catholic,* (forthcoming).

29 "Laity, Marriage, Family Life and Youth: Women's Spirituality in the Workplace: A Compilation of Diocesan Focus Group Reports," available at http://www.usccb.org/laity/women/focusgroups.shtml (last accessed August 2009).

30 Ibid.

31 Tracy L. Scott, "Choices, Constraints, and Calling: Conservative Protestant Women and the Meaning of Work," *International Journal of Sociology and Social Policy* 22 (1/2/3) (2002): 1–38, see p. 15.

32 Scott, "Choices, Constraints, and Calling," p. 19.

33 Ibid., pp. 19–20.

34 Ibid., p. 26.

35 Ibid., p. 14.

36 Ibid., p. 28.

37 Daphne C. Wiggins, *Righteous Content: Black Women Speak of Church and Faith* (New York: New York University Press, 2004), p. 79.

38 Pew Hispanic Center, "Changing Faiths: Latinos and the Transformation of American Religion" (2007).

39 Laura M. Padilla, "Latinas and Religion: Subordination or State of Grace?" *U.C. Davis Law Review* 33 (4) (1999–2000): 978.

40 Hasia R. Diner, *The Jews of the United States, 1654 to 2000* (Berkeley: University of California Press, 2004), p. 301.

41 Penny Edgell Becker, "Congregations Adapting to Changes in Work and Family: A Report from the Religion and Family Project." Working Paper (University of Minnesota Religion and Family Project, 1999).

42 Margaret Bendroth, "Last Gasp Patriarchy: Women and Men in Conservative American Protestantism," *Muslim World* 91(1/2) (Spring 2001): 45–54.

43 Sally K. Gallagher, "The Marginalization of Evangelical Feminism," *Sociology of Religion* 65 (3) (2004): 228.

44 Gallagher, "The Marginalization of Evangelical Feminism," pp. 228–230.

45 Randall Balmer, *Thy Kingdom Come: How the Religious Right Distorts the Faith and Threatens America: An Evangelical's Lament* (New York: Basic Books, 2006), pp. 25–35.

46 Balmer, *Thy Kingdom Come*, p. 10.

47 Gallagher, "Marginalization of Evangelical Feminism," p. 229; W. Bradford Wilcox and John P. Bartkowski, "The Evangelical Family Paradox: Conservative Rhetoric, Progressive Practice," *The Responsive Community* 9 (3) (1999): 34–39.

48 Darren E. Sherkat and Christopher G. Ellison, "Recent Developments and Current Controversies in the Sociology of Religion," *Annual Review of Sociology* 25 (1999): 372.

49 Penny Edgell, *Religion and Family in a Changing Society* (Princeton, NJ: Princeton University Press 2006), p. 5.

50 Ibid, pp. 133, 138.

51 "Sacred Places, Civic Purposes: Child Care Conference Event Transcript," available at http://pewforum.org/events/?EventID=6 (last accessed August 2009).

52 Roger Neugebauer, "Status Report #6: Trends in Religious-Affiliated Child Care" *Exchange* 184 (Nov/Dec 2008): 12–14.

53 National Center for Education Statistics, "Initial Results from the 2005 NHES Early Childhood Program Participation Survey" (2006), p. 59.

54 Monica Rohacek, Gina Adams, and Kathleen Snyder, "Child Care Centers, Child Care Vouchers, and Faith-Based Organizations" (Washington: Urban Institute, 2008).

55 Neugebauer, "Status Report #6: Trends in Religious-Affiliated Child Care."

56 Penny Edgell Becker, "Congregations Adapting to Changes."

57 Ram A. Cnaan, Edwin I. Hernández, and Charlene C. McGrew, "Latino Congregations and Social Service: The Philadelphia Story" (Notre Dame University: Institute for Latino Studies: February 2006).

58 Conversation with faith leaders in Atlanta, GA, July 20, 2009.

59 John Green, "American Congregations and Social Service Programs: Results of a Survey" (Albany: The Roundtable on Religion and Social Welfare Policy, 2007).

60 Ihsan Bagby, Paul M. Perl, and Bryan T. Froehle, "The Mosque in America: A National Portrait" (Washington: Council on American-Islamic Relations, Apr. 26, 2001), p. 42.

61 Cnaan, Hernández, and McGrew, "Latino Congregations and Social Service."

62 Ebaugh and Chafetz, "Agents for Cultural Reproduction," p. 595.

63 Ibid., p. 598.

64 Patricia Leigh Brown, "Megachurches as Minitowns," *The New York Times*, May 9, 2002, available at http://www.nytimes.com/2002/05/09/garden/megachurches-as-minitowns.html.

65 Ibid.

66 Sandra M. Schneiders, "Religion vs. Spirituality: A Contemporary Conundrum," *Spiritus* 3 (2) 2003: 175.

67 Ibid., pp. 164–166.

68 Denise N. A. Bacchus, "Coping with Work-Related Stress: A Study of the Use of Coping Resources Among Professional Black Women" *Journal of Ethnic and Cultural Diversity in Social Work* 17(1) (2008): 70, 74.

69 Ibid., p. 69.

70 Wuthnow, *After the Baby Boomers*, p. 133.

71 Ibid.

72 Pew Forum on Religion & Public Life, "U.S. Religious Landscape Survey" (2008), p. 2.

73 Arnold Jacob Wolf, "Against Spirituality," *Judaism* 50 (3) (June 2001): 362–365.

74 Ibid., p. 365.

75 Ibid.

76 Schneiders, "Religion vs. Spirituality," p. 171.

77 Ibid., p. 172.

78 Ibid.

79 Ibid., p. 177.

Life's Teachers

By Patricia Kempthorne, founder and executive director, Twiga Foundation, Inc., promoting family consciousness at home, in the workplace, and in the community

I am the daughter of a liquor salesman who served in World War II and who didn't believe life was fair. I was told marketing and finance were the keys to success, but I should be a home economics teacher or an English teacher. So I sought a business degree just to prove I could. I have built coalitions and started businesses. I have worked with women and men in an attempt to change the way we balance our work life and our life's work. I took on too many committee meetings and too much commitment to prove I had a right to be here on earth.

I am the spouse of a mayor, a U.S. senator, a governor, and a cabinet member and have only been married once. I am the mother of two extraordinary children and the grandmother of the most precious grandson possible.

I don't know for sure what my grandmother felt at 24 as she crossed the Atlantic and the span of this nation as a homesteader and bride in an arranged marriage. I give this educated, articulate, and adventuresome women credit for the courage she passed on to us to keep taking risks and push against the tide.

I can't imagine what my mother at 26 was hoping for when leukemia quickly took her life and left a grieving husband and three young children. I read a letter she wrote a week before we lost her that praised the rain for refreshing the earth and her family for sharing her burdens.

I know more about and admire the tenacity of my daughter today, a stay-at-home mom, finishing her MBA and working her keyboard in the virtual world, often with her son on her lap, to grow her business and expand her opportunities.

Because of all of them, because of what I learned from freedoms fought for and paths taken, and because of the composure and compassion I observed and then exercised when confronting challenges, I believe this is the best time for both women and men to define our purpose and our roles in the future for our families, our workplaces, and our communities. Working side by side and challenging one another with reason and passion, life will reveal itself and will lead us to that purpose

I believe this is the best time for both women and men to define our purpose and our roles in the future for our families, our workplaces, and our communities.

Goals and Values

By Anna Deavere Smith, an artist in residence at the Center for American Progress and a Tony Award-nominated and Pulitzer Prize-winning actress

As a child in an African American community at the advent of the civil rights movement and the women's liberation movement, I saw most of the educated women around me trapped in segregation, condensing their talents into primarily two directions: teaching or nursing. The women around me had modest means, but they were extraordinarily generous with their time and their concern. If the women around me had not dedicated their professional lives to educating all African American children, then legislation and social activism would not have had their necessary partner and the transformation we saw would not have been possible.

The capacity to have concern for the vulnerable, and to animate that concern into actions that protect and lift up the vulnerable, is a talent. It is a talent just as being able to decimate someone on the tennis court, in a court of law, or in business is a talent. Which talent should we cultivate in women and in men? That's our challenge today. And women must help make the right choice for all of us.

Are we hoping that women will be in more positions of power, running companies, sitting on high courts, serving in the military? Is the goal to have a woman president, more women four star generals, more women's names in the names of law firms, more women on Wall Street, more woman leading correctional facilities? In other words, is the goal to look at ways for women to gain influence in our culture by competing and potentially dominating in traditional ways?

Or will an increased presence of women mean a shift in values? Will the increased presence of women result in increased concern for the vulnerable and a healthier atmosphere for social justice? A more robust public sphere? Will the increased presence of women ensure an atmosphere where all children get a fair chance in education and everyone has proper health care?

Not necessarily. And indeed that might not even be a goal for some people. Since the women's liberation movement of the '60s, more women run companies (not enough to be sure), govern states, serve in the military, sit on high courts, run prisons and prison systems, and compete in sports, including boxing and wrestling. Yet we do not see a full transformation of values. If anything, our culture's overarching values—greed and competition—have increased over the past two decades.

The capacity to have concern for the vulnerable, and to animate that concern into actions that protect and lift up the vulnerable, is a talent.

The reason: Power still rests with men. Their values reward those who dominate and even abuse the vulnerable—values that restrict care to immediate families rather than larger communities. Because of this, we as a people lack imagination about extending circles of care beyond me and mine. If this were not the case, we would have more equitable education and health care systems in this country. This needs to change. Women can make it happen.

Lusty

By Miriam W. Yeung, executive director, National Asian Pacific American Women's Forum

One morning last summer my pregnant partner rolled out of bed and exclaimed, "Call the midwife!" At exactly 3 hours and 50 minutes from that moment, my daughter, Penelope, pushed her way out into this big bad world and gave a "lusty" cry to let us all know that she had arrived.

Lusty. Now isn't that an interesting word? Commonly used to describe the strong, robust cry that you want your newborn child to score on the Apgar Scale, according to the American Heritage Dictionary, lusty can also mean:

1. Full of vigor or vitality; robust
2. Powerful; strong: a lusty cry
3. Lustful
4. Merry; joyous.

Wow, what an adjective! But then why do I feel so shy about using it?

Maybe it's my good immigrant Asian girl upbringing that cautions me to never talk about or acknowledge anything remotely having to do with sex, which of course is what most Americans think of when they hear the word—never mind the definitions in the dictionary. I think maybe it's not classy. And maybe I'm afraid that bringing it up will reinforce bad stereotypes about lesbians.

Or maybe it's because lusty women are the number one thing misogynists hate. And like it or not, we've all internalized aspects of misogyny (and racism and homophobia) for so long that we come to deny our most basic feelings and instincts.

The fact is, lustiness is exactly what we need in a woman's nation. While we can celebrate women entering the workforce at equal rates to men, no woman's nation is going to be complete without reproductive justice and sexual liberation. Women need the ability to make the best choices for themselves about their bodies, their families, and their communities. And for that to happen, there needs to be a lot more flexibility, creativity, and acknowledgement of the ways families really work.

I consider myself lucky in the creativity department. My partner Abigail is a pre-kindergarten teacher in a progressive New York City public school and I run a small national nonprofit. Both jobs require quick thinking and deep reserves of ingenuity. Without those pesky predefined gender roles, we've always shared our family responsibilities almost entirely equitably (I'm better at building Ikea furniture but she's more brave about mice). We both cut our teeth as AIDS activists so we have a deep appreciation for the ways networks of friends come together as chosen family to take care of each other.

Our daughter Penelope has a wonderful network of adults who love her and most of them, like me, are not biologically related to her at all. But sometimes love is not enough. Though I was there at conception, I have no legal relationship to Penelope until I "adopt" her. While New York City offers Abigail and me a lot of rights as domestic partners, we're nobodies if we venture outside of the five boroughs. And while we're lucky that there are so many lesbian and gay parents around us that we're never the only ones, or the first ones, I know that this is not true for many of the other 10 million children raised by lesbian, gay, bisexual, or transgender parents in the United States. In the end, while there may be some challenges in our biracial lesbian household, we're grateful that both of us are creating the home that works for our lives and that we get to create a world where our daughter can have as many opportunities as any other kid.

When I think about what kind of world I want my daughter to grow up in, I hope it's a lusty one. I hope that she will be able to be her highest, biggest, fullest, most robust self in the world. I hope she feels her vitality through working hard at jobs that enhance her. I want her to define her gender in ways that make her feel whole and authentic. I want her to come to understand, appreciate, and help build a just and peaceful world. I want for her a world in which she'll be able to safely proclaim her sexual desire, her lust, no matter her sexual orientation. And I wish her the same joy that I've been able to attain through my communities of families, biological and chosen.

As women in this nation, let's be reminded by our first moments of life to cry powerfully, live vigorously, and celebrate our sexualities joyously. Let's all remember to be a little more lusty.

LYNN GOLDSMITH, CORBIS

Where Have You Gone, Roseanne Barr?

The media rarely portray women as they really are, as everyday breadwinners and caregivers

By Susan J. Douglas

It's October 2009, and after a hard day at work—or no day of work since you've been laid off—and maybe tending to children or aging parents as well, you click on the remote. On any given evening, in fictional television, you will see female police chiefs, surgeons, detectives, district attorneys, partners in law firms and, on "24," a female president of the United States. Reality TV offers up the privileged "real" housewives of New York, Atlanta, and New Jersey, all of whom devote their time to shopping or taking their daughters to acting coaches. Earlier in the evening, the nightly news programs, and the cable channels as well, feature this odd mix: highly paid and typically very attractive women as reporters (and on CBS, even as the anchor) and, yet, minimal coverage of women and the issues affecting them.

Many of us, especially those who grew up with "Leave It to Beaver" and "Father Knows Best," are delighted to see "The Closer" (Kyra Sedgwick) as an accomplished boss and crime solver, Dr. Bailey (Chandra Wilson) as the take-no-prisoners surgeon on "Grey's Anatomy," and Shirley Schmidt (Candice Bergen) as a no-nonsense senior partner on reruns of "Boston Legal." Finally, women at or near the top, holding jobs previously reserved for men, and doing so successfully!

But wait. What's wrong with these fantasy portraits of power? And what are the consequences of such fantasies? In short, what happened to everyday women in the media? Where is Roseanne Barr when we need her?

Fantasies of power

The profound gap between media images and lived reality

So here is the unusual conjuncture facing us in the early 21st century, and especially amid the Great Recession: Women's professional success and financial status are significantly overrepresented in the mainstream media, suggesting that women indeed "have it all." Yet in real life, even as most women work, there are far too few women among the highest ranks of the professions and millions of everyday women struggle to make ends meet and to juggle work and family. "Roseanne" humorously balanced that almost impossible mix, engaging audiences of millions, men and women alike, because of its cheeky take on everyday situations. By contrast, what much of the media give us today are little more than fantasies of power.

Here is the unusual conjuncture facing us in the early 21st century, and especially amid the Great Recession: Women's professional success and financial status are significantly overrepresented in the mainstream media, suggesting that women indeed "have it all." So what much of the media have been giving us, then, are little more than fantasies of power.

Why should policymakers pay attention to media images of women? Because the media—and especially (although not exclusively) the news media—may not succeed in telling us what to think, but they certainly do succeed in telling us what to think about. This is called agenda setting, and thus it matters if the real lives of most women are nowhere on the agenda, or if the agenda promotes the fantasy that full equality is now a reality for all women. And policymaking matters because the news media typically follow the lead of political elites in Washington.

If the president, or Congress, make an issue such as "ending welfare as we know it" a top priority, the news media will cover the debates around welfare, which will invariably focus some attention on poor women and their families. Without prominent politicians emphasizing the ongoing pay gap between men and women, or the continuing child care crisis in our country, and proposing major legislation to address such issues, the news media will rarely take up such topics on their own.

This essay argues, then, that it is time to consider the rather profound contradictions between image and reality currently facing us, and to examine the consequences they might have on public policy and on the lives of women and their families. These contradictions include:

- Women's occupations on television that bear scant resemblance to the jobs women actually hold
- Successful, attractive women journalists in front of the camera that masks how vastly outnumbered women are by men as experts and pundits
- The hype of the nontrend of mothers "opting out" of the workplace rather than the real lives of mothers as breadwinners
- Young women in America portrayed as shallow, cat-fighting sex objects obsessed with their appearances and shopping
- The dismissive coverage of powerful, successful women versus their real achievements
- The denigration of feminism—which is a movement important to the well-being of men, women, and children—as somehow irrelevant to the realities of the workplace and family life in the 21st century

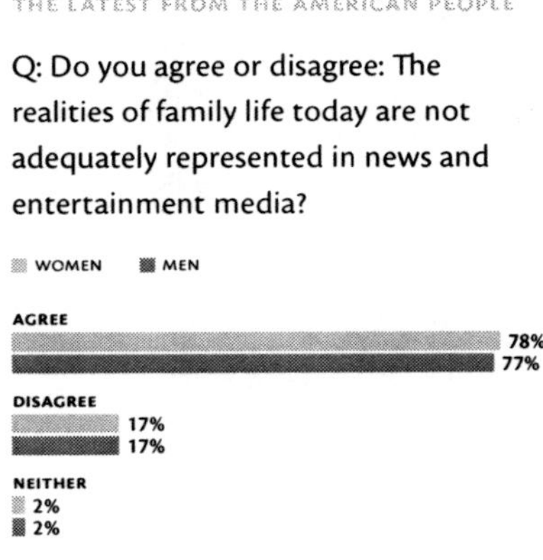

Source: Rockefeller/*Time* poll, 2009.

What might the repercussions of these misrepresentations be? Well, it's misleading for the media to imply that full equality for women is real—that now they can be or do anything they want—but then

BRIDEZILLA? In this photo from WE TV, 20 brides-to-be dive into a giant wedding cake in New York's Times Square in search of a winning raffle ticket. The event kicked-off season two of WE: Women's Entertainment's original series, "Bridezilla," the reality program that seriously overplays the planning of weddings. [DIANE BONDAREFF, WE TV, AP]

simultaneously suggest that most women prefer domesticity over the workplace. This reinforces the notion that women and men together no longer need to pursue greater gender equality at work and at home. Roseanne Barr, for one, would never stand for it.

That's why this essay argues that we need to remember what the feminists of the 1970s taught us—ridiculing unrealistic media images can be fun as well as important.

If you immerse yourself in the media fare of recent years, what you see is a rather large gap between how the vast majority of girls and women live their lives, the choices they must make in life, and what they see—and don't see—in the media. Ironically, it is just the opposite of the gap in the 1950s and '60s, when images of women as stay-at-home housewives, or blonde bombshells, effaced the exploding number of women entering the workforce, attending college, and becoming involved in politics. Back then the media illusion was that the aspirations of girls and women weren't changing at all when in fact they were. Now, the media illusion is that equality for girls and women is an accomplished fact when it isn't. Then the media were behind the curve; now, ironically, they're ahead.

The discrepancy between the reality of most women's economic situations and what we see on our nation's TV, computer, and silver screens is deep and profound.

At the same time, there has been a resurgence of retrograde dreck clogging our cultural arteries—"The Man Show," *Maxim* magazine, "Girls Gone Wild," and "The Bachelor"—that resurrect stereotypes of girls and women as sex objects obsessed with romantic love and pleasing men.[1] And, finally, representations of women as working-class or middle-class breadwinners, such as those we used to see in "Roseanne," "Grace Under Fire," "One Day at a Time," "Kate & Allie," and "Cagney & Lacey," have virtually vanished from the small screen.

The situation is equally contradictory online. Sites such as Catalyst.org, for example, seek to advance professional opportunities for women, yet one of the most successful and important news and entertainment websites, the Huffington Post, also showcases, on its main page, stories about actresses posing nude. And then there's the "Jezebel" controversy, in which bloggers claiming to speak for a new generation of liberated young women write under the handle "slut machine" and dismiss the prevalence and impact of date rape.[2]

Of course, women online are also engaged in far more positive efforts to inform Americans about the hard realities of work and life today. Case in point:

PunditMom, the blog that makes clear the connection between mothering and politics. But overall, the discrepancy between the reality of most women's economic situations and what we see and hear on our nation's TV, computer, and silver screens is deep and profound.

These gaps between image and reality have both honorable and ignoble roots. Certain show creators, writers, and producers have indeed sought to develop "role model" characters who demonstrate that women can hold jobs previously reserved for men, including that of president of the United States. News organizations, local and national, have recognized the importance and appeal of female reporters and anchors.[3]

Of course, advertisers, the main support of most American media, want to present "aspirational" images of financially comfortable, even wealthy people so we will envy the future selves we will become if we buy their products. Thus, women's magazines need to provide a congenial environment for such ads and to offer visions of the individual empowerment that will result from exercise, the right makeup, and shrewd consumerism. The film industry, focused on the young and especially the teenage audience, devotes the bulk of its output to superheroes, science fiction, and "chick flicks" in which the women are desperate to get married.

The mainstream news media, faced with cutbacks and declining audiences, have reduced their hard-news coverage and investigative reporting in favor of lifestyle, celebrity, and soft-news features.

But let's not forget the persistence of plain old sexism. Talk radio is dominated by conservative men who are either openly sexist or have no interest in how the economy or public policy affect women. The mainstream news media, faced with cutbacks and declining audiences, have reduced their hard-news coverage and investigative reporting in favor of lifestyle, celebrity, and soft-news features. Websites that aggregate and then comment on this kind of news coverage rarely replace it with reporting of their own. And advertisers' niche marketing, which divides women up by age, race, class, and lifestyle, allows mainstream and alternative media alike to target younger audiences with more stereotypical images.

Why should we care about something as evanescent and often banal as media imagery, or the contradictions between this imagery and women's everyday lives? Because the media, in their many forms, have become such powerful and ubiquitous institutions in our society, shaping public understandings of which issues and which people are important and which ones are not. The media are not, as some in the industry would have us believe, "mirrors" simply reflecting reality.

The media are funhouse mirrors that magnify certain kinds of people, values, attitudes, and issues, while minimizing others or even rendering them invisible.

Rather, the media are funhouse mirrors that magnify certain kinds of people, values, attitudes, and issues, while minimizing others or even rendering them invisible. Through the repetition of particular images and the erasure of others, the media play a central role in constructing a national "common sense" about who we are and who we should be. And these distorted reflections contain and perpetuate significant class biases by either ignoring or silently ridiculing most women who make less than $100,000 a year and aren't media perfect in appearance.

Because of the privileged position that rich, successful, or exceptional women now hold in the media, there exists a blackout, however unintended (or not), of how the majority of women, and especially those whose median earnings are about $36,000 a year or less, live their lives.

Dr. Meredith Grey, meet my hairdresser

Women's occupations on television versus the jobs women actually hold

For decades, television drama has been dominated by crime-fighting shows, police and detective stories, hospital dramas, and soap operas, with some programs hybrids of these genres. Although it took a while (in the aftermath of the women's movement), by the 1990s the success of "Law & Order," "L.A. Law," and "E.R." led to more celluloid female professionals, including law firm partners, female doctors, surgeons and hospital administrators, and female cops and police officers, especially in the 10 p.m. prime-time slot. By 2009, here's a partial lineup of whom we had met:

- Lt. Anita Van Buren on "Law & Order"
- Detective Olivia Benson on "Law & Order: SVU"
- President Mackenzie Allen in "Commander in Chief"
- President Allison Taylor on "24"
- Deputy Police Chief Brenda Johnson on "The Closer"
- Detective Claudette Wyms in "The Shield"
- White House Press Secretary C.J. Cregg on "The West Wing"
- Dr. Lisa Cuddy, the hospital administrator and benighted boss of Dr. House in "House"

All these women, concentrated in high-profile, male-dominated lines of work. Hey, do women have it made, or what?

And the way they get to talk to their male bosses or co-workers! Lt. Anita Van Buren (S. Epatha Merkerson) tells a doctor who demands to see his patient, a suspect in a murder case, "Until you have more stars on your collar than I do, Doctor, you can't demand a damn thing." In "Grey's Anatomy," Dr. Bailey (Chandra Wilson) is equally fearless when taking on her superiors. She notifies her boss Dr. Burke (Isaiah Washington), "I think you're cocky, arrogant, bossy, and pushy, and you also have a God complex, you never think about anybody but your damn self."

These are delicious fantasies for women—to succeed and be taken seriously in male-dominated professions, and to be able to talk back to male privilege. That's one of the reasons all these shows are successful. Nonetheless, they overrepresent how far women have in fact come in the workplace, underrepresent the kind of work most women do, and misrepresent how women can, and do, comport themselves on the job.

The most telling case in point: the top five jobs for women in the United States are not surgeon, lawyer,

FANTASY. Women characters on TV are concentrated in high-profile, male-dominated lines of work. From top, Dr. Lisa Cuddy on "House," Lt. Anita Van Buren on "Law & Order," and White House Press Secretary C.J. Cregg on "The West Wing."

{PHOTO CREDITS FROM TOP: ADAM TAYLOR, NBCU PHOTO BANK VIA AP IMAGES; WILL HART, NBCU PHOTO BANK VIA AP IMAGES; NBCU PHOTO BANK VIA AP IMAGES} police lieutenant, district attorney or cable news pundit. In fact, the top five jobs for women in 2008 were, in first place, secretaries, followed by registered nurses, elementary and middle school teachers, cashiers and retail salespersons. Further down the list? Maids, child care workers, office clerks, home health aids, and hairdressers.[4]

Or consider that in 2008, the median earnings for women was $36,000 a year, 23 percent less than that of their male counterparts.[5] And even more privileged women who attend college still earn 80 percent of what men make one year out of college. (And 10 years out? 69 percent.)[6] Of the top Fortune 500 companies in 2008, only 15 had a female chief executive, and only 1 percent of police chiefs are women.[7] And mothers, as financial journalist Ann Crittenden amply documents, pay an enormous price in lost wages once they have children, a price fathers rarely pay.[8]

Also, various studies suggest that rather than verbally smacking down their co-workers—let alone their superiors—the majority of female supervisors are "team builders," often more open and accessible than men, more tolerant of and able to deal with different styles and personalities, more likely to solicit advice. They are, again in contrast to the tough-talking broads on TV, actually more likely to praise co-workers and to mentor and motivate them.[9]

It is male managers, according to these studies, who are more likely to punish co-workers, despite everything we've learned from "The Devil Wears Prada." This doesn't mean that women are better managers than men, but that many of them are different because of how women have been socialized. Certainly most women managers are quite at odds

FACT. In reality, women are more often secretaries, teachers, maids, or hairdressers.

(PHOTO CREDITS FROM TOP: VANESSA VICK, REDUX; BOB BIRD, AP; DAVID J. PHILLIP, AP)

with the leathery, acid-tongued female law enforcement officers and other types so dominant in the media.

But if some think that females in power are more intimidating or unsympathetic or acerbic than men in power, it's not hard to see how these stereotypes are reinforced every day in the media. At the same time, all these confident, linguistically brawny women personify the assumption that, whether they deserved it or not, women have smashed through the glass ceiling. Who in their right mind would think there would ever be a need for a revitalized feminist politics with hard-bitten, flinty, successful women like these at the top?

Terry Who?

Women journalists in front of the camera versus women as experts and pundits on all issues

The success and prominence of certain women in television news—Katie Couric, Diane Sawyer, Gwen Ifill, Christiane Amanpour, Maria Bartiromo, Judy Woodruff—has certainly been a welcome change over the past 20 years. In 2007, women were 40.2 percent of the television news workforce. Nonetheless, significant inequities remain. In 2006, only 28 percent of the broadcast evening newscast stories were reported by women. In newspaper newsrooms, while women were 37 percent of the workforce in 2008 (and minority women were 17 percent), 65 percent of all supervisors were men, and they are also 58 percent of copy editors, 61 percent of reporters, and 73 percent of photographers.[10]

> The preponderance of those hosting or featured on television talk shows are white men who have shown scant interest in the challenges facing working-class or lower-middle-class women in particular.

"Terry Who?" is Terry O'Neill, the president of the National Organization for Women, the largest women's advocacy group in the United States. Yet where is she and other prominent women who would happily discuss the challenges of work and life faced by women and men today on CNN, the network news, or other television talk shows? Women as news sources, experts, or commentators on these profound changes in our economy and society have been utterly marginalized. As a result, virtually unnoticed by the media are the enormous changes in family life wrought by massive male layoffs and more women becoming breadwinners; the increasing, pressing need for child care and quality after-school programs; and the persistence and consequences of pay inequity.

Importantly, the preponderance of those hosting or featured on television talk shows are white men who have shown scant interest in the challenges facing working-class or lower-middle-class women in particular. Men outnumbered women by a four-to-one ratio on the Sunday-morning talk shows in 2005 and 2006. Of the 35 hosts or co-hosts on the prime-time cable news programs, 29 were white men. As the Media Report to Women, an organization that covers women and the media, noted, "Women did not make up at least half of the guests on a single one of the three cable networks, and on some networks they comprised as little as 18 percent."[11]

Paris Hilton, all-American girl?

Images of young women as shallow, cat-fighting sex objects versus the real girls of America

The turn of the millennium marked a rise in television shows, movies, music videos, and magazines resurrecting sexist stereotypes of young women as little more than sex objects, defined first and foremost by their faces and bodies, as obsessed with boys, relationships, and finding Mr. Right, as addicted to shopping and defined by what they buy, and as shallow, materialistic twits who love getting into catfights with each other, especially over men. So we get TV shows about young women desperate to become the next "top model," plastic surgery and makeover shows, "reality" TV shows about rich women desperate to stay young in Orange County, Atlanta, or New York, and celebrity magazines obsessed with "Who Wore it Better."

Just a glance across the media landscape reveals these pervasive sexist images. Young women on MTV's "The Real World" are categorized as "sluts," "bitches" (including "the black bitch"), and party girls. Rap music videos—with the derogatory term "video ho's"—reduce African American women to gyrating hootchie

CBS EVENING
with

CLAIMING THE SPOTLIGHT. The success and prominence of certain women in television news—among them Katie Couric, Diane Sawyer, Christiane Amanpour, Gwen Ifill, and Lisa Ling—has been a welcome change over the past 20 years. In 2007, women were 40.2 percent of the television news workforce.

{PHOTO CREDITS CLOCKWISE FROM TOP LEFT: TODD HEISLER, *THE NEW YORK TIMES*; MARK PETERSON; RAMIN TALAIE, CORBIS; LAIF, REDUX; MARK LEONG, REDUX} mamas. And the latest bachelor on "The Bachelor" is presented with 25 women he gets to sample until he chooses the one he likes best.

How did this happen, given the successes of the women's movement and the understanding that sexism is reactionary? The chief culprit is the use of an arch irony—the deployment of the knowing wink that it's all a joke, that we're not to take this too seriously. Because women have made plenty of progress because of feminism, and now that full equality is allegedly complete, it's OK, even amusing, to resurrect sexist stereotypes of girls and women.[12] After all, TV shows such as "Are You Hot?" or magazines like *Maxim* can't possibly undermine women's equality at this late date, right?

THE LATEST FROM THE AMERICAN PEOPLE

Q: How would you rank these three things in importance for a daughter of yours?

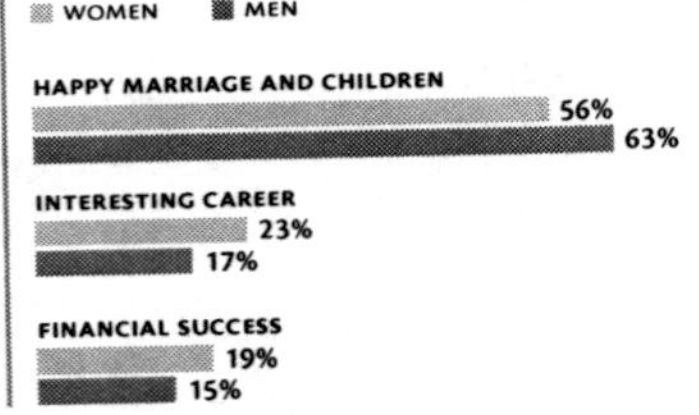

Source: Rockefeller/*Time* poll, 2009.

But the line this kind of media fare sells is that true power comes from getting men to lust after you and other women to envy you. Such representations reinforce the notion that a girl's appearance is more important than her achievements or aspirations—not a very useful message in the real world of women as breadwinners.

These kinds of images also promote the notion that given these allegedly inherent female traits, girls may simply be unsuited for professional careers or positions of power. So images may have very real consequences on girls' ambitions, especially girls from low- and medium-income families, on their notions of feasible career choices, and on their accepting being tracked into lower-paying, dead-end jobs. Research shows that after being exposed to certain sexist media fare that objectifies women, in a subsequent task girls choose not to assume leadership positions in team groups.[13]

Other studies show that after being required to focus on their bodies, girls do less well in certain kinds of cognitive tasks.[14] And researchers also document that stereotypical imagery has a negative impact on what boys think girls and women can and cannot do.[15] Indeed, another experiment shows that when applying for a managerial position, the women who appeared more sexy got rated as less competent and less intelligent than the more conservatively dressed applicants.[16]

The tensions between media fare and the lives and experiences of most everyday young white women and women of color couldn't be starker. The vast majority of ordinary young women in America cannot shop till they drop, do not like being objectified by boys, and will need to earn a living and be taken seriously at work.

Smart, hardworking, accomplished young women who care about ideas, politics, social justice, and their future careers are very few and far between in America's mass media, yet they are going to college in record numbers, and at some elite institutions getting a greater share of honors degrees than men.[17]

Back to June Cleaver?

Mothers "opting out" of the workplace versus mothers as breadwinners

Several years ago we were told that a big new trend was sweeping the land. According to an instantly infamous article in the Sunday *New York Times Magazine* from October 2003, women were now "opting out" of work.[18] The cover headline asked "Q: Why Don't More Women Get to the Top? A: They Choose Not To." The subtitle read, "Abandoning the Climb and Heading Home." Reportedly the newspaper got more mail about this story, most of it hostile from furious women, than any other in recent history.[19]

The magazine article sparked intense debate at the time, yet ever since the debut of "the mommy track" in the early 1990s, the women of America have been subjected to these kinds of stories about mothers seeing the light and chucking it all for Junior's sake.

What made this particular piece distinct was a statistical blip that showed a small decline in the number of working mothers in the workforce. The article, written by Lisa Belkin, herself a former *New York Times* reporter who decided to quit and write freelance instead, cited the experiences of several highly privileged white women

TGICREENY, FLICKR

How different it all is from, you know, the sort of media images that we have of the 1950s family where he would be the sole breadwinner and he'd give his wife an allowance. Now two people sit down and say, 'Here's how much money we're making, how are we gonna make these decisions together as a unit.' I think about how different that is.

Michael in Seattle

who were Princeton alums (as is Belkin). Their decision to "opt out" was then held up as a new, national trend embraced by all women of all races and classes.

The biggest problem with this and similar stories was the emphasis on "choice." Supposedly sensible, devoted mothers who truly cared about their kids simply chose to "opt out." But despite the headline, what we learned inside the article was that the first two women we met, one an attorney, the other a television reporter, were confronted with speed-up at work—55- to 75-hour weeks—at the same time they were having children. Both asked for shorter and more flexible hours and were turned down. Their "choice" was to maintain their punishing schedules or to quit. As one of these women admitted, "I wish it had been possible to be the kind of parent I want to be and continue with my legal career."

The real story here was not about mothers "choosing" not to work. It was about the ongoing inhumanity of many workplaces whose workaholic cultures are hostile to men and women alike.

Then there was the old selective use of statistics. There was no empirical evidence at all that mothers were "opting out."[20] The article emphasized findings from a recent survey in which 26 percent of women in senior management said they did not want a promotion. So that meant nearly three-quarters did. We then learned that *Fortune* reported that in a survey of 108 women in high-powered jobs, "at least 20" had chosen to leave. Doesn't that mean that four-fifths have not made this "choice"?

Katha Pollitt of *The Nation*, Heather Boushey, then at the Center for Economic and Policy Research, and others debunked Belkin's other statistical sleights of hand in the piece, which allowed her to overstate how many mothers were actually "opting out" of the workforce.[21] In fact, the most interesting thing about the article was its buried lead. The real story here was not about mothers "choosing" not to work. It was about the ongoing inhumanity of many workplaces whose workaholic cultures are hostile to men and women alike. After all, there aren't many women (and men) today who can afford to opt out of the family-unfriendly rat race and have the financial strength to start their own businesses suited to their family needs.

At the same time, the standards for what constituted being a good-enough mother had become unattainable. There was the emergence of what Smith College professor Meredith Michaels and I termed "the new momism" in our book *The Mommy Myth*—the insistence that no woman is truly complete or fulfilled unless she has kids, that women remain the best primary caretakers of children, and that to be a remotely decent mother, a woman has to devote her entire physical, psychological, emotional, and intellectual being, 24/7, to her children.[22]

The new momism is driven by fear, stoked by so many stories about missing children, dangerous products, and child care centers supposedly staffed by child molesters. It has also been driven by marketing, the desire to sell anxious mothers as many products as possible to protect their children from germs, and stoke their intellectual and physical development as early as possible—hence, piping Mozart into your womb while pregnant—and to sell magazines with such angst-producing headlines as:

"Are You a Sensitive Mother?"
"Is Your Child Eating Enough?"
"Is Your Baby Normal?"

No wonder 77 percent of mothers with children at home said they believe it's harder to be a mother now than it was 20 or 30 years ago, and 50 percent felt mothers were doing a worse job today than mothers back then, according to a 1997 Pew Research Center poll.[23] Even mothers who deliberately avoid TV and magazines, or who pride themselves on seeing through them, have trouble escaping the standards of perfection, and the sense of threat, that the media ceaselessly atomize into the air we breathe.

While important websites such as Catalyst, MomsRising, Feministing and those for the National Organization for Women and the Feminist Majority all seek to address these issues at home and abroad, many user-generated sites and blogs such as Adventures in Motherhood, Mothers & More, and Motherhood Uncensored, to name only a few, focus disproportionately on motherhood, its challenges, its joys, and the need to confess one's failings. This is powerful testimony to the tyranny of the new momism and women's need to talk back to it and connect with each other in honest and mutually sustaining ways.

TOO EMOTIONAL. When Senator Hillary Clinton teared up during the New Hampshire primary, she was declared too emotional. (ELISE AMENDOLA, AP)

TOO HOT. Governor Sarah Palin suffered from sexist attention during the presidential campaign from conservative men who proudly called her a "hottie." (LYNNE SLADKY, AP)

TOO ANGRY. When the media at first had no idea what to make of Michelle Obama, she was tagged as an "angry black woman." (STEVE HELBER, AP)

Mothers, often isolated from one another because of geography or work patterns and forced to think of themselves as lone heroes (or failures), have found on the Internet a place where they can try to connect with each other and not feel so alone. The proliferation of all the "momoir" books and these online sites documents the struggle that mothers—including working mothers—face, how neglected they remain by our government, and the extent to which motherhood in particular remains the unfinished business of the women's movement.[24]

And it rhymes with witch...

The dismissive coverage of powerful, successful women versus their achievements

On top of all this, there are the representations of powerful women as impossible divas: greedy, unscrupulous, hated by their staffs, unloved by their families. Just think Miranda Priestly in "The Devil Wears Prada." But what about the corporate thieves of Enron—Kenneth Lay, Jeffrey Skilling, Andrew Fastow, and others—all of whom bilked thousands of Enron employees and investors out of their life savings? These guys did not come in for the same ridiculing and schadenfreude-filled media coverage that Martha Stewart faced when she was charged with covering up an insider trading deal of far less shattering financial importance. Yes, it's true, the Enron boys weren't celebrities. But they also weren't women.

Let's consider how the media dealt with the three most important women in the 2008 presidential contest: Hillary Clinton, Sarah Palin and Michelle Obama. Millions of women were outraged over the sexist coverage of Hillary Clinton during her presidential campaign. This smart and experienced U.S. senator was caricatured by a brigade of middle-aged, upper-middle-class white male commentators throughout the presidential primaries. Clinton was cast by white, male TV commentator Joe Scarborough as "very shrill."[25] And according to Tucker Carlson, she made men "involuntarily" cross their legs out of castration anxiety.[26] Glenn Beck cut to the chase and simply called her a bitch.[27] MSNBC's Chris Matthews asserted that the New York Senator got where she was only because people felt sorry for her because her husband cheated on her.[28]

There are the representations of powerful women as impossible divas: greedy, unscrupulous, hated by their staffs, unloved by their families.

At first, Sarah Palin was spared such coverage. Indeed, in the wake of the commentary Senator Clinton received, it was verboten in the mainstream press to ask whether a mother of five, including a 4-month-old infant with Down's Syndrome, could run for and hold such a high office. But in the online world Governor Palin's many substantive and personal contradictions were the subject of immediate and intense ridicule from the left and lots of sexist attention from conservative men who proudly declared her a "hottie."

But after the election, former aides to her running mate, Senator John McCain (R-AZ), began leaking all sorts of innuendo. The Alaska governor thought Africa was a country, not a continent. She was a diva and had tantrums. She was difficult and uncooperative. She was suffering from postpartum depression. And that

> The 2008 campaign was allegedly all about gender—at least on an individual basis—but collectively it wasn't about gender at all. There was scant attention paid to how the health care crisis affects women and their families, the ongoing child care crisis, pay inequity, women's health, or reproductive rights.

it was Palin, not her handlers, who insisted on a $150,000 wardrobe makeover.[29] How much of this was true remains unclear, but it was all easy to believe because she was a woman, and an ambitious one at that.

And then there is our current first lady. For much of the 2008 campaign the media had no idea what to make of the elegant, Princeton- and Harvard-educated Michelle Obama (except, of course, her clothes and bare arms). But the stereotype of the "angry black woman" was so pervasive, so available, that Fox News, *National Review* and the Internet rumor mill had no trouble trying to pin it on her. Even *The New Yorker* magazine had its take on the stereotype, running its "fist-bump" cover, with Obama drawn in Black Panther garb with an assault rifle slung over her shoulder.[30] After Barack Obama's inauguration, black journalist and talking head Juan Williams—juiced on the fumes of "The O'Reilly Factor"—referred to Mrs. Obama's "militant anger" and described her as "Stokely Carmichael [a 1960s black activist]...in a dress."[31]

Michelle Obama has had to pay dearly for the prevailing stereotype of black women as "angry," domineering and emasculating, according to her hometown newspaper the *Chicago Tribune*. She went on daytime talk show "The View" to chat with its women cohosts, she read to schoolchildren, she planted the famous White House garden, she tended to her kids, she shopped at J. Crew. She became the "mom-in-chief." By May 2009, her favorability ratings had soared to 72 percent, higher even than her husband's.[32]

The great irony of the 2008 campaign was that it was allegedly all about gender—at least on an individual basis—but collectively it wasn't about gender at all. Between all the anxiety about Hillary Clinton's cleavage and her tears during the New Hampshire primary campaign, or how "hot" Sarah Palin was, or how angry Michelle Obama was, there was scant attention paid to how the health care crisis affects women and their families, the ongoing child care crisis, pay inequity, women's health, or reproductive rights. The media were sexist to all three and in the process ignored what really matters to women and men in American today as they try to balance work and life.

Those "radical" feminists

The demonization of feminism versus its importance to the well-being of men, women, and children

Feminism is now embedded in American life. The understanding that women can and should be able to hold the same jobs as men has led to TV shows such as "The Closer" and "Grey's Anatomy." At the very same time, feminism and feminists have been so thoroughly and effectively demonized in American society—Rush Limbaugh, for example, equating them with Nazis[33]—that it is hard to think of a political group or movement that has had such a great impact on American life while at the same time being so discredited.

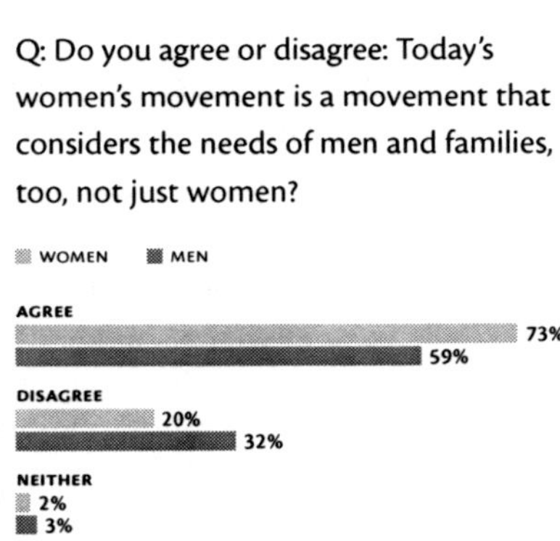

Source: Rockefeller/*Time* poll, 2009.

This rests on a new "common sense" in the media about the status of women. Allegedly, the women's movement has been such a complete success that full equality with men is a fact, and so feminism is supposedly irrelevant now. Feminists have been stereotyped—in the news, books, movies, and television shows—as strident, humorless, deliberately unattractive, anti-family women who hate men and wish to make young women as unhappy as they are. Consequently, not only is feminism unnecessary because all its goals have supposedly been achieved, but also it is objectionable because it will make those who embrace it unattractive, unloved, and miserable.

In real life, of course, as Jessica Valenti, the co-founder of the website Feministing, put it, "The smartest, coolest women I know are feminists."[34] Most feminists bear zero resemblance to the stereotype describe above. Just think Ellen DeGeneres, Geena Davis, Whoopi Goldberg, Barbara Ehrenreich, Wanda Sykes, Toni Morrison, Katha Pollitt, Representative Maxine Waters (D-CA), Margaret Cho, Billie Jean King, Isabel Allende, and Naomi Klein.

That may be the biggest challenge facing women today—to re-imagine and embrace collective action that cuts across the lines of race, class, and sexuality.

Similarly, in the everyday world most women display a feminist sensibility that detracts not at all from their humor, looks, outlook on life, or the workaday world they engage in. But this common sense about feminism keeps feminist voices and women's issues out of much of the media. What dominates instead is a discourse of individualism—each woman is a product that she alone must make and shape. In this imagined world, any and all successes and failures are up to her and her alone—and so ingrained is this view that it is hard to imagine another model, another way of thinking.

And that may be the biggest challenge facing women today—to re-imagine and embrace collective action that cuts across the lines of race, class, and sexuality. This new, all-encompassing movement would hold the government, our workplaces and our educational, cultural, and religious institutions responsible for building a more just and humane society based on real equality.

Where do we go from here?

Women as mindless consumers, young women as airheads or enmeshed in catfights, powerful women as difficult and unloved and, yet, women who have cracked the glass ceiling, all appear on our nation's media screens. But you note I have not yet used the word "breadwinner" because that role, implying as it does active support of a family in multiple forms, is more absent from the media today than when "Cagney & Lacey" or "Roseanne" were on the air in the 1980s and 1990s.

Women as breadwinners today include low- and middle-income women as well as the upper-middle-income and wealthy women more often portrayed in the media. Women as breadwinners reminds us of the central economic role of African American, Hispanic and other minority women and low- and middle-income women in our economy. These women—the majority of us—are invisible, erased. And when

A DIFFERENT TAKE IN THE MEDIA Ellen DeGeneres: one of the pioneers of daytime talk shows that really matter to women. [CHRIS PIZZELLO, AP]

women as breadwinners are not seen, our needs are not even acknowledged. That's why our media would be more reflective of real life and real work, and our society would be better off if we:

- Increase the presence of family-friendly and female experts in the news media
- Expose sexist media fare and promote media literacy among our youth
- Make the role of women as breadwinners more visible

To achieve these ends, I recommend that we work together to pressure the media much, much more than we have in the past, and the news media especially, to increase the presence of women, including experts on issues affecting women.

Where are the routine women's voices, backed by studies about pay inequity, health care, inadequate child care, homeless women and their families, on "Meet the Press" or CNN? This is a huge fight, given the stereotypes about feminists and the dismissing of women's issues.

We need to match the reality with the image of women as citizens and breadwinners and render visible what has been so effectively eclipsed.

Finally, we need to talk back to the media more. Let's remember that it was a group of high school girls in Pennsylvania, so outraged by the Abercrombie & Fitch T-shirt for girls that read "Who needs brains when you have these?" that got the shirts removed from stores.[35] But this must also be a more sustained, long-term activity, involving the promotion of media literacy for children and fighting against the sexist stereotypes—and the advertisers who support them—that target young people. We would do well to trumpet the analysis of the Women's Media Center, the reporting of Women's eNews, and the pushback of Media Matters.

In short, we need to match the reality with the image of women as citizens and breadwinners and render visible what has been so effectively eclipsed. Pay inequity, dead-end jobs, sexual harassment, abuse of overtime pay, speed-up at work, out-of-date maternity leave policies, inadequate or nonexistent child care—these are all burdens carried by tens of millions of women with minimal help or acknowledgment. And these are all problems that government, employers, and society can help overcome.

It's time for leaders across the country to emphasize the discrepancies between image and reality, and to get women's issues and a feminist perspective back in the media spotlight. Let's first consider these misleading images and the real lives of women, then identify the pressure points in the media where women and men together can apply humor and satire, and justified outrage whenever appropriate to chastise the overt and inadvertent stereotyping of women today.

And we should also identify when and where we can praise the media for giving voice to women's real needs and concerns. Because despite everything, the media do this too—just not often enough. This is one of main effects of today's media—by overemphasizing certain kinds of people, policies, values, and solutions, it makes imagining alternatives all the much harder. It is time for us to take on the current "common sense," to smash it, and to dare the country and the media not to take us seriously.

ENDNOTES

1 Ariel Levy, *Female Chauvinist Pigs: Women and the Rise of Raunch Culture* (New York: Free Press, 2006).

2 See Sarah Hepola, "Jezebels Without a Cause," *Salon*, July 8, 2008, available at http://www.salon.com/mwt/broadsheet/2008/07/08/jezebels/?source=refresh.

3 United States Commission on Civil Rights, "Window Dressing on the Set: Women and Minorities in Television" (1977).

4 Bureau of Labor Statistics, "Quick Stats on Women Workers, 2008" (2009), available at http://www.dol.gov/wb/stats/main.htm.

5 U.S. Census Bureau, September 10, 2009, http://www.census.gov/Press-Release/www/releases/archives/income_wealth/014227.html.

6 American Association of University Women, "Behind the Pay Gap" (2007), available at http://www.aauw.org/research/behindPayGap.cfm.

7 "Women CEOs of the Fortune 1000," available at http://www.catalyst.org/publication/322/women-ceos-of-the-fortune-1000 (last accessed September 2009); Jacqueline Mroz, "Female Police Chiefs, a Novelty No More," *The New York Times*, April 6, 2008, available at http://www.nytimes.com/2008/04/06/nyregion/nyregionspecial2/06Rpolice.html.

8 Ann Crittenden, *The Price of Motherhood: Why the Most Important Job in the World is Still the Least Valued* (New York: Owl Books, 2002).

9 Alice Eagly, Mary Johannesen-Schmidt, and Marloes L. van Engen, "Transformational, Transactional and Laissez-Faire Leadership Styles: A Meta-Analysis Comparing Women and Men," *Psychological Bulletin*, 129 (3) (2003): 569–591.

10 Media Report to Women, "Industry Statistics" (2009), available at www.mediareporttowomen.com/statistics.htm.

11 Ibid.

12 Angela McRobbie, "Notes on Postfeminism and Popular Culture: Bridget Jones and the New Gender Regime." In Anita Harris, ed., *All About the Girl* (New York: Routledge, 2004); Rosalind Gill, *Gender and the Media* (Malden, MA: Polity Press, 2007).

13 Paul G. Davies and others, "Consuming Images: How Television Commercials That Elicit Stereotype Threat Can Restrain Women Academically and Professionally," *Personality and Social Psychology Bulletin*, 28 (12) (2002): 1615–1628.

14 Barbara L. Fredrickson and others, "That Swimsuit Becomes You: Sex Differences in Self-Objectification, Restrained Eating, and Math Performance," *Journal of Personality and Social Psychology*, 75 (1) (1998): 269–284.

15 Peter Glick and Susan T. Fiske, "The Ambivalent Sexism Inventory: Differentiating Hostile and Benevolent Sexism," *Journal of Personality and Social Psychology*, 70 (3) (1996): 491–512.

16 American Psychological Association, "Report of the APA Task Force on the Sexualization of Girls," (2007), p. 30.

17 Jay Mathews, "Study Casts Doubt on the 'Boy Crisis,'" *The Washington Post*, June 26, 2006, available at www.washingtonpost.com/wp-dyn/content/article/2006/06/25/AR2006062501047.html; Tamar Lewin, "At Colleges, Women Are Leaving Men in the Dust," *The New York Times*, July 9, 2006, available at http://www.nytimes.com/2006/07/09/education/09college.html.

18 Lisa Belkin, "The Opt-Out Revolution," *The New York Times*, October 26, 2003, available at http://www.nytimes.com/2003/10/26/magazine/26WOMEN.html.

19 "Letters to the Editor," *The New York Times Magazine*, November 9, 2003, p. 14.

20 Heather Boushey, "'Opting Out?' The Effect of Children on Women's Employment in the United States," *Feminist Economics*, 14 (1) (January 2008): 1–36.

21 Katha Pollitt, "There They Go Again," *The Nation*, October 30, 2003, available at http://www.thenation.com/doc/20031117/pollitt; Boushey, "'Opting Out?'"

22 Susan J. Douglas and Meredith W. Michaels, *The Mommy Myth: The Idealization of Motherhood and How It Has Undermined Women* (New York: The Free Press, 2004).

23 Pew Research Center For the People & the Press, "Motherhood Today—A Tougher Job, Less Ably Done" (1997), available at http://people-press.org/report/109/motherhood-today-a-tougher-job-less-ably-done.

24 See, for example, Ayelet Waldman, *Bad Mother: A Chronicle of Maternal Crimes, Minor Calamities, and Occasional Moments of Grace* (New York: Doubleday, 2009).

25 "Hardball with Chris Matthews for Feb. 10," available at: http://www.msnbc.msn.com/id/11326818, last accessed September 2009.

26 Katharine Q. Seelye and Julie Bosman, "Critics and News Executives Split Over Sexism in Clinton Coverage," *The New York Times*, June 13, 2008, p. A1, available at http://www.nytimes.com/2008/06/13/world/americas/13iht-13women.13681561.html.

27 Media Matters For America, "CNN's, ABC's Beck on Clinton: "[S]he's the stereotypical bitch" (March 15, 2007), available at http://mediamatters.org/research/200703150011.

28 Howard Kurtz, "Hardbrawl: Candid Talker Chris Matthews Pulls No Punches," *The Washington Post*, February 14, 2008, p. C1, available at http://www.washingtonpost.com/wp-dyn/content/article/2008/02/13/AR2008021303418.html.

29 Ed Pilkington, "Palin Returns to Alaska Amid Criticism from Disgruntled McCain Aides," *The Guardian*, November 6, 2008, available at http://www.guardian.co.uk/world/2008/nov/06/sarah-palin-wasilla-hillbillies; Jonathan Martin, "Palin Story Sparks GOP Family Feud," *Politico*, June 30, 2009, available at http://dyn.politico.com/printstory.cfm?uuid=33D91FFD-18FE-70B2-A87D66E6D1BFE37B.

30 Bary Blitt, "The Politics of Fear," cover of *The New Yorker* magazine, July 21, 2008, available at http://www.newyorker.com/online/covers/slideshow_blittcovers?slide=1#showHeader.

31 Media Matters For America, "Juan Williams Again Baselessly Attacked Michelle Obama, Claiming 'Her Instinct is to Start with This "Blame America" ... Stuff" (January 27, 2009), available at http://mediamatters.org/research/200901270002.

32 Stacy St. Clair, "Michelle Obama Image Makeover: First Lady's Approval Ratings Soar as She Embraces Traditional Role—With a Modern Twist," *Chicago Tribune*, April 28, 2009, available at http://www.chicagotribune.com/news/local/chi-michelle-obama-28-apr28,0,3727662.story.

33 Media Matters For America, "Repeating 'Feminazi' Comment, Limbaugh Reprises Familiar Theme" (January 6, 2006), available at http://mediamatters.org/mmtv/200601060006.

34 Jessica Valenti, *Full Frontal Feminism: A Young Woman's Guide to Why Feminism Matters* (Emeryville, CA: Seal Press, 2007), p. 15.

35 Caryl Rivers and Rosalind Barnett, "Girls Must Be Girls," AlterNet, November 29, 2005, available at http://www.alternet.org/rights/28884.

Sexy Socialization

Today's media and the next generation of women

By Stacy L. Smith, Cynthia Kennard, and Amy D. Granados

The next generation to enter the American workforce is growing up today bombarded with numerous media choices. As Susan Douglas details in the preceding chapter, "Where Have You Gone, Roseanne Barr?" the media present skewed portraits of women and work. Here, we turn to the influence the media exert on children and teenagers and what that may mean for the next generation entering the workforce, particularly the media itself.

The typical 8-to-18-year-old spends roughly six and a half hours per day with various media.[1] Whether looking at animated films approved for general audiences, R-rated blockbusters, or innovative video games, girls and women often appear as eye candy. These ever-present idealized portrayals may be inescapable for female viewers, whether they are 8 or 18 years of age. Of equal concern is what boys and young men might be learning about girls and women and how to relate to them. All this will inform the future workplaces of America.

Let's start with content delivered in traditional formats and move to new media platforms. The first message young Americans may extract from the media is that girls and women are missing in action. Analyzing 400 films released between 1990 and 2006, one study found that males appear on screen 2.71 times more frequently than females.[2] Assessing popular video games, this gender gap can widen to as much as five males to every one female in some games.[3] Television is closer to presenting a more balanced picture,[4] with prime-time women occupying 37 percent to 40 percent of all roles.[5] Despite significant gains, the American woman today remains noticeably absent across media watched by kids and teenagers.

When females are present, storylines often reveal that women are valued more for how they look rather than for who they are. This is the second message children and teenagers may glean from the media, particularly in animated content. Looking across 100 popular G-rated films, a recent study found that 33.1 percent of females are thin, 34.6 percent possess an unrealistically small waist, and 16.3 percent have an unattainable hourglass figure.[6] Such disfigured dames have little room for a womb or any other internal organ.

Storylines often reveal that women are valued more for how they look rather than for who they are.

Children's media diets do change with age and maturity. Music, magazines, websites, video games, and mobile media may become more or less important in late elementary school and early adolescence. Music videos have been heavily criticized, with concern emanating from depictions of that objectify women, explicit lyrical references to sex, and highly suggestive "bump and grind" dance choreography.[7] One study shows that women are more likely than men to be shown in provocative outfits in music videos.[8] Roles in this genre also vary by gender: Men are more likely to be shown as "sex animals" and women are more likely to be shown as "sex objects."[9]

The fashion-centric media only add to the succession of sexy images seen across other platforms. Beauty magazines, corresponding websites, and reality shows—think "Project Runway" and "America's Next Top Model"—may be particularly important agents of socialization for adolescent females. *Elle*, *Vogue*, and *In Style* feature no shortage of thin, waif-like women. Some of these haute couture models have been criticized for their slim, "heroin chic" looks.[10]

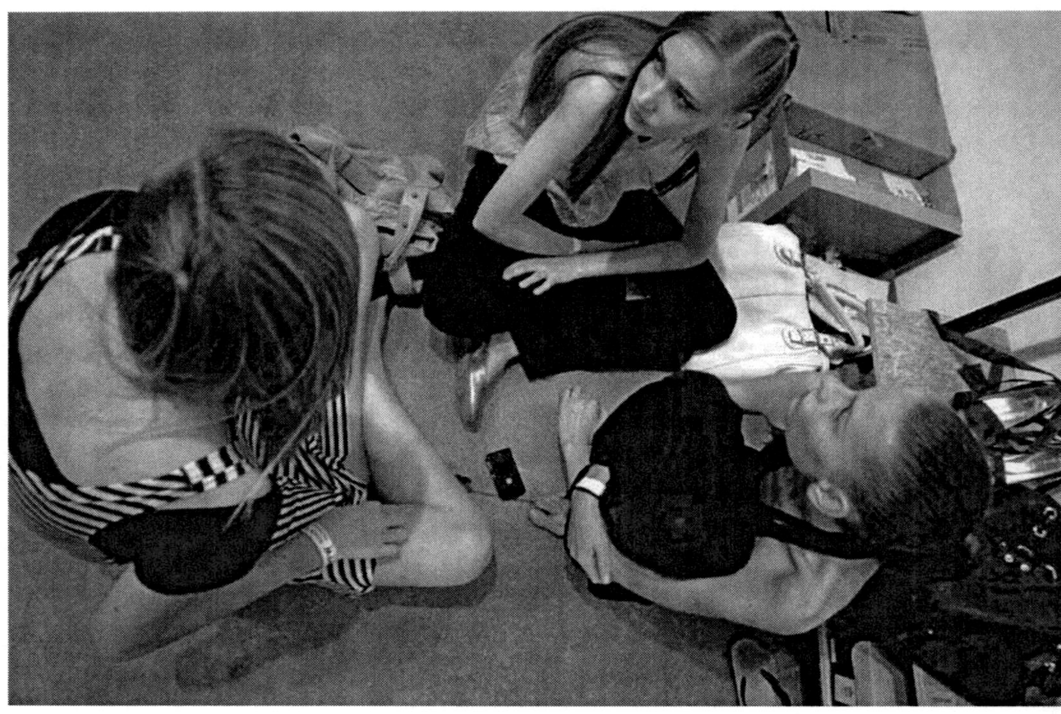

UNFASHIONABLY EMACIATED. High fashion models with unhealthy bodies are a threat to the young women who emulate them. [ANA LAURA CASTRO]

One investigation found that models working in high fashion became taller but their weight remained unchanged across most of the 20th century.[11] More than 25 percent of these women between the 1930s and the 1990s met the standard set by the American Psychological Association for anorexia nervosa. In stark contrast, the typical 18-to -29-year-old American woman became taller and heavier—thereby widening the discrepancy between what is a real and a quixotic body size.

As adolescent females turn to fashion, many young males may seek out and play video games. Such content is the breeding ground for the construction of many gals with improbable features, among them Lara Croft from the "Tomb Raider" series and Helena from "Dead or Alive 4." Studies show that females in top-selling video games are more likely than their male counterparts to be clothing challenged, adorned in sexualized attire, and wearing garments inappropriate for the task at hand.[12]

What impact does repeated exposure to these types of portrayals have on viewers? Before answering this question, it is important to underscore that media messages are factors among many that may contribute with other influences to the actual socialization of youth. Research also reveals that not all children and teens are affected by the media in the same way. But here we will outline several possible outcomes that may be associated with viewing skewed, sexy media portrayals on the next generation of American women—those who may one day dominate the workforce.

First, the media may affect perceptions of self-worth of girls and teenagers. Second, the media may affect girls' thoughts and feelings about their bodies.[13] Third, the media may affect how females construct their identities virtually in the public sphere. This last point is particularly relevant as girls continue to dominate some elements of online content creation,[14] such as blogging and social networking, which means they may become attracted to media industries as they enter the workforce.

> Models working in high fashion became taller but their weight remained unchanged across most of the 20th century.

When girls and young women become their own producers and distributors of online content they may look to women in the media to inform their personal branding style. Isn't it ironic, then, that real narratives about women and girls are marginalized in fictional media while the sexual conquests, materialism, and globetrotting of ingenues and reality stars are deemed newsworthy across print, broadcast, and online sources?

These mixed messages could have serious career implications. A recent survey of 3,169 professionals revealed that over a fifth have used social networking sites to help inform their hiring decisions.[15] Among those turning to such sites, a third has disqualified potential applicants based on what they saw or read on personal profiles. Just after drug/alcohol use (41 percent), the study showed that the second highest reported "area of concern" among managers (40 percent) was seeing "provocative or inappropriate photographs or information" online about a potential employee.

So, what is to be done? The main hope lies on females working behind the scenes across media platforms in production, distribution, and exhibition. Research demonstrates that when women direct films, write/produce TV shows, or even cover the news, the way in which females are presented changes dramatically.[16] Yet there may be a long wait for complex and wide-ranging portrayals of females, as breaking into decision-making media positions has proven difficult for many women.

Female decision-makers in the entertainment industry are the exception and not the rule. Few executive studio positions have been filled by women and the number of females working as directors, writers, and producers of film is low and

HOPE FOR THE FUTURE. Young women in the fashion business may one day deliver more real presentations of women. [FRED R. CONRAD, *THE NEW YORK TIMES*]

has not changed meaningfully over the last decade. Fewer than 10 percent of all films are directed by a female auteur.[17] While near financial parity exists in television, a substantial wage gap prevails for writers of film. This is evidenced by the approximate $40,000 discrepancy in median salary for men and women screenwriters in 2005, the last year for which complete data are available.[18]

In the digital world, a profusion of stories about girls and women in new media may be easier to accomplish over time. This may happen despite the fact that only two women reside in the president or CEO positions at technology companies—Carol Bartz at Yahoo! Inc. and Gina Bianchini at Ning Inc. Perhaps early socialization to technology focusing on relationship building and interpersonal connectivity will attract more teen- and college-aged females into careers involving blogging, online newsgathering, reporting and dissemination, and webisode construction.

Future female media content creators may well have the opportunity to tell a multitude of stories about girls and women across the lifespan. To achieve this end, we need to sensitize the next generation of American citizens to current media biases surrounding the prevalence and portrayal of females. Such educational efforts could also target areas where women may have less direct experience than men. For instance, webisodes or fictional narratives addressing salary negotiation, management training, and long-term career planning could instruct and may help to narrow the wage gap between males and females in some professions.

These types of stories may also help to populate—over time—the executive suite of major media and digital corporations with females. Surely these attempts could harness the prosocial potential of new and old media and may even take a step toward inoculating some of the next generation of males and females in the workforce from perpetuating what has been the status quo.

By Stacy L. Smith, Ph.D., faculty fellow, Center on Communication Leadership and Policy, Annenberg School for Communication, University of Southern California; Cynthia Kennard, senior fellow, Center on Communicational Leadership and Policy, Annenberg School for Communication, University of Southern California; and Amy D. Granados, doctoral student, Annenberg School for Communication, University of Southern California.

ENDNOTES

1 Kaiser Family Foundation, "Generation M: Media in the Lives of 8–18 Year-Olds" (2005).

2 Stacy L. Smith and Crystal Allene Cook, "Gender Stereotypes: An Analysis of Popular Films and TV" (Los Angeles: Geena Davis Institute for Gender and Media, 2008).

3 Children Now, "Fair Play? Violence, Gender and Race in Video Games" (2001); Edward Downs and Stacy L. Smith, "Keeping Abreast of Hypersexuality: A Video Game Character Content Analysis" (Paper presented at the annual conference of the International Communication Association to the Mass Communication Division, New York, 2005); Dmitri Williams and others, "The Virtual Census: Representation of Gender, Race, and Age in Video Games," *New Media Society* 11 (5) (2009): 815–834.

4 Smith and Cook, "Gender Stereotypes: An Analysis of Popular Films and TV."

5 Jack Glascock, "Gender Roles on Prime-Time Network Television: Demographics and Behaviors," *Journal of Broadcasting and Electronic Media* 45 (4) (2001): 656–669; Martha. M. Lauzen and David M. Dozier, "The Role of Women on Screen and Behind the Scenes in the Television and Film Industries: Review of a Program of Research," *Journal of Communication Inquiry* 23 (4) (1999): 355–373; Nancy Signorielli and Aaron Bacue, "Recognition and Respect: A Content Analysis of Prime Time Television Characters Across Three Decades," *Sex Roles* 40 (7/8) (1999): 527–544.

6 Smith and Cook, "Gender Stereotypes: An Analysis of Popular Films and TV."

7 Kathy SaeNgian, "Researcher Cites Negative Influences of Hip-Hop," *Pittsburgh Post-Gazette*, June 13, 2008, available at http://www.post-gazette.com/pg/08165/889550-51.stm; Nekesa Mumbi Moody, "BET's 'Uncut' exposes plenty of female flesh," *Star-Ledger*, April 13, 2004, retrieved September 25, 2009, Lexis-Nexis.

8 Christine Hanson and Ranald Hanson, "Music and Music Videos." In Dolf Zillmann and Peter Vorderer, eds., *Media Entertainment: The Psychology of its Appeal* (Mahwah, NJ: Lawrence Erlbaum, 2000), p. 183.

9 Hanson and Hanson, "Music and Music Videos"; Kate Conrad, Travis Dixon and Yuanyuan Zhang, "Controversial Rap Themes, Gender Portrayals and Skin Tone Distortion: A Content Analysis of Rap Music Videos," *Journal of Broadcasting and Electronic Media* 53 (1) (2009): 134–156.

10 "Skinny Models Banned from Catwalk," available http://www.cnn.com/2006/WORLD/europe/09/13/spain.models/index.html (last accessed September 2009).

11 Carol Byrd-Bredbenner and Jessica Murray, "A Comparison of the Anthropometric Measurements of Idealized Female Body Images in Media Depicted to Men, Women, and General Audiences," *Topical Clinical Nutrition* 18 (2) (2003): 117–129.

12 Berrin Beasley and Tracy C. Standley, "Shirts vs. Skins: Clothing As an Indicator of Gender Role Stereotyping in Video Games," *Mass Communication & Society* 5 (3) (2002): 279–293; Downs and Smith, "Keeping Abreast of Hypersexuality: A Video Game Character Content Analysis."

13 Shelly Grabe and others, "The Role of the Media in Body Image Concerns among Women: A Meta-Analysis of Experimental and Correlational Studies," *Psychological Bulletin* 134 (3) (2008): 460–476.

14 Kate Spicer and Abul Taherreport, "Girls and Young Women are Now the Most Prolific Web Users," *The Sunday Times*, March 9, 2008, available at http://technology.timesonline.co.uk/tol/news/tech_and_web/the_web/article3511863.ece.

15 "Employers Using Social-Networking Sites to Research Job Candidates," available at http://www.marketingcharts.com/interactive/employers-using-social-networking-sites-to-research-job-candidates-5998 (last accessed September 2009).

16 Cinny Kennard and Sheila Murphy, "Characteristics of War Coverage by Female Correspondents." In Philip Seib, ed., *Media and Conflict in the 21st Century* (New York: Palgrave MacMillan, 2005); Lauzen and Dozier, "The Role of Women on Screen and Behind the Scenes in the Television and Film Industries: Review of a Program of Research"; Stacy L. Smith, Marc Choueiti, Amy D. Granados and Sarah Erickson, "Asymmetrical Academy Awards: A Look at Gender Balance in Best Picture Nominated Films from 1977–2006" (Los Angeles: University of Southern California, Annenberg School for Communication, 2008).

17 Martha M. Lauzen, "The Celluloid Ceiling: Behind-the-Scenes Employment of Women on the Top 250 Films of 2008" (San Diego: Center for the Study of Women in Television and Film, 2009).

18 Darnell M. Hunt, "Whose Stories Are We Telling? The 2007 Hollywood Writers Report" (Los Angeles: Writers Guild of America, West, 2007), p. 20.

A Second, Quiet Revolution

By Dan Mulhern, first gentleman of Michigan, author of "Everyday Leadership: Getting Results in Business, Politics and Life," and radio talk show host

I am profoundly grateful that women fought for the right to live and lead in the public spaces outside the home. The struggle has been epic, fought on many fronts—political, academic, economic, and more—over more than a century. And it's working! Women have been liberated and the country has been blessed with an extraordinary influx of long-lost talent.

The pioneers gave my wife shoulders to climb—to break through the glass ceiling that kept women out of offices like the one she occupies as governor of the State of Michigan. Like most guys who have experienced a daughter, mom, wife, or friend excel in this way, I thought this was awesome. I've had my moments, with my (male) ego struggling in the shadows of a great woman. I learned what "first ladies," executives' wives, and just about every girl or woman on the globe felt for decades when someone looked past them as though they weren't there. These moments helped me appreciate the ways in which we marginalize people and why inclusion is not only nice and just but makes incredible sense.

I look forward to the unfolding of a second, quiet revolution. Women are now free to live in the public world, but we men are not inquiring about (let alone demanding or fighting for) the corresponding freedom to do "women's work." We did not shout: "Why can't I raise the kids?" Or, "Why are we stereotyped as aggressive, testosterone driven, and incapable of answering questions like 'how do you feel?'" Why does society still belittle those men who care deeply about fashion or aesthetics, food or relationships? Why do we still socialize men to not feel the vulnerable emotions that come with their lives every bit as much as women's lives: sadness, empathy, whimsy, silliness, or fear? Most emblematic: Why are men not allowed to cry?

My dad suffered with lung cancer. The way he'd been socialized—the oldest son, Korean War vet, corporate manager—made it nearly impossible for him to deal with all the emotions churning within him: regret, joy, sadness, love, and of course fear. The male socialization that blocked access to his feelings also made it so hard for him to receive and validate and share the intense feelings of my mom—her sadness and fear as well as her depth of love.

Women have won a new opportunity not only for themselves but for men. Men now have the chance to be great supporters of powerful women, to relate to them in whole new ways, to nurture and empathize with our children, and central to it all, to develop our own full humanity. So, I say thanks to the feminists, the suffragettes, the quiet courageous women, and the good men who opened two-way doors to exciting new worlds.

Men now have the chance to be great supporters of powerful women, to relate to them in whole new ways, to nurture and empathize with our children, and central to it all, to develop our own full humanity.

"I think really we need to redefine what femininity is. You can still be in a position of power, you can still run your household and you can still be feminine. That's really I think where we are getting this new definition of what femininity is."
Devon in Silicon Valley

"So we were the two girls in the room and we could either try to be like the guys or we could say, 'I am different.' Part of being different is understanding a little more about how other women buy things and how to relate to other people in terms of your employees and how to build an organization that is a different kind of culture and that can be a strength. And so I just don't want to lose the female diversity, the power of female diversity, because I think that the more we try to sort of put that away, the more we lose a real, a differentiating advantage that we bring together." Heidi in Silicon Valley

"I was brought up in a traditional home. My parents migrated from Mexico and I have these Latino uncles who were tough and macho. And as a little kid, it was like, wow, these guys. I had that image of what I was supposed to be. But also, at the same time today, I feel really fortunate that I belong to a local church. And I get together with men every Saturday. And I get to tell these guys what's going on. And then I realize that we've all got these different difficulties. But we encourage each other. And we pray for each other. And it's like, hey, you know, I'm a guy. And I want to be a guy. And I don't know that the definition has changed. But I know what I want for my family. And so I've got this support group that is trying to help me be what my definition of a guy should be."
Victor in Seattle

"I remember asking a pastor one time, 'you always say that men are the head, men are in charge, yet the people I see running things around here are moms.' And women. But it has gotten more confusing now that women are more empowered. They don't have to play that role." Ward in Seattle

Let the Conversation Begin

"I think you have to start talking to your spouse and setting the ground rules. What exactly is she expecting from you and what do you expect from her? And that way, you are going to avoid any conflict. If you have that clear, I guess it would always work out. Now if there's no conversation, I doubt sincerely that that struggle is gonna be something easy to be solved." Rodrigo in Los Angeles

"Yes, I wish we could all have a man take care of us. And, yes, being the primary breadwinner is not something that is conducive to raising children—we don't have the time. But you know, two of us have to work in order to make ends meet." Bea in Los Angeles

"You know, all of us grew up thinking this was a man's world, that these doors were just gonna open to us because we had a Y chromosome. And suddenly we have to adjust to the fact that, you know, that's not the case. And the recession has made it even more intense for us. And so every family, I think, is trying to figure out, like, what does this mean?" Michael in Seattle

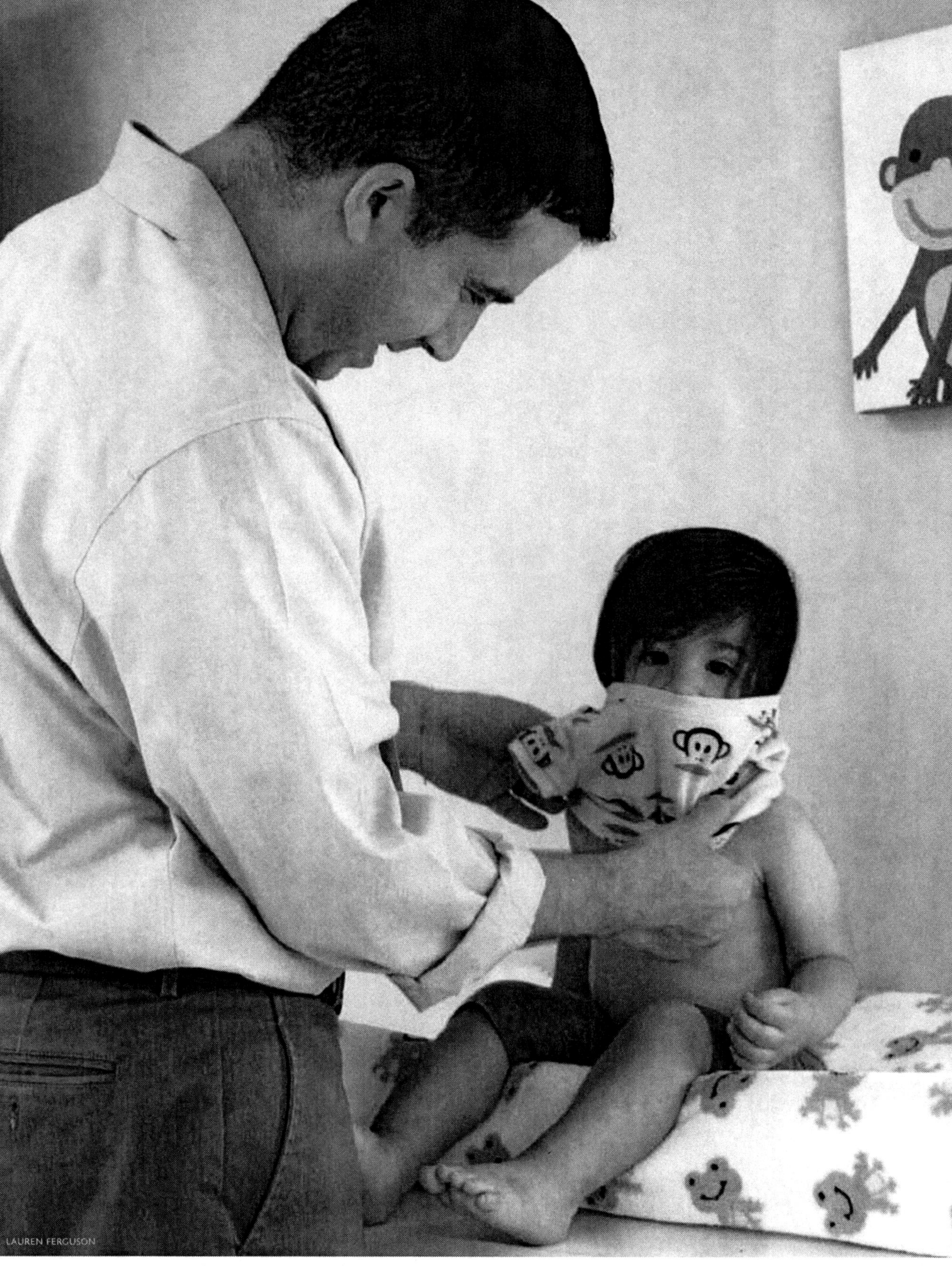

LAUREN FERGUSON

Has a Man's World Become a Woman's Nation?

By Michael Kimmel

"This is a man's world," sang James Brown in 1964, with a voice both defiantly assertive and painfully anguished. He starts off proudly, with a litany of men's accomplishments: men made the cars, the trains, the electric lights and the boats that carried the loads and took us out of the dark. Men even made the toys that children play with. But lest he encourage only smug self-satisfaction, Brown changes course at the end of the song. "But it wouldn't be nothing...without a woman or a girl." Without women, Brown ends, men are "lost in the wilderness...lost in bitterness...lost, lost," his voice trailing off in confusion and despair.

This essay is about that wilderness 45 years later—a wilderness in which some men today are lost, others bitter, and still others searching for new forms of masculinity amid what they believe is the excessive feminization of American society and culture—not because of the absence of women in their lives that Brown noticed but rather, ironically, because of their increased presence. At work and at home, in private and in public, women's increasing equality has been an issue to which men have had to respond.

If women's entry into the labor force stirred up men's ability to anchor their identity as family provider, women's emergence as primary breadwinner is a seismic shift, shaking some men's identities to their foundations. Coupled with the equally seismic shift in the structure of the workplace, we see a major reason why many contemporary observers see a "crisis" of masculinity—a general confusion and malaise about the meaning of manhood.

How have men responded? While some noisily and bitterly protest, and others continue to fight a rear-guard action to undo women's gains, most American men simply continue to go about their lives, falling somewhere between eager embrace of women's equality and resigned acceptance. And among this majority of American men, some interesting developments are now clear. These men by and large are closer to their wives and children and happier for the effort (as are their families), and they are healthier both physically and mentally. And yes, they have more sex.

Declaring America to be a woman's nation, while deliberately provocative, does not mean we are, but just as surely it does mean we no longer live in a man's world, underscoring a significant trend of the gradual, undeniable, and irreversible progress toward gender equality in every arena of American life—from the public sector (economic life, politics, the military) to private life (work-family balance, marital contracts, sexuality). Women have successfully entered every arena of public life, and today many women are as comfortable in the corporate boardroom, the athletic playing field, the legal and medical professions, and the theater of military operations as previous generations of women might have been in the kitchen.

> Declaring America to be a woman's nation, while deliberately provocative, does not mean we are, but it underscores a significant trend of the gradual, undeniable, and irreversible progress toward gender equality in every arena of American life.

And they've done it amazingly fast. It is within the last half-century that the workplace has been so dramatically transformed, that the working world depicted in the hit TV show "Mad Men" (about Madison Avenue advertising executives in the early 1960s) looks so anachronistic as to be nearly unrecognizable. For both women and men, these dramatic changes have come at such a dizzying pace that many Americans are searching for the firmer footing of what they imagine was a simpler time, a bygone era in which everyone knew his or her place.

My father tells me that when he was in college, he and his friends would occasionally pose this question to each other: "Will you let your wife work?" And, he tells me, they all answered it in pretty much the same way. "She shouldn't *have to* work. I should be able to support my family all by myself."

Today, among my male students, the question itself is meaningless. They assume their wives will work, and certainly do not anticipate being asked to grant permission for their wives to do so. They expect to be part of a two-career couple, for financial, if not political, reasons.

The transformation of American public life prompted by these changes in women's lives has of course had a profound impact on the lives of American men—whether or not they recognize it. Indeed, these changes have reverberated to the core of American manhood. Some of the responses receive disproportionate media coverage than their number might warrant. But a guy changing a diaper or drying a dish is far less media-genic than a bunch of Wall Street bankers drumming as they bond around a bonfire, or some deranged divorced dad dressed up as Batman and scaling a state capitol building to promote "fathers' rights."

THE LATEST FROM THE AMERICAN PEOPLE

Q: Do you agree or disagree: Compared to your father, you are more comfortable having women work outside the home?

AGREE 70%

DISAGREE 23%

Source: Rockefeller/*Time* poll, 2009.

I'll try to map a range of men's responses, but the evidence is clear that most American men are quietly acquiescing to these changes, with sweeping implications for our economy and our nation.

Real men provide for their families

Since the country's founding, American men have felt a need to prove their manhood. For well over a century, it's been in the public sphere, and especially the workplace, that American men have been tested. A man may be physically strong, or not. He may be intellectually or athletically gifted, or not. But the one thing that has been non-negotiable has been that a real man provides for his family. He is a breadwinner.[1]

A man who is not a provider—well, he doesn't feel like much of a man at all. Two general trends—structural and social—define the dramatic erosion of the foundation of that public arena for men, leading some men to their current malaise and confusion over the meaning of manhood. James Brown may have been right in 1964 that men made the boats, trains, cars, and electric lights. But the dramatic structural shifts that have accompanied globalization mean that there are very few cars, boats, trains—and even toys—being made domestically any longer.

In the past three decades, manufacturing jobs have been hardest hit as lay-offs in the steel, automobile, and other brick-and-mortar industries downsized,

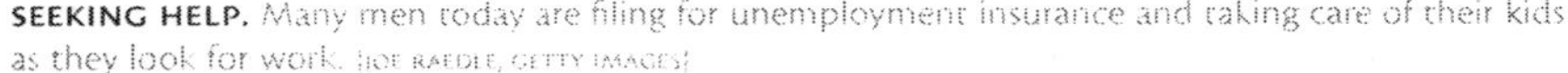

SEEKING HELP. Many men today are filing for unemployment insurance and taking care of their kids as they look for work. (JOE RAEDLE, GETTY IMAGES)

outsourced, cut back, laid off, and closed. Add to that the gradual erosion of our social safety net (health insurance, medical benefits, retirement and pension accounts, Social Security) instituted by the New Deal and we are now living in a new era of "social insecurity." As one 62-year-old machinist told a journalist, "we went to lunch and our jobs went to China."[2]

If women's entry into the labor force stirred up men's ability to anchor their identity as family provider, women's emergence as primary breadwinner is a seismic shift, shaking some men's identity to its foundation.

This decline in manufacturing has been precipitous—and permanent. "Foreman says these jobs are going, boys, and they ain't coming back," sang Bruce Springsteen in "My Hometown"—a 1984 tune that resonates even more today as the Great Recession bleeds even more manufacturing jobs out of the U.S. workforce.

Heather Boushey, in her chapter in this report, also captures the anxiety experienced by blue-collar men of all races who are losing the majority of jobs in this recession and almost all men who are seeing their wages fall. These job losses and wage cuts narrow the gender gap in pay not because women are getting ahead but rather because traditional male-dominated industries are suffering.

Even in economic recovery, as President Obama observed, these jobs "will constitute a smaller percentage of the overall economy," so that, as a result, "women are just as likely to be the primary bread earner, if not more likely, than men are today."[3] So the very foundations on which masculinity has historically rested have eroded; the entire edifice seems capable of collapse at any moment. Or so it seems to a variety of different types of men who rail against our changing society.

Lost in the bitterness

To some men, women's entry into the public arena is experienced not as "entry" but as "invasion." The men who today oppose women's entry into firehouses and police stations, military combat units, and corporate boardrooms echo those who opposed their entry into the Citadel and Virginia Military Institute, the Augusta Country Club, and the locker room a decade ago—men who themselves echoed those who opposed women's right to vote, join a union, serve on a jury, drive a car, or enter the workforce a century ago.

Demographically, they range from younger working-class guys—firefighters and factory workers who sense greater competition for jobs—to middle-class, middle-aged corporate types who believe that the politics of women's entry (affirmative action, an end to wage discrimination, comparable worth) hurt them. Both groups mourn the loss of the casual locker-room frivolity that marked the all-male workplace, and are afraid of, and angry about, sexual harassment guidelines, which they regard as the Politically Correct police. Most are white, and offer the same dire predictions—loss of camaraderie and casual cohesiveness—that whites feared 40 years ago about integration.

> To some men, women's entry into the public arena is experienced not as "entry" but as "invasion."

Men who oppose women's equality today often express a *defensive resistance*. They're interested in preserving certain arenas as all-male havens. Women, we might be told, are not qualified for the positions they seek; they are not strong enough, not tough enough, not [fill in the blank] enough to make the grade. This defensive resistance lies close to the surface; a gentle scratch can elicit a furious response. "I will have none of the nonsense about oppressed and victimized women; no responsibility for the condition of women...none of the guilt or self-loathing that is traditionally used to keep men functioning in harness," fulminates Richard Haddad, a champion of men's rights.[4]

While researching my recent book, *Guyland*, I happened on a Brooklyn bar that has been home to generations of firefighters and their pals. There's an easy ambience about the place, the comfort of younger and older guys (all white) sharing a beer and shooting the breeze. Until I happen to ask one guy about female firefighters. The atmosphere turns menacing, and a defensive anger spills out of the guys near me. "Those bitches have taken over," says Patrick:

WOMEN FIREFIGHTERS. In 2008, women made up 4.1 percent of firefighters, but you wouldn't know it from firehouse conversations. [JUSTIN SULLIVAN, GETTY IMAGES]

> *They're everywhere. You know that ad 'it's everywhere you want to be.' That's like women. They're everywhere they want to be! There's nowhere you can go anymore—factories, beer joints, military, even the firehouse! [Raucous agreement all around.]*[5]

Not long ago, I appeared on a television talk show opposite three such "angry white males" who felt they had been the victims of workplace discrimination. They were in their late twenties and early thirties. The show's title, no doubt to entice a large potential audience, was "A Black Woman Stole My Job." Each of the men described how they were passed over for jobs or promotions for which they believed themselves qualified.

Then it was my turn to respond. I said I had one question about one word in the title of the show. I asked them about the word "my." Where did they get the idea

LEARNING FROM THEIR DAUGHTERS. Coaching girls sports teams is increasingly common among fathers, bringing daughters and dads closer together. [NICOLE BENGIVENO, *THE NEW YORK TIMES*]

it was "their" job? Why wasn't the show called "A Black Woman Got *a* Job" or "A Black Woman Got *the* Job"? These men felt the job was "theirs" because they felt entitled to it, and when some *other* person (a black female) got the job, that person was really taking what was "rightfully" theirs.

That sense of entitlement—and entitlement thwarted—is what lies beneath the surface of these men's resistance to women's equality. These men employ what we might call a "wind chill" theory of gender politics: It doesn't matter what the temperature actually is, it matters only how it feels. Gender equality is felt to be a zero-sum game: If women win, men lose. And to hear them tell it, men are losing.

Once the domain of real men, the participation of women and girls in sports is one of our era's most significant gender transformations.

But they rarely just "tell it." Urged on by anti-feminist media pundits, usually what we hear are screams. Just flip on virtually any talk radio station in America and listen to the callers as they rail against a system that no longer favors them. Eavesdrop on the myriad "men's rights" groups that advocate for men as the new victims of reverse discrimination. Or tune into sports radio, the most gender-specific spot on your radio dial.

As women race onto the athletic field in record numbers, some men run off into sports talk. Once the domain of "real" men, the participation of women and girls in sports is one of our era's most significant gender transformations. In 1971, fewer than 300,000 high school girls played interscholastic sports, compared with 3.7 million boys. By 2005, the participation of boys had increased by about half a million, but girls' participation had soared to 2.9 million. But though women may play sports, they don't tend to spend much time talking about them.

Sports talk radio often expresses the defensive male bonding that lies just below the surface of the easy camaraderie of that imagined locker room. Here's how one regular listener explained it to communications scholar David Nylund:

> *It's a male bonding thing, a locker room for guys in the radio. You can't do it at work, everything's PC now! So the Rome Show [Jim Rome is the most famous sports talk radio DJ] is a last refuge for men to bond and be men... I listen in the car and can let the maleness come out. I know it's offensive sometimes... but men need that!*[6]

Sometimes, this leads to some dizzying reversals of both conventional wisdom and common sense. Are feminists concerned about domestic violence? Proclaim "gender symmetry," and then argue that women hit men as much as men hit women. Women concerned about sexual assault? "The way young women dress in the spring constitutes a sexual assault upon every male within eyesight of them," wrote one retired professor. Women seek to protect their right to choose? Attempt to establish a "man's right to choose," and then prevent a woman from aborting "his" child while ignoring any responsibility for the child once born. Or how about women in the workplace campaigning against wage discrimination or sexual harassment? Insist that the wage gap favors women and that sexual harassment is actually an expression of women's sexual power.[7]

In the eyes of these anti-feminist men's rights groups, it's no longer a man's world. They share this report's perception that America has become a woman's nation. And, in their view, it's time to take it back.

This anti-feminist political agenda is best, and most simply, made by Harvard political scientist Harvey Mansfield, in an op-ed in *The Wall Street Journal*. "The protective element of manliness is endangered by women having equal access to jobs outside the home," he writes. "Women who do not consider themselves feminist nonetheless often seem unaware of what they are doing to manliness when they work to support themselves. They think only that people should be hired and promoted on merit, regardless of sex."[8]

While it can't be true that only feminists actually believe in meritocracy, some who would support men evidently want to keep that playing field as uneven as possible. That's certainly what groups such as the National Organization for

Men, Men's Rights International, and others seek as they organize men around perceived injustices against men by the feminist cabal that supposedly now rules Washington. In the eyes of these anti-feminist men's rights groups, it's no longer a man's world. They share this report's perception that America has become a woman's nation. And, in their view, it's time to take it back.

The "masculinists"

To other men, women's increased empowerment only highlights the loss of masculine vigor among American men. Their response was not to attempt to roll back women's gains but rather to return to a nostalgic notion of masculinity, one rooted in ostensibly natural, primal, sacred, or mythic qualities. If women have invaded all the previously all-male institutions, men needed to find, as Virginia Woolf might have put it, "a room of their own"—an all-male space where men can relax with other men, free from the constant policing that accompanies political correctness, and retrieve their inner sense of their own masculinity, in the presence of other men. For these "masculinists," gender politics are a project of reclamation, restoration, and retrieval—not of some lost power over women, but of a lost sense of internal efficacy and sense of power.

To some men, women's increased empowerment highlights the loss of masculine vigor among American men. Their response was not to attempt to roll back women's gains but rather to return to a nostalgic notion of masculinity.

In the last decades of the 20th century, thousands of middle-aged, middle-class white men found themselves literally "lost in the wilderness" as they trooped off dutifully on what were called "mythopoetic" retreats with poets such as Robert Bly and story-tellers such as Michael Meade. These "weekend warriors" sensed that men had lost their vitality, their distinctively male energy in a world of alienating office cubicles, yucky diaper-changing and sappy date movies.[9]

For masculinists, power is not about economic or political aggregates or different groups' access to resources. Nor is it to be measured by comparing wages or representatives on corporate boards or legislative bodies. Rather, power is an interior experience, a sense of dynamic energy. As a result, they tend not to engage with policy initiatives designed to push women back. At their best, they are indifferent to women's collective experience; they may even take inspiration from women's empowerment. They seek instead to combat their sense of emasculation not with impotent rage against feminized institutions, but rather by restoring their sense of power in reclaiming masculine myths.

THE PROMISE KEEPERS. Persuading men to find Jesus and take control of their families.
[MARC ASNIN, REDUX]

Other guys find that lost all-male Eden in cyberspace. While cinematic and pornographic fantasies of men's power have long been with us, the proliferation of video and computer games in which avatars wreak havoc on women, gays, and other "others" is still somewhat shocking. For significant numbers of younger men, remote corners of cyberspace are the newest incarnation of the Little Rascals' "He-Man Woman Haters Club," the tree house with the sign that says "No Gurls Allowed."

These types of masculinists tend to rely on archaic notions of the essential, natural, and binary masculine and feminine. As a result, they may become momentarily enamored with anti-feminist policy initiatives, such as the re-segregation of schools into single-sex classes, ostensibly to promote boys' engagement with education, but often to set back decades of feminist efforts to make classrooms and athletic fields more equal. (These anti-feminists are not to be confused with those popular voices in minority communities—backed by many policy analysts—all of whom are engaged with the crisis facing many *minority* boys in school, which is both real and serious.) For these mostly white masculinists, their zeal to support fathers' connection with family life and especially with the experience of fatherhood often draws them into "angry dad" campaigns against custody or divorce laws, in which men are said to be the victims of reverse discrimination.

The most interesting arenas of contemporary masculinism, however, are in some of America's churches. The most visible of these renewed revirilization efforts is the group Promise Keepers, which holds massive 50,000-to-75,000 men-only rallies in sports stadiums (because that's where men feel comfortable gathering) with ministers (called coaches) and their assistants (dressed in zebra-striped shirts as if they were football referees) who seek to return men to the church.

Founded in 1990 by Bill McCartney, former football coach at the University of Colorado, Promise Keepers is an evangelical Christian movement that seeks to bring men back to Jesus. Mostly middle class from the South and Midwest, they wed what you might think is a more "feminine" notion of evangelical Christianity—ideals of service, healing, and racial reconciliation—with a renewed assertion of men's God-ordained position as head of the family and master of women. While mostly white, they have a real presence of African Americans in leadership positions.

In return for men keeping their promises to be faithful husbands, devoted fathers, and general all-around good men, the movement's "bible," "The Seven Promises of a Promise Keeper," suggests that men deal with women this way:

MINDING THE FAMILY SINGLE-HANDEDLY. Scott Elgin is raising his three-year-old daughter Emilie on his own in St. Petersburg, Florida after Emilie's mother developed a drug addiction. {JULIA ROBINSON}

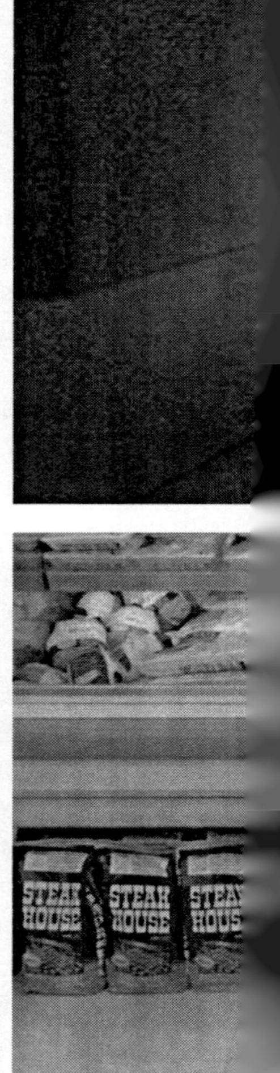

STEAK
HOUSE

> *[S]it down with your wife and say 'Honey I've made a terrible mistake. I've given you my role in leading this family and I forced you to take my place. Now I must reclaim that role.' . . . I'm not suggesting that you ask for your role back. I'm urging you to take it back. . . . There can be no compromise here. If you're going to lead you must lead.*[10]

THE LATEST FROM THE AMERICAN PEOPLE

Q: Do you agree or disagree: With the rise of women in society and the workplace, men no longer know their role?

	AGREE	DISAGREE
WHITE MEN	27%	70%
BLACK MEN	29%	67%
LATINO MEN	30%	64%
MEN EARNING <$60,000 PER YEAR	32%	62%
MEN EARNING >$60,000 PER YEAR	23%	76%

Source: Rockefeller/*Time* poll, 2009.

Others have followed suit, from "The Power Team," hyper-muscular zealots who pump up their gendered theology along with their biceps, performing such feats of strength as breaking stacks of bricks, to "J-B-C Men" who promise a "shock and awe" gospel and bonding at the movies (J-B-C stands for "Jesus - Beer - Chips!"). Or Seattle evangelist Marc Driscoll, who rails against the "Richard Simmons, hippie, queer Christ" offered by mainline Protestant churches.[11]

The formal elements of the so-called "Masculinist Movement," such as the Promise Keepers, have been predominantly white and upper- or middle-class.[12] Men of color, however, have also participated in the Movement in different ways, some formal and some less formal. The 1995 Million Man March was a formal (and for some, troubling) engagement with masculinist politics. As scholar Maurice Orlando Wallace described it, the march was "ambitious and unprecedented," but it focused on the crisis of black America as one centered on "an embattled black masculinity," which "provoked rigorous dissent from African American feminists" and others.[13]

To the new masculinists, it may no longer be a man's world, but they'd like, at least, to find small pockets of all-male purity in which they can, again, be men among men.

Fatherhood as politics

After enumerating men's accomplishments in the workplace in his hit song, James Brown shifts his tone to a softer, more yearning, and plaintive tone. "Man thinks about a little baby girl, and a baby boy/ Man makes them happy,' cause man makes them toys." Here Brown signals the other defining feature of American manhood: fatherhood. After all, if one's identity is wrapped up in being a family provider, one has to have a family to provide for.

In the 21st century, reconnecting men to family life is politicized terrain, filled with moral urgency, legalistic outrage, and social movements. Some advocates of the "new fatherhood" paint with far broader strokes than simply enabling married couples to better balance work and family. David Blankenhorn's *Fatherless America* credited absent fathers with causing myriad social problems, ranging from juvenile delinquency, drug taking, sexual irresponsibility, crime and violence to unemployment. "Boys raised by traditionally masculine fathers generally do not commit crimes," Blankenhorn adds. "Fatherless boys commit crimes."[14] His work was a catalog of specious correlations masquerading as causal arguments, but it struck a nerve about men's responsibility, or lack thereof.

In the 21st century, reconnecting men to family life is politicized terrain, filled with moral urgency, legalistic outrage, and social movements.

With divorce so common, one arena in which fatherhood has become highly politicized is during and after divorce. Many of the organizations promoting involved "fatherhood responsibility," especially in communities of color, seek to keep men engaged in family life because it's good for the children, good for women, and good for the men themselves. For other men, mostly white and middle class, the stroke of the pen finalizing divorce turns hordes of doting daddies into furious fathers who feel aggrieved by a process they believe denies them the access to their children to which they feel entitled.

These "father rights" guys blend easily into more general anti-feminist organizations in advocating for public policy reforms. Case in point: Fred Hayward, founder of Men's Rights, Inc., argued that women were "*privileged* because they are more frequently *allowed* to raise children, while men are being *oppressed* by denial of access to children."[15]

Fathers' rights groups use a language of equality to exact their revenge against their ex-wives, their ex-wives' lawyers, and the entire legal system, demanding mandatory joint custody and an end to alimony and child support payments. "Society cannot take away a father's right to his children and expect him to cheerfully pay child support," writes one activist. "Society cannot expect a father to make enough money to support two separate households. Society cannot afford to support mothers who choose not to work."[16] Fathers must have equal rights—the right to custody and the right to financial freedom without burdensome alimony and child support.

Well-documented racial disparities in enforcement of child support laws create a perception that some fathers are significantly more irresponsible, creating (or enabling) the very dynamics they are supposed to remedy.

In reality, the fathers' rights groups are tapping into a problem that very few men report having. Most parents get the custody arrangements they say they want, and while, all things being equal, the legal system does tend to privilege ex-wives' claims over ex-husbands' claims, all things are rarely, if ever, equal. In a recent study of 1,000 divorces in two California counties, for example, psychologist Eleanor Maccoby and law professor Robert Mnookin found that about 82 percent of mothers and 56 percent of fathers received the custody arrangement they wanted, while 6.7 percent of women and 9.8 percent of men requested more than they wanted and 11.5 percent of women and 34.1 percent of men requested less than they wanted.[17]

This suggests that "gender still matters" in what parents ask for and what they do to get it. That mothers were more likely to act on their desires by filing for a specific request also indicates that men need to ask for more up front to avoid feeling bitter later.[18]

But one consequence of current custody arrangements is paternal withdrawal. Whether this is because the father is bereft about losing regular contact with his children, or because once the marital bond is severed he considers himself to have escaped from a conflict-ridden family situation, it appears that many men "see parenting and marriage as part of the same bargain—a package deal," write sociologists Frank Furstenberg and Andrew Cherlin. "It is as if they stop being fathers as soon as the marriage is over."[19]

In one nationally representative sample of 11-to-16-year-old children living with their mothers, almost half had not seen their fathers in the previous 12 months. Indeed, we see a widespread "masculinization of irresponsibility"—the refusal of fathers to provide economically for their children, which has led to the "feminization of poverty," with excruciatingly high poverty among single-mother families.

DIVIDING UP THE CHORES. Families today divide up the housework and the bill paying, but women continue to do more child care. [GARY KAZANJIAN, AP]

JP LAFFONT / SYGMA / CORBIS

> Well, the local union that I represent is in Flint. And one of the things that we saw as things were going on, obviously tensions rose as people were fearful for their jobs. And what we wanted to do was make sure that we responded in a way that would let them know that there were options. Because the feeling is the lack of options creates a desperation. And we did not want that desperation to turn on their fellow employees or their families or on themselves.
>
> *Art in Detroit*

What predicts continued paternal involvement in their children's lives after a divorce is the quality of the relationship between the ex-spouses prior to the divorce.

This masculinizaton of irresponsibility is compounded by class and race. Poorer communities desperately need child support programs to enable and assist fathers in staying connected. Well-documented racial disparities in enforcement of child support laws create a perception that some fathers are significantly more irresponsible, creating (or enabling) the very dynamics they are supposed to remedy. Take just one example. In Dane County, Wisconsin, arrest rates for African Americans for nonpayment of child support are about 35 times those of white residents. Nearly one in two of those arrested for this reason were African Americans in a county whose African American population in 2000 was 4 percent of the total county population.[20]

Found, not lost

The anti-feminists may shout loudest, and the new masculinists may be the most mediagenic of men's responses to increased gender equality, but they represent only a small fraction of American men. The largest, if least acknowledged, response to women's equality is the quiet acceptance of gender equality at both the public and private level. In the public sphere, the majority of American men support wage equality, comparable worth, women's candidacies for public office.

The anti-feminists may shout loudest, and the new masculinists may be the most mediagenic of men's responses to increased gender equality, but they represent only a small fraction of American men.

On the domestic front, surveys consistently show "substantial and persistent" long-term trends increasing the endorsement of gender equality in families. With only modest attitudinal adjustment, most American men have adapted to the dual-career couple model that now characterizes most marriages. Some are even delighted to have the additional family income. Most American men subscribe to a general "ethical imperative" and see women's equality as right, just, and fair. They just don't think it has all that much to do with them as men.[21]

But it does. As I will show below, when fatherhood is transformed from a political cause to a personal experience, from an ideological position or an existential state of being to a set of concrete practices, men's lives are dramatically improved. As are their children's.

When fatherhood is transformed from a political cause to a personal experience, from an ideological position or an existential state of being to a set of concrete practices, men's lives are dramatically improved. As are their children's.

This acceptance isn't the result of some grand ideological transformation in the meaning of manhood. Some part of it is simply financial. "These days, Ward Cleaver wouldn't be able to afford a house in the suburbs or Beaver's tuition—unless June went to work too," writes Nicholas Kulish in *The New York Times*. Indeed, despite some evidence that the Great Recession may spur increases in reactive defensiveness among men, it may, in fact, propel the trend toward greater acceptance of equality. One recent survey found that a decline in men's breadwinner status tends to promote egalitarian gender ideologies.[22]

Plus, it is the inevitable result of countless micro-level decisions made by families every day: about their daughters' and sons' education, an increased intolerance for bullying or harassment, a sense of fairness about wage equality and reducing discrimination. It's not that men woke up one morning and decided to scrap their traditional definition of masculinity. Rather, they gradually, and without fanfare or struggle, drifted into more egalitarian relationships because they love their wives, partners, and children.

Support for gender equality begins at home. Across race, class, and (nonevangelical) religious ideologies, support for the more conventional male-breadwinner/female homemaker ideology has fallen dramatically since the late 1970s. A new report by the Families and Work Institute finds that while 74 percent of men (and 52 percent of women) subscribed to that conventional model in 1977, just over two-fifths of men (42 percent) and less than two-fifths of women (39 percent) subscribe to it today.[23]

What's more, men's attitudes about women's ability to balance work and family also shifted in a decidedly positive direction. In 1977, less than half of men (49 percent) agreed with the statement, "A mother who works outside the home can have just as good a relationship with her children as a mother who does not work." Thirty years later—a short time in terms of attitude shifts—two-thirds of men agree (as do 80 percent of women).

It's not that men woke up one morning and decided to scrap their traditional definition of masculinity. Rather, they gradually, and without fanfare or struggle, drifted into more egalitarian relationships because they love their wives, partners, and children.

This change is more pronounced the younger the respondent. Just over a third of "Millennial" employees who were 28 or younger in 2008 support that traditional family model today, while slightly more than half (53 percent) of mature workers (63 and older in 2008) support it—though 90 percent of mature workers subscribed to the conventional model in 1977. And while 70 percent of men in dual-career couples still subscribed to the more conventional model in 1977, only about 37 percent of them subscribe to that today.[24]

While most American men's participation in family life, that is doing housework and child care, tends to be expressed by two two-word phrases—men "help out" and "pitch in"—men's share of housework and especially child care has also increased significantly in the past few decades. Men are both more likely to do more housework, and also more likely to hug their children and tell them that they love them, than in previous decades. It took several decades for the norm to be a dual-career couple; it will take several more decades before the norm is also a "dual-carer" couple.

HANDLING THE PLAY DATES. Fathers do more than barbecue these days. [JAMES ESTRIN, *THE NEW YORK TIMES*]

The average father today spends three hours a day on the weekend with his family, up significantly from estimates in earlier decades. While women still do the majority of routine housework, "husbands of working wives are spending more time in the family than in the past." In 1924, 10 percent of working-class women said their husbands spent "no time" doing housework; today that percentage is less than 2 percent. Between the mid-1960s and the mid-1970s, men's household labor increased from five to seven hours per week, while women's share decreased by about five hours, from 27 hours to 22 hours per week.[25]

Though we tend to think that sharing housework is the product of ideological commitments—progressive, liberal, well-educated middle-class families with more egalitarian attitudes—the data suggest a more complicated picture that has less to do with ideological concerns.

When couples were asked to keep accurate records of how much time they spent doing which household tasks, men still put in significantly less time than their wives. The most recent figures from the National Survey of Families and Households at the University of Wisconsin show that husbands were doing about 14 hours of housework per week (compared with 31 hours for wives). In more traditional couples in which she stays home and the husband is the sole earner, her hours jump to 38 and his decline slightly to 12.

Reasonable, since they've defined housework as "her" domain. But when both work full-time outside the home, the wife does 28 hours and the husband does 16.[26] This is four times the amount of housework that Japanese men do, but only two-thirds of the housework that Swedish men do.[27]

Though we tend to think that sharing housework is the product of ideological commitments—progressive, liberal, well-educated middle-class families with more egalitarian attitudes—the data suggest a more complicated picture that has less to do with ideological concerns. In every single subcategory (meal preparation, dishes, cleaning, shopping, washing, outdoor work, auto repair and maintenance, and bill paying), for example, black men do significantly more housework than white men. In more than one-fourth of all black families, men do more than 40 percent of the housework. Men's "share" of housework comes closer to an equal share.

In white families, only 16 percent of the men do that much. And blue-collar fathers, regardless of race (municipal and service workers, policemen, firefighters, maintenance workers), are twice as likely (42 percent) as those in professional, managerial, or technical jobs (20 percent) to care for their children while their wives work. This difference comes less from ideological commitments and more from an "informal flex time," a split-shift arrangement with one's spouse, which is negotiated by about one-fourth of all workers in the United States, and one-third of all workers with children under age 5.[28]

Such findings are echoed among Mexican-origin families. Fathers in these families did more housework when the family income was lower or when wives contributed a larger share of family income, an indication that among this population, too, economic reality can modify ideological assumptions.[29] Among immigrant groups, class position tends to be more important than ethnicity as well—though it might tend in a different direction. Taiwanese immigrant men, for example, in the professional class tend to hold more egalitarian attitudes and perform more housework and child care than do Taiwanese men in the working class.[30]

As a result of these complex findings, researchers increasingly adopt an intersectional approach, exploring how race, class, ethnicity, and immigrant status interact to produce distinct patterns. It may be that class position—regardless of race, ethnicity, or

THE LATEST FROM THE AMERICAN PEOPLE

Q: Families today are very busy juggling multiple and conflicting schedules, duties, and responsibilities. How often do you and your spouse/partner need to coordinate your family's schedule?

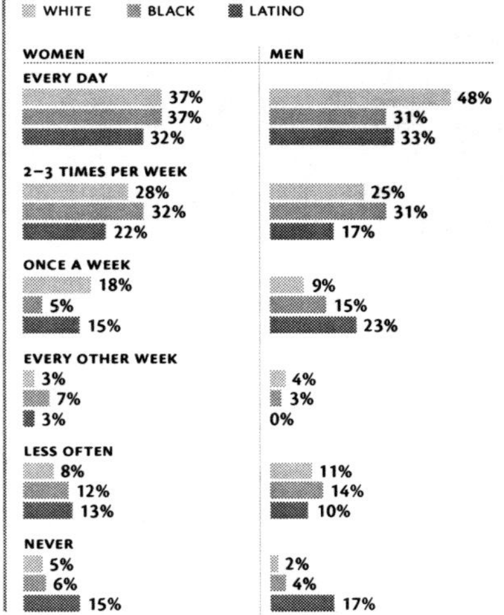

Source: Rockefeller/*Time* poll, 2009.

LUNCH TIME. Family friendly working hours would help this father with his family chores and policeman's duties. {KEVIN HORAN, TIME LIFE PICTURES, GETTY IMAGES}

immigrant status—may be the best predictor of both ideological orientations and actual behaviors, though the two may be contradictory or mutually reinforcing.[31]

Housework aside, when it comes to being fathers, men are evidently willing to do more. A poll in *Newsweek* magazine found that 55 percent of fathers say that being a parent is more important to them than it was to their fathers, and 70 percent say they spend more time with their children than their fathers spent with them. What's more, they are actually *doing* it. According to the 2008 study by the Families and Work Institute, the amount of time fathers spend with their children under the age of 13 on workdays has increased from two hours a day in 1977 to three hours a day in 2008—an increase of 50 percent. Women's rate has remained constant over that 30-year period, at 3.8 hours per workday. Millennial fathers spend 4.3 hours per workday (their wives spend five hours). Men are not merely walking their walk; they almost seem to be jogging it.[32]

President Obama has also weighed in on the state of American fatherhood. In June 2008, during the presidential campaign, he took African American men to task for high rates of absenteeism in the lives of their children. And, as we've seen, after the dissolution of a relationship, many fathers dramatically reduce, or altogether lose, contact with their children. But while the couple is together—in both black families and white, native-born and immigrant, religious and secular—men are, today, more involved in child care than possibly any other generation in American history.

To be sure, there are some racial and ethnic differences. According to one 2005 U.S. Census Bureau study, 20 percent of white fathers are primary caregivers for their children when the mother is at work, compared to 11.3 percent of Asians, 12.7 percent of African Americans, and 15 percent of Hispanics. Note, though, that these differences are for primary caregiving, not caregiving in general, and that the rates are not so dramatically different. What's more, in all cases the trajectory is up.[33]

Men's increased participation in child care has its challenges, of course. Men are reporting significantly higher levels of work-family conflict than they did 30 years ago.

Men's increased participation in child care has its challenges, of course. Men are reporting significantly higher levels of work-family conflict than they did 30 years ago (and their rates now surpass women's). Three of five fathers in dual-earner couples report significant work-family conflict, up from just over a third (35 percent) in 1977.[34]

What's more, with men's child care participation increasing so much faster than their housework, a dangerous disequilibrium is developing in which dad is becoming the "fun parent." He takes the kids to the park and plays soccer with them; she stays home. "What a great time we had with dad!" the kids announce as they burst through the kitchen door to a lunch that mom prepared while also folding the laundry and vacuuming the living room.

But when men do share housework as well as child care, the payoff is significant. Research by sociologists Scott Coltrane and Michele Adams looked at national survey data and found that when men increase their share of housework and child care, their children are happier, healthier, and do better in school.[35] They are less likely to be diagnosed with ADHD, less likely to be put on prescription medication, and less likely to see a child psychologist for behavioral problems. They have lower rates of absenteeism and higher school achievement scores.

THE LATEST FROM THE AMERICAN PEOPLE

Q: Do you agree or disagree: Men today are less interested in playing the macho role than they were in years past?

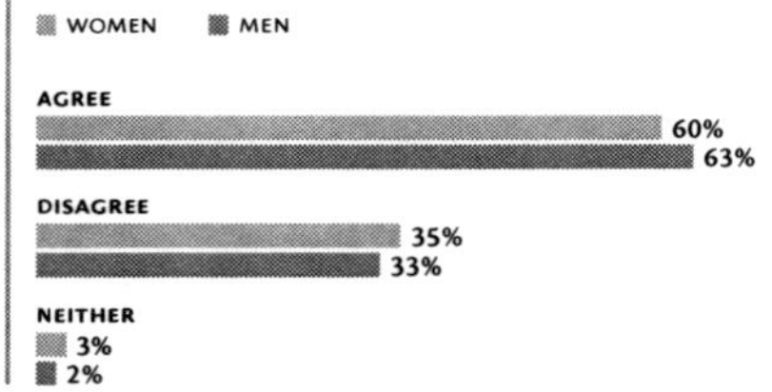

Source: Rockefeller/*Time* poll, 2009.

"When men perform domestic service for others, it teaches children cooperation and democratic family values," said Coltrane. "It used to be that men assumed that their wives would do all the housework and parenting, but now that women are nearly equal participants in the labor force, men are assuming more of the tasks that it takes to run a home and raise children."[36]

Perhaps the most telling correlation is that when school-aged children do housework with their fathers, they get along better with their peers and have more friends. And they show more positive behaviors than if they did the same work with their mothers. "Because fewer men do housework than women," said Adams, "when they share the work, it has more impact on children." Fathers model "cooperative family partnerships."

When men share housework and child care, it turns out, their wives are happier. This is intuitively obvious. Historically, working mothers reported higher levels of self-esteem and lower levels of depression than full-time housewives. Yet they also reported lower levels of marital satisfaction than do their husbands, who are happier than the husbands of traditional housewives. This was because under such arrangements, women's workload increased at home, while the men benefited by having almost the same amount of work done for them at home and having their standard of living buttressed by an additional income.[37]

But wives of egalitarian husbands, regardless of class or race and ethnicity, report the highest levels of marital satisfaction and lowest rates of depression, and are less likely to see therapists or take prescription medication. They are also more likely to stay fit, since they probably have more time on their hands.[38]

The benefits for the men? Men who do more housework and child care are physically healthier. They smoke less, drink less, and take recreational drugs less often. They are more likely to stay in shape and more likely to go to doctors for routine screenings, but less likely to use emergency rooms or miss work due to illness.

They're also psychologically healthy. They are less often diagnosed with depression, and see therapists and take prescription medication less compared to men who do not share housework. They report higher levels of marital satisfaction. They also live longer, causing the normally staid British financial magazine *The Economist* to quip, "Change a nappy, by God, and put years on your life." "When males take full responsibility for child care," sociologist Barbara Risman points out, "they develop intimate and affectionate relationships with their children." Nurturing their children is good for men's health.[39]

And they have more sex. Research by psychologist John Gottman at the University of Washington found higher rates of marital sex among couples where men did more housework and child care. This last finding was trumpeted by *Men's Health* magazine with the headline "Housework Makes Her Horny" (although I suspect that is not true when she does it). It is probably worthwhile pointing out that there is no one-to-one correspondence here; I would advise male readers of this essay against immediately rushing home to load the washing machine. Instead it points to wives' lower levels of stress in balancing work and family, coupled with a dramatic reduction in resentment that they alone are doing the second shift.

"Nothing without a woman or a girl"

There's an old adage that the Chinese character for "crisis" is a combination of the characters for "danger" and "opportunity." While some men see increased gender equality as a dangerous reversal of traditional gender arrangements, most men are going along for a rather apolitical ride, seeing neither danger nor opportunity. They're doing more housework and child care, supporting their wives' career aspirations, and sharing the decision-making about family life and career trajectories, not because of some ideological commitment to feminism, but because of a more commonplace commitment to their families and loved ones.

In a sense, they know the fix is already in. Women are in the labor force—and every other public arena—to stay. So the choice for men is how we will relate to this transformation. Will we be dragged kicking and screaming into the future? Flee to some male-only preserve, circle the masculine wagons, and regroup? Or instead, will the majority of us who are now somewhere between eager embrace and resigned acceptance see instead the opportunity for the "enthusiastic embrace" of gender equality?

Chances are we will—not only because it is inevitable (which it is) and not just because it's right and just and fair (which it is). We will because we also see that men who embrace equality will live happier, healthier lives, lives animated by love and connection with our wives, our partners, our children, and our friends. And so will the children of these and most other men, who grow up with working mothers—and have sisters, friends, and girlfriends who expect to be equal at work and at home.

Men who have renegotiated a more gender-equitable path forward in their lives and their work have reaped significant benefits, yet many men continue to struggle with lost incomes, lost breadwinner status, and downward economic mobility that threatens their ability to see women's progress for what it is. There is a role for government in helping all men understand there is a clear path forward where masculinity and gender equality are complementary, not adversarial:

- Most men are "apolitically accepting" of the new status quo, but there needs to be public space to develop a politically forward-thinking agenda where men and women together can champion the reforms presented throughout this report.

Men need to help create this public space, not rely on women to do so. Men need to speak out in the public sphere as fathers and partners, just as women have embraced their role as workers in their homes.

- As a result, both men and women both need the kinds of support that makes it possible to have dual-earner, dual-carer families, but these issues are most often misperceived as "women's issues" in Washington and statehouses around the nation. Men need family-friendly policies, including on-site child care, health care reform, flexible working hours, and parental leave so that they can have the sorts of relationships they say they want to have.

- Policymakers need to support the choices of the majority of men who are pursuing gender equality within their homes. Men today are nearly as likely as women to take time off from work to care for ailing family members, but men remain less likely to take time off to bond with a new child. Policies that redefine what it means to be a good provider and a good citizen should encourage men and women to be both breadwinner and caretaker in their families.

Becoming a woman's nation can be a vast improvement for everyone over remaining a man's world. Gender equality is not a zero-sum game, but rather win-win.

ENDNOTES

1 Michael Kimmel, *Manhood in America: A Cultural History, 10th anniversary edition* (New York: Oxford University Press, 2006), p. 20.

2 "A NewsHour with Jim Lehrer Transcript: The Jobless Recovery," available at http://www.pbs.org/newshour/bb/economy/jan-june03/jobs_6-23.html (last accessed August 2009).

3 Reihan Salam, "The Death of Macho," *Foreign Policy*, June 22, 2009, available at http://www.foreignpolicy.com/articles/2009/06/18/the_death_of_macho.

4 Richard Haddad, "Feminism has Little Relevance for Men." In Keith Thompson, ed., *To Be a Man: In Search of the Deep Masculine* (Los Angeles: Jeremy Tarcher, 1991), p. 100.

5 Michael Kimmel, *Guyland: The Perilous World Where Boys Become Men* (New York: HarperCollins, 2008), p. 12.

6 David Nylund, *Beer, Babes, and Balls: Masculinity in Sports Talk Radio* (Albany, NY: SUNY Press, 2008), pp. 118–119.

7 Warren Farrell, *The Myth of Male Power* (New York: Simon and Schuster, 1993), pp. 298, 301.

8 Harvey Mansfield, "Why a Woman Can't Be More Like a Man," *The Wall Street Journal*, November 3, 1997, p. A 22.

9 Michael Kaufman and Michael Kimmel, "The New Men's Movement: Retreat and Regression with America's Weekend Warriors," *Gender Issues* 13 (2) (June 1993): 3–21.

10 Tony Evans, "Reclaiming Your Manhood." In Al Janssen ed., *The Seven Promises of a Promise Keeper* (Colorado Springs, CO: Focus on the Family Publishing, 1994), pp. 79–80.

11 Molly Worthen, "Who Would Jesus Smack Down?" *The New York Times Magazine*, January 11, 2009, p. 20.

12 Billy Hawkins, "A Critical Reading of a Promise Keepers Event: The Interworkings of Race, Religion, and Sport," *Sociology of Sport Online* 3 (1) (2000), available at http://physed.otago.ac.nz/sosol/v3i1/v3i1a2.htm.

13 Maurice O. Wallace, *Constructing the Black Masculine: Identity and Ideality in African American Men's Literature and Culture, 1775–1995* (Durham, NC: Duke University Press, 2002), p. 5.

14 David Blankenhorn, *Fatherless America: Confronting Our Most Urgent Social Problem* (New York: HarperCollins Publishers, 1995).

15 Anna Gavanas, *Fatherhood Politics in the United States* (Urbana, IL: University of Illinois Press, 2004); Jocelyn Crowley, *Defiant Dads: Fathers' Rights Activists in America* (Ithaca, NY: Cornell University Press, 2008); Marcy Sheiner, "What do Men Really Want...and Why Should we Care?" *East Bay Express*, July 10, 1992, p. 11.

16 Jon Conine, *Fathers' Rights: The Sourcebook for Dealing with the Child Support System* (New York: Walker, 1989), p. 2.

17 Eleanor Maccoby and Robert Mnookin. *Dividing the Child: Social and Legal Dilemmas of Custody*. (Cambridge: Harvard University Press, 1992).

18 Robert Griswold, *Fatherhood in America: A History* (New York: BasicBooks, 1993), p. 263; Nancy Polikoff, "Gender and Child Custody Determinations: Exploding the Myths." In Irene Diamond, ed., *Families, Politics and Public Policy: A Feminist Dialogue on Women and the State* (New York: Longman, 1983), pp. 184–185; Robert H. Mnookin and others, "Private Ordering Revisited: What Custodial Arrangements are Parents Negotiating?" In Stephen Sugarman and Herma Kaye, eds., *Divorce Reform at the Crossroads* (New Haven: Yale University Press, 1990), p. 55; Eleanor Maccoby and Robert Mnookin, *Dividing the Child: Social and Legal Dilemmas of Custody* (Cambridge: Harvard University Press, 1992), p. 101.

19 Frank Furstenberg and Andrew Cherlin, Divided Families: What Happens to Children When Parents Part (Cambridge, MA: Harvard University Press, 1994), p. 38.

20 "The Effect of Child Support and Criminal Justice Systems on Low-Income Noncustodial Parents," available at http://www.cffpp.org/publications/effect_child.html#coopreq (last accessed August 2009).

21 Arland Thornton and Linda Young-DeMarco, "Four Decades of Trends in Attitudes Toward Family Issues in the United States: The 1960s through the 1990s," *Journal of Marriage and Family* 63 (4) (2001): 1009–1037.

22 Nicholas Kulish, "Editorial Observer: Changing the Rules for the Team Sport of Bread-Winning," *The New York Times*, September 23, 2005, available at http://www.nytimes.com/2005/09/23/opinion/23fri4.html; Jiping Zuo and Shenming Tang, "Breadwinner Status and Gender Ideologies of Men and Women Regarding Family Roles," *Sociological Perspectives* 43 (1) (2000): 29–43.

23 Ellen Galinsky, Kerstin Aumann and James T. Bond, "Times Are Changing: Gender and Generation at Work and at Home" (New York: Families and Work Institute, 2008), p. 10.

24 Ibid, p. 11.

25 Randall Collins and Scott Coltrane, *Sociology of Marriage and the Family: Gender, Love and Property (4th edition)* (Chicago, IL: Nelson-Hall, 1995), p. 378.

26 Lisa Belkin, "When Mom and Dad Share it All," *The New York Times Magazine*, June 15, 2008, p. 47.

27 Almudena Sevilla-Sanz, "Household Division of Labor and Cross-Country Differences in Household Formation Rates." Working Paper 325 (University of Oxford Department of Economics, May 2007).

28 Bart Landry, *Black Working Wives: Pioneers of the American Family Revolution* (Berkeley: University of California Press, 2000); Scott Coltrane, "Research on Household Labor: Modeling and Measuring the Social Embeddedness of Routine Family Work" *Journal of Marriage and the Family* 62 (4) (2000): 1208–1233; Margaret Usdansky, "White Men don't Jump Into Chores," *USA Today*, August 20, 1994; Julia Lawlor, "Earning It: For Many Blue Collar Fathers, Child Care is Shift Work, Too," *The New York Times*, April 26, 1998, available at http://www.nytimes.com/1998/04/26/business/earning-it-for-many-blue-collar-fathers-child-care-is-shift-work-too.html.

29 Katy Pinto and Scott Coltrane, "Divisions of Labor in Mexican Origin and Anglo Families: Structure and Culture," *Sex Roles* 60 (7-8) (2009): 482–495; Beth Shelton and Daphne John, "Ethnicity, Race, and Difference: A Comparison of White, Black, and Hispanic Men's Household Labor Time." In Jane Hood, ed., *Men, Work, and Family* (Thousand Oaks, CA: Sage, 1993).

30 Yen Le Espiritu, "Gender and labor in Asian immigrant families," *American Behavioral Scientist* 42 (4) (1999): 628–647.

31 Scott Coltrane and Kristy Y. Shih, "Gender and Household Labor." In Joan C. Chrisler and Donald R. McCreary, eds., *Handbook of Gender Research in Psychology* (Springer, forthcoming); Heather Dillaway and Clifford Broman, "Race, Class, and Gender Differences in Marital Satisfaction and Divisions of Household Labor Among Dual-Earner Couples: A Case for Intersectional Analysis," *Journal of Family Issues* 22 (3) (2001): 309–327.

32 Jerry Adler, "Building a Better Dad," *Newsweek*, June 17, 1996; Tamar Lewin, "Workers of Both Sexes Make Trade-Offs for Family, Study Shows," *The New York Times*, October 29, 1995, p. 25; Galinsky and others, "Times Are Changing," p. 14.

33 "Who's Minding the Kids? Child Care Arrangements: Spring 2005," available at http://www.census.gov/population/www/socdemo/child/ppl-2005.html (last accessed August 2009), table 2B.

34 Galinsky and others, "Times Are Changing," p. 18.

35 Scott Coltrane, personal communication, July 25, 2009.

36 "When Dads Clean House, It Pays Off Big Time," available at http://newsroom.ucr.edu/news_item.html?action=page&id=611 (last accessed August 2009).

37 Arlie Hochschild, *The Second Shift* (New York: Penguin Books, 2003); Paul Amato and Alan Booth, "Changes in Gender Role Attitudes and Perceived Marital Quality," *American Sociological Review* 60 (1) (1995).

38 Coltrane, "Research on Household Labor: Modeling and Measuring the Social Embeddedness of Routine Family Work."

39 "Sex, Death, and Football," *The Economist*, June 13, 1998, p. 18; Robert D. Mintz and James Mahalik, "Gender Role Orientation and Conflict as Predictors of Family Roles for Men," *Sex Roles*, 34 (1-2) (1996): 805–821; Barbara Risman, "Can Men 'Mother'? Life as a Single Father," *Family Relations* 35 (1) (1986); Caryl Rivers and Rosalind Barnett, "Fathers Do Best," *The Washington Post*, June 20, 1993, p. C5.

Our Fathers—Teaching Us to Soar

By Sukhinder Singh Cassidy, CEO-in-residence, Accel Partners

When I was young, I often felt as if I lived between several worlds—the world of my professional parents (doctors), that of my culture (East Indian/Sikh), and that of my friends growing up in Canada. It was a world full of contradictions. There were clear expectations around the home: Being able to cook, clean, and take care of the house for our Indian guests. Yet no limitations set on what I could achieve academically or otherwise in life. Mine was a childhood of continual opportunity and ambiguity surrounding my possible identities as a woman, an Indian-Canadian woman, and as a potential professional.

To me, living in a woman's nation seems like that experience on steroids. Instead of managing three identities across 18 years, I often feel as if I'm juggling 10 identities on any given day of the week. And everywhere I look, I now see others—my husband, friends, and co-workers—each managing their own increasing "portfolio of identities" that defies a singular description. I'm grateful for the childhood training that prepared me well for this multiple identity syndrome.

Yet digging deeper, it's also clear to me that my father was the even more powerful force in my childhood. It used to be said that behind every successful man there is a powerful woman, but the adage today should be "behind every powerful woman, there is likely a powerful man and role model."

In my case, I credit both my parents, who shared a medical practice for over 30 years, with inspiring me professionally. It was my father, however, who taught me to soar, and who fostered the belief that truly anything was possible for my life. As early as first grade, I remember his love for science, helping me put together my first science project—a working model of the human eye. Yet he was also an artist—a lover of both charcoal and watercolors, as well as a businessman who loved running his practice and financial investing.

As importantly, he took the time to answer my questioning on religion and culture with an open-mindedness that led me to believe intellectual pursuit could co-exist with faith.

His overarching message to me was that it was possible for me to control my own destiny and live by my own expectations. He encouraged me to work for myself, which led me to help found a technology company in my twenties. And in my thirties, I married a man of a different race and culture knowing my father would have embraced him wholeheartedly into our family.

It used to be said that behind every successful man there is a powerful woman, but the adage today should be "behind every powerful woman, there is likely a powerful man and role model."

In fact my father also married and embraced an unconventional woman of her times. My mother was raised in Punjab in the 1930s by her father and brother (my grandmother died when my mom was 8 years old). My mother was an anomaly, becoming a doctor and waiting until she was 32 to marry when most women in India married young and stayed home.

Today, I look at my husband and my daughter and I have no doubt whatsoever about the incredible role he will play in the woman she becomes. He is already comfortable in a world where we together choose and interchange the roles we play in our children's lives day by day. But I'm newly grateful for the unique ways he shows her what's possible in ways only a father can. If who we are today has been shaped by a generation of men who taught us to soar despite prevailing expectations, I'm awestruck by the opportunity for our husbands and partners to teach the next generation how to fly even further.

PABLO CORRAL VEGA, CORBIS

A MAN'S VIEWPOINT

Genders Full of Question Marks

Men and women both struggle to answer new questions

By Jamal Simmons

When it comes to American women, men are a gender full of question marks. Ask 10 men to explain what women want or what is expected of men in a relationship today and in response you will get 10 more questions. Ask women what they want and be prepared for various questions, too. In my experience, women can or will do just about anything required, but just because a woman can or must do a thing does not mean she wants to.

My mother went to work and night school to become a nurse after she and my father split up. When I was 7 she decided to move to California to start over. She packed everything in her silver Ford Mustang and drove across the country to work as a nurse. I stayed with my father for six months and finished the school year in Detroit before following her out there. She made the choices that were best for her and her young child, but when asked what she wanted, she says now that she would have preferred to have a husband who made it possible for her to spend more time raising her children.

But it may be impossible for men to know what women want because the question presumes there is a uniform answer. Instead, it appears different women answer the question differently at various points in their lives. There are many women who start a career before their children are born, then choose to stay home for some time while their children are growing up and return to the workplace later. Others choose a career or entrepreneurial endeavor that will allow them to work from home or nearby so they can spend more time with their children. And still other mothers work throughout the lives of their children, balancing work and child care as best they can alongside their husbands and often on their own—because they are single or divorced or because their husbands are unemployed.

This uncertainty is tough for many men to handle—even for those who rely on their women to take care of them and their children. Most men grew up in a world where there were rules to follow. Whether playing football, basketball, or Dungeons and Dragons, the rules were standard and your abilities were the variable. Life was supposed to be the same way. Go to school, do well, get a good job, meet a good woman, and make enough money to raise a family.

But relationships these days are different. The woman you commit to today may have the same name and Social Security number as the woman you are with tomorrow, but she may want completely different things in her life at different times in your life with her. The only remaining rule seems to be: Stay flexible.

Relationships these days are different. The woman you commit to may want completely different things in her life at different times in your life with her. The rule seems to be: Stay flexible.

In America today, flexibility is almost always an option for women. Technology has mostly liberated women from the constraints of biology. Medicine has reduced the risks of child birth and enabled women to return to active roles more quickly, and advances in birth control have enabled them to have more control over the timing of pregnancy. Without the biological constraints of unplanned pregnancy, nursing, or more dangerous child birth, American women have been able to choose whether or not they want to leave the home and enter the workforce alongside men. Those who chose "yes" forced the doors of education open, enabling women to compete and collaborate with men in the workplace and stand out.

This is not to imply that the playing field is now level. Of course it is not. Women still make less money for the same work, face more harassment, and often have to work harder and be smarter to get the same rewards. The obstacles are important, but just like the situation for African Americans and other minorities, the obstacles have always been there. What is different about today is the greater number of opportunities that exist for women to excel.

Today many women face the question:
"Now that I know I can compete, do I want to?"

For so long the battle was to create this reality. Today many women face a different question. "Now that I know I *can* compete, do I *want* to?" It is this choice that has really thrown both genders for a loop. Many of my female friends have had to face questions their grandmothers had not, among them:

- Is my career worth not being there for my children full time?
- Is my career and lifestyle more important to me than having biological children at all?
- How do I respond when another mom from a play group comes up to my child at the grocery store and wonders who I am, because they have only ever seen her with the nanny?

Whew!

On the other hand, my male contemporaries face unexpected questions too. What is a husband who was attracted to the drive of a successful lawyer or businesswoman allowed to say or feel when that professional peer decides to get off the career track and channel her energy into the home front? Conversely, how is he allowed to react when she suddenly decides to go back to work when the kids are still toddlers, expecting him to step it up with child care and home chores without sounding like a misogynist? Or how does he handle the blow to his conception of manhood when he loses his job and she becomes the main breadwinner, expecting him to raise the kids and take care of the house?

Men have been raised with our own expectations, many of them are traditional, but others quite different than our fathers and grandfathers. In addition to my mother, I was raised around very strong women. All of my aunts earned paychecks, as did both of my grandmothers, and each had a very strong influence over their husbands and families. As a child, it never occurred to me that women would not leave home to work.

My parents decided early in my childhood that I would do anything a girl was expected to do. My mother wanted me to be able to take care of myself. If I found a woman willing to take care of me, fine, she would say, but I would never need her to. So I learned to cook, clean, and do laundry. My father, with whom I spent every summer and lived with in high school, required each of his sons to cook dinner one night each week, and Saturday mornings were for thoroughly cleaning the house. Meanwhile, we were still expected to know how to change tires, paint, and do basic plumbing, yard work, and other "manly duties."

Sometimes we get our ideas from popular culture. For some of my contemporaries, Marian Cunningham, the stay at home mom on "Happy Days" was the model, for others it was the tough-talking working class "Roseanne." For me it was Claire Huxtable on "The Cosby Show." Claire was beautiful and in great shape after five kids, without ever going to the gym, rolling her hair at night or putting on eye cream. She was a successful lawyer while making it home every night for dinner, often cooking it herself. Never too tired, Claire was always ready for a romantic evening, even though she worked a full day and had just solved a family crisis. What was there not to love?

If the image of Claire gave some of us unrealistic expectations, Bill Cosby's Cliff helped prepare us to be partners much different from my grandfathers, who spent many hours in easy chairs watching sports, news, or old movies while my grandmothers, who worked outside the home, too, cooked and took care of the house. Cliff Huxtable loved to play with the kids and thoughtfully reprimanded them when needed. He kissed his wife in every episode and hugged his children—even the boy. And when Claire came in from work, Cliff always asked her about her day. He was a good dad, playful husband, and thoughtful friend.

The advances women have made are all around us. Hillary Clinton is the third female Secretary of State and almost nobody even raises an eyebrow about men not being alone on that list anymore. Women such as Carly Fiorina, the former chief executive of Hewlett-Packard Co., and her counterparts Meg Whitman at eBay Inc. and Ursula Burns at Xerox Corp. have led Fortune 500 companies. Michele Rhee is chancellor of the Washington, D.C. schools and Shirley Franklin is mayor of

THE PERFECT FAMILY. Cliff and Claire Huxtable of "The Cosby Show" inspired many to seek a middle-class lifestyle. [NBCU PHOTO BANK VIA AP IMAGES]

Atlanta. Oprah Winfrey is the most successful woman in entertainment and Katie Couric is a network news anchor. Except for the White House, women have reached the pinnacle of nearly every field. There is more work to be done to reach parity, but women are making progress at breaking through the glass ceiling.

Despite these successes, society still has traditional expectations of women. Imagine the sight of an unruly child running alone through the grocery store or a father with a daughter whose hair is not combed neatly. Someone will inevitably ask: Where is her mother?

Despite the sight of all of the dads at the park with their kids on Saturday, pushing strollers down the street, or opening gifts at the now fashionable co-ed baby shower, men still have societal expectations, too. Imagine a family getting out of an old dented car, or five people living in a one-bedroom apartment. Someone will think: Why can't *he* take better care of his family?

In the end, both genders are trying to figure out how to navigate this new world. We are on new terrain and it means men must be as flexible as the women in our lives. Women have a responsibility also to be clear about what they want and need and give us fair warning when or if that changes. Men are not mind readers and we have expectations of our own based upon the most recent data available. Just keep us posted.

With love and commitment, men and women can find the balance of work and family that makes sense for each couple, answering the questions we have and navigating the waters of this new terrain together.

While we celebrate the advances women are making and ponder the conflicts society's changes pose, men and women cannot lose track of the things each of us truly seeks from our relationships—regardless of the division of labor and which partner is earning the most money. Ideally, most of us want:

- Someone who will be honest about their ideas, expectations, intentions, and frailties
- A safe place to be vulnerable and someone we can trust to be there to help take on the unexpected challenges of life
- A partner who will help raise children with the values that we share
- A faithful lover and friend to explore whatever part of the world we choose together

Recently I was invited to a recommitment ceremony for the grandparents of a friend. At the ceremony the pastor told the story of how they got engaged. A student at Howard University, the gentleman met a lovely young woman who he began to court. After six months he turned to her and asked, "What would you do if I offered you an engagement ring?" She responded, "I would wear it."

A week later he bought her a ring and she put it on. Needless to say, the gentleman was not well known for his romantic side, but they went on to raise two children, enjoy the adoration of four granddaughters, and spend a fulfilling life together of friends and service to their community.

After 63 years together, the wife was coping with advancing Alzheimer's disease and her husband was her primary caregiver, choosing her clothes, making her meals, and administering her medication. Knowing that his wife was feeling uncertain about her future and the strain her illness was putting on him, the husband decided to plan the recommitment ceremony. Long ago they had committed to be together in sickness and in health. This was the sickness part and while she was still able to appreciate it he wanted her to know that the love he felt for her 63 years ago was still strong.

In the end, that type of dedication is what most of us—men and women—really look for. With love and commitment, men and women can find the balance of work and family that makes sense for each couple, answering the questions we have and navigating the waters of this new terrain together.

Jamal Simmons emerged from the 2008 election as one of the new young voices in the world of political analysis.

Suddenly a Single Father

By Matt Logelin, project manager, Yahoo! Inc, and a blogger on family issues

A few days after my wife died in childbirth, a woman visiting her grandchild in the same neonatal intensive care unit where my newborn daughter slept heard about my story and said, "So...are you going to give the baby up for adoption?" The implication, of course, being that a man cannot provide the kind of nurturing and care that is innate in a woman.

I have to be honest. I worried about a lot of things in the seconds/minutes/hours/days after Liz died. I worried about raising Madeline all alone. I worried about whether or not I'd be able to afford the house we purchased 10 months earlier. I worried about having to someday explain a menstrual cycle to my daughter. But I never once worried that I couldn't raise her as well or better than anybody else. After my encounter with the woman at the hospital, I resolved to be the best parent that ever walked the earth.

As a man and a single father living in a woman's nation, I face an interesting double standard. On the one hand, I often get treated as if I'm completely incompetent when it comes to raising my child. A woman in the grocery store recently admonished me for not putting socks on my daughter. Mind you, I live in Los Angeles and it was 97 degrees outside that day. And on a recent flight—round-trip flight number 22 for my daughter and me—a flight attendant asked me if I was babysitting for my wife. Even the women in my life offer up the most basic parenting advice, as if I've not yet figured out everyday things like diapering and feeding my child.

On the other hand, I get incredible accolades when I accomplish even the smallest feat with my daughter. If her bloomers match her dress, women compliment my sense of style, telling me that their husbands could never pull off something like that. If I can get a hair clip to remain in Madeline's hair for more than 10 minutes, I'm treated as if I've accomplished something on par with solving world hunger. It's as if, because I've taken in active role in my daughter's life, I'm some sort of super parent.

It's not just the people I know or encounter in my everyday life. Society also mythologizes the good, single father. A man who steps up to his role as father is looked at in awe. Mothers? It seems that most people think nothing of the remarkable work done by these women. They're just doing "their" job, right? Women are expected to be good mothers. Men are expected to be, well, men.

Women are expected to be good mothers. Men are expected to be, well, men.

I've faced some difficult situations in the 16 months since my daughter was born and my wife died, and though I promised to be the best parent ever, my daughter would tell you that I have a long way to go—as soon as she learns to talk.

MAX WHITTAKER/THE NEW YORK TIMES

Sharing the Load

Quality marriages today depend on couples sharing domestic work

By Stephanie Coontz

Back in the early 1960s, if a woman wanted a job she consulted the ads under the category "Help Wanted/Female." There she would find openings for a "pretty-looking cheerful gal" to greet clients at an ad agency, or "an Ivy League grad with good typing skills," or even an executive secretary, provided she met the main requirement: "You must be really beautiful."[1] Being young and single was usually another job requirement.

Many employers then would not hire married women, and psychiatrists warned of the strain on marriages if a woman got used to earning her own money or making her own decisions. In fact, most Americans believed—in the words of one respondent to a Gallup survey in December 1962—that "being subordinate to men is a part of being feminine." And these beliefs were codified in law. Many states had "head-and-master" laws affirming that wives were "subject" to their husbands. Only four states allowed a wife the right to a separate legal residence, and in no state was it illegal for a man to rape his wife.[2]

That was the context in which Betty Friedan published her shocking best seller, *The Feminine Mystique,* in February 1963, which urged women to seek work outside the home. In October of that year, President John F. Kennedy's Commission on the Status of Women added to the controversy by issuing lengthy recommendations for more fully incorporating women into the public sphere.

By then, though, many housewives—and even more of their daughters—were already beginning to look beyond the home. Most Americans worried about what that might mean for the future of marriage, since conventional wisdom held that women who pursued higher education or a career were unlikely to marry, and if they did, their marriages were likely to end in divorce.

There was a kernel of truth to the idea that "female emancipation" undermined marital "solidarity." The reason: When marriage was based on a woman's lack of alternative options rather than on mutual respect or interdependence, then a woman who acquired educational and economic resources was indeed a threat to the stability of marriage. Economists called this the "independence effect."

As more wives went to work in the 1980s, and as the women's movement challenged old inequities at home and on the job, the divorce rate began to fall.

For the first 70 years of the 20th century, female college graduates were much less likely to marry than women with less education. And if a married woman took a job, the couple was more likely to ultimately divorce. In the late 1960s and 1970s as women poured into the labor force, divorce rates soared. By 1980 nearly half of American marriages were ending in divorce. The "independence effect" seemed inexorable.

But a funny thing happened on the way to the 21st century. As more wives went to work in the 1980s, and as the women's movement challenged old inequities at home and on the job, the divorce rate began to fall. From a peak of 22.8 divorces per 1,000 couples in 1979, the divorce rate dropped to 16.7 divorces per 1,000 married couples by 2005, and those more recently married seem to be following the same trend.[3] Today, divorce rates tend to be highest in states where fewer wives have paid jobs and lower in states where more than 70 percent of married women work outside the home.[4]

Education is now a plus for marriage, too. The difference in marriage rates between female college graduates and women with less education has almost entirely disappeared, and divorce rates for educated women have fallen more rapidly than for other groups. The result: educated women are now more likely to be married at age 35 than their less-educated counterparts.[5]

High-earning women—once considered the most divorce-prone of all females—have gained a similar advantage. Analyzing the 2000 and 2001 Current Population Surveys, Heather Boushey (then an economist as the Economic Policy Institute and now the co-editor of this report as senior economist for the Center for American Progress) found that women between the ages of 28 and 35 who worked full time and earned more than $55,000 a year, or who had graduate or professional degrees, were just as likely to be married as other working women of the same age. Sociologist Christine Whelan reports that among women aged 30 to 44 earning more than $100,000 per year, 88 percent are married, compared to 82 percent of other women. And Whelan's mate selection studies reveal that men now find career women and educated women much more attractive as marriage partners than in earlier decades.[6]

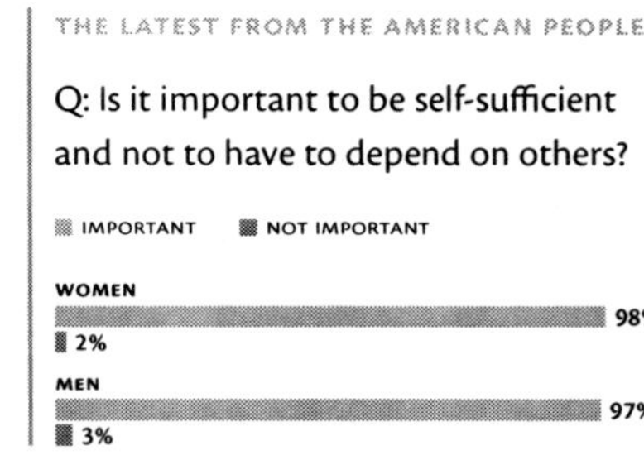

Source: Rockefeller/*Time* poll, 2009.

Today, the independence effect seems to increase marital quality and stability. When a woman is capable of making her own way in the world, she can be more selective in choosing a marriage partner and has more negotiating tools inside the marriage. This creates fairer marriages with improved marital quality for husbands as well as wives. Educated couples, especially those with egalitarian gender views, report the highest marital quality of all.

Stay-at-home wives also benefit from the independence effect. It was the women's movement, not defenders of so-called traditional marriage, that convinced legislators to overturn the prevailing marriage laws in 1963—when 42 states and the District of Columbia all held that if a couple divorced and the wife had been a homemaker, she was not entitled to share the earnings her husband had accumulated during their marriage.[7]

Similarly, the pressure on husbands to take on more responsibilities at home was initiated by working wives, but these new expectations trickled down to male-breadwinner-only families as well, with the result that all men now do significantly more housework and child care than in the past. That's good for children, who get more time with both their fathers and their mothers today than they did in 1963. And it's good for couples, too, despite the stresses of trying to preserve quality couple time as expectations of parenting have expanded and wives spend more time at work.

Although there are many variations by racial and ethnic status, income, and occupation in the division of housework and the values that couples hold about both of them doing these chores, one of the biggest predictors of a wife's marital satisfaction is whether she feels that the division of housework is fair. Meanwhile, one of the biggest predictors of a husband's satisfaction is how often he has sex. And researchers report that women feel more sexual attraction to husbands who do more housework and child care.[8]

When a woman is capable of making her own way in the world, she can be more selective in choosing a marriage partner and has more negotiating tools inside the marriage.

Despite the group differences in men's housework, the trend has almost universally been toward greater participation. Twenty-nine percent of wives reported in 1980 that their husbands did no housework at all. Twenty years later this had fallen to 16 percent. That makes for healthier and more stable marriages. Sadly proving the point is the new countertrend—marriages where the husband earns all the income and the wife does all the housework are now more likely to split up than marriages where husbands and wives share breadwinning and homemaking.[9]

The movement of wives into the workforce has been especially positive for well-educated couples with secure middle-class jobs, with husbands and wives both reporting increased marital satisfaction. Although highly work-committed, dual-earner couples experience more stress in juggling work and family obligations, couples where both husband and wife have challenging and rewarding jobs also

LIVING TOGETHER, WORKING TOGETHER. Couples who share domestic chores and have dual careers can survive the toughest challenges, as this couple did after Hurricane Katrina. {NICOLE BENGIVENO, *THE NEW YORK TIMES*}

report the highest sexual satisfaction. It helps, of course, that many of these dual-income parents can also afford to pay for outside—or sometimes live-in—child care and housekeeping. Nonetheless, employed wives earning all kinds of different incomes are less likely to suffer from depression than full-time homemakers with comparable household incomes.[10]

For couples with fewer resources to cope with the economic uncertainties of the last two decades, women's growing economic roles have been more problematic, resulting in lower personal satisfaction and greater marital distress. This is especially true among lower-income couples and those with less education, who consequently have less access to secure, remunerative, or flexible jobs. Balancing rigid work schedules with unpredictable family obligations—while also keeping up with everyday household cooking and chores—is difficult enough, but for most economically secure couples there have been enough enhancements from women's work to generally raise the quality of most marriages. The couples who have experienced the most declines in marital satisfaction are those in which the wife would rather stay at home and works solely due to financial constraints, while the husband wants to be the sole provider and household authority but cannot achieve that goal, and yet does not help with housework when his wife has to go to work.[11]

Trying to turn the clock back to a largely mythical Golden Age of marriage in the past will not solve these stresses. The threat to successful marriages today is not that women have changed too much but that other individuals and institutions have changed too little. We are no longer in the thrall of the feminine mystique, but two other mystiques continue to impede our progress.

Finding creative ways to allow men and women to integrate, combine, and sometimes alternate their responsibilities to work and to family could be the single most effective "pro-marriage" program of the 21st century.

One is the masculine mystique, which still leads some men to resist sharing household chores and to feel threatened by their wives' work commitments or earnings successes. Pandering to this—as some politicians and pop psychologists advise—is not the answer. The men most likely to experience psychological and health setbacks when they lose their job or when their wives earn equal or higher salaries are those who are more invested in their identity as breadwinners than as family members. And men or women in dual-earner couples who adopt less egalitarian ideas over time become more psychologically vulnerable in their marriages.[12]

By contrast, men whose attitudes become more egalitarian during the course of their marriage report higher marital satisfaction, as do their wives.[13] Perhaps that's why the masculine mystique is on the defensive, and why more men are in fact beginning to accept and even embrace women's equality.

A far more insidious mystique that has yet to be seriously challenged by any of our social institutions is what sociology professor Phyllis Moen and psychology professor Patricia Roehling call the "career mystique." This postulates that a successful career requires people to devote "all their time, energy, and commitment throughout their 'prime' adult years" to their jobs and to delegate all care-giving responsibilities to someone else.[14]

Finding creative ways to allow men and women to integrate, combine, and sometimes alternate their responsibilities to work and to family could be the single most effective "pro-marriage" program of the 21st century. Now that women have so many more options outside marriage and men have so much less arbitrary authority within it, our government, our employers, and our society need to:

- Recognize that the institution of marriage circa the 1960s will never again provide most employees with an unpaid second worker to free the first one up from all domestic responsibilities and care-giving obligations.

- Understand that despite the stresses and trade-offs associated with the multiplication of family diversity, today's "independence effect" is good for the married and unmarried women and men alike. Enhancing gender equality will reduce—not increase—tensions between men and women.

- Structure our laws and institutions so that when marriages do break up, more couples are able to negotiate less conflicted partings. Encouraging fathers to take parental leave and use flex time from day one will engage fathers in more child care and develop strong family identities during their marriages, which means they will be far less likely to cut off contact with their children after divorce.

- Embrace flexible working hours, family leave, and child care and elder care time so that married couples and other individuals with care-giving obligations, no matter what their income status, can balance the demands of work and family equitably.

Family diversity is here to stay, and every kind of family has strengths that we can help them build upon. But the marriages that do last today—and more *are* lasting in each new generation of newlyweds since the baby boomers—are fairer, more intimate, and more respectful than couples from previous eras would have ever dared to dream. If only we could say the same about the work policies and social support systems that families need.

ENDNOTES

1 Advertising section, *The New York Times*, April 7, 1963.

2 George Gallup and Evan Hill, "The American Woman: Her Attitudes on Family, Sex, Religion and Society," *Saturday Evening Post*, December 22, 1962. For more on the views and social status of women in 1963, see Stephanie Coontz, *"'The Feminine Mystique' and Women in the 1960s* (New York, Basic Books, forthcoming 2010) and Coontz, *Marriage, a History: How Love Conquered Marriage* (New York: Viking Press, 2005).

3 Betsey Stevenson and Justin Wolders, "Marriage and Divorce: Changes and their Driving Forces," *Journal of Economic Perspectives* 21 (2)(2007): 27–52.

4 Zvika Neeman, Andrew F. Newman, and Claudia Olivetti. "Are Career Women Good for Marriage?" Institute for Economic Development Discussion Paper 167, Boston University (April 2007.). Evidence from other countries also indicates that "the independence effect" tends to be strongest when the terms of marriage are unfair to women. One cross-cultural study finds that increases in women's power and resources are a threat to marital stability only in societies where there is widespread gender inequality, with men dominating the realm of production and women responsible for most reproductive and nurturing activities. In societies where women and men share productive and reproductive labor, by contrast, especially when men are heavily involved with infants, divorce rates are lower, and increases in female resources do not have such destabilizing effects. Llewellyn Hendrix and Willie Pearson, "Spousal Interdependence, Female Power, and Divorce: A Cross-Cultural Examination," *Journal of Comparative Family Studies* 26 (1975) pp. 217–32. See also Burton Pasternak, Carol Ember, and Melvin Ember, *Sex, Gender, and Kinship: A Cross-Cultural Perspective* (Upper Saddle River, NJ: Prentice-Hall, 1997), p. 199.

5 Adam Isen and Betsey Stevenson, "Women's Education and Family Behavior: Trends in Marriage, Divorce and Fertility," November 24, 2008, available at bpp.wharton.upenn.edu/betseys/papers/Marriage_divorce_education.pdf; Evelyn Lehrer, "Are Individuals Who Marry at an Older Age Too Set in Their Ways to Make Their Marriages Work?," Council on Contemporary Families Fact Sheet, May 28, 2007, available at http://www.contemporaryfamilies.org/subtemplate.php?t=briefingPapers&ext=marryolder; Paul Amato, Alan Booth, David Johnson, and Stacey Rogers, *Alone Together: How Marriage in America is Changing* (Cambridge: Harvard University Press, 2007).

6 Heather Boushey, "Baby Panic Book Skews Data," Women's eNews, July 3, 2002 (disputing evidence presented by Sylvia Hewlett, *Creating a Life: Professional Women and the Quest for Children* (New York: Hyperion, 2002)); Christine Whelan, *Why Smart Men Marry Smart Women* (New York: Simon and Schuster, 2006), p. 143; Boxer, Christie F. and Christine B. Whelan, 2008. "Changing mate preferences 1939–2008" Unpublished working paper, The University of Iowa, Iowa City, IA.

7 Coontz, "*The Feminine Mystique*."

8 Oriel Sullivan and Scott Coltrane, "Men's changing contribution to housework and child care," Discussion Paper on Changing Family Roles, Briefing paper prepared for the 11th Annual Conference of the Council on Contemporary Families, April 25–26, 2008, available at http://www.contemporaryfamilies.org/subtemplate.php?t=briefingPapers &ext=menshousework ; Suzanne Bianchi, John Robinson, and Melissa Milkie, *Changing Rhythms of Family Life* (New York: Russell Sage, 2006).

9 Amato and others, *Alone Together*, p. 150; Lynn Prince Cooke, 'Traditional' Marriages Now Less Stable Than Ones Where Couples Share Work and Household Chores, available at http://www.contemporaryfamilies.org/subtemplate.php?t=briefingPapers&ext=LynnCooke, retrieved August 8, 2009.

10 Amato and others, *Alone Together*, p. 138; Rosalind Barnett and Caryl Rivers, *She Works, He Works* (New York: HarperSanFrancisco, 1996); E. Wethington and R. Kessler, "Employment, Parental Responsibility, and Psychological Distress," *Journal of Family Issues* 10 (1989), 527–46; Janet aHyde, John DeLamateur, and Erri Hewitt, "Sexuality and the Dual-Earner Couple: Multiple Roles and Sexual Functioning," *Journal of Family Psychology* 12 (1998), 354–68.

11 Amato and others, *Alone Together*, pp. 172–3; Robert Brennan, Rosalind Barnett, and Karen Gareis, "When She Earns More Than He Does: A Longitudinal Study of Dual-Earner Couples," *Journal of Marriage and Family* 63 (2001), pp. 178–81.

12 Jacquelyn James , R. Barnett, and R.T. Brennan, "The Psychological Effects of Work Experiences and Disagreements about Gender-Role Beliefs in Dual-Earner Couples: A Longitudinal Study," *Women's Health Research on Gender, Behavior, and Policy* 4 (1998), 341–48; Barnett, Gareis, and Brennan, "Reconsidering Work Time; A Longitudinal Within-Couple Analysis," *Community, Work & Family* 12 (2009), 105–133: Barnett, personal communication, August 12, 2009; Kristen Springer, Kristen, "The Ups and Downs of Income in Marriage: Health Effects of Husbands' Economic Dependence Across the Lifecourse," Paper delivered at the Gerontological Society of America Annual Meeting, November 2008.

13 Ibid.

14 Phyllis Moen and Patricia Roehling, *The Career Mystique: Cracks in the American Dream* (Lanham, MD: Rowman and Littlefield, 2005), p. 5.

Single in a Marriage-Centered World

By Page Gardner, president, Women's Voices Women Vote, a non-profit organization dedicated to involving American women on their own in our democracy

This may come as a surprise to most Americans—a majority of households in the United States are headed by an unmarried person and almost half of all women 18 years of age and older are unmarried—whether they are never married, divorced, separated or widowed. Who is the unmarried woman today? She may be middle-aged, but she is more likely to be young or old. She may be rich, but she is probably struggling to make ends meet.

She may be white, but compared to her married counterpart, she is more likely to be a woman of color. She may be an educated, career-oriented professional, but she probably doesn't have a college degree and is stuck in a low-wage job. She may or may not have children, but as an unmarried woman she is largely on her own. No matter her life's circumstances, she has decisions to make, a household to run, and a future to plan on her own.

The unmarried woman is a young woman just out of high school and starting out in life, learning to navigate the waters of adulthood while remaining single. Like many of her peers today, if she marries it will likely be many years later than her mother did. If she doesn't marry by 30, like one-quarter of all women, she will continue on her own in a world where the unmarried woman is more likely to be unemployed, to lack health insurance, and to spend much more of her income on the basic necessities of life.

The unmarried woman is also the single mom—divorced, separated or never married—working a double shift to pay rent. She wonders how she will take care of her kids on her own on her low wages—because unmarried women make on average barely more than half of what a married man makes, and unmarried women with children earn less than women without kids.

The unmarried woman is the single mom's child care worker, grocery clerk, schoolteacher, nurse's aide, and hairdresser. She has been on the front lines of the current economic crisis, from housing to health care. If she is still employed, her hours and income may be down, and retirement savings is a foreign concept.

The unmarried woman is also your widowed grandmother. Women of her generation didn't work much, so she probably has little if any savings of her own; it all depended on her husband. Will her husband's savings be enough for the rest of her life? More than half of her income comes from Social Security, and she hopes she doesn't become a burden on her children.

Other women are choosing independence, to be on their own, but many are trapped by circumstance. Many are divorced, but may not have received a fair share of the marital assets. Marriage is now more than ever more an institution for the privileged: those with higher education and the highest salaries. Being—or becoming—an unmarried woman means much greater economic vulnerability but also economic control over the few resources she has, greater hardship but more personal independence. Yet generations of social focus on marriage makes many government-bestowed benefits inaccessible.

When people recognize that very soon there will be more unmarried than married women in our country, this social focus on marriage may change. Our public policies certainly need to recognize and reflect this new America.

Being—or becoming—an unmarried woman means much greater economic vulnerability but also economic control over the few resources she has, greater hardship but more personal independence.

NICOLE BENGIVENO, *THE NEW YORK TIMES*

A YOUNG WOMAN'S VIEWPOINT

Transcending 9 to 5

How American women *and* men are reworking our country

By Courtney E. Martin

My paternal grandmother, Maryanne, dreamed of becoming a writer. For a short spell in the 1950s, she edited manuscripts for a literary agent—male, of course. Hunched over stacks of paper at a Formica-topped kitchen table while dinner got a little burnt nearby, she was blissfully happy. It was the closest she would ever come to realizing her dream. For the majority of her life, she worked exclusively in the home exclusively as a "homemaker."

My maternal grandmother, Joan, boldly went where few 18-year-old girls from Kearney, Nebraska, dared to go in the early 1940s—Chicago, Illinois. She attended a teachers college while volunteering at Jane Addams' Hull House, the progressive community house founded by the Nobel Prize-winning social activist in the late 1880s. My grandma Joan would ring her own heavy school bell for just a few years, as a kindergarten teacher, before starting a family and staying home forevermore.

My own mother thought that the perfect job for her, circa 1965, would be secretarial work. She heard that if you finished your work early enough, you could read novels all day at your desk. Then the late 1960s turned everything upside down, and suddenly my mom was protesting the Vietnam War right alongside my dad, earning top grades as an undergraduate at Colorado State University, and applying to social work graduate school.

She worked throughout my childhood—mostly a juggling act of consulting, part-time, and unpaid community work. She was often sick with an autoimmune disorder, but deeply fulfilled nevertheless. My parents' commitment to shared parenting proved noble, but ultimately unrealized—with my dad logging long hours at his inflexible law firm.

My partner's mother, a Caribbean immigrant, worked nights as a nurse while raising four kids on her own in Bedford Stuyvesant, Brooklyn. She would sew suits from scratch for the doctors at the hospital for extra money and occasionally make elaborate weddings dresses for their daughters. She didn't fret over failed promises or her own unfulfilled dreams; she worked tirelessly so that her children could thrive. And they did. They became a blues singer, a nurse, a technology expert, and—my partner—a film editor.

The majority of Americans know that women, in most cases, must earn a living, and that, just like men, we find fulfillment in an honest day's work.

On the precipice of my 30s, I look back at my matrilineal history and that of my partner's family—and more broadly at the historical shifts described in this book—and I feel profoundly grateful. There is no longer any real debate over whether women *should* work. Perhaps some on the fringes still wonder, but the majority of Americans know that women, in most cases, *must* earn a living, and that, just like men, we find fulfillment in an honest day's work—whether we fix plumbing, care for the elderly, or design websites. If we are lucky, we even find a vocation where, as theologian and novelist Frederick Buechner puts it, our "deep gladness meets the world's deep need."

There have been such significant gains in so many of the areas examined in these pages—government, business, education, health, religion, and, yes, even the still-frustrating arenas of pop culture and mainstream media. You've just read many of the exciting headlines:

- Women are indeed half of all U.S. workers
- Workplaces are beginning to change to allow workers to be able to earn an income for their family and still meet their family responsibilities

- Studies prove that women-led businesses have an improved bottom line
- Women are more educated than ever before
- Religious institutions are being compelled to evolve to accommodate the working woman
- Women's access to contraception has put them in a position to design their lives as never before
- Men want to be present fathers!

For all of this and so much more, I raise a glass and toast those who have spoken up, stood out, and refused to settle for indignity or injustice.

I thank the icons, such as Anita Hill and Lilly Ledbetter, who took great personal risk to expose large-scale injustice. I thank the lesser-known, but no less courageous, fighters, among them Bernice Sandler, the architect of Title IX, and Sarah

FEMINIST ICONS. Women marching for the vote on May 1, 1912. (BETTMANN, CORBIS)

COMING OF AGE. Today's young women stand on the shoulders of earlier feminist leaders.
[BOB THOMAS, CORBIS]

Claree White, a union organizer at the Delta Pride catfish plant,[1] who led one of the largest strikes of African American workers in Mississippi. I thank the women all across the country who have dreamed despite their deferment and worked tirelessly so that the next generation could live less restrictive lives.

The women (and men) of my generation have come of age at a time when feminist values are simply in the water. On "Free to Be... You and Me," the early 1970s children's record album, Harry Belafonte and Marlo Thomas sang to a new generation, "Some mommies are ranchers, or poetry makers/Or doctors or teachers, or cleaners or bakers/Some mommies drive taxis, or sing on TV/Yeah, mommies can be almost anything they want to be."[2] Immigrant mothers have served as courageous models—caring for their families while working double shifts, all with an eye on their children's education and upward mobility; their daughters watch them and learn that femaleness is about dynamism and determination. Even if our parents didn't call themselves feminists, we—the daughters of the 1980s and 1990s—were raised with a new and improved edict of equality: *You can do anything you want to do, just like your brothers.*

It's a good thing we've been so pumped up on post-gender idealism, because there are some big battles ahead. As the authors of these pages attest, we need comprehensive policy reform that reflects an accurate picture of the American worker—not Mr. Cleaver putting in his eight hours and then wandering home for dinner on the table at 5:30 p.m., but men and women customizing their 15-plus hour days out of a unique mix of work (both in office and remotely), caretaking (for both children and aging parents), community activism, religious and spiritual practices, entertainment, and exercise.

Even if our parents didn't call themselves feminists, we—the daughters of the 1980s and 1990s—were raised with a new and improved edict of equality: You can do anything you want to do, just like your brothers.

It will take a truly diverse and cohesive coalition to make sure these reforms are not seen as "women's issues," but critical quality-of-life concerns for all. Likewise, we must work across class, ethnicity, religion, and political party if we want to shape policy that benefits all Americans, not just the privileged few who sit in the hallowed halls of power or have the resources to lobby. From the federal level on down, we need policies that honor Americans' ideals for their own lives and support their human right to have safe working conditions, economic stability, access to education, quality health care, and time with their loved ones and communities.

Men need to own their responsibility in championing these causes alongside women. For too long, women have taken on a disproportionate amount of the burden of shifting government and workplace policies to be more family friendly—causing the unintended side effect of having these efforts framed as niche issues.

Labor unions—a great force throughout American history—have helped, pushing for the passage of family and medical leave and state-paid family leave laws, and we'll continue to need their collective voices on our side. More gender-balanced leadership and widening the fairly narrow rights framework to a more broad-based quality of life framework would be exciting.

Of course, the notion that motherhood could somehow be niche is so preposterous as to be comical. After all, we all have a mother! And beyond that, there is nothing niche about wanting to have a well-rounded life, about needing flexibility and support, about wanting to be there when your 2-year-old says her first word or your father his last. Thanks to the feminist movement, young men are increasingly seeing these issues as directly related to their own lives. Recent studies confirm that men, just like women, have an optimum fertility window,[3] and even those who don't want children are waking up to the precious gift of having a rich life outside of work. The challenge ahead is for men to grapple for the language and the framing that inspires them to join the fight. Women, for our part, must make room for our male partners and colleagues to own their share.

Men need to own their responsibility in championing these causes alongside women. For too long, women have taken on a disproportionate amount of the burden of shifting government and workplace policies to be more family friendly.

There are also some battles ahead that are far less direct—the stuff of self-examination, social and cultural shape-shifting, open interpersonal communication, experimentation, and scariest of all, bold and unapologetic dreaming. Women must face the ways in which they take on too much of the burden of housework and then resent their partners for it. Men must grow comfortable leaving work meetings early for family obligations and being transparent with colleagues about it. Supervisors must try out policies that acknowledge their workers as whole human beings and neighbors must collaborate on child care, meal preparation, and extracurricular opportunities to ease the burden of raising children in isolation.

We must all envision the more equitable, humane, and balanced America we want to live in and then fight like mad to make it a reality. I see all of these less definitive shifts buzzing beneath the surface of so much of this comprehensive report—the not-so-subtle subtext to all the analysis about workplace structure, government policy, and health care reform.

We must all envision the more equitable, humane, and balanced America we want to live in and then fight like mad to make it a reality.

You see, we can reform our government, social, and workplace institutions, but until we re-imagine our own lives, we will forever be caught in the crossfire of thwarted personal expectations. My generation must carry on our backs the burden of so many unresolved interpersonal and social issues and so many unanswered questions about the best way to shape a life, a family, a nation.

Take my own history as an example. I have never had a role model of a marriage where two partners truly shared caregiving responsibilities. I've had tremendous mentors in the daily effort to maintain a committed partnership and a messy, loving family, and the humble search for work that is both satisfying and economically secure. But I also come from a long line of women with physical and mental health issues, unrealized potential, and unspoken regrets. I feel as if I carry this complex mix—the enlightened mentoring and the swallowed failures—around with me as I try to envision my own life as a working woman and, some day, mother.

Of course, those institutional reforms will enable me and my generation to make decisions within a healthier, more just context. The women of my generation will face far fewer double-binds than our mothers or grandmothers. The men of my generation will enjoy a far broader, though still not universal, cultural assumption that they are not only workers but also nurturers and partners. But I still believe that it is incumbent upon all of us to reinvent the most intimate of spheres in order to fully realize the potential afforded by these institutional reforms.

SHARING LIFE, SHARING HAPPINESS. Men who do more housework and child care are healthier, physically and psychologically. {TODD HEISLER, *THE NEW YORK TIMES*}

What does this new future look like?

It is my friend Charlton, staying home with his newborn baby boy while his wife works, reveling in all the new discoveries that both of them—father and son—enjoy in that precious time. It is my friend Megan, walking into her boss's office and negotiating the salary she deserves without apology. It is my dad, retired and learning to cook for the first time, smiling from ear to ear when my mom tells him how delicious his stir-fry tastes. It is my friends Rachel and Yvette, sustaining a loving partnership via Skype and a thousand beautiful emails despite the

U.S. government's refusal to recognize their union and grant Yvette a visa. It is partners across the country, sitting down with one another and having honest conversations about what they need in order to be fulfilled individuals *and* happy families—and most important, honoring their commitments even when it bucks cultural conventions. It is—and this is hard to admit—women letting go of some of the unhealthy expectations that we've had of ourselves and giving men more room to contribute, fail, learn, and own their part in the domestic sphere.

As men remake the role of father—from antiquated "big daddy" protector to emotionally attuned, involved mentor—and as women remake the role of mother—from martyred queen of the home to full human being with a capacity to lead in many areas—our country's ideas about leadership will also continue to evolve.

Just as policy reform can create a more comfortable climate within which individuals can make courageous choices, those courageous choices can then influence a more enlightened politics at large. As men remake the role of father—from antiquated "big daddy" protector to emotionally attuned, involved mentor—and as women remake the role of mother—from martyred queen of the home to full human being with a capacity to lead in many areas—our country's ideas about leadership will also continue to evolve.

It's such an exciting moment. We are balanced on the precipice of a whole new way of working and living, not just for women, but for everyone. If we can hold tight to our vision of what a more humane, healthy, and just America looks like, pull up our sleeves and do the hard work—side by side—that manifesting this vision will require, then the rewards could be breathtaking.

We could birth differently. No longer forced to have a baby and then rush back to work, women and men together could share the first, sacred months of life and head back to work with their bonds secured. We could learn differently, finally honoring our rhetoric in this country about providing equal education for all and supporting more diversity within every field. We could work differently, expecting dignity and fair wages in our workplaces and using the best technology has to offer to be more efficient within our truly customizable work schedules.

We could govern differently. Lawmakers could craft policies that support individuals and families, not just the bottom line. We could care differently, coordinating not just with our equally harried partners but also with federally subsidized child care centers, more cohesive neighborhood groups, and religious and spiritual communities.

We have leaders at the highest levels who—both symbolically and fundamentally—support Americans, men and women, in their quest for fulfilling work and personal lives. We have momentum.

We could worship differently. "Bowling alone" no more, we could depend on our religious and neighborhood communities to feed our spirits while starving our sense of alienation. We could even die differently, surrounded by those who love us, those who are supported to be present during the moments that matter most in our lives.

My grandmothers, and my mother especially, lived amazing, courageous lives, but they were limited by the times in which they were born—the economic constraints, the fearful clinging to joyless gender norms, the lack of a collective analysis and an inspired vision. My generation faces its own challenges today—the Great Recession, a dangerous and insecure world, the threat of environmental ruin, the residue of decades of gender disparity—but the world today also boasts ripe conditions for thoroughgoing change.

We have the opportunity that comes from crisis—the battered economy has shaken up just about everything. Our environmental crisis points toward our undeniable interconnection. We have leaders at the highest levels who—both symbolically and fundamentally—support Americans, men *and* women, in their quest for fulfilling work *and* personal lives. We have momentum.

Alice Walker once wrote, "And so our mothers and grandmothers have, more often than not anonymously, handed on the creative spark, the seed of the flower they themselves never hoped to see—or like a sealed letter they could not plainly read."[4] In these pages, I have read the sealed letter. It is a call to action to my entire generation to agitate for the world that our mothers and fathers, grandmothers and grandfathers, didn't get to live in, but dreamed of—for us.

Courtney E. Martin is the award-winning author of Perfect Girls, Starving Daughters: How the Quest for Perfection is Harming Young Women.

ENDNOTES

1 Kristal Brent Zook, "Catfish and Courage," *Essence*, April 21, 2003, available at http://www.essence.com/news_entertainment/news/articles/catfishandcourage.

2 Harry Belafonte and Marlo Thomas, "Parents Are People," *Free to Be...You and Me*, Bell, 1972.

3 Steven Reinberg, "Late-Life Fatherhood May Lower Child's Intelligence," *US News and World Report*, March 9, 2009, available at http://heath.usnews.com/articles/health/healthday/2009/03/09/late-life-fatherhood-may-lower-childs-intelligence.html.

4 Alice Walker, *In Search of Our Mother's Gardens* (New York: Harvest Books, 2003), p. 240.

MICHAELEC, FLICKR

Battle of the Sexes Gives Way to Negotiations

Americans welcome women workers, want new deal to support how we now work and live today

By John Halpin and Ruy Teixeira
with Susan Pinkus and Kelly Daley

"A Woman's Nation Changes Everything" documents in detail the many transformational changes in our economy and our society today because of the massive influx of women into the American workforce over the past few decades. But how do Americans overall feel about these changes? What effect, if any, do all these changes have on the beliefs and behavior of men and women? Is discord rising between the sexes or are men and women finding ways to co-exist and even reach consensus on important matters? How are modern families adjusting to the changes at home and in the workplace? Do men and women agree or disagree in their understandings of how families, work environments, and public policy should be structured?

The Rockefeller Foundation, in collaboration with *Time* magazine, set out to answer these and other questions about women and society in a landmark study of public opinion that was completed less than a month before the publication of this report. The research team, led by the authors of this chapter, set out to determine just how men and women view one another in this new era and how changes in the economy are influencing attitudes about gender relations, the family, and the workplace. Working with public opinion research firm Abt SRBI to design and execute our study, we interviewed more than 3,400 adults across the country to get a clearer picture of the state of gender relations today.

The results are striking. Contrary to much of the conventional wisdom about the battle of the sexes, our research finds basic alignment between men and women in terms of what they want in life and what they believe about one another. First and foremost, both men and women overwhelmingly agree that the rise of women in the workforce is a positive development for society—a viewpoint that crosses generational, ideological, partisan, and racial and ethnic lines.

Compared to earlier generations, men say they are perfectly comfortable with women working outside the home, women earning more money than men, and more men being stay-at-home dads. In turn, women say they are less dependent on men for financial security than women were in their mothers' generation and that many of the tensions between working and having a family life can be bridged.

Tellingly, these new attitudes are apparent in conversations across kitchen tables throughout our country. Both men and women say they are negotiating more than earlier generations about the rules of relationships, work, and family—a clear sign that the battle of the sexes has given way to a new era of gender diplomacy and mutual discussion about their increasingly harried and stressful lives. Both sexes disagree that men no longer know their role in work and life or that men and women are confused about how to interact with one another in this new era.

Yet our public opinion research also shows that mutual understanding doesn't mean changes in behavior have been equally forthcoming. Both sexes agree that women continue to bear a disproportionate burden in taking care of children and elderly parents, even when both partners in a relationship have jobs. Women overwhelmingly report that they are solely responsible for the care of their children and many say that they alone are responsible for the care of aging parents.

Given the ongoing difficulties many people face in balancing work and family life, it is not surprising that large numbers of Americans—men and women alike—view the decline in the percentage of children growing up in a family with a stay-at-home parent as a negative development for society. A majority of men—and even a bare majority of women—agree that it is still best for a family if the father works outside the home and the mother takes care of the children.

But rather than pining for family structures of an earlier generation, we heard loud and clear from Americans in this study that government and businesses have failed to adapt to the needs of modern families. Men and women are ready and

Survey methodology

The Rockefeller Foundation, in collaboration with *Time* magazine, contacted 3,413 adults nationwide by telephone from August 31 to September 15, 2009, including 1,599 men and 1,814 women. Telephone numbers were chosen randomly in separate samples of land-line and cell phone exchanges across the nation, allowing listed and unlisted numbers to be contacted, and multiple attempts were made to contact each number. Cell phone exchanges and ported numbers were hand-dialed. The survey includes "over samples" (polling parlance for measures to ensure all subsets of a population are captured in the poll) of African Americans and Hispanics selected from census tracts with higher than 8 percent concentration of each respective group. The sample includes a total of 446 African Americans and 383 Hispanics. The resulting interviews were weighted into proportion by probability of selection. The sample was adjusted to census proportions of sex, ethnicity, age, education, and national region.

The margin of sampling error for adults is plus or minus two percentage points. For both men and women, it is three points; for African Americans, it is five points; and for Hispanics, it is six points. For smaller subgroups, the margin of error may be higher. Survey results may also be affected by factors such as question wording and the order in which questions are asked. Interviews were conducted in English and Spanish. Questionnaire design and interviewing was conducted by Abt SRBI of New York. Center for American Progress senior fellows John Halpin and Ruy Teixeira coordinated the polling and analyzed the poll results.

willing to work out the details of their stressful lives. Many Americans will choose more traditional arrangements, and many may not. But regardless of family structure, Americans across the board desire more flexibility in work schedules, paid family leave, and increased child care support. Ever practical and pragmatic, our survey demonstrates that Americans understand that everything has changed in their work and lives today and that consequently they are working things out as best they can while looking to their government and their employers to catch up.

Americans strongly accept increasing role of women in our economy

In our survey, we asked Americans to evaluate the ramifications of the central premise of this report—everything changes in work and life because women today make up nearly one-half of the U.S. workforce. As Figure 1 highlights, more than three-quarters of Americans (77 percent) view this change positively, with more than 4 in 10 (42 percent) saying that it has been a "very positive" change for

American society. Less than one-fifth of Americans (19 percent) say the rise of women in the economy has had a negative impact on society.

Positive views cut across the demographic and ideological spectrum, with strong majorities of men (75 percent), women (77 percent), whites (76 percent), African Americans (81 percent), Latinos (84 percent), liberals (87 percent), and moderates (86 percent) viewing women's increased role in the economy positively. Even more traditional elderly and conservative audiences believe women working equally alongside men in the workforce is a net positive for society, albeit at lower overall levels than other groups.

Although every age and gender group thinks that more women going to work is a positive change for society, women under 45 are most enthusiastic about this development (55 percent very positive) followed by younger men (44 percent very positive). Less than 4 in 10 (38 percent) women over the age of 45 say they have

FIGURE 1

The American public overwhelmingly views the rise of women in workforce as good for society

Q: Forty years ago, just one-third of all workers were women. Today, about one-half of all workers are women. Do you think this change has been positive or negative for American society?

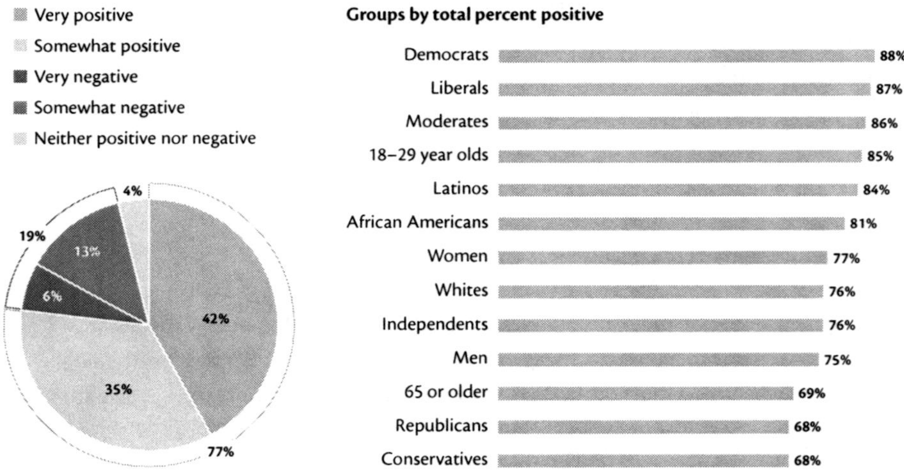

very positive feelings about this, but three-quarters of them (75 percent) hold at least a somewhat positive view of more women working in the economy.

One might think the movement of millions of women into the economy would cause friction between the sexes, particularly for men who might feel wrongly displaced from employment or left out altogether from the modern economy. To the contrary, the demonstrated lack of discord over this profound social shift in American life more likely signals convergence between the sexes due to the alignment of their views about major life goals and family desires.

As Figure 2 shows, both men and women today agree almost down the line with one another about what is most important to them in their own lives. More than 9 in 10 men (92 percent) and women (96 percent) place being healthy at the top of their list in terms of what is very important to them, followed by being self-sufficient, being financially secure, and having a fulfilling job. Although women

FIGURE 2

Men and women agree on most life goals

Q: I'm going to read you a list of some things that different people value. Some people say these things are very important to them. Other people say they are not so important. Please tell me how important each thing is to you personally.

Percent saying "very important"

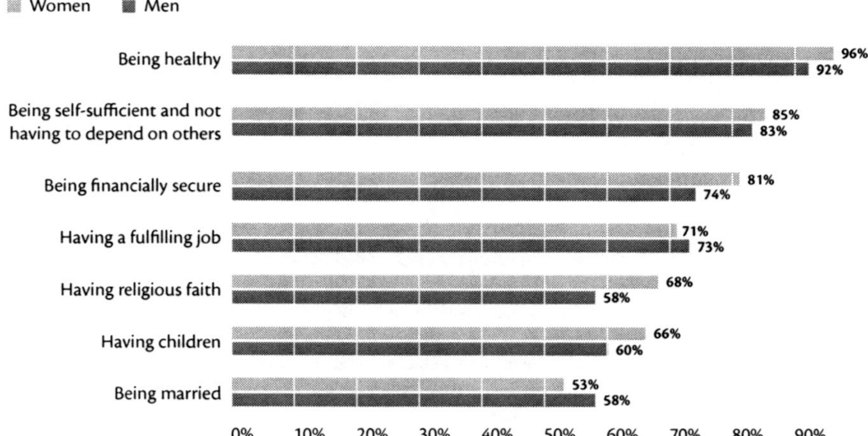

place a slightly higher premium on faith than do men (68 percent very important for women; 58 percent for men) and less of an emphasis on marriage (58 percent very important for men; 53 percent for women), the sexes are generally aligned on major life goals.

Similarly, men and women appear to look for the same traits and attributes in their mates. As seen in Figure 3, 82 percent of men and 75 percent of women told us that it is very important to them for their romantic partners to give them love and affection, and nearly 7 in 10 men (68 percent) and more than 6 in 10 women (62 percent) want their partners to have a family. And to whom will they turn in order to make family decisions and provide for the family? Our survey shows that both men and women are looking less to their partners to make major household decisions or to support them financially, though women are still twice as likely as men to look to their partners for financial support (30 percent very important versus 15 percent very important, respectively).

This last finding may be partially explained by the continued desire among both mothers and fathers for their daughters to have a traditional family structure over more individualistic measures of financial and career success. Looking at Figure 4, we find that 63 percent of fathers and 56 percent of mothers rank "a happy marriage and kids" as their chief desire for their daughters, compared to less than one-third of men and less than half of women who rank "financial success" and "an interesting career" as top goals for their daughters.

FIGURE 3

Men and women are looking for similar things from their partners

Q: Whether or not you have a romantic partner in your life right now, please tell me how important you feel it is for you personally to have that person do the following.

Percent saying "very important"

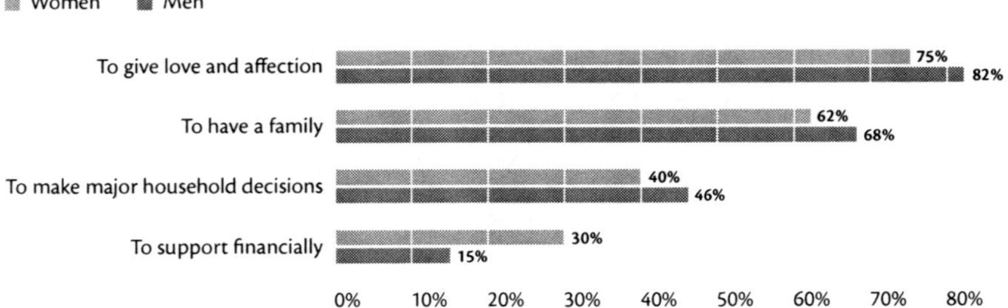

FIGURE 4

Mothers and fathers both want a traditional family arrangement for their daughters

Q: [FOR THOSE WITH DAUGHTERS OR STEPDAUGHTERS] Everyone naturally wants the best of all things for their children, but I'd like to know how you would rank these three things in importance. For a daughter of yours, which would you most want her to have? (Percent ranked "first")

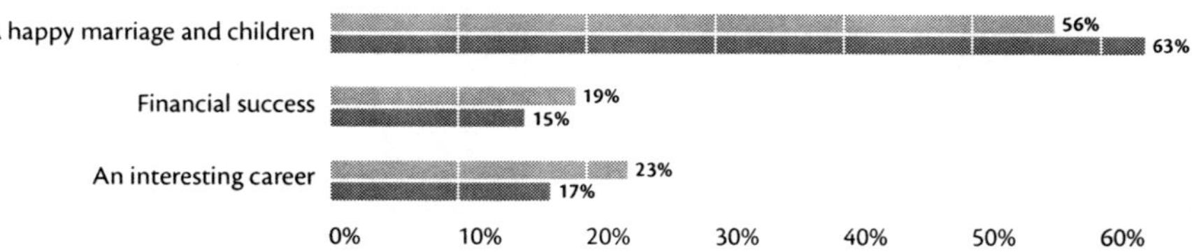

Although every age and gender group expresses a desire for their daughters to have a happy marriage with children above other goals, 30 percent of women under the age of 45 say they want their daughters to have an interesting career compared to 16 percent of men under 45. Only 18 percent of men and 19 percent of women ages 45 or older rank an interesting career as their top desire for their daughters. Intriguingly, looking below the surface we find that less than half of single men with kids (48 percent) and single women with kids (47 percent) rank a happy marriage and children as their top desire for the daughters.

FIGURE 5

Men and women are equally happy in their own marriages/relationships

Q: All things considered, how would you describe your marriage or partnership?

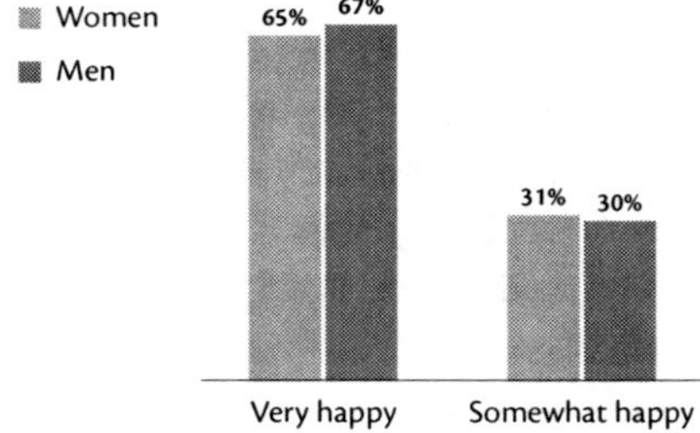

The ongoing importance of marriage for married parents is not that surprising, given what they told us about their own life experiences—roughly two-thirds of married men and women (67 percent and 65 percent, respectively) describe their own marriages as very happy, clearly a condition they would like for their own offspring.

Perhaps the strongest alignment between men and women in terms of their day-to-day lives involves the level of anxiety they are experiencing

FIGURE 6

Americans are stressed in their daily lives; parents are coordinating more

Q: In general, how often do you experience stress in your daily life: never, rarely, sometimes, or frequently?

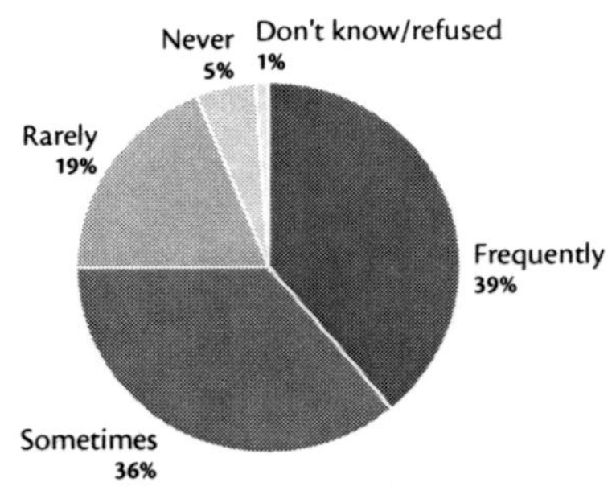

Q: Families today are very busy, juggling multiple and sometimes conflicting schedules, duties, and responsibilities. How often do you and your spouse/partner (need to) coordinate your family's schedules, duties, and responsibilities?

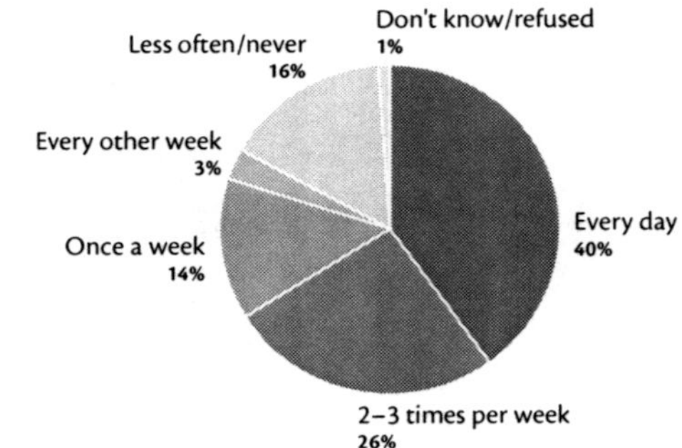

and the constant negotiations that must go on between partners to bring some order to their daily schedules. As Figure 6 shows, 75 percent of Americans report experiencing stress in their daily lives, with nearly equal percentages of men and women (39 percent and 40 percent, respectively) saying this stress occurs frequently. Given the hectic nature of modern life, no wonder two-thirds of Americans say they are coordinating their duties and responsibilities with their spouses or partners at least two to three times per week. Forty percent of Americans say they are negotiating these details daily.

The battle of the sexes is over

What can we conclude from these data? First, the profound shift in women's role in the U.S. economy has not led to massive conflict between men and women. In fact, the opposite happened—men and women view this change in quite favorable terms. Second, the lack of acrimony over this shift is partially a result of men and women largely sharing the same life ambitions, goals, and realities. Third, both sexes appear to be converging in their beliefs about gender relations and the role of women in society and the workplace rather than fragmenting along gender lines.

Although some divisions remain between genders and across ideological lines, the real story emerging from this study is the consistent and strong agreement of the sexes on many attitudinal measures of modern life. The bulk of our study asked people whether they agreed or disagreed with a range of statements about the status of men and women in society. Strikingly, we learned that strong majorities of both men and women agreed with one another on 24 of 31 measures—an agreement rate of more than 75 percent. In many cases, the attitudes of women were stronger than those of men, but the overall agreement rate is astounding—further highlighting the convergence of opinion between men and women.

Table 1 presents a comprehensive overview of the many areas of consensus between the sexes, ranked by the total level of agreement (or disagreement) among women. To get a sense of the areas where men and women are in greatest alignment these days, consider the following measures where the sexes are separated by only five percentage points or less:

- You are comfortable with women in households earning more money than men. (89 percent of men and women agree)
- Husbands and wives today are negotiating more than earlier generations about the rules on relationships, work, and family. (83 percent of men and 84 percent of women agree)
- Mothers cannot be as productive at work as fathers. (82 percent of men and 81 percent of women disagree)
- The realities of family life today are not adequately represented in news and entertainment media. (77 percent of men and 78 percent of women agree)
- Mothers cannot be as productive at work as people without children. (82 percent of men and 81 percent of women disagree)
- You are confused about the way men and women are supposed to interact these days. (72 percent of men and 71 percent of women disagree)
- Women need to behave more like men to be taken seriously in the workplace. (74 percent of men and 71 percent of women disagree)

TABLE 1

Basic alignment between genders on women and society; women stronger on many measures

Q: For each statement, please tell me whether you strongly agree, somewhat agree, somewhat disagree, or strongly disagree. (Total percent agree, unless indicated; ranked by total for women)

	Women		Men	
	Strongly	**Total**	**Strongly**	**Total**
You are comfortable with women in households earning more money than men.	65	**89**	61	89
Despite changes in the modern family, women today still bear the primary responsibility for taking care of sick or elderly parents.	52	**86**	27	66
Compared to previous generations, it is now more acceptable for men to be stay-at-home dads.	41	**85**	32	79
In households where both partners have jobs, women take on more responsibilities for the home and family than their male partners.	55	**85**	28	67
Husbands and wives today are negotiating more than earlier generations about the rules on relationships, work and family.	51	**84**	46	83
Women who have children are just as committed to their jobs as women who do not have children.	57	**83**	44	73
Mothers cannot be as productive at work as fathers. (Disagree)	63	**81**	56	82
The realities of family life today are not adequately represented in news and entertainment media.	47	**78**	47	77
It is possible for a woman to have a fulfilling life if she remains single.	54	**78**	38	67
Mothers cannot be as productive at work as people without children. (Disagree)	56	**77**	45	72
Today's women's movement is a movement that considers the needs of men and families too, not just women.	34	**73**	22	59
You are confused about the way men and women are supposed to interact these days. (Disagree)	46	**71**	46	72
Women need to behave more like men to be taken seriously in the workplace. (Disagree)	48	**71**	47	74
[WOMEN ONLY]: Compared to your mother, you are less dependent on your spouse for financial security.	48	**70**	–	–
[MEN ONLY]: Compared to your father, you are more comfortable having women work outside the home.	–	–	40	70
There would be fewer problems in the world if women had a more equal position in government and business.	39	**69**	24	54
Compared to past generations, men are becoming more financially dependent on women.	23	**65**	19	61
Women who work outside the home have less time and attention for their marriage or relationship.	26	**63**	25	65
With the rise of women in society and the workplace, men no longer know their role. (Disagree)	29	**61**	38	68
Men today are less interested in playing the macho role than they were in years past.	19	**60**	19	63
Men have lost the battle of the sexes. (Disagree)	26	**58**	31	62

- Compared to past generations, men are becoming more financially dependent on women. (61 percent of men and 65 percent of women agree)
- Women who work outside the home have less time and attention for their marriage or relationship. (65 percent of men and 63 percent of women agree)
- Men today are less interested in playing the macho role than they were in years past. (63 percent of men and 60 percent of women agree)
- Men have lost the battle of the sexes. (62 percent of men and 58 percent of women disagree)

On several other measures, we find that majorities of both men and women agreed with a certain statement but women were much stronger in their beliefs than were men. This is particularly true for matters related to the distribution of labor within households.

Fifty-two percent of women, for example, strongly agree (86 percent total agree) with the statement: "Despite changes in the modern family, women today still bear the primary responsibility for taking care of sick or elderly parents." Only 27 percent of men strongly agree (66 percent total agree) with this statement. Similarly, 55 percent of women strongly agree (85 percent total agree) that "In households where both partners have jobs, women take on more responsibilities for the home and family than their male partners," versus 28 percent of men who strongly agree (67 percent total agree).

Balancing family life and the workplace seems to spark less disagreement. Fifty-seven percent of women, for example, strongly agree (83 percent total agree) that working mothers are just as committed to their jobs as women without children, with 44 percent of men strongly agreeing (73 percent total agree). Despite the more intense opinions of women on some issues, it is notable and important that majorities of men are at least somewhat in alignment with the attitudes of women on many measures of gender relations and the workplace.

Furthermore, as Figures 7 and 8 highlight, men and women are basically aligned in their attitudes about one of the more contentious issues between the sexes—the traditional family structure. Fifty-six percent of men agree (39 percent disagree) that "it is better for a family if the father works outside the home and the mother takes

FIGURE 7

Traditional family structure favored by a majority of men and a plurality of women

Q: It is better for a family if the father works outside the home and the mother takes care of the children?

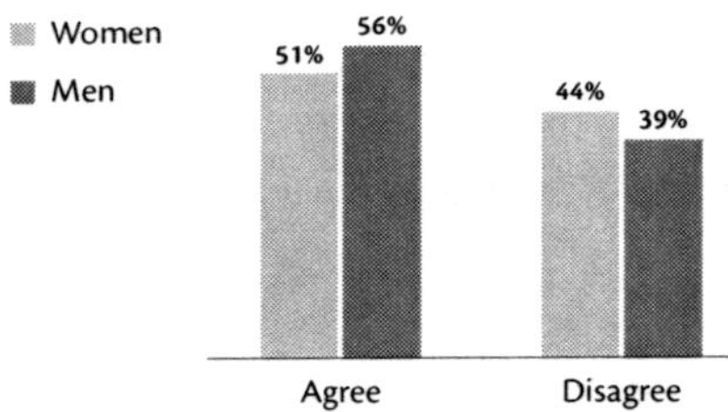

care of the children." At the same time, a bare majority of women agree with this notion—51 percent versus 44 percent disagreeing. Generational differences are clear on this measure. Women under age 45 are less inclined to agree that it is better for a family if the father works outside the home and the mother takes care of the family—less than one in five younger women strongly agree with this idea.

Perhaps more telling, we presented respondents with the fact that today less than 30 percent of children grow up in a family with a stay-at-home parent compared to a majority of kids who grew up in this family environment in the mid-1970s. A full 65 percent of Americans—including 70 percent of men and 61 percent of women—believe this change has had a negative effect on American society compared to only 28 percent who view this change positively. Although concerns are widespread about the demise of the proportion of children growing up in a family with at least one parent at home, lower percentages of single and full-time working women, African Americans, and Latinos view this development as a negative change for society.

The battle is over, but differences remain to be negotiated

Despite general agreement among Americans on many measures involving women's changing role in society, lingering differences still exist. Most of the differences are small and stem from divergent attitudes between men and women, and between liberals and conservatives, about the overall status of women and the relationship of working women to their children.

As Figure 9 highlights, there are four statements that produced noticeable gender gaps. In the first of these, 54 percent of men agree that it is "harder for a mother who works outside the home to establish as warm and secure a relationship with her children as a mother who does not work outside the home." A roughly similar percentage of women, 56 percent, *disagree* with this sentiment. Women of all ages

FIGURE 8

Public worried about effect on children without stay-at-home parent

Q: In the mid-1970s, a majority of children grew up in a family with a stay-at-home parent. Today about 30 percent of children grow up in a family with a stay-at-home parent. Do you think this change has been very positive, somewhat positive, somewhat negative, or very negative for American society?

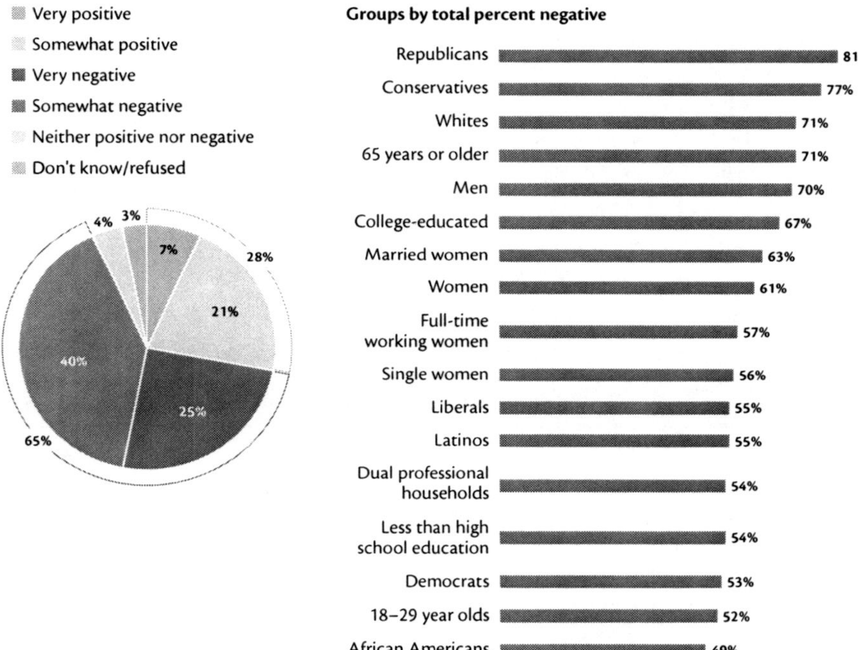

disagree with this notion while younger men (52 percent agree, under 45) and older men (55 percent agree, 45 or older) feel the opposite way.

Similarly, a majority of men (60 percent) believes that "there are no longer any barriers to how far women can advance in the workplace," compared to only 50 percent of women who believe this is the case. On the flip side of the gender coin, a strong majority of women (68 percent) agrees that "men resent women who have more power than they do" versus only 48 percent of men. And 52 percent of women agree that "all things considered, men continue to have it better in life than women do," while 53 percent of men disagree they occupy an elevated position in life.

FIGURE 9

Gender gaps still persist on important family and social status issues

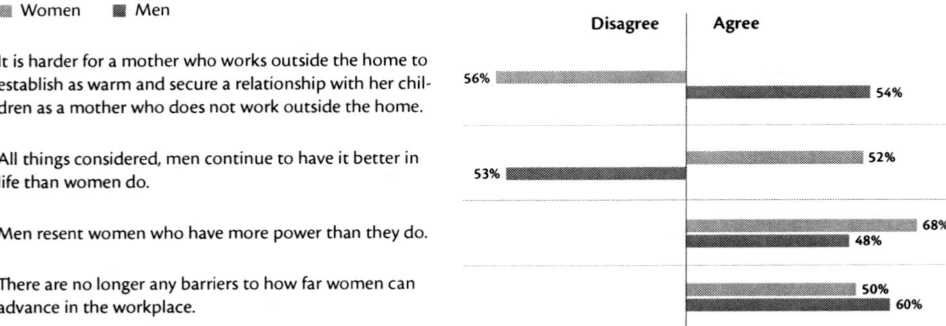

TABLE 2

Ideological and partisan gaps on key measures (percent total agree)

	Liberal	Conservative	Difference	Democrat	Republican	Difference
The government should provide more funding for child care to support parents who work.	84	49	**+35**	84	46	+38
There would be fewer problems in the world if women had a more equal position in government and business.	78	47	**+31**	75	44	+31
It is better for a family if the father works outside the home and the mother takes care of the children.	41	68	**-27**	45	67	-22
It is harder for a mother who works outside the home to establish as warm and secure a relationship with her children as a mother who does not work outside the home.	41	55	**-14**	41	54	-13
There are no longer any barriers to how far women can advance in the workplace.	48	61	**-13**	53	58	-5
All things considered, men continue to have it better in life than women do.	53	42	**+11**	53	42	+11

Ideological differences are even more pronounced than gender ones on many of these same measures. As Table 2 shows, there is a 27-point gap between conservatives and liberals on whether it is better for a family if the father works outside the home and the mother takes care of the children. And there is a 14-point gap between conservatives and liberals on the notion that it is harder for a working mother to establish as warm and secure a relationship with her children as one who does not work.

FIGURE 10

Women are more skeptical of female bosses than are men

Q: Female bosses are harder to work for than are male bosses.

Percent agreeing

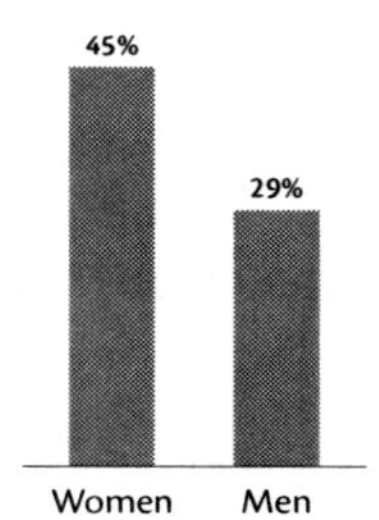

In contrast, there is an 11-point gap between liberals and conservatives on the idea that men still have it better in life. Fifty-three percent of liberals believe this is the case but only 42 percent of conservatives agree with them.

There is one final and somewhat counterintuitive difference between the sexes that is worth noting, given many stereotypes about the workplace. Figure 10 shows that only 29 percent of men agree that female bosses are harder to work for than are male bosses, compared to 45 percent of women. The tension between female employees and their female bosses appears to be more concentrated among white-collar workers and management professionals—49 percent of white-collar women and 47 of women professionals agree with this notion versus 38 percent of blue-collar women.

Behavior hasn't caught up with attitudes

The attitudes we have documented so far paint a picture of a more consensual and mutually respectful relationship between men and women. Men and women both accept the increasing role of women in the economy and do not view this change as a threat to the status of either gender. They are negotiating more about the details of their lives and understand that women are still bearing a larger share of child care and elder care. Both sexes also believe that it is okay for women to earn more than men and to contribute more to household income.

But we also find that the self-reported reality of men's and women's lives does not match the more progressive attitudes expressed in other areas of the study. Case in point: Figure 11 highlights a full 69 percent of women—including 64 percent of married women with kids and 86 percent of single women with kids—say they are mostly responsible for taking care of their children. In contrast, only 13 percent of men report a similar set-up. Forty-one percent of women also say that they are mostly responsible for taking care of their elderly parents compared to less than one-quarter of men who do so.

FIGURE 11

Behavior lagging behind attitudes—women still bear the burden of kids and elderly parents; men still bringing home more of the family income

Q: In your household, who is mostly responsible for taking care of your children?

Self Spouse Both Other

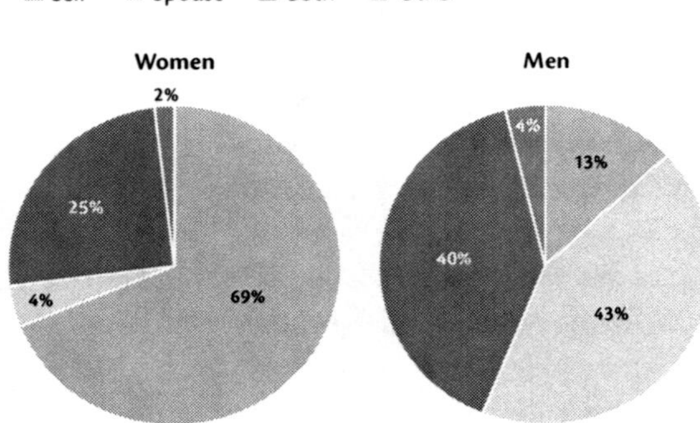

Q: Personally speaking, who in your household has the most responsibility for caring for your elderly parents: you or your spouse or partner, or do both of you share that responsibility equally, or some other family member?

Percent responding "self"

Women 41%

Men 23%

Q: Are you the primary breadwinner in your household?

Percent responding "yes"

Women 40%

Men 70%

Q: [IF MARRIED OR PARTNER] What share of your family's income do YOU personally earn?

Percent responding "more than half or almost all"

Even with these greater family responsibilities, women report greater difficulties than men in getting time off from work to care for their children and elderly parents. Forty-two percent of women say they face difficulties getting time off to care for kids compared to 36 percent of men, and 27 percent of women find similar hurdles getting time to take care for parents compared to 18 percent of men (see Figure 12).

In terms of household earnings, 70 percent of men overall say they are the primary breadwinners in their households compared to 40 percent of women overall. This broadly reflects the analysis in other parts of this report, which demonstrates that workplace practices and expectations among employers that men are the primary breadwinners in households result in workplace behaviors that are often detrimental to women. Even more striking, 65 percent of men report that they bring home more than half or almost all of their household income compared to only 19 percent of women. There are definite class differences in terms of the primary breadwinner status, with trends inverted for blue-collar and white-collar women: 57 percent of blue-collar women say they are the primary breadwinners compared to 44 percent of women professionals.

Despite more enlightened attitudes and greater negotiations between the sexes, American women clearly have yet to reach parity with men on many in terms of household duties and earnings.

Americans overwhelmingly want better balance between work and life

Americans understand that they are unlikely to return to the traditional arrangements of an earlier generation given the changing nature of work and family, but they are not yet convinced that the modern workplace has adapted to the new reality and the needs of modern families.

For starters, both men and women desperately want changes to their work structures. Presented with a list of possible things that would need to change in order to improve work and family life, 54 percent of women and 49 percent of men say that more flexible work hours and schedules would be their top choice. This is well above other options, such as more paid time off, better child care options or longer school hours.

In addition, we found broad and deep support among men and women for significant changes in governmental and business policies to better address the needs of modern families. As Figure 13 highlights, 53 percent of Americans *strongly* agree (84 percent totally agree) with the statement "businesses that fail to adapt to the needs of modern families risk losing good workers." Seventy-six percent of Americans agree that businesses should be required to provide paid family and medical leave, and 73 percent of Americans say businesses should provide their employees with more child care benefits. A similar proportion of Americans—74 percent—says that employers should be required to give workers more flexibility in their work schedules.

FIGURE 12

More women than men having trouble getting time off from work

Q: Has there ever been a time when you wanted to take time off from work to care for (your child/your elderly parent), but you were unable to do so?

Percent responding "yes"

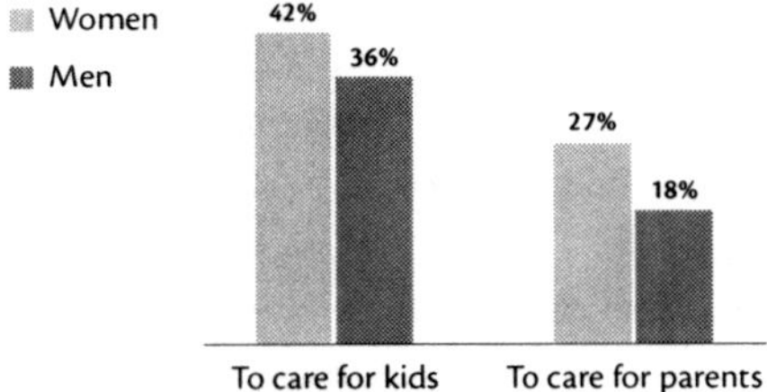

TABLE 3

Men and women overwhelmingly want more workplace flexibility

Q: Which of these things, in particular, would need to change in order for working parents to balance evenly their job or business, their marriage, and their children?

	Women	Men
More flexible work hours/schedules	**54**	**49**
More paid time off	15	16
Better or more child care options	13	12
Longer school hours or school year	8	10

FIGURE 13

Public strongly supports policy changes to improve work-life balance

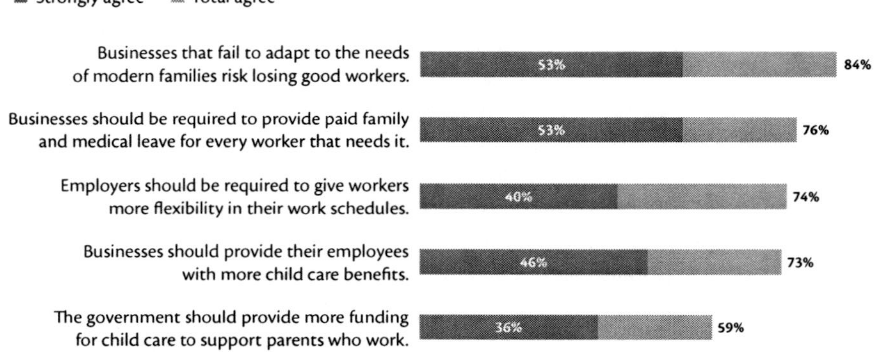

With the exception of increased government funding for child care, support for new measures to improve work-life balance cuts across partisan and ideological lines. For example, 73 percent of conservatives and 61 percent of Republicans agree with the statement that businesses should be required to provide paid family and medical leave, with 88 percent of liberals and 90 percent of Democrats similarly agreeing. Likewise, more than 6 in 10 conservatives (64 percent) and Republicans (63 percent) agree that employers should be required to give workers more flexibility in the workplace, with agreement topping 80 percent among liberals and Democrats.

Indeed, if there is one clear message emerging from this survey, it is that the lives of Americans have changed significantly in recent years, yet the parameters of their jobs have yet to change to meet new demands. Political and business leaders who fail to take steps to address the needs of modern families risk losing good workers and the support of men and women who are riding the crest of major social change in America with little or no support.

The battle of the sexes is over. A new era of negotiation between the sexes is upon us. It is time for our major government, business, and social institutions to enter the dialogue.

Profile of the modern woman

Looking back at the descriptions of women in the 1963 report issued by the Presidential Commission on the Status of Women, it is striking how much progress has been made in terms of the opportunities for women but also how difficult women's lives continue to be even in this more enlightened age. The original report provided a fascinating portrait of the "two images" of women—one from the turn of the 20th century and another from the suburban perspective of the 1960s:

- In terms of the home, the turn-of-the-previous-century woman lived within a more community-based environment and knew how to cook and bake, sew, garden, and be a home nurse and teacher in addition to raising children. In terms of work, this early-20th-century woman had no bargaining power and faced low wages; and if she was an immigrant woman (and there were many), then she had to work on horrible terms with no labor laws to protect her or government social services to help her.

- The 1960s woman, in turn, had supermarkets and stores, a range of entertainment options, sports, arts, television, and time for volunteering and active work in the church or neighborhood. The typical woman got married young, had children, and then had many years to do something else after the children were grown. Many post-war women gave up their own educational opportunities to support their husbands on the GI Bill, who after completing college had a wide array of well-paying, full-time career options to choose from to support the family single-handedly.

Almost a half-century later, as women cross the threshold to comprise half of the American labor force, what can we say about the modern American woman? How do working women differ from nonworking women in their characteristics, attitudes, and experience of daily life? Who are the female primary breadwinners? Characteristics of the respondents appear in Table 4.

Work status

- Fifty-seven percent of our female respondents are working or looking for work. Among those who are not working, nearly half are retired (48 percent), and just under one-third are keeping house or are full-time parents.

- There were few differences across racial/ethnic categories by working status, except for Latina women, who are 17 percent of working women, versus 10 percent of nonworking women. Marital/partnership status is similar between nonworking and working women, with a slightly higher percentage of married or partnered

Profile of the modern woman *(continued)*

women working (70 percent versus 64 percent nonworking). There is a larger disparity between education levels of working and nonworking women.

- Just over half of the nonworking women have spouses or partners who work, and 46 percent have nonworking spouses/partners, attributed mostly to the fact that many of these couples are retired (38 percent of the spouses of nonworking women are retired). The vast majority (86 percent) of partnered working women have a spouse who also works.

- Fifty-two percent of professional women are married or partnered to another professional.

- Three quarters of nonworking women in our survey have their own children under the age of 18, while only 40 percent of working women do.

- Primary responsibility for taking care of children more often lies with nonworking women (83 percent versus 63 percent). More spouses/partners of working women are sharing the responsibility for children, 31 percent versus 13 percent of nonworking women.

Values

- Working women and nonworking women share similar values about their goals in life, as show in the table below.

Women's values by working status

	Percent very important		
	Working	**Not working**	**All women**
Financial security	82.4	80.1	81.4
Self-sufficiency	86.0	84.5	85.4
Being married	48.4	59.9	53.3
Having children	63.2	70.6	66.3
Having a fulfilling job	75.3	68.4	72.4

- Although both working women and nonworking women value the importance of being married, working women are less likely to state that it is very important to them (48 percent) than are nonworking women (60 percent).

Changes for women

- Eighty-four percent of working women believe the increase of women in the workforce over the past 40 years has been positive, versus 74 percent of nonworking women, with the largest difference being in the extreme answer categories "very" positive.

- Working women say they are less dependent than their mothers were on their spouses for financial security than nonworking women.

- Not surprisingly, nonworking women have more traditional attitudes about mothers working outside the home: 34 percent of nonworking women "strongly agree" that it is better for a family if the father works outside the home and the mother takes care of the children versus 18 percent of working women. Responses are the same for "somewhat agree" to this statement.

- While working women and nonworking women share similar positive opinions about advancements of women in the workplace, their attitudes differ somewhat about motherhood and working. Nonworking women are more likely to strongly agree that it is harder for a mother who works outside the home to establish as warm and secure a relationship with her children as a mother who does not work outside the home. They have somewhat more traditional aspirations for their daughters as well: 63 percent of nonworking women ranked a "happy marriage and children" as most important for a daughter of theirs, versus 50 percent of working women.

- Working and nonworking women share very similar opinions about the role of a romantic partner in their lives and they are equally happy in their marriages and partnerships.

- Both working and nonworking women agree that more flexible work schedules are needed to accommodate working families.

Managing daily life

- Although more women are working today, they do not differ from nonworking women in the frequency with which they need to coordinate their family's schedules, duties, and responsibilities. While very few women disagree with their spouses about coordinating their daily lives "all" or "most of the time," twice as many nonworking women say this occurs all the time (11 percent) than women who work.

- The vast majority of working women have had to rearrange their work schedules in order to accommodate their family's needs.

- Sixty percent of working women have wanted to take time off of work to care for their children but have been unable to do so. Nearly two-thirds of these women consider themselves the primary caretaker of their children. Half of these women are in professional or managerial positions, versus 20 percent in blue-collar or pink-collar jobs.

- Working women more often report that they experience stress in daily life. Nearly half of working women experience stress "frequently" and less than one-third of nonworking women experience stress "frequently." Having kids under age 18 does not appear to affect the stress levels of working women.

Breadwinners

- Forty-one percent of working women from our survey are the primary breadwinners in their households, comprising mostly single women: Less than 40 percent of female breadwinners are married or partnered. Among the female breadwinners, 62 percent of the married partners have a spouse or partner who works, versus 77 percent of the women who are not breadwinners. Sixty percent of the female breadwinners in our survey are under 55 years old and are low or middle income: 55 percent earn less than $40,000 per year.

- Seventy percent of the breadwinners do not have children under 18 in the home. Yet they share characteristics with women who are not primary breadwinners. The distribution of education is similar, with slightly higher percentages of nonbreadwinners with college educations or more (44 percent of nonbreadwinners have college or more, versus 37 percent or more who don't).

- Change in the share of women's contribution to the family income is similar across female breadwinner status, with about one-quarter experiencing a decrease in their contribution to family income in the last year and with about 45 percent maintaining the same family income.

- Breadwinners coordinate with spouses and partners about their family activities and responsibilities at similar rates as nonbreadwinners, and they disagree at similar rates.

- The experience of stress in daily life does not differ between women who are primary breadwinners and those who are not; nor does this vary between those with kids under 18 and those without.

TABLE 4

Demographic profile of women today

Females only	N	%
Age		
18–29	248	14.3
30–44	431	24.9
45–64	684	39.4
65+	354	20.4
Total	1716	100.0
Income		
Less than $40K	623	40.8
$40–60K	312	20.4
$60–100K	314	20.5
$100K+	279	18.3
Total	1,528	100.0
Education		
Less than high school	140	8.1
High school grad—includes tech	475	27.5
Some college	406	23.5
College graduate	417	24.1
More than college	292	16.9
Total	1,730	100.0
College		
Less than college	1,022	59.0
College+	709	41.0
Total	1,730	100.0
Political ideology		
Liberal	526	31.4
Moderate	450	26.9
Conservative	639	38.2
Don't think that way	60	3.6
Total	1,674	100.0
Political affiliation		
Democrat	743	43.5
Independent	376	22.0
Republican	404	23.6
Don't think that way	50	2.9
Something else	135	7.9
Total	1,708	100.0
Work status		
Working	907	52.4
Not working	825	47.6
Total	1,732	100.0

Females only	N	%
Marital Status		
Married/partnered	1,177	67.9
Single	557	32.1
Total	1,734	100.0
Children		
Yes	1,407	81.0
No	330	19.0
Total	1,737	100.0
Children (under 13) in supervised care		
One	90	20.5
Two	71	16.2
Three	16	3.7
More than three	4	0.9
None	257	58.6
Total	438	100.0
Could not take time off work to care for family (ever)		
Yes	140	42.3
No	191	57.7
Total	331	100.0
Rearranged work schedule to accommodate family (ever)		
Yes	293	88.3
No	39	11.7
Total	331	100.0
Spouse/partner rearranged work to accommodate family (ever)		
Yes	319	83.9
No	60	15.8
Total	380	100.0
Elderly parents		
Yes	865	49.7
No	866	49.8
Total	1,731	100.0
Most responsibility for caring for your elderly parents		
You/respondent	357	41.2
Spouse/partner	16	1.9
Both equally	134	15.6
Some other family member	147	17.0
No need/they are independent	192	22.2
Other	14	1.6
Total	861	100.0

Females only	N	%
Ever a time wanted time off work to care for elderly parents, but unable		
Yes	134	26.9
No	359	72.3
Total	493	100.0
Frequency of coordination of family responsibilities with spouse		
Every day	159	35.0
2–3 times a week	126	27.8
Once a week	72	15.7
Every other week	15	3.3
Less often	49	10.7
Never	33	7.2
Total	453	100.0
Frequency of disagreement over family coordination		
All the time	29	6.9
Most of the time	26	6.3
Some of the time	194	46.1
None of the time	168	40.0
Total	417	100.0
Which, in particular, would need to change for working parents to balance work and family		
Longer school hours or longer school year	132	7.6
More flexible work hours/schedules	937	53.9
More paid time off	266	15.3
Better and/or more day-care options	228	13.1
Total	1563	100.0
In general, how often do you experience stress in your daily life		
Never	73	4.2
Rarely	297	17.1
Sometimes	675	38.8
Frequently	690	39.6
Total	1,735	100.0
Are you the primary breadwinner in your household		
Yes	695	40.0
No	999	57.6
Total	1,694	100.0

Females only	N	%
What share of your family's income do you personally earn		
Almost all or all	99	8.4
More than half	126	10.7
About half	322	27.4
Less than half	398	33.8
None or almost none	197	16.8
Total	1,142	100.0
Change in share of contribution to the family income over the past year		
Increased	320	27.2
Decreased	298	25.3
Stayed the same	534	45.4
Total	1,152	100.0
Total family income		
Less than $10,000	87	5.0
$10,000 to $19,999	181	10.4
$20,000 to $29,999	147	8.5
$30,000 to $39,999	209	12.0
$40,000 to $49,999	167	9.6
$50,000 to $59,999	145	8.3
$60,000 to $74,999	139	8.0
$75,000 to $100,000	174	10.0
More than $100,000	279	16.1
Total	1528	100.0
One or more child in supervised care		
Yes	181	41.3
No	257	58.7
Total	438	100.0

Sojourner Truth
(1797–1883)

Epilogue

By Oprah Winfrey

We women have been having conversations since the birth of this nation. We know when it's time for a conversation to begin. Expressing ourselves as women, expressing ourselves as people of success and power and influence, it reminds me of a convention held in Akron, Ohio in 1852, where Sojourner Truth, a former slave whom I consider one of my great mentors, gathered together suffragettes asking, pleading, and fighting for the right to vote. Sojourner Truth, a proud, six-foot-tall Amazon-like figure, walked up to the podium and said:

> *Well, children, where there is so much racket, there must be something out of kilter. I think that 'twixt the negroes of the South and the women at the North, all talking about rights, the white men will be in a fix pretty soon. But what's all this here talking about? If the first woman God ever made was strong enough to turn the world upside down all alone, these women together ought to be able to turn it back, and get it right-side up again!*

Those are the words of Sojourner Truth, who believed that without media, without mass marketing, without any social programs, women joined together had the possibility of turning the world right-side up.

Now, in 2009, there's so much racket again. Today, it's about women becoming half of all the American workers, about making more money than men, about what men think about this, and about what our families, our government, and our politicians, bosses, clergy, and aging parents are going to do. Men and women, families of all kinds, are negotiating about household responsibilities, child care, work, and sex. There's a lot of noise going on in this country and in this report about what it means to live in a woman's nation.

It seems to me it's an important conversation to have. Are our political, government, faith, and media leaders out of touch with the realities of how most families live and work today, just like they were out of touch in the day of Soujourner Truth? Some might say our nation has now been turned right-side up, but no one seems to recognize this outside of the families living and working every day. There is something a-kilter.

We have earned the right to celebrate the kind of power that isn't about landing the corner office, but about stoking an internal fire.

Where do we go from here? One thing is for sure: Women have a new kind of power in the workplace, in the marketplace, in the boardroom, and in the bedroom. Women have as many definitions of power as there are women to use it.

Forget the idea that being powerful is about how rich or important you are, or whether or not you get your own coffee in the morning. What I find powerful is a person with grace, with courage, with the confidence to be her own self and to make things happen. We have earned the right to celebrate the kind of power that isn't about landing the corner office, but about stoking an internal fire.

For me, there is no real power without spiritual power. A power that comes from the core of who you are and reflects all that you were meant to be. A power that's connected to the source of things. When you see this kind of power shining through someone in all its truth and certainty, it's irresistible, inspiring, elevating. I can feel it in myself sometimes, mostly when I'm sharing an insight that I know will have an impact on someone's life and I can see that they "get it." I get real joy from helping other people experience those "aha" moments. That is where my power lies.

"When we align our thoughts, emotions, and actions with the highest part of ourselves, we are filled with enthusiasm, purpose, and meaning," writes Gary Zukav in his best-selling book *The Seat of the Soul*. "When the personality comes fully to serve the energy of its soul, that is authentic empowerment."

Fulfilling your purpose with meaning is what gives you that electrifying "juice" and makes people stand in wonder at how you do it. The secret is alignment: when you know for sure that you're on course and doing exactly what you're supposed to be doing, fulfilling your soul's intention, your heart's desire, or whatever you choose to call it (they're all the same thing). When your life is on course with its purpose, you are your most powerful. And you may stumble, but you will not fall.

I know for sure that in every challenging experience there's an opportunity to grow, enhance your life, or learn something invaluable about yourself. Every challenge can make you stronger if you allow it. Strength multiplied equals power.

We have the power as women, as families, as a nation to rise to the challenges of our time. To hear each other out. To talk it out. To let the conversation begin. Together, we ought to be able to "turn it back, and get it right-side up again!"

Acknowledgements

Maria Shriver and John D. Podesta would like to thank The Rockefeller Foundation, Hewlett-Packard Company, Cisco Systems, Inc., Visa, Pacific Gas & Electric Company, Marcy Carsey and all of our financial partners for their generous support of this groundbreaking report. Without their belief in us, the report would not have been possible.

From Maria Shriver

This book is filled with facts, and here's one more: This report wouldn't even exist without Karen Skelton. She pushed this project from the very beginning. She spearheaded it, massaged it, shepherded it—in short, she made it happen. We've been working together for six years, and while Karen may labor behind the scenes, there's nothing behind-the-scenes about her. She's a brilliant political strategist, writer, attorney, talent scout, and leader of women and men—and a spectacular mother and friend. She juggles policy, political clients, polls, and prose, and still finds time for yoga and church. She makes normal multitaskers look like they're standing still.

Leslie Miller—who also jumped in before we had a plan or partners—is a veteran communications strategist with enormous talents that enabled us to expand the reach of the project. Leslie is the calm in the storm. She takes the whirlwind of moving pieces, people and targets and creates order and direction.

One of this project's greatest assets is the extraordinary John Podesta. I am honored to partner with him and to call him my friend. This endeavor wouldn't have been possible had the Center for American Progress—led by John—not been open to this collaboration.

Laura Nichols, our CAP ally from the beginning, is a rare jewel—sparkling, brilliant, strong, fierce, loyal. She led a team at CAP that exceeded all expectations and standards of professionalism. Without her we would not have been able to seamlessly blend academic expertise with cultural and current trends. She saw no challenges without solutions, seized opportunities, sought consensus, and became the Super Glue to a phenomenal cross-country marriage.

This report is groundbreaking in large part due to the work of CAP's Heather Boushey and Ann O'Leary. They and their colleagues have all worked incredibly hard around-the-clock to make this project work. And Ed Paisley's patient and seasoned editing, along with Shannon Ryan's savvy and stylish layout, made this report stand out like no other report of its kind.

Becky Beland assisted in every aspect of execution with the kind of discipline, commitment, and perseverance that gives you confidence in the next generation of up-and-coming women. Senior Advisor Olivia Morgan managed, befriended, learned from, and nurtured our impressive senior advisory council.

This team led a group of highly accomplished, passionate people who all believed in this project from the get-go and birthed it. I am grateful for Yasmine Abboud, Coby Atlas, Lyndie Benson, the team at the Dewey Square Group, Tina Frank, Alexandra Gleysteen, Debby Goldberg, Adam Greenfield, Noel Greenwood, Shannon Marven, Nancy McFadden, Jan Miller, Terri New, Barbara O'Connor, Susan Pinkus, Matt Rallens, Amy Rosenberg, Kristina Schake, and Erin Stein. From the University of Southern California Annenberg Center on Communication Leadership and Policy, I am grateful to Geoff Cowan, Geoff Baum, Cinny Kennard, Stacy Smith, Alison Trope, and Rebecca Shapiro.

We thank our partner, the Berkeley Center on Health, Economic & Family Security at UC Berkeley School of Law, led by Ann O'Leary, for the academic rigor and resources they brought to the project.

We thank Debbie Fine, CAP's general counsel, and our team of Lawrence Shire and Peter Grant from Grubman, Indursky & Shire, PC, and Munger, Tolles & Olson LLP's Steve Guise, for welcomed and wise legal judgments.

Much appreciation goes to all the roundtable participants who shared their personal stories with me and the people who worked to make the roundtables and other meetings around the country happen. I would especially like to thank Sukhinder Singh Cassidy and Accel Partners, Aileen Lee from Kleiner Perkins Caufield & Byers, Sue Bostrom and Cisco, Howard Schultz and the Starbucks Headquarters in Seattle, The Henry Ford in Dearborn, Michigan, Governor Jennifer Granholm and First Gentleman Dan Mulhern, Atlanta Mayor Shirley Franklin, North Avenue Presbyterian Church in Atlanta, Helen Torres, Daniel Zingale, and The California Endowment.

Thanks to everyone who wrote a personal essay for this project, whose diverse voices let us better understand how living in a woman's nation changes everything.

All of us stand on someone else's shoulders. I am well aware I wouldn't be writing this without the courageous women who've gone before me—women who fought for Title VII, Title IX, for choice, and those women who paved the way for me to be a journalist. I also thank my mentor, who knows who she is. I tell my daughters, "Because someone else fought for you, you have the luxury of just opening the door and walking through. Be grateful, work hard yourself, and pass it on."

Among those upon whose shoulders we stood on for this report are the amazingly diverse men and women who agreed to advise us along the way, our A Woman's Nation Advisory Committee:

Madeleine K. Albright
Anna Burger
Majora Carter
Sister Joan Chittister
John Chambers
Katherine Chon
Eve Ensler
Marty Evans
Bill Frist
Judy Gold
Daniel Goleman
Christie Hefner
Antonia Hernández
Yvonne Hunt
Patricia Kempthorne
Billie Jean King
Wendy Kopp
Judy Lichtman
Monica Lozano
Todd McCracken
John Miller
Pat Mitchell
Janet Murguía
Christiane Northrup
Suze Orman
Condoleezza Rice
Cheryl Saban
Ruth Simmons
Sukhinder Singh Cassidy
Mena Trott
Andrea Wong

Finally, we extend an enormous thank you to our media partners, without whom we would not be heard: NBC News, Telemundo, and *Time* magazine.

From Editors Heather Boushey and Ann O'Leary at the Center for American Progress

We would like to thank Maria Shriver and John Podesta for their leadership on this project. Without their collaboration, none of this would have happened. Maria's team, Karen Skelton and Leslie Miller, showed a dedication to making this report sing and getting every last piece right. We are grateful to them. Laura Nichols at CAP led our team on this effort and we are so grateful for her tireless effort to manage this project on a tight timeline and keep us all on track. This report could not have happened without the dedication and talent of Ed Paisley, who spent countless hours and weekends working with us, wowing us constantly with his skill, dexterity, and patience throughout. And we are incredibly appreciative of Shannon Ryan's willingness to go above and beyond the call of duty and for her beautiful layout of the Report.

Tremendous thanks go to the Economic Policy team at the Center for American Progress and the Berkeley Center on Health, Economic & Family Security at UC Berkeley School of Law for providing research support and lending their resources and staff to getting this report finished in time. In particular, we couldn't have done this without the leadership and good humor of Michael Ettlinger, vice president of CAP's economic policy team.

A big shout out to the fabulous women at the Center for American Progress for all their help and support—Jessica Arons, Becky Salay, Ilia Rodriguez, Debbie Fine, Allison Lessne, Anna Soellner, Sarah Rosen Wartell, and all the rest.

As editors, we are especially grateful for such terrific authors. They worked with us throughout accelerated timelines and detailed editing process. We are so glad that each and every one of you has contributed to this process and it has been a privilege to work with you throughout.

Lauren Smith has been the day-to-day backbone of this project and we are grateful for her humor, her dedication, her skills, and especially her tireless effort to make sure that every sentence of this report said what it meant to say. To make sure every fact and footnote was just right, we couldn't have done this without our fantastic team of research assistants—Justin Masterman, Eleanor Blume, Zoe Savitsky, Tracy Petznick—and CAP's dedicated economic policy interns, Maddie Esposito, Jillian Moreno, Regina Topolinskaya, and Ilana Fischer. And special thanks to K.C. Summers, a former (and long-time) editor at

The Washington Post who is now a freelance writer and editor in Washington, for her deft and concise copy editing work.

We have imposed on countless colleagues to help us with this work and we are grateful for their time and expertise. We thank Judy Lichtman and Karen Minatelli from the National Partnership for Women and Families, and Marcia Greenberger and Duffy Campbell from the National Women's Law Center for giving us invaluable advice at the start of this project. We extend sincere gratitude to Lee Badgett, Ellen Bravo, Stephanie Coontz, Katie Corrigan, Liana Fox, Angie Kelley, Aarti Kohli, Alan Rosenblatt, Malika Saada Saar, Liz Weiss, and Joan Williams, who gave us guidance throughout the writing process on bringing the chapters together and helping us do our best to incorporate more voices and perspectives. We are grateful to John Schmitt, who put together the data used in many of the chapters and to Jeff Chapman for running the data on breadwinner mothers.

As is so often the case with large projects like this, we stand on the shoulders of giants. The community of scholars who work on these issues have provided us with the body of research underpinning the findings of this report and the advocates work tirelessly to create a world that values combining work and care. We are honored to be a part of this community and are grateful for their support in this project.

Finally, we are indebted to our families. Goodwin Liu and Todd Tucker have stood by our sides despite long hours and weekends and vacations full of editing. Both have provided invaluable input into the chapters and the project has been improved from their masculine perspectives. Goodwin has taken on even more than his normal share of 50-50 parenting during this project, encouraging me (Ann) with emailed photos of our 2-year old from the zoo or the playground as I worked away on weekend mornings.

From individual chapter authors

"The New Breadwinners," by Heather Boushey

Thanks go first and foremost to Ann O'Leary for her superb editing and incisive commentary on my chapter, as well as being a model colleague and friend throughout this entire process. Lauren Smith has provided invaluable service for this chapter and I am thankful for all her help. Thanks to Michael Ettlinger and the rest of CAP's economic policy team for their guidance, support, and assistance. I am grateful for Jeff Chapman's time and expertise, as well as the work of John Schmitt. A number of wonderful colleagues provided comments on earlier drafts and I am grateful for their help: Randy Albelda, Lee Badgett, Ellen Bravo, Stephanie Coontz, Angie Kelley, and Liz Weiss. I cannot thank Ed Paisley and Shannon Ryan enough for their incredible work and attention to detail in editing my chapter and graphs. The biggest thanks goes to Todd Tucker for his edits, love, and support.

"Family Friendly for All Families," by Ann O'Leary and Karen Kornbluh
The authors would like to thank Heather Boushey for her partnership and commitment to editing and providing guidance on our chapter, and her friendship and encouragement throughout this project. We would also like to thank Ellen Bravo, Judy Lichtman, and Goodwin Liu for their guidance and helpful comments. Ed Paisley made our chapter sing and we thank him tremendously. We thank Zoe Savitsky, Tracy Petznick, Eleanor Blume, Justin Masterman, and Lauren Smith for their tremendous research assistance. Finally, Ann would like to thank the faculty and staff at Berkeley CHEFS for their support and encouragement.

"Sick and Tired," by Jessica Arons and Dorothy Roberts
The authors would like to thank Melissa Alpert, Eleanor Blume, Jonathan Hillel, Justin Masterman, Valerie Shen, and Lauren Smith for their research assistance; the Kirkland & Ellis Fund for research support; Claire Brindis, Karen Davenport, Shira Saperstein, and Judy Waxman for their helpful feedback; and Heather Boushey, Ann O'Leary, and Ed Paisley for their guidance and keen editing.

"Better Educating Our New Breadwinners," by Mary Ann Mason
The author would like to thank Cynthia Brown, Delaine Eastin, Catherine Hill, Lisa Maatz, Jorge Ruiz de Velasco, and Louis Soares for their guidance and advice. The author would also like to thank the tremendous team of research assistants at Berkeley CHEFS, especially Tracy Petznick and Eleanor Blume, for their diligence and hard work on this chapter. Finally, the author thanks Ann O'Leary, Heather Boushey, and Ed Paisley for their hard work in shaping and guiding this chapter to the very end.

"Got Talent? It Isn't Hard to Find," by Brad Harrington and Jamie J. Ladge
The authors would like to thank Annie Soisson of Tufts University for the excellent review and thoughtful insights she provided on this chapter. We would also like

to acknowledge the work of the Boston College Center for Work & Family, whose research and corporate engagement over the past 20 years has supported working individuals and their families and has provided a strong foundation for our work.

"The Challenge of Faith," by Sally Steenland and Kimberly Morgan
The authors would like to thank Stephanie Boddie, Shaun Casey, Penny Edgell, and Susan Thistlethwaite for providing helpful comments on the chapter, and Mary Ellen Konieczny, Brian Steensland, and Bradford Wilcox for offering helpful ideas on our research. We'd like to thank Jonathan Duffy, Nan Futrell, and Zoe Savitsky for assisting with research. Thanks also to Lauren Smith for shepherding our chapter through many drafts and to Justin Masterman for finalizing late changes and organizing footnotes. And finally, thanks to Heather Boushey, Ann O'Leary, and Ed Paisley for their guidance, support, and good edits.

"Where Have You Gone, Roseanne Barr?" by Susan Douglas
This essay draws from my book *Enlightened Sexism: The Seductive Message That Feminism's Work Is Done*, so I would like to thank my editor at Henry Holt, Paul Golob, for his invaluable assistance in honing my arguments. Thanks also to Heather Boushey, Ed Paisley, and Ann O'Leary for their comments and revisions.

"Has a Man's World Become a Woman's Nation?" by Michael Kimmel
The author would like to thank Scott Coltrane, both for his pioneering research and his help in sifting through it. I would also like to thank Amy Aronson, and Ann O'Leary and Heather Boushey, for exemplary editorial shepherding.

About the Contributors

Maria Shriver is First Lady of California, an award-winning journalist and producer, best-selling author and mother of four. As First Lady, Shriver has created groundbreaking programs and initiatives that empower people to become "architects of change" in their own lives and in the lives of others. Shriver has used her voice to advocate on behalf of women, the working poor, the intellectually disabled and families like hers who are struggling with Alzheimer's disease.

Under Shriver's leadership, The Women's Conference has grown into the nation's premier forum for women, annually uniting more than 100 internationally acclaimed leaders and visionaries with 20,000 women from all walks of life to share enriching stories of transformation and success, inspirational life lessons, practical tips and life-changing tools. The Women's Conference expanded in 2009 to two full days. In 2004, Shriver created The Minerva Awards—named after the goddess Minerva on the California State Seal who epitomizes courage, wisdom, and strength—given annually at the conference to recognize and reward the achievements of women who make extraordinary contributions to their communities and the state. To extend the reach of the conference, Shriver also launched a dynamic online community at WomensConference.org with the goal of providing a daily gathering place for women everywhere to become architects of change.

With a career in journalism spanning more than two decades, Shriver has been a network news correspondent and anchor for CBS and NBC, winning Peabody and Emmy Awards. She is the author of six *New York Times* best-selling books. She recently executive produced HBO's "The Alzheimer's Project," an Emmy Award-winning four-part documentary series that took a close look at cutting-edge work being done in the country's leading Alzheimer's laboratories and examined the effects of this disease on patients and families. Shriver is a graduate of Georgetown University, with a degree in American Studies.

Heather Boushey is senior economist at the Center for American Progress. Boushey studies working families and trends in the U.S. labor market. She has written extensively on labor issues, including tracking the recession and its impact on workers and their families, women's labor force participation, trends in income inequality, and work-family policy issues. She has testified for Congress and the Equal Employment Opportunity Commission about issues facing working families in this recession.

Prior to joining the Center, Boushey was a senior economist with the Joint Economic Committee of the U.S. Congress. She was formerly a senior economist with the Center for Economic and Policy Research. Boushey received her Ph.D. in economics from the New School for Social Research and her bachelor's degree from Hampshire College.

Ann O'Leary is a senior rellow at American Progress and is the executive director of the Berkeley Center for Health, Economic & Family Security at University of California, Berkeley, School of Law. CHEFS' mission is to develop and advance creative solutions to address the economic risks faced by working Americans, with a focus on improving access to health care, developing better protections for workers who are voluntarily or involuntarily on leave from their jobs, and supporting working parents in a flexible workplace.

O'Leary previously served as a deputy city attorney for the City of San Francisco and clerked for the Honorable John T. Noonan Jr. on the Ninth Circuit Court of Appeals. From 2001 through 2003, she served as legislative director for then-Senator Hillary Rodham Clinton, and from 1994 through 2000 she served in a number of positions in the Clinton administration, including as special assistant to the president on the Domestic Policy Council and as senior policy advisor to the deputy secretary of education. O'Leary received her bachelor's degree from Mount Holyoke College, her master's degree from Stanford University, and her law degree from UC Berkeley School of Law.

Karen Skelton is the executive co-producer and program director for the California Governor and First Lady's Women's Conference, managing all aspects of programming for the world's premier live event for women. She founded the California office of the Dewey Square Group, one of the country's leading public affairs firms, growing this multimillion dollar consulting practice from the ground up—specializing in political strategies and communications, energy and environmental policy, and government relations.

Skelton previously worked in the White House during the Clinton administration on the political staff and as a member of the defense team that argued against the impeachment of the president of the United States. Skelton served as the first director of political affairs for then-Vice President Al Gore, initiating and managing his first national political program in preparation for his 2000 election campaign. As a lawyer, Skelton prosecuted criminal cases at the U.S. Department of Justice as a special assistant U.S. attorney, and as a trial lawyer in the Division of Environmental Enforcement. She was named chief counsel of the Federal Highway Administration in January 1999. Skelton received her bachelor's degree with honors in English from UCLA, a master's from Harvard's John F. Kennedy School of Government, and her J.D. from the University of California, Berkeley School of Law. She currently serves on the boards of the California Arts Council and the UC Berkeley Institute for Governmental Studies.

Ed Paisley is vice president for editorial at the Center for American Progress. He is a 20-year veteran of business and finance journalism who joined the Center after successfully launching the specialist Wall Street print and Web publication *The Deal* as its managing editor. At *The Deal,* he was also responsible for the publication's award-winning coverage of technology finance and international finance.

Before moving to New York to launch *The Deal* in 1999, Paisley spent a decade in East Asia as an editor and journalist covering business, finance, and politics for the *Far Eastern Economic Review* and *Institutional Investor* magazine. Prior to that, he worked for *American Banker* newspaper in Washington, DC, covering domestic and international financial regulation. Paisley earned a master's degree in East Asian history from Georgetown University in 1984 and a bachelor's degree in American studies from George Mason University in 1982.

Laura Nichols is a senior fellow at the Center for American Progress and a member of the Center's executive team. As one of the original architects of American Progress, she has contributed to building the institution, overseeing the construction of its communications operations, and leading its strategic planning since its founding in 2003. As senior fellow, she contributes to the Center's new media efforts and serves as a liaison to the progressive community, donors, and Capitol Hill. She is also a partner in First Tuesday Media, a media company based in Los Angeles that organizes the entertainment industry to produce political and advocacy media.

Nichols spent eight years as advisor, strategist, and spokesperson for former House Democratic Leader Richard Gephardt. In those roles, she served as Gephardt's spokesperson and was responsible for developing and managing communications strategies on a wide variety of policy issues for House Democrats. Nichols also served as press secretary to the Democratic Congressional Campaign Committee and former U.S. House Rep. Vic Fazio. She began her career in politics as the Iowa press secretary in 1988 for Gephardt's presidential campaign. Nichols is a graduate of the University of Missouri.

Leslie Miller is the co-executive director of "A Woman's Nation" project. She created, built, and managed the cultural components, media partnerships, and national reach of *The Shriver Report.* She is a veteran communications and political strategist and has worked for some of the most respected and high-profile organizations around the globe, including being a part of a senior communications team with the Obama presidential campaign.

Prior to joining the campaign, Miller led the Dewey Square Group's California practice in San Francisco for six years, where she specialized in government affairs and was strategic communications counsel. While there, Miller advised Fortune 500 companies and national foundations to develop internal community affairs programs and external affairs plans, and was a co-strategist in developing a bipartisan organization focused on transforming the political process in California. Miller also is a former producer for NBC News in Washington, DC. She covered the 1996 and 1998 elections, Congress, and the Clinton administration. Miller received her bachelor's degree from the University of California, Berkeley, and resides in California.

Chapter Contributors

Jessica Arons is the director of the Women's Health and Rights Program at American Progress and a member of the Faith and Progressive Policy Initiative. Prior to joining American Progress, she worked at the ACLU Reproductive Freedom Project, the labor and employment law firm of James & Hoffman, the Supreme Court of Virginia, the White House, and the 1996 Pennsylvania Democratic Coordinated Campaign. She currently serves on the boards of the DC Abortion Fund and the ACLU of Virginia. Arons is an honors graduate of Brown University and the William & Mary School of Law.

Stephanie Coontz teaches history and family studies at The Evergreen State College in Olympia, WA, and is director of research and public education for the Council on Contemporary Families, which she chaired from 2001 to 2004. She is the author of several books, including *Marriage, A History: From Obedience to Intimacy, or How Love Conquered Marriage* (Viking Press, 2005) and *The Way We Never Were: American Families and the Nostalgia Trap* (Basic Books, 1992 and 2000). She recently completed a new book on the history of women from the 1920s through the 1960s and the impact of Betty Friedan's *The Feminine Mystique* (forthcoming 2010, Perseus Books). Coontz has testified about her research before the House Select Committee on Children, Youth and Families in Washington, DC, and addressed audiences across America, Japan, and Europe. Coontz received her bachelor's degree in American History at the Honors Program at the University of California Berkeley and her master's degree in European History at the University of Washington in Seattle.

Kelly Daley is a senior analyst at Abt SRBI, where she specializes in survey questionnaire design and data analysis across a variety of subject matters including public health, civic engagement, and women's studies. Prior to joining Abt SRBI, she was co-director of the University of Chicago Survey Lab. She has been responsible for multiple survey research projects, cognitive testing, pilot studies and qualitative work including focus groups, observational field work, and in-depth interviews. Daley holds a Ph.D. in sociology from the University of Chicago and a master's degree in policy studies from The Johns Hopkins University. Her Ph.D. dissertation examined the impact of the women's movement and the sexual revolution on the attitudes and behaviors of women who came of age prior to 1960. Prior to her graduate studies, she worked with numerous San Francisco nonprofit organizations to help improve access to health care and raise awareness of women's health issues.

Susan Douglas is the chair of the Department of Communication Studies at the University of Michigan, as well as the Catherine Neafie Kellogg Professor and Arthur F. Thurnau Professor of Communication Studies. She is author of a number of books, including most recently *Enlightened Sexism: The Seductive Message That Feminism's Work Is Done* (Henry Holt, forthcoming, March 2010), as well as *The Mommy Myth: The Idealization of Motherhood and How it Has Undermined Women* (with Meredith Michaels, The Free Press, 2004). Douglas received her bachelor's degree from Elmira College (Phi Beta Kappa) and her master's degree and Ph.D. from Brown University. She has lectured at colleges and universities around the country and was the media critic for *The Progressive* from 1992 to 1998.

Maria Echaveste joined University of California's Berkeley School of Law as a lecturer after co-founding a strategic and policy consulting group, serving as a senior White House and U.S. Department of Labor official, and working as a community leader and corporate attorney. She is also a senior fellow with the Law School's Chief Justice Earl Warren Institute on Race, Ethnicity and Diversity. From 1998 to 2001, she served as assistant to the president and deputy chief of staff to President Bill Clinton. Echaveste is also a non-resident fellow of the Center for American Progress working on issues such as immigration, civil rights, and education. She continues to provide strategic and policy advice to a variety of corporate, non-profit and union clients through her consulting firm, NVG, LLC. Echaveste received a Bachelor of Arts in anthropology from Stanford University in 1976 in 1980, and her J.D. from the University of California, Berkeley.

John Halpin is a senior fellow at the Center for American Progress focusing on political theory, communications, and public opinion analysis. He is the co-director and creator of the Progressive Studies Program at CAP, an interdisciplinary project researching the intellectual history, foundational principles, and public understanding of progressivism. Halpin is the co-author with John Podesta of *The Power of Progress: How America's Progressives Can (Once Again) Save Our Economy,*

Our Climate, and Our Country, a 2008 book about the history and future of the progressive movement. Prior to joining CAP, he was a senior associate at Greenberg Quinlan Rosner Research, providing strategic guidance and public opinion research for political parties and candidates including Al Gore's 2000 presidential campaign, the British Labor Party, the Austrian Social Democrats, and a range of congressional, state legislative, and initiative campaigns. Halpin received his undergraduate degree from Georgetown University and his master's degree in political science from the University of Colorado, Boulder.

Brad Harrington is the executive director of the Boston College Center for Work & Family and an associate professor of organization studies in the Carroll School of Management. Prior to his arrival at Boston College, Harrington was an executive with Hewlett-Packard Company for 20 years. His roles there included global director of management and organization development, chief quality officer and member of the executive committee for HP's Medical Products Business, and quality director for Hewlett-Packard United Kingdom, Ltd., as well as a number of human resource management positions. Along with Professor Douglas T. Hall of Boston University, he is the author of *Career Management & Work/Life Integration: Using Self-Assessment to Navigate Contemporary Careers* (Sage Publications, 2007). Harrington holds a bachelor's degree in business administration from Stonehill College, a master's degree in psychology from Boston College, and a Ph.D. in human resource development and organization development from Boston University.

Michael Kimmel is among the leading researchers and writers on men and masculinity in the world today. A professor of sociology at the State University of New York, Stony Brook, his many books include *The Politics of Manhood* (1995), *The Gender of Desire* (2005), and *The History of Men* (2005). His documentary history, *Against the Tide: Pro-Feminist Men in the United States, 1776-1990* (Beacon, 1992), chronicled men who supported women's equality since the founding of the country. His most recent best-selling book, *Guyland* (HarperCollins, 2008), charts the emergence of a new stage of development among young people. Kimmel consults regularly with non-governmental organizations, corporations, and governments concerning men's issues. He was in the first coeducational class at Vassar College, where he received his bachelor's degree. He received his master's degree at Brown and his Ph.D. at the University of California Berkeley.

Karen Kornbluh was a visiting fellow at the Center for American Progress working on environmental technology financing and work-family policies when she wrote this chapter. Previously, she served as policy director in then-Sen. Obama's Senate office, beginning in 2005. Prior to that, Kornbluh founded the Work and Family Program at the New America Foundation, where she was also a Markle technology fellow and published widely on the need to update government policies for the new family and new economy. From 1994 to 1997, she filled several roles at the Federal Communications Commission, including assistant chief of the International Bureau, director of the Office of Legislative and Intergovernmental Affairs, and deputy chief of the Mass Media Bureau. Kornbluh received a master's degree from Harvard University's John F. Kennedy School of Government and a bachelor's degree from Bryn Mawr College.

Jamie J. Ladge is a faculty member in the College of Business at Northeastern University, where she teaches in the areas of management and organizational development. Ladge is a faculty affiliate of the Boston College Center for Work and Family and an Alfred P. Sloan Work-Family Career Development Award Grantee for the 2009-2011 academic years. Her primary research interests are at the intersection of careers, identity, and work-life integration. Her most recent research work has been published in academic journals such as *Organizational Dynamics, Journal of Vocational Behavior,* and *Negotiation and Conflict Management Research Journal*. She also has published a number of Harvard Business School cases and was recently cited in a 2009 article in *The Wall Street Journal* on parents re-entering the workplace. Ladge earned her B.S. from Babson College, an M.B.A. from Simmons College, and an M.S. and Ph.D. from Boston College.

Courtney E. Martin is the award-winning author of *Perfect Girls, Starving Daughters: How the Quest for Perfection is Harming Young Women* (Berkley Books, 2008). She is also a widely-read freelance journalist and regular blogger for Feministing. She is a senior correspondent for *The American Prospect* and her work has appeared in *The Washington Post, Newsweek,* and *The Christian Science Monitor,* among others. In addition, Martin consults with social justice organizations, including the Ms. Foundation for Women, the National Council for Research on Women, and the Bartos Institute for the Constructive Engagement of Conflict. Martin has a master's degree from the Gallatin School at New York University in writing and social change and a bachelor's degree from Barnard College in political science and sociology. She is a fellow of both the Woodhull Institute for Ethical Leadership and the Women's Media Center.

Kimberly Morgan is associate professor of political science and international affairs at The George Washington University. She received her Ph.D. in political science from Princeton University in 2001 and was a post-doctoral fellow at New York University and Yale University before coming to George Washington. She teaches courses on European politics, comparative politics, and comparative social policy. In 2008-09, Morgan was a fellow at the Woodrow Wilson International Center for Scholars. Her book *Working Mothers and the Welfare State: Religion and the Politics of Work-Family Policies in Western Europe and the United States* was published in 2006 by Stanford University Press, and her articles have appeared in numerous academic journals. Currently, she and Massachusetts Institute of Technology Professor Andrea Louise Campbell are completing a book titled *The Delegated Welfare State: Medicare, Markets, and the Governance of American Social Policy* (forthcoming, Oxford University Press).

Mary Ann Mason is currently professor and co-director of the Berkeley Center on Health, Economic & Family Security at the University of California Berkeley School of Law. Mason's scholarship spans working families, in particular the issues faced by the surging numbers of professional women in law, medicine, science, and the academic world. Her most recent book (co-authored with her daughter Eve Mason Ekman) is *Mothers on the Fast Track: How a New Generation Can Balance Family and Careers* (Oxford, 2007). Among her other books are two major works on child custody, *From Father's Property to Children's Rights: The History of Child Custody in the United States* (Columbia University Press, 1994) and *The Custody Wars: Why Children are Losing the Legal Battle—and What We Can Do About It* (Basic Books, 1999). Mason received a bachelor's degree cum laude from Vassar College, a Ph.D. in American history from the University of Rochester, and a J.D. from the University of San Francisco.

Susan H. Pinkus is the president of S.H. Pinkus Associates, a public opinion company. She was previously director of the LATimes poll at the *Los Angeles Times*. She is a past member of Executive Council of American Association of Public Opinion

Researchers and past president of Pacific Chapter. She is also a member of the National Women's Media Foundation, the World Association for Public Opinion Research, and a trustee on the National Council on Public Polls. She is on the Board of Directors at the Roper Center and serves on the Journalism Advisory Committee at SUNY Albany. Pinkus earned her bachelor's degree at the State University of New York at Albany, and completed post-graduate work toward an MBA at City University of New York, Baruch College.

Dorothy Roberts is the Kirkland & Ellis Professor at Northwestern University School of Law, with joint appointments in African American Studies, Sociology, and the Institute for Policy Research. She is author of the award-winning books *Killing the Black Body: Race, Reproduction, and the Meaning of Liberty* (Vintage Books, 1998) and *Shattered Bonds: The Color of Child Welfare* (Basic Books, 2003), as well as six co-edited texts and more than 70 articles and essays in books and scholarly journals, including *Harvard Law Review, Stanford Law Review,* and *Yale Law Journal*. Roberts also serves on the boards of directors of the Black Women's Health Imperative, National Coalition for Child Protection Reform, and Generations Ahead, as well as on the executive committee of Cells to Society: The Center on Social Disparities and Health, the Braam foster care oversight panel in Washington State, and the Standards Working Group of the California Institute for Regenerative Medicine. Roberts received a bachelor's degree from Yale College and a J.D. from Harvard Law School.

Jamal Simmons emerged from the 2008 election as one of the new young voices in the world of political analysis. With an extensive background in Democratic politics and international affairs, he was a strong supporter of Barack Obama's campaign and became a fixture on CNN's political coverage. Simmons is a principal at the Raben Group, where he provides strategic and communications counsel to the firm's clients. Previously, Simmons was a senior aide to several Democratic political campaigns and served as chief of staff to Rep. Carolyn Cheeks Kilpatrick (D-MI), senior advisor to Sen. Max Cleland (D-GA), and as a political appointee in the Clinton administration under U.S. Trade Representative and Commerce Secretary Mickey Kantor. Simmons received his bachelor's degree from Morehouse College and his master's in public policy from the Kennedy School at Harvard University.

Sally Steenland is senior policy advisor to the Faith and Progressive Policy Initiative at American Progress. In 2005, she organized the Initiative's "national conversations," a series of town-hall meetings and discussions across the country on pressing issues of faith and policy. She guides the Initiative's work on a variety of policy issues, including faith and science, the role of religion in the public square, diversity and tolerance, economics, the environment, and cultural and social matters. Previously, Steenland was deputy director of the National Commission on Working Women, where she wrote major studies on women's employment and women in the media and directed projects involving women in nonprofessional jobs. Steenland received a bachelor's degree in English from Calvin College in Grand Rapids, MI, and a master's in education from Howard University.

Ruy Teixeira is a senior fellow at both the Century Foundation and American Progress, where he co-directs the Progressive Studies Program. He is the author or co-author of six books, including *Red, Blue and Purple America: The Future of Election Demographics* (Brookings Institution Press, 2008); *The Emerging Democratic Majority* (Scribner, 2002); *America's Forgotten Majority: Why the White Working Class Still Matters* (Basic Books, 2000); and *The Disappearing American Voter* (Brookings Institution Press, 1992), as well as hundreds of articles, both scholarly and popular. Teixeira's recent writings include "New Progressive America," "The Decline of the White Working Class and the Rise of a Mass Upper Middle Class" (with Alan Abramowitz), "The Politics of Definition" (with John Halpin), "Back to the Future: The Emerging Democratic Majority Re-emerges" (with John Judis), and the New Politics Institute reports, "The Next Frontier: A New Study of Exurbia" and "The Progressive Politics of the Millennial Generation."

{COVER PHOTO CREDITS FROM LEFT: LOU BOPP, STOCKSHOP; MATT EICH, AURORA PHOTOS; LYNDIE BENSON; DAVIS FACTOR, CORBIS; DANA SPAETH, GETTY IMAGES}

Join the Conversation

www.awomansnation.com

LaVergne, TN USA
13 November 2009
164054LV00001B/1/P